WHEN WRITING TEACHERS
TEACH LITERATURE

WHEN WRITING TEACHERS TEACH LITERATURE

Bringing Writing to Reading

Edited by
Art Young
Clemson University
and
Toby Fulwiler
The University of Vermont

Boynton/Cook
HEINEMANN
Portsmouth NH

Boynton/Cook Publishers, Inc.
A subsidiary of Reed Elsevier, Inc.
361 Hanover Street
Portsmouth, NH 03801-3912

Offices and agents throughout the world

"The Skokie Theatre" from WILD GRATITUDE by Edward Hirsch. Copyright © 1985 by Edward Hirsch. Reprinted by permission of Alfred A. Knopf, Inc.

Excerpt from "Livvie" from THE WIDE NET AND OTHER STORIES. Copyright 1942 and renewed 1970 by Eudora Welty. Reprinted by permission of Harcourt Brace & Company.

Excerpt from "Mother to Son" from SELECTED POEMS by Langston Hughes. Copyright 1926 by Alfred A. Knopf., Inc. and renewed 1954 by Langston Hughes. Reprinted by permission of the publisher.

"The Young Housewife" from COLLECTED POEMS: 1909–1939, Volume I by William Carlos Williams. Copyright © 1938 by New Directions Publishing Corp. Reprinted by permission of New Directions Publishing Corp.

"Sex Without Love" from THE DEAD AND THE LIVING by Sharon Olds. Copyright © 1983 by Sharon Olds. Reprinted by permission of Alfred A. Knopf, Inc.

Editor: Peter R. Stillman
Production: Renée M. Nicholls
Cover Design: Tom Allen/Pear Graphic Design

Library of Congress Cataloging-in-Publication Data
When writing teachers teach literature : bringing reading to writing /
   edited by Art Young and Toby Fulwiler.
       p.   cm.
   Includes bibliographical references.
   ISBN 0-86709-363-3
       1. Authorship—Study and teaching.   2. Literature—Study and
   teaching.   I. Young, Art, 1943–   II. Fulwiler, Toby, 1942–
   PN181.W48   1995
   808′.042′07—dc20   95-18517
                                                                    CIP

Printed in the United States of America on acid-free paper
OPI Docutech 2007

In the memory of James Britton,
friend and mentor,
who brought reading and writing to many.

Contents

Introduction

Toby Fulwiler and Art Young

English Studies are changing, what with the literary canon fractured, fallen, and conflicted; with the teaching of critical theory and cultural studies replacing the teaching of literary texts; and with rhetoric and composition pedagogy pushing its way broadly across the curriculum and deeply into the provinces of literature. The authors of this collection agree, but not with alarm. These essays confirm the value of new voices in the canon and in the classroom, of diverse theoretical perspectives that merge with interactive pedagogical practices, and especially, of the emergence of writing along with reading as the central business of English Studies.

English Studies

In the old days, most English instructors were graduate-school trained in literary study and not trained at all in pedagogy of any kind. So it was hardly surprising that when literature instructors had to teach writing classes, they taught them as they would literature classes: Each week they asked students to read a short essay by E. B. White ("Once More to the Lake") or Virginia Woolf ("Death of a Moth"); discussed this essay during class; then assigned students to go home and write one like it. When the student essays were completed, instructors collected, corrected, and graded them. Next week a new essay was read and discussed, and the students wrote another one themselves.

Both editors of this book remember this pedagogical model from both sides of the desk, having been taught this way in the early 1960's and then teaching this way ourselves in the late 1960's. In retrospect, it seems obvious that literature training influenced the teaching of literature and composition alike; we did what was done to us—sometimes quite well—and we helped student writers where we could with what little we knew. The good writers continued to write well, the less good got a little better and were relieved when the course ended and formal instruction in writing was forever behind them.

Today, many college teachers of English find themselves trained as scholars to study literary texts, but trained as writing teachers to study how students learn. Preparation for teaching literature has commonly focused on lecture demonstrations and Socratic discussion of canonical texts, while not attending, in any deliberate way, to the conditions, needs, and abilities of the learners trying to read those texts. The focus is on the text, not the learner: Here is the text, read it, learn about it, tell back what you learned. If you disagree with the instructor's interpretation, be prepared to defend your interpretation with specific evidence from the text.

Composition training, however, focuses not only on published and student texts, but also on the learners who read and create texts. Instructors trained to teach writing learn to help students from diverse backgrounds and cultures, with wide-ranging abilities, learn to compose and advance their thoughts in a variety of contexts, for a variety of purposes, to a variety of audiences. And, of course, you see in this last sentence the editors' biases about teaching and learning: that the best teaching is not the mere transmission of knowledge, but the transmission of the means of creating knowledge and the excitement that accompanies that. However, as this book will attest, the times are changing, as composition pedagogy is being applied to the teaching of literature in a variety of college classrooms, with what we see as remarkably happy results.

The way in which many literature instructors, including the editors of this book, learned to apply composition-based pedagogy to their literature teaching was not, ironically, a direct result of teaching writing, but rather of developing and participating in writing-across-the-curriculum programs, and directing and attending interdisciplinary writing workshops. If ideas about teaching with writing could work in biology and history classes, maybe they could even work in literature classes.

Writing Across the Curriculum

Many volumes now have been written detailing the emergence, in the 1960's and 1970's, of composing process ideas on the teaching of writing in composition classes (e.g., Berlin, North). Additional volumes have examined the extension, in the 1970's and 1980's, of those same ideas into other disciplines through the movement called writing across the curriculum (e.g., Fulwiler and Young, Russell). This volume narrows the focus still further by examining the influence of writing-across-the-curriculum pedagogy as it circles back into the discipline from whence it came, English Studies, emerging as an alternate and viable pedagogy for the teaching of literature.

In retrospect, it seems logical that when English instructors began teaching writing in their composition classes according to the way it was actually produced by experienced writers, these same ideas would spread into other disciplinary areas where writing also was assigned and assessed. The ideas

that have translated best—that seem to have had the most staying power—
are writing to learn, the composing process, and collaborative learning.

The phrase "writing to learn" implies that writing is valuable not only
as traditionally assigned in school, as a mode of communication to other
people, but as a mode of learning for the person doing the writing. The now
classic studies of James Britton, *The Development of Writing Abilities*, and
Janet Emig, "Writing as a Mode of Learning," promoted the idea that the
act of writing helped writers discover, remember, invent, extend, and revise
ideas. Translated into classroom assignments, writing-to-learn practices
included journal writing, freewriting, and discovery drafting, as well as
numerous invention strategies such as brainstorming, list-making, and
clustering—all of which were assigned to benefit the writer, not to be graded
by the teacher. In a literature classroom, teachers used such strategies to
help students create and analyze literary meaning for themselves, individually and collectively.

Teaching the often messy, sometimes unexplainable process of composing has revolutionized the teaching of writing. Following the advice of early
process teachers such as Donald Murray (*A Writer Teaches Writing*) and Ken
Macrorie (*Writing to Be Read*), students learned to start with discovery
drafts, to revise and rewrite those drafts, and later to edit and proofread. Students learned to generate ideas and produce writing after the fashion of most
professional writers. Learning the composing processes that best suited their
individual needs helped many students learn to write, learn to like to write,
and learn to actively engage the material about which they were writing.

Learning to collaborate with one another in peer writing, research, and
discussion groups has radically increased the sense of community in classes
where these techniques are employed. Under influences as diverse as Peter
Elbow (*Writing Without Teachers*) and Kenneth Bruffee ("Collaborative
Learning and 'The Conversation of Mankind' "), composition teachers have
made small-group work a staple of writing classes, increasing students' sense
of critical responsibility, awareness of audience, and understanding of the
social construction of knowledge. At the same time, learning to collaborate
has helped students learn to compose, revise, and edit more effectively by
expanding their sense of audience from the teacher alone to the other students in the class. When applied to literature classes, collaboration means
that the creation of literary knowledge becomes a social and democratic
enterprise in which all participate, rather than a dissemination enterprise in
which the teacher speaks and the students listen, record, and recall.

These process-oriented pedagogies that center on the student-as-learner
were pioneered in composition classes and are being exported with often
remarkable success to literature and other classes across the academic curriculum. Many of the chapters in this volume describe in detail one or more of
these writing-across-the-curriculum ideas as they intersect with the teaching
of literature.

Social Context and Classroom Community

Writing and reading are social acts that are dramatized in educational settings. College literature classrooms are settings in which literary experience is collaboratively created and re-created by reading, writing, talking, and listening. This book does not focus on theory—neither literary theory nor composition theory—but rather focuses on the classroom community in which theories and practices join together and perform in ways not always consistent and predictable. Nor do we focus on the larger cultural contexts in which classrooms are situated that often determine what goes on in them: English departments, two-year colleges, religiously affiliated colleges, research universities, public educational systems, and various social and political, local and global constituencies. We do not focus on them, but we are always mindful of them as we read the stories of these teachers in their individual classrooms.

The authors in this collection are reflective practitioners, and their essays imply theories that inform practices even as they describe practices that sometimes explode theories. Some of these teachers might be described by others, or might even describe themselves, as expressivists or feminists or Marxists or postmodernists or some other "ist" or combination of "ists." Some are primarily concerned with the development of the individual self through personal writing in response to literature; others are concerned with the development of literary knowledge through critical thinking, persuasion, and consensus; yet others are concerned with creating the knowledge of discourse practices and cultural understandings often necessary for action in support of social justice; and still others are concerned with creating a postmodern classroom that, in Lester Faigley's words when speaking about the varieties of postmodern theory, "emphasizes the multiplicity of subjectivities and resists the impulse to speak for the Other and to turn the Other into the same person as the speaker" (46).

Therefore, while these practitioners do not explicitly discuss the merits and demerits of various theories, they do raise important theoretical and pedagogical concerns. In the college literature classroom, should the language of the learner be privileged, or the language of the academy, or some in-between language? What are the consequences for the study of literature when a teacher privileges academic discourse? or personal response? or multiplicity of response? or consensus? What should be the role of the literature teacher in the classroom and what are the consequences? expert authority? mentor? facilitator? all of the above? Answers to such questions often emerge as teachers reflect on their practices and their theoretical assumptions and thus gain a better understanding of the reasons they teach literature as they do and the meaning of that teaching. From such experiences come possibilities for educational change. Teachers in this collection comment explicitly on how such pedagogical reflections transformed their teacherly lives.

The Practicing Teacher

This book examines what happens at the point where the study of literature intersects with the teaching of writing. This happens when writing teachers teach literature classes, when they teach poetry, fiction, or drama in composition classes, or when they teach some of the more recent hybrid courses in which composition and literature are stressed equally (e.g., "Reading and Writing Autobiography" and "Reading and Writing the Nonfiction Essay"). In assembling this volume, we asked twenty-three instructors well known as teachers of writing to describe how they teach literature: What do they do differently from what they did before they came to see themselves as writing teachers? How does their teaching of literature differ from the teaching of colleagues who view themselves as primarily literature teachers? And in either case, what is the net result, for both the learners and the texts they read, of applying composition pedagogy to literary study?

We have organized this collection into five thematic sections, placed brief "interchapters" between essays, and ended with a provocative "Afterword" by Gerald Graff. The interchapters are brief, informal speculations by people who teach literature and attended a session we co-chaired at the 1994 Conference on College Composition and Communication (CCCC) Convention in Nashville. We asked participants to write a response to the prompt "how does the teaching of writing influence how you teach literature." What we have then is numerous teachers' voices on this topic—teachers from two-year colleges, four-year colleges, research universities, from Hawaii to Vermont—teachers who teach literature in different settings to diverse student populations. We also are pleased that Gerald Graff agreed to read the manuscript and write a critical reflection on our enterprise. We knew he is more closely identified with the teaching of literature than the teaching of writing; we knew of his abiding interest in both the history and future of English Studies; we knew of his continuing interest in both composition and literature (he regularly participates in both CCCC and Modern Language Association annual conventions); and we knew that with his wealth of knowledge and his critical acumen, he would provide fresh insight and critical perspective on this collection of essays. And that he has done.

Essays in the first section, "Conflicts in the Contact Zone," raise questions about the current field of English Studies, highlighting some of the points of agreement, intersection, and departure among those who teach both literature and composition. But more importantly, perhaps, they focus on both the literature teacher's role and the students' roles in creating literary knowledge in classroom contexts. Our title suggests two prominent models for engaging students in the experience of reading and valuing literature: Gerald Graff's "teach-the-conflicts" model and Mary Louise Pratt's "contact-zone" model.

John Trimbur focuses on student experience in "taking" English courses in high school and college. He begins his introductory literature class by asking students to write on the questions "What is literature?" and "Why have you been required to study literature?" And thus we too begin at the beginning—suggesting ways that teachers and students can become involved in situating literature in their lives, in their common classroom experiences, and in the social dynamics of their society. In so doing, we can appreciate Trimbur's rationale and strategies for taking students seriously as thinkers about literature.

Deborah H. Holdstein shows us the conflicts close to home by inviting us to a dinner party where various English faculty munch and chew their way through departmental politics, process versus product, and "theoretical perspectives often as unyielding as a recalcitrant oyster shell." What exactly do English faculty, some specializing in literature, some in composition, have in common and what can each contribute to the conversation about teaching literature?

Charles Moran describes his own thirty-year evolution within the English profession, from "professor" of literature to reflective practitioner, from ivy-league to public university, from teacher-centered to student-centered. His experiences with conflicts between literature and composition in his department, his profession, and his daily "life-as-teacher" have come together to teach him anew what it means to be a teacher of English.

This section concludes with James A. Reither's description of a course in which students learn the work of the profession and the processes of how to do it. Reither suggests that literary studies courses often get "precisely the writing they deserve" because they do not engage the students in the genuine discourse of the discipline. He suggests an appealing alternative based on Kenneth Burke's notion that to change the texts produced by students, you have to change the situation that motivates the textual production. In Reither's course, students publish a book that represents their contribution to the discipline's knowledge about the workings of language and literature.

The second section, "Student Writing and Teacher Learning," moves more specifically into the work of the profession, focusing especially on the making of literary knowledge as a collaborative endeavor among students and teachers of literature. In each of these essays, what literature is and what it means to those who read it are questions answered by students and teachers who together take equally seriously the literature they read and the literature they produce. For example, Joseph F. Trimmer's journal presents his day-to-day experiences in one literature class that wrote its own contemporary literature anthology. Students took responsibility for selecting, interpreting, and teaching literary selections, and they arranged to interview the authors to combine any new information with that found in library reference sources in the headnotes they wrote. And most interestingly, in addition to the work of previously published and often notable authors, each student included a literary selection from his or her own portfolio of writing.

Lynn Z. Bloom describes a graduate seminar in autobiographical literature in which, after twenty years of teaching, she manages to integrate the critical with the creative, the writing with the reading, the process with the product. Students studied published autobiographies and, at the same time, composed portions of their own and shared them with each other. They wrote literature to learn literature. A breakthrough occurs in this particular class during one workshop session in which the teacher offers a piece of her own autobiographical writing "in process" and invites response and critique from her fellow writers.

Richard J. Murphy, Jr. continues the exploration of teachers learning from their students by focusing closely on the teaching of a single literary work, the eighteenth-century novel *Clarissa*. Murphy has taught Richardson's novel six times over the years, but recently the student voices have become louder and more interesting. What students say in writing and talking about the novel has expanded Murphy's own understanding of this text in ways the critical canon surrounding the work has not. And in listening closely to his students discussing *Clarissa*, Murphy discovers anew some of the ways people read literature that in turn suggests new ways for him to teach literature. What students write about *Clarissa* will make subsequent readings of the novel a very different experience for him and for them.

In the concluding essay of this section, Cheryl Glenn tells us about her daily challenges (as recorded in the journal she keeps) of teaching a survey course in Restoration and Romantic literature with extensive and varied writing assignments, oral presentations, and frequent student-teacher conferences. Like Trimmer, Bloom, and Murphy, she found that student-raised questions and personal explorations pushed her own understandings of the literature and the course in new directions. For Glenn, teaching the reading process is interconnected with teaching the writing process, in which "rough reads" are analogous to rough drafts, in which reading-intensive and writing-intensive become one.

The essays in "Writing and Rewriting Literature" describe courses in which student writing becomes an active part of re-seeing, re-inventing, and re-writing the texts under study in a college classroom. They suggest ways in which writing, imagining, and performing can revise and enrich initial readings of texts through meanings negotiated in classroom settings. These authors collectively argue that such interactive strategies are important to making one's own encounters with literary texts. They construct assignments that enable students to experience literature directly rather than vicariously through the teacher's reading. Wendy Bishop asks the question of herself and of us: "How to draw the student-generated canon into a working relationship with the contemporary academic canon?" In constructing her answer, Bishop shows us the alternative voices running though her head as well as through her class as she walks a fine line between teaching the accepted poetic canon and listening to the students teach her and each other their own poetic canons.

Charles Schuster describes in detail how the activity of rhetorical "reader's theater" helps students interpret and transform literary texts into personally meaningful performances. He suggests that literary study is most meaningful to students when they come to view it as an expression of performance. And for his students, Schuster wants for them not only to be informed and cognizant members of the writer's audience, but also "coauthors" who participate in the performance through the parallel act of creation.

In "A Merging of Lives," Brad Peters takes issue with Richard Marius's contention that students need to study a text for the meaning in the text itself rather than to construct the meaning of a text in relation to their own lives. While Marius believes that student "autobiographical writing demeans our profession," Peters believes that such writing might unlock the mysteries of our profession (understanding, engaging, and experiencing a wide variety of texts) for our students. Through five different assignments that form a "companion text" to *I Know Why the Caged Bird Sings* by Maya Angelou, Peters demonstrates that the intersection between published literature and personal writing is the most important contact zone for many students.

What's important about literary study for Diana George and Saralinda Blanning is for students "to love and appreciate literature as they do," not as we do. In two very different courses, a first-year composition class and an upper-level British novel survey, they taught the novels *Dr. Jekyll and Mr. Hyde* and *Frankenstein*. They encounter students, mostly engineering majors, who say they didn't know literature had anything to do with life. In such a context, students arrive at new understandings of this literature through invention and re-writing exercises, through collaborative learning and oral performance, through connecting popular culture to academic culture and to their own lives. Thus they disagree with Maxine Hairston and Erika Lindemann, who have argued that the composition classroom should not attempt to bridge the gap to the literature classroom.

Brenda M. Greene cites Wayne Booth, J. Hillis Miller, and Robert Scholes in arguing that the best way for students to arrive at a critical understanding of literature is to reinvent it for themselves. Greene asks her students from New York City, the majority of whom have a Caribbean heritage, to write monologues and dialogues from the point of view of marginalized characters in such works as *Wide Sargasso Sea, Heart of Darkness*, and *The Awakening*. From such experiences, students learn to deconstruct these texts while they construct their own readings and writings.

In the fourth section, "Writing for Personal Knowledge," five essayists explore the role of personal or expressive writing to enhance students' understanding of literary texts and of their own experiences with literature. We begin this section with Peter Elbow, who gives four explicit examples related to our book's subtitle, "Bringing Writing to Reading." In suggesting that the process of reading a literary text may begin with students' writing (rather than always having the writing follow the reading), Elbow articulates the differences between discussing literature and writing about it. He explains how a writing workshop-style literature class, one that takes students through the process of reading and experiencing a literary text (similar to a writing workshop that takes them through the process of composing a text), allows students to arrive at their own interpretations and improve the quality of subsequent classroom discussion.

In "Reading People: The Pragmatic Use of Common Sense," Thomas Newkirk suggests that student understanding of literature is more enjoyable and profound when teachers draw out and acknowledge the tacit theories of interpretation that students bring with them to the formal study of literature. His goal is to demystify the reading of literature and to make it a rewarding everyday activity, like reading people.

In their essays, Douglas M. Tedards and Carl R. Lovitt show how intensive journal writing can lead students to new understandings of the works they read. Describing a section on modern American poets from his course "Major American Authors II," Tedards demonstrates how he uses three kinds of journal entries—expressive, analytical, creative—to change students' poor attitudes toward modern poetry and toward their own writing. In a sophomore survey of contemporary literature, Lovitt explores the public and private domains of keeping a personal journal of literary responses. Working with students who confessed that reading literature did not have meaning for their lives, he explores the potential of the private domain of journal responses to a literary work read outside of class.

Helen J. Schwartz teaches older students (over twenty-five) who are commuters and city dwellers with job and family responsibilities. In "New Technologies for New Majority Students of Literature," she introduces the concept of electronic mail (e-mail) as a new and especially flexible medium in which to have students informally explore the meaning of literature to themselves and others. Schwartz demonstrates how e-mail can create conversation about literature and collaboration in thinking about it in nonresidential college settings.

The essays in the final section, and Gerald Graff's "Afterword," focus on student writing that strengthens students' critical proficiency in expressing their ideas about literature. In what ways can classroom practices develop in students the ability to think critically as well as welcome them as novice practitioners into the community of those who use academic discourse to read and write about literature? The first two essays answer this question in very different academic settings. Linda H. Peterson describes how a collaborative writing workshop in a senior literature seminar for Yale University English majors introduces students to the discourse conventions of literary studies and to the process by which disciplinary knowledge is developed and put to use. One product of the workshop and of the course is an insightful and well-argued "senior essay" about literature. Thus, this senior-level seminar becomes a writing-intensive course in reading and writing in the discipline. Jeffrey Sommers, on the other hand, explores ways to use writing to improve students' critical understanding of texts in a culturally diverse two-year college setting. Sommers uses the multiple literacies of students in his Jewish-American Writers course to strengthen their language abilities in academic contexts and "to allow students freedom to move across forms of literacy and experience cultural mediation."

In "Portfolios, Literature, and Learning: Story as a Way of Constructing the World," Kathleen Blake Yancey makes a case for improving the quality of student writing about literature by introducing the portfolio as a means of assessment. In a computer classroom setting, students in an experimental composition and literature course read novels such as *The Great Gatsby* and, among other writing, they drafted and revised four major essays. Students and teacher together decided the portfolio contents and "created the criteria that would govern the evaluation of the portfolio."

William E. Coles, Jr., explores the value of using writing to foster critical thinking in large-enrollment (more than forty-five) literature sections. In contrast to several other authors in this collection, who use a variety of freewriting techniques to engage students with literary texts, Coles demonstrates a ten-minute writing assignment in which students work hard to "craft sentences that discriminating readers will be able to see making very deliberate and very precise relationships between ideas." While the goal of many freewriting exercises is to have writers fill up half a page or more of text in response to a prompt (thus discovering ideas at the point of utterance), the goal of Coles's assignment is for students to write no more than two well-crafted sentences in response to a prompt (thus using time and space limitations as an enabling constraint to generate, craft, and express thought).

The final essay in this section is Toby Fulwiler's "Song of the Open Road: A Motorcycle Rider Teaches Literature." Riding a motorcycle teaches one to attend as much "to the journey (the learning) as the destination (the knowledge)." In a dialogue with a startled listener who doesn't immediately see the connection between motorcycle riding and teaching literature, Fulwiler describes his interactive, multi-genre (journals, letters, critical essays, portfolios) approach to teaching a sophomore survey of American literature. And thus concludes our collection on bringing writing to reading by reminding us that our journey in learning and teaching English is not over and that the open road awaits.

Works Cited

Berlin, James. 1987. *Rhetoric and Reality: Writing Instruction in American Colleges, 1900–1985*. Carbondale: Southern Illinois University Press.

Britton, James, Tony Burgess, Nancy Martin, Alex McLeod, and Harold Rosen. 1975. *The Development of Writing Abilities*. London: Macmillan Education.

Bruffee, Kenneth. 1984. "Collaborative Learning and the 'Conversation of Mankind.'" *College English* 46: 635–652.

Elbow, Peter. 1973. *Writing Without Teachers*. New York: Oxford.

Emig, Janet. 1977. "Writing as a Mode of Learning." *College Composition and Communication* 28:122–128.

Faigley, Lester. 1992. *Fragments of Rationality: Postmodernity and the Subject of Composition*. Pittsburgh: University of Pittsburgh Press.

Fulwiler, Toby, and Art Young. 1990. *Programs that Work: Models and Methods for Writing Across the Curriculum*. Portsmouth, NH: Boynton/Cook.

Graff, Gerald. 1992. *Beyond the Culture Wars: How Teaching the Conflicts Can Revitalize American Education*. New York: W. W. Norton.

Macrorie, Ken. [1968] 1984. *Writing to Be Read*, 3rd ed. Portsmouth, NH: Boynton/Cook.

Murray, Donald. 1968. *A Writer Teaches Writing*. Boston: Houghton-Mifflin.

North, Stephen M. 1987. *The Making of Knowledge in Composition: Portrait of an Emerging Field*. Portsmouth, NH: Boynton/Cook.

Pratt, Mary Louise. 1991. "Arts of the Contact Zone." *Profession* 91: 33–40. New York: Modern Language Association.

Russell, David R. 1991. *Writing in the Academic Disciplines, 1870–1990: A Curricular History*. Carbondale: Southern Illinois University Press.

I

Conflicts in the Contact Zone

1

"Taking English"
Notes on Teaching Introductory Literature Classes

John Trimbur
Worcester Polytechnic Institute

Picture the students who walk into the "Introduction to Literature" class I teach every fall—largely first-year students, mostly men (I teach in an engineering school that is about 80 percent male), dressed almost identically in jeans or shorts, tee shirts, sneakers, athletic caps worn backward or forward. These students generally come from white ethnic working-class and middle-class homes in southern New England. Most attended public high schools, where they finished in the top ten percent of their graduating class. Sixty percent or so are likely to have been raised Catholic. They are culturally conservative and vaguely liberal to centrist in their politics. They tend to be sweet, naive, and a little bit clueless, especially when it comes to English.

This is not to say these students haven't studied English. They have, repeatedly, year after year, K through 12. Almost all of them have taken four years of English in high school, often in honors and AP courses, where they tend to get tracked. Some have enjoyed their high school English courses, and some remember an English teacher or two with fondness. Some have had charismatic teachers of the *Dead Poets Society*-type and are still in the thrall of literature as a romantic cult of beautiful and tragic young men. Others figure they're just not good at English, never were and never will be—they must have missed out when the literature gene got passed around, perhaps disproportionately, they figure, to their female counterparts. Still others look forward to English as a respite from the science and mathematics courses that make up the first-year curriculum in an engineering college. They see English as a place where there are no right or wrong answers and you "get to discuss."

But, whatever their experience in English courses might have been in the past, my students have very little idea why they've been asked over and over again in twelve years of schooling to take English and to read and study works of literature. Instead, they bring to class that first day a range of expectations both conventional and contradictory. Some, for example, think the class will be creative writing. Others expect to read some poems and short stories and give their personal responses or search for "hidden meanings." A number think we'll be studying grammar and punctuation. My point here is that the title of the course, "Introduction to Literature," does not seem to register. They read the title, I believe, as "English" in a decidedly undifferentiated way that encompasses virtually everything they've been asked to do in the past in school under the auspices of "English."

If you asked these students, as I usually do the first day of class, why they have decided to take a literature course ("Intro to Lit" is not a required course), they would probably tell you that they want to improve their reading and writing and "communication skills" because, as one student said this past fall, we live in a "fast-paced age of information and rapid technological change." Almost all the students agree that "effective communication" is somehow key to the careers they hope to pursue, though they have only the vaguest notion of the kinds of reading and writing professionals do in the workplace. What they do know is that it's a tough world out there—a place of heightened competition, diminished expectations, downsizing, and temporary contracts. They are acutely aware of the threat of downward mobility and the crisis of the middle classes and that to avoid dead-end McJobs, they need any edge they can get. One of these edges they call "English," and these students share the common belief that "taking English" can invest them—and their speaking, reading, and writing habits—with the kind of propriety, refinement, and grammaticality that serves to distinguish the professional managerial classes from the working and lower classes.

At the same time, however, my students also believe that "English" can play a very different role in their lives—that in fact it can make them better persons. A number of students say that the reason they're "taking English" is to learn about other cultures and other peoples. As one student put it this past fall, literature is about "learning lessons about life and how people solve moral problems."

The fact that the reasons my students give for "taking English" are both conventional and contradictory should not be surprising. For one thing, cultural beliefs about the connections among literacy, upward mobility, and social distinction are deeply entrenched in the popular consciousness. For another, from Matthew Arnold on, the study of literature has persistently been figured as strategic cultural work to elevate the tastes and opinions of the middle classes and to prepare them for moral leadership in society. So my students seem to intuit that "English" is not only about writing for success in the workplace but also about character-building, perfecting an ethical self, and learning class consciousness. Now, if my students have updated some of these constructions of "English" to meet what they see as the pragmatic, bottom-line realities of the American job market, I don't want to suggest that they are simply cultural dupes reproducing the twin ideologies of literacy and literature. There are some other reasons they so readily fall back on the view that "English is good for you."

Of all the disciplines, English in general and literary studies in particular have been remarkably reticent about explaining to their charges what these fields are about, what kind of problems they investigate, and why they do so. It may well be, as Jeanne Fahnestock and Marie Secor suggest, that the rhetorical address of literary studies is largely epideictic or ceremonial— a "subtly ritualized form of communication" that celebrates its own activities without naming them, where literature takes shape as that which "goes without saying" (and to have to ask is not so much wrong as a sign of poor taste). Moreover, as Susan Peck MacDonald says, because literary studies, as opposed, say, to the sciences and social sciences, deal with texts as "ill-defined problems," a good deal of the problem formulation that gives disciplines their objects of inquiry remains tacit, a matter of what Charles Bazerman (1988) calls a "complex state of mind beyond naming" (40). For these reasons, it is no wonder my students believe, as Bazerman continues, that the literary work "only gains importance in subjective experience" (42). In other words, as my students might say, when it comes to "taking English," either you get it or you don't, depending on the kind of person you are.

These difficulties are compounded by the fact that English teachers themselves may not be altogether clear about what the study and teaching of "English" is really about. This too should not be surprising because the study and teaching of English is currently caught up in what Jurgen Habermas calls a "legitimation crisis." The role of English studies in transmitting an Arnoldian model of life—a *culture generale d'esprit*—has increasingly been challenged not only by canon-busting critics, feminism, African-American studies, postcolonialism, and queer theory, but also by the performance principle and an achievement ideology of careerist individualism (precisely the contradiction my students have articulated). What had formerly been self-evident and self-justifying has now become problematic, a topoi in a discourse of crisis. In a legitimation crisis, as Habermas describes it, the authority of cultural tradition loses its power to secure the level of loyalty needed to produce the tradition intact. This reproduction normally occurs, as it were, behind the backs of the actors—students and faculty alike— seemingly without a thought. At times of crisis, however, faculty and students go about their business teaching and studying, but they are not quite sure why. The old motives inscribed in the activity of "English" no longer appear to be sufficient, and no practical equivalent to the problematized system of authority has emerged. The crisis of legitimacy thus spills over into a crisis of motivation.

The poet Robert Hass describes this crisis state as a failure of memory: "After a while, I would have a sense that I used to know what the point of teaching and learning literature was, but that I couldn't remember anymore. It was a sensation like losing a set of car keys. I couldn't remember where I'd been and I couldn't go anywhere" (38). Literature courses continue to take place, and literary works get read and discussed. What is missing, though, is a sense of authorization: the sense among faculty that legitimizes their work and makes it meaningful and the sense among students that what they are learning somehow counts. The forms of teaching and learning remain but they are hollow. No one is sure what animates them, what they mean, or what authority is capable of eliciting consent to the whole enterprise.

This is where proposals for reform come in, to give reasons, re-inscribe motives, and restore memory. The "heritage model" offered by figures such as Allan Bloom, William J. Bennett, and Lynne Cheney propose that students should know literature to understand their common culture and get in touch with what is universal about it. This model, of course, has been repeatedly (and justifiably) criticized for assuming that what's common to American or Western culture is somehow by definition universal. But the alternatives, such as Gerald Graff's "teach-the-conflicts" model, though it usefully foregrounds the legitimation crisis of "English," nonetheless in at least one important respect share a key assumption with defenders of the canon such as Bloom, Bennett, and Cheney. That is, both models represent students as novices for whom the study of literature amounts to learning the practices of experts, whether it is Arnold's "disinterested endeavour to learn and propagate the best that is known and thought in the world" or the politically interested readings of feminist, postcolonial, Marxist, and other critics that have thrown the issue of literature into such turmoil.

To my way of thinking, what both models leave out is student experience—both as disciplined pupils in twelve years of English classrooms and as ordinary readers of popular culture. By seeking to clarify the problem of "English," these models neglect how contradictory student experience has been—and how useful pedagogically it can be to raise this contradictory experience to consciousness and to reinterpret it. Instead, both models assume that the effective meanings of literature can be read off the surface of the text—whether those of the canon or of canon-busting critics—by the procedures of experts. And what gets lost are the histories of ordinary readers and accounts of ordinary experience.

Now I want to be careful here not to hold up ordinary experience as a more authentic form of truth or a more immediate kind of consciousness than the codified knowledges of expertise. This is one of the senses of the term "experience" Raymond Williams notes in *Keywords* that invests it with an idea of wholeness and inviolability derived from the "inner" and "personal" experiences of both radical Protestantism and Romantic aesthetics. But "experience," as Williams says, also denotes "the product of social conditions or of systems of belief" (128), the determinants rather than the irreducible grounds of subjectivity. To my mind, the usefulness of thinking about student experience is that it asks us to engage the tension between these two senses of the term—to represent students neither as essential selves (whose experience can "correct" the institutions of schooling) nor as academic initiates (whose innocence is about to be "corrected" by the experience of the teacher). Instead, experience points to the spot where the everyday lives of students intersect with schooled knowledge and the discourses of experts, where students internalize, resist, and evade what their teachers tell them. To put it another way, students' sense of "English" both reproduces and exceeds its cultural codings. As students learn from the earliest grades on up to separate work from play, academic life from social life, reading for comprehension from reading for pleasure, they learn that literature and literacy are deeply contradictory phenomena.

One of the reasons that "English" is experienced as contradictory is that "English" refuses to present itself as the experience readers have of written and other texts, but instead offers itself as a set of skills (reading, writing, usage, punctuation, and so on) and a body of material called "literature"— and these representations collide, in oblique ways, with how students experience themselves as readers. Many of my students are voracious readers. But much of the reading they do—science fiction, thrillers, cyberpunk, bestsellers, romances—is disqualified ahead of time, in their own and their English teachers' minds, from the domain of "English." Moreover, a surprising number of my students not only consume such popular genres, they also produce them both alone and collaboratively through self-sponsored writing. My point here is that "English," at least as it is presently constituted, makes little effort to recognize where or how its own particular concerns intersect with students' experience as readers and their productive work as writers. Instead, if "Intro to Lit" anthologies are any indication, "English" simply begins with the assumption that students should study the genres—fiction, poetry, drama.

One of the rationales for organizing "Intro to Lit" courses around the genres is that such introductory courses need to lay the groundwork for a student's further literary studies. By this account, students need to acquire a shared vocabulary and set of analytical methods to make the literature curriculum coherent. There is, of course, some logic to this view, but the problem is that the emphasis on the *introductory* character of the course, by being so resolutely prospective, actually serves to erase student experience, to render it mute and inaccessible. In contrast, I suggest "Intro to Lit" courses should begin not at the beginning—by diving into the genres—but in the student's past, by unpacking the conventional and contradictory meanings and experiences of "English" that students carry with them.

To do this, on the first day of class, after I've asked students why they are taking "Intro to Lit," I ask them to write for five minutes on each of these two questions: "What is literature?" and "Why have you been required to study literature?" I read through the student texts and in the next class show overhead transparencies of a few of the responses in order to prompt discussion of the issues each question raises. I have found that the student writings invariably unlock the contradictory character of "English" and make students' experience of these contradictions available for analysis and reinterpretation. Let me give some examples of how this works. The following is a response a student wrote to the question "What is literature?":

> Literature is anything someone writes for other people to read in the form of a text. There will be questions to answer after each reading. This definition is not really correct, however, because policemen refer to their pamphlets as literature also. Literature could be ancient (Shakespeare), informative (Bill James' *Abstracts*), or modern (Fitzgerald, Hemingway). Literature is just anything someone throws together for others to read.

There are a number of things to notice here. First, when I initially read that "literature is . . . in the form of a text," I wondered whether the student was invoking a poststructuralist language of textuality. But when I read the next sentence, it became clear that the student meant text as textbook. In other words, from the perspective of a reader constituted as a pupil of "English," literature appears in anthologies assigned by teachers and is inseparable from a pedagogy that examines student reading: "There will be questions to answer." At the same time, this definition of literature is not entirely satisfactory to the student, for, as he notes, "policemen refer to their pamphlets as literature also." In this response, the student's experience of literature as schooled readings that the teacher will examine collides with the student's knowledge of the world. This collision, moreover, is marked discursively by the "however" that reveals the student's awareness of the contradictory meanings of the term "literature": as something in "English" books and as forms of writing people use at work. In the grouping of imaginative literature—Shakespeare, Fitzgerald, Hemingway—with nonfiction (Bill James' *Abstracts* consists of baseball statistics) and in the final sentence, there is a growing feeling of exasperation over trying to contain and delimit the term "literature": It "is just anything someone throws together for others to read."

Another response begins along similar lines, when the student says, "Literature could be any kind of writing to express what the writer thinks." Nonetheless, in the next two sentences, the student begins to draw a distinction. "For some reason, however, I have a hard time thinking of paperbacks in the drugstore as literature. Ibsen or Faulkner is literature, but Stephen King or thrillers are just books." Again the use of "however" marks the point where contradictory senses of the term "literature" collide, in this case, the categorization of forms of writing into serious literature and popular fiction.

Here is a third example of a response to the question "What is literature?" that reveals a different set of contradictions:

> Literature is anything you are assigned to read in a humanities course, be its purpose to analyze society or confuse freshmen. All the good writers are dead. Which makes their writing classic literature. No, I'm just kidding. To be considered, a book must have a good standing in the academic community. Why go on? You're probably going to give the next question. I'm right. You just did.

Notice here that the student begins by locating literature in the domain of school authority—as "anything you are assigned to read"—and then parodies the uses of this authority as a means to "confuse freshmen." In the next two sentences, the student offers further parody of what makes "writing classic literature," namely that "the good writers are dead." But then, after a disclaimer—"No, I'm just kidding"—the student moves from parody to analysis (and invokes what teachers will recognize as Stanley Fish's notion of interpretive communities as constitutive of the category literature) when he says, "To be considered literature, a book must have a good standing in the academic community." Finally, the student remarks on the relation of his work—"Why go on?—to my authority as a teacher:"You're probably going to give the next question." And by noting that I "just did," the student asserts his own control over and knowledge about classroom life: "I'm right."

The last example I offer here was written in response to the question "Why have you been required to study literature?" and, like the others, is notable for its contradictory qualities. Here's what the student wrote:

> The purpose of studying literature is to expose students to works they might not otherwise have taken the trouble to read. All of life is a learning process. The thoughts of an author written one hundred years ago can inspire us and teach lessons about life today. Unfortunately, books in literature courses are chosen according to the ethics of the time. This borders on the verge of censorship.

Again, I want to call attention to the turn the student makes in his writing. After what I see as a remarkably "orthodox" view of the purposes of studying literature (to "expose students," to "inspire us," to "teach us lessons about life"), the student abandons the liberal humanist view that "all of life is a learning process," to consider how "books are chosen according to the ethics of the time." Like the preceding student, this writer has not needed Stanley Fish to know that what we call literature is inextricably bound up in relations of power and the cultural authorization of expert readers. Given the opportunity to articulate understandings that grow out of the everyday experiences of schooled pupils of "English," this student is neither naive nor clueless when it comes to considering why he has so persistently been called upon to study literature.

My point may be obvious by now. The conventional and contradictory understandings of why they are "taking English" that students bring with them into "Intro to Lit" classrooms can serve as a rich repository of experience and practical knowledge. I think my students were surprised when I showed anonymous transparencies of what they had written—not just because I was taking them seriously as thinkers about literature, but because there was so much to talk about. These writings called on us to negotiate our problematical and contradictory understandings of the meanings of literature in school and society. And in this sense, what my students had written co-determined the curriculum by making available the experiences of schooled pupils of "English" and ordinary readers—thereby locating our work together in what Mary Louise Pratt calls the "contact zone," where expert and popular understandings of literature collide, intertwine, resist, and parody each other in complex and potentially rewarding ways.

Works Cited

Bazerman, Charles. 1988. *Shaping Written Knowledge: The Genre and Activity of the Experimental Article in Science*. Madison: University of Wisconsin Press.

Fahnestock, Jeanne, and Marie Secor. 1991. "The Rhetoric of Literary Criticism." In *Textual Dynamics: Historical and Contemporary Studies of Writing in Professional Communities*, edited by Charles Bazerman and James Paradis. Madison: University of Wisconsin Press.

Habermas, Jurgen. 1975. *Legitimation Crisis*. Boston: Beacon.

"An Interview with Robert Hass." 1983. *Louisiana English Journal* 22: 36–42.

MacDonald, Susan Peck. 1987. "Problem Definition in Academic Writing." *College English* 49.3: 315–31.

Pratt, Mary Louise. 1991. "Arts of the Contact Zone."*Profession 91:* 33–40.

Williams, Raymond. 1983. *Keywords*. Revised ed. New York: Oxford.

I sacrifice some content to make room for revision and peer-group work. This sacrifice was hard at first, but soon enough I began to realize that "field coverage" was not my only (or even my primary) goal. I wanted my students to learn, and to enjoy the learning to the extent that they would be inclined to read (and maybe even to write) poems and stories beyond the temporal and somewhat artificial borders of college.

Much of the writing I assign in literature classes is designed to assist students in learning rather than memorizing. Examples of such assignments would be journals and short response papers, and the aim of such writing is almost always exploratory, involving question-posing and speculation rather than reporting of information. Such assignments may be linked to longer, more formal papers, and thus constitute part of an ongoing process, but not always. As for the "formal" papers I assign—well, I'm happy to say they have become increasingly less "formal," far less academic.

Because I have been interested for some time in personal voice (however disputed that term may now be and no matter how variously defined), I frequently ask students to write personally about their experience with the assigned literature, and I will frequently couple that personal dimension to a specific audience—say, for example, readers of a metropolitan newspaper's Sunday Supplement or college-level readers of an anthology of literature targeted for non-English majors.

More recently, I have been asking for group collaborative essays, and my exams are frequently collaborative as well—students work together to MAKE an exam, not take it. Both learning to ask good questions and composing them lucidly seem to generate more enthusiasm and interest than the traditional testing format. I believe I am a better literature teacher now because of the composition strategies I have brought to my literature classroom; at the same time, I am able to reinforce, especially in upper division courses, the writing skills promoted in first-year English.

Randall Freisinger
Michigan Technological University

2

The Dinner Party: Munching the Conflicts
(Or, My Dinner with Double-Entendre)

Deborah H. Holdstein
Governors State University

As I began to think about the subject for this collection, I found myself in something of a quandary. As a composition specialist who "gets" to teach literature, I confess to being something of a half-breed, or "false coinage"—what Cynthia Ozick, for vastly different reasons, called T. S. Eliot (119). Indeed, one might say with some justification that I am a literature specialist who "gets" to teach composition. In my youth, I had been drawn to the study of English because of literature; the study of poetry in particular (initially French poetry at that) would be my lifelong *metier*.

But since I had few designs on becoming a poet (and by birthright no claim on becoming a French poet), then I could certainly afford poetry and those capable of creating its beauty the reverence they richly deserved. And to a large extent, I still feel that way. My retraining in composition evolved because I was fortunate enough to encounter its significance during and after graduate school. The exigencies of the job market and capitalist greed (that is, my need to pay the rent) served to reinforce my established interest and commitment to composition studies. Can one legitimately claim membership in the composition club and still revere the literary products of genius?

I hold within me other manifestations of the philosophical and practical conflicts between the lit-types and the compo-types, the institutionally based divisions between theory and practice, the implication of this volume that we in composition somehow bear profound and significant insights about the teaching of literature that our counterparts do not (and wouldn't even care to admit to, if they did). How might I discern the ways in which twenty years

24

of learning about and teaching the writing process have influenced my teaching of literature?

I Looked to Brainstorm, and I Found a Fight

3:45 P.M. Having typed into my Macintosh a clean copy of Edward Hirsch's poem, "The Skokie Theatre," I then hurry to begin documenting my students' responses to the text and our productive discussion about the poem—all this for the purposes of this essay. ("I'd better get the table set," *that* part of me urges.) As one might linger before leaving a loved one, I pause by the old Mac Plus—just a few minutes more, please!—to continue brainstorming notes toward my own draft before I abandon thoughts of poetry, teaching, and writing for the intricacies of Caribbean Chicken, charcoal briquets, and random acts of parenting. I prepare for the dinner party, a gathering of friends. Tonight, everyone coming happens to be a faculty member in one of several English departments in the Chicago area.

But this afternoon I cannot shut down my brainstorming as easily as I've shut down the Mac. I am preoccupied during food preparation, carrying with me rather annoying questions about the nature and purpose of this essay, indeed, this collection. "I know," I bubble to no one in particular. "I'll talk about this essay tonight. I'll get advice." It seemed like the perfect time to sound out a few ideas—colleagues from literature, critical theory, rhetoric, and a few souls marginally connected to composition.

They arrive, each bearing her or his designated part of the evening's gastronomic game plan and, as I would later be reminded, theoretical perspectives often as unyielding as a recalcitrant oyster shell. We make the usual small talk, sit or stand around comfortably in the large kitchen. I wait, patiently, for someone to ask the question—"What are you working on these days, Deb?" Jana, a feminist critic with specialization in nineteenth-century American literature, gives me what I want. The door, metaphorically speaking, has opened.

I confidently and proudly announce the subject for this collection—*When Writing Teachers Teach Literature*. But before we can even approach the doorway of intellectual discourse, I am instead subject to this:

"Must be a rather thin book," says my spouse, a philosopher. (His wry humor undoubtedly attracted me in the first place.)

"Who *cares* if writing teachers teach literature. So *what*?" says Antonio, a critical theorist.

"They shouldn't be allowed to, should they? I mean, what do they know about literature if they teach writing?" says Jana.

"One could also say, however, that this is *way* arrogant, *n'est-ce pas*?" asks Judy, a specialist in African-American literature whose latest enthusiasm is the slave narrative. "A collection like this implies by its title that writing teachers must have some sort of unique angle on the teaching of

literature that we in literary studies do not. Who on earth would the audience
for this book be?''

Eric, the other composition specialist (besides me), pipes up, attempting
to make nice. ''I would assume—isn't this the case, Deb?—that a writing
teacher teaching literature would make the course writing-centered, no matter the subject, and that student engagement with the text would be as important, if not more important, than the literary text.'' Well, it's the last part of
that remark that really blows things up.

Jana turns red, nearly choking on her own spinach dip. ''What is it about
you compo people—having to think that all texts are equally good? What's
the deal with all that? Are you all so touchy-feely, so tree-huggy, that your
poor little students can't stand the thought that something by Keats might
have more merit, strictly speaking, than their essays about a summer vaca-
tion? Isn't that what the decline of education is all about?''

Uh, this is, as they say, getting out of hand. I am speechless, in the
ridiculous position of hosting a citywide version of a department meeting (of
people from different departments, no less) in what now seems to be the flimsy
guise of a dinner party. I just cannot extricate us from fairly negative implications for these mostly literature-based colleagues over the prospect of some
formal delineation of the ways in which composition teachers teach literature.

''Hey, you guys,'' I say, invoking my best New Yawk accent, ''all I
want is some feedback.'' But it's not a pretty sight to see one's friends grow
increasingly slack jawed by the discussion. ''It is not violating the purposes
of teaching, of communicating the value of things literary—however we
define that, even *you* have trouble defining that—to share certain values
about our students and about teaching our students.''

''Yes?'' volunteers Judy. ''Like what, for instance?''

''Is it possible for those of you 'in literature,' or at least more in the
mainstream of English departments, to share our assumptions about important concepts and issues that affect our students? Student empowerment,
finding one's voice, owning one's text, writing as process, collaborative
learning and multiple authorship, peer discussion and revision. . . . ?''

''Great,'' Antonio responds. ''Caring about everything and anything but
the text at hand. Nobody thinks of the text as wholly sacred anymore—this
is poststructuralism, you know—but can't your students be challenged by
their engagement with the text? You've mentioned everything except reading and responding!''

''Let her finish,'' Eric says. ''Maybe there are a few ways to do things,
just as there are multiple ways to read a text. Maybe you're projecting your
own insecurity about teaching.''

''You're *all* getting ahead of me,'' I retort.

''So what you're saying is, that we in literature teach in outmoded fashion. We're reactionary, oppressive. We don't take our theory and put it into
practice.''

I confess to Antonio that I have always suspected he is little more than a closet New Critic, despite his publications centering on poststructuralist theory. I suggest that his theory might be a mere cover for his true longing for the Tradition. He is, I offer, someone eagerly awaiting the time when it is again safe to use the words "irony" and "paradox"in the same sentence. Haven't they heard of Hairston? Clifford and Schilb?

And my hackles are raised, my Irish is up. I am defensive, veering dangerously close to the "I'll show ya" mentality of adolescence.

"If the shoe fits, kiddo! Given the things you've said, I doubt that you even *care* if your teaching is effective or not, if you're even reaching your students. And unfortunately you've got institutional sanction for the way you feel!"

I grow calm, more or less, but Eric really puts a scare into the group: "Would you even consider letting your students 'mess with the text' for the ultimate benefit of their access to that text?"

Jana jumps in, "Isn't that just taking students away from the text? Aren't you then just using the text as an occasion for writing rather than as the subject for writing?" As I serve the "jerk" chicken, the name for which I *swear* is no comment on my beloved friends and colleagues, I bless Jana for at least getting us back to productive discussion.

"Isn't it possible that the teaching of literature by those coming out of composition-influenced perspectives would just offer something *different* in the ways they teach literature, not necessarily something *better?*" Quiet prevails. Are they thinking or just chewing? Maybe it's a bad evening for conversation, but I have to admit I'm rather pleased to have these conflicts aired. Visions of Gerald Graff and "teaching the conflicts" *redux* flash before my eyes—his tale of the OMP (Old Male Professor) and the YFP (Young Female Professor) debating the questionable value (in YFP's view) of male-derived, canonical texts. Fortunately, Graff himself rings the doorbell, awash in apology for lateness, and arrives in time to join the fray. The fact that Graff isn't a writing specialist—indeed, he might well be perceived as "the enemy"—doesn't trouble me at this point. He'll never have the last word anyway, nor will he try to take it. I need time. At this juncture, I even have time to put away the kitchen knives.

"Wait a minute," I announce to everyone, as I turn to head for my study. "Just listen to what we did in class the other day, actually over several days. It brought my students away from the text for the purpose of taking them back."

"Yeah, yeah," several of my pals yawn. "You've really *left* us, haven't you, Deb? Maybe you're not even a half-breed anymore," says Antonio.

"Look," I say. "You eat. I'll read to you. You know, in graduate school twenty years ago, everyone was still under the influence of Wellek and Warren's *Theory of Literature*. On the first day of my first class, I was taught that literature is the reflection of all that concerns *man*kind.' Here's one of many possible ways to enact that as truth, even if we have discarded the rest of that book, especially if we debate about what those concerns are and what counts as literature. In the particular class I want to tell you about—if you'll just eat and hush for a second—the focus on writing *and* the text led us naturally into a bunch of issues I *know* most of you care deeply about!''

"Don't tell me we're going to talk teaching," Jana said.

"Why not?" volunteered Graff.

"Look, that's the problem with composition and the reason you're not taken seriously; isn't it true that in the 1960's all you people talked about was which teaching technique is better? Wasn't that all at the expense of solid, theoretical underpinning?" Judy asked.

"That's not composition now, and it hasn't been for the last twenty years," Eric says, with Graff nodding in assent. "But that doesn't mean that compositionists will sell out—all theory and no practice. Good theories, as it's been said, are eminently practical."

"It's just that all this talking about teaching makes me uncomfortable," adds Jana.

Antonio joins in: "It's ridiculous, that's what it is. This whole collection you're writing for sounds like some sort of sanctioned justification to debunk literature, to take pot shots at literary and critical theorists."

"You know, Deb, your colleagues are going to think that you need to water down literature because your students simply aren't up to the task of reading it and writing about it," Judy asserts.

I rise, physically and metaphorically. "You, of all people, Judy! And Jana! People who have spent their estimable professional lives asserting the place for and value of un-canonical texts and alternative approaches to literary study! Shame on both of you!" Applause from Eric and, surprisingly, my philosopher-spouse. Muffled giggles from Graff. Tentative nod of resignation from Antonio. My son and daughter, passing through, pledge to agree with whatever I say, subject unheard.

"OK. I'm going to say this, and you won't like it," Antonio says. "Let's face it; *somebody's* got to be concerned with teaching. It's better left to the writing teachers."

"You, too, are being ridiculous. Keep eating! Wait here!"

I emerge a few minutes later and begin to read aloud— it *is* my house—the following poem, "The Skokie Theatre," by noted poet and critic Edward Hirsch:

Twelve years old and lovesick, bumbling
and terrified for the first time in my life,
but strangely hopeful, too, and stunned,
definitely stunned—I wanted to cry,
I almost started to sob when Chris Klein
actually touched me—oh God—below the belt
in the back row of the Skokie Theatre.

Our knees bumped helplessly, our mouths
were glued together like flypaper, our lips
were grinding in a hysterical grimace
while the most handsome man in the world
twitched his hips on the flickering screen
and the girls began to scream in the dark.
I didn't know one thing about the body yet,
about the deep foam filling my bones,
but I wanted to cry out in desolation
when she touched me again, when the lights
flooded on in the crowded theatre
and the other kids started to file
into the narrow aisles, into a lobby
of faded purple splendor, into the last
Saturday in August before she moved away.
I never wanted to move again, but suddenly
we were being lifted toward the sidewalk
in a crush of bodies, blinking, shy,
unprepared for the ringing familiar voices
and the harsh glare of sunlight, the brightness
of an afternoon that left us gripping
each other's hands, trembling and changed.

"Great poem. I like it," Jana volunteers, face brightening. Murmurs of assent as coffee begins perking and we all clear the table.

"If Mrs. Civin, my junior high school English teacher, were here," I almost shout, "she'd show us by her example that revering the literary text doesn't mean that students are diminished by its greatness. Our job as teachers is to help our students find the authority, the power, to reach the text as text, to more than appreciate it, to analyze, critique, question it and whatever issues surround or contextualize it. That Mrs. Civin, she taught me to revere the magic of literature, that the text is a worthy, transforming enterprise. Composition has taught me—in practical terms that critical theory often leaves out—that texts are explorable, malleable, and that my students and I have the authority to tackle them, to make them our own."

The mood enlivened by chocolate truffles and strong coffee, I persist, assuming the goodwill of my crowd. "OK, so listen. We read the poem without a title or author, and my students wonder, despite their insider information about me, whether I espouse what to them is a highly alternative sexual orientation when we get to the pronoun 'she,' as in '. . . before she moved away.' This leads nicely into a discussion about ideology and the assumptions we as readers bring to a text."

"With undergraduates?," Jana asks. "At *your* school?"

"Why not?" Judy defends me for the first time that evening.

"To get them into the poem," I continue, ignoring all, "I had my students choose one of three phrases from the text: '. . . cry out in desolation,' 'faded purple splendor,' or 'trembling and changed.' Then I had them write whatever came to mind.''

"Oh, typical," Antonio drools.

"So what?" resurrects Judy.

"Oh, yeah?" I challenge. "Listen up: In addition to a warm-up that brought a variety of interesting glimpses of my students' memories, I asked them to write something else: a response to Edward Hirsch thirty years later from the Chris Klein mentioned in the poem, something she writes after seeing the poem in print for the first time.''

"Ooohh," Judy comments, "I'd love to tackle that one myself! Maybe she's a cop!''

I pass around a copy of one of the student responses, the following poem by one of my graduate students, Juan N. His poem initiated a fruitful sidebar discussion about the relationships between art and literature and issues of gender and writing, all this in addition to lively, satisfying discussion of both poems themselves:

October: Clear Light

falls into my kitchen,
the ring descends
around me once more.

The world turns slowly
toward the sun.
I have dreamed of blue plates,
it seems, and set the simple table.
Blue cups of cold cider.
The loaf of fresh bread. Gravity
to hold each in its place.

I have a daughter
playing now in the yard
with friends, a husband
who will enter being led
by her hand: I will call
from the window where
dried peppers twist in a breeze,
where the Indian Summer sun
will redden my face
like certain women.

Edward, Vermeer's "Milkmaid"
was your favorite portrait of me,
remember? Milk pouring
from a pitcher into a wide bowl,
the maid—white as her milk,
pure with this act of milk—
standing before a window
and bathed in morning light.

You said the clarity of light
was the clarity of God,
that our bodies were pitchers
and bowls to be filled,
and your hands were as generous
as Vermeer's with his maid.

But the capture of light is like milk: it pours
through the hands, falling
through the maiden
and the artist's brush. It splashes
up the sides of the bowl,
licking peach halves and sighing
over strawberries that bloom suddenly
in a creamy pool.
And the painted kitchen
cannot contain it,
flickers now and dims
like a movie on a screen,
narrowing and holding our gaze
until the final point.

More silence. Thoughtful munching and sipping. Antonio and Judy struggle to voice the same thought: "But you're lucky to have had such a thoughtful student. Certainly they're not all like that!?"

"Of course not," I snap. "But even the less 'successful' efforts—and I never expected something like Juan's poem anyway—get us into a discussion of any number of things, for instance, the narrator of the Hirsch poem. By looking at it with Juan's poem, we were then able to compare the two narrators, what the poems imply about their experiences, their attitudes, whether or not the Chris Klein of Juan's text was even possible—what would have had to have happened between then and now. But in every case, we've been able to talk solidly and well about the original text." I hold up a stack. "Here are responses from undergraduate and graduate classes. I can't read them all to you, but I also liked one by another student, Kathy Z. She wrote a 'Dear Eddie' letter that raised potentially interesting social issues and issues of gender that again took us back to the original Hirsch poem. Students asked any number of things and answered the questions among themselves for later full-class discussion. For example, 'Did this really happen?' 'Why does he use the word _____ instead of _____ ?' Kathy writes: '. . . the thirty-odd years that happened to me/never happened to you. . . . The sounds of family drift around me . . . am I still twelve years old to you?'"

Judy wonders aloud, "Don't your students think this is all kind of corny, especially the graduate students? Do they take this sort of thing seriously? Don't they respond rather cynically?"

I am momentarily distracted by the search for another truffle.

"That's exactly what I was afraid of—I'm still locked into my own concerns about the teaching techniques becoming too intrusive, about my own disparaging connotative associations with 'activities.' But I made the issue part of our conversation in class, *asking* students directly what they thought of the activity, explaining what I was doing and why I was doing it. And I was pleasantly surprised to hear that both my graduates and undergraduates said that the writing made them feel much more comfortable with the poem, extremely eager to read it again and again, talk about it, dissect it, write more about it.''

We are beyond argument. We can agree that my students had become invested in the literary text by initially having taken away fragments of it to explore, that this was one of many ways to explore language and texts, and that these investments urged students back again to the original text. We laugh together when I recall that one student saw the writing as a "personal, non-electronic superhighway towards close reading of the text itself.''

The successful airing of these conflicts notwithstanding, most of my friends finish dessert having retreated to their original concerns. After such poorly chosen words as "quaint" and "interestingly energetic," several of my guests pronounce that my "experiment," as it is then dismissively categorized, appears excellent. But to their minds it remains an isolated one.

As she leaves, however, Jana has something to tell me. She emphatically whispers to me as we stroll toward my front door, conspiratorially arm-in-arm. "I'll think about some of this and consider ways to make writing more prominent, more . . . *something* . . . when I teach literature and critical theory.''

"Hey," I offer, "maybe you and I will co-edit that next great collection of essays, *When Literature Teachers Teach Writing*.''

Jana smiles, eyes darting about, face reddening. "OK," she warns, raising a parental finger, "just as long as you don't make me *talk* about it.''

Works Cited

Hirsch, Edward. 1985. "The Skokie Theatre." In *Wild Gratitude* by Edward Hirsch, p. 23. New York: Knopf.

Ozick, Cynthia. 1989. "A Critic At Large (T. S. Eliot): T. S. Eliot at 101." *The New Yorker* 20 November: 119–128, 130, 132–144, 149–154.

T eaching writing for more than twenty years, both in composition classes and in a writing center, plus writing about people, places, and events for the popular press have convinced me that we can indeed write a way into a better understanding of our world. As a writing teacher and a writer, I consider every class a writing class. In literature classes, therefore, before we write formal papers, we write and talk to share in the construction of meaning. Students tell stories and become, like the authors in their textbook, writers.

How does the world look from inside a character's head? Why does a poet write free verse rather than a villanelle? Where is the fictional place that fiction takes place? I want to know. And I want my literature students to want to know.

We write a letter of unsought advice to our old school friend, J. Alfred Prufrock; or we compose an entry in the secret diary of the winged man in "A Very Old Man with Enormous Wings"; or perhaps we create a dialogue between ourselves and Thoreau on the possibility of living according to one's conscience in 1994; or we send e-mail to Emerson and to each other.

To understand the story's dangerously loving husband, we construct a letter from Dr. John to a medical colleague after the events of "The Yellow Wallpaper"; to learn more about real contexts for imaginary situations, we add another "story" to explain the untold tale of Maxine Hong Kingston's aunt in "No Name Woman." What would the emissary say in his blank verse reply to the Duke of Ferrara? And so we write and talk about what we've written in our literature class, moving inside the style and substance of the plays, poems, and stories with which we started.

Donna Reiss
Tidewater Community College

3

One Teacher, Two Cultures
A Study of Influence and Change

Charles Moran
University of Massachusetts
at Amherst

I began my life-as-teacher in 1958, teaching literature to tenth grade boys at
St. George's School, in Newport, Rhode Island. Shortly afterward, I was
trained as a specialist in literary scholarship at Brown University. After the
Ph.D. I taught literature at the University of Massachusetts for a decade and
then changed fields, beginning in 1976 to identify myself with the field of
rhetoric and composition. I believe that now, in 1993, I teach literature differently than I did in 1958–59. I believe, further, that the difference is in part
the result of my move from the culture of literary criticism to that of composition studies.

But how to support these claims? I need to provide evidence that I have
indeed changed as a teacher of literature. I need, further, to find support for
my second claim: that my move into the field of rhetoric and composition has
been one of the forces that has driven this change. I begin with my first
claim—that my practice as a literature teacher has changed. I don't have
access to first-hand accounts of my teaching in 1958. I wish I did, but such
accounts are extraordinary in any time and in any case. What I do have is
the actual copies of the textbooks I taught from in 1958. What I propose,
therefore, is an archaeological dig, a sifting of this material in search of evidence of past teaching practice. In effect I become myself a site, one that has
been inhabited over the years by a series of teachers.

I thank the members of the Department of Language, Literature, and Communications at Northern State University, Aberdeen, South Dakota, and in particular the chair, Jay Ruud, and the
writers whose work I have quoted, for their generosity in allowing me to represent our work in
this chapter.

Setting Out: 1958–59

The evidence I have to work with in this period is slim, because the documents that might help me here are ephemeral: syllabi, class notes, and class documents from 1958–59 are long gone. Were they not, I'd have to have an attic that could, as the saying goes, eat Chicago. I don't generally trust my recall of something as embodied as teaching style, but I have memories that are so vivid that they may indeed be connected to what I actually did. As a teacher who was only five or six years older than his all-male, sometimes-huge students, I was, or felt myself to be, challenged often by students in a range of ways. I therefore needed all the authority I could get. I remember making a practice of putting my grade book on the desk when I walked into the room, of taking attendance slowly and carefully, of using students' last names ("Mr. Prescott?" "Present, Sir!") and of establishing myself, behind the desk and under the clock, as the authority in the room. If anyone challenged me, I was ready. I had been a student at this school and had watched teachers as they worked. This was what they did. I followed suit.

Certainly this need for authority would help determine the way I taught literature. So would the teaching I'd seen from the other side of the desk; so would the New Criticism that I'd absorbed at Princeton. But how *did* I teach literature? The evidence I have is the markings in the literature text I taught from in 1958, Brown and Perrin's *A Quarto of Modern Literature*, fourth edition. This is the only text I have kept from my first teaching years. It has survived nine moves and dozens of book purges. I believe I have held onto this text because I worked at it so hard and, in its presence, through teaching, learned to love literature. I had been a chemistry major at first in college, and then an English major. At St. George's School, teaching with George Carey and Geoff Spranger, I deeply encountered literature for the first time. George, Geoff, and I, known to the students as the "Three Musketeers" and, I'm sure, less-publicly by names unprintable, would read the next day's poetry, prose, or drama and discuss it long into the night, sometimes even in Newport's then-real bars.

In returning to the *Quarto* in 1993, I was struck by how different this textbook is from the apparatus-heavy anthologies of today. The *Quarto* is a "pure" anthology, one in which the work of art is presented without context, a presentation that practically ensures an apolitical, art-for-art's sake approach, particularly in the hands of a brand new, new-critically-trained teacher. The selection of works presented—chiefly those that respond readily to formalist analysis—reinforces the mode of presentation. As I re-encountered the first selection in the anthology, John Galsworthy's short story "The Apple Tree," I had hoped that some memory of how I must have taught this story would surface, but whatever memory traces there may be would not be stirred. I did find it remarkable that Ashurst looks backward, with regret, from the ripe old age of 47, and that his wife, Stella, is, from his perspective, "still at forty-three a comely and faithful companion." I'm now 57, and my wife, Kay, is still, at fifty-something, a more-than-comely and faithful companion. Ashurst and Stella seem to be children, really. And yet I remember them as being so old. "The Apple Tree" appears to me now, in 1993, an entirely new story.

The story is marked, sometimes in pencil, sometimes in blue ink, and occasionally in red ink, suggesting that I taught from this text more than once. At the head of the story is this marginal note: "Time sequence ABBA"—which suggests that I was reading for structure. At the end of the book, on a blank page I've listed and diagrammed the five metrical "feet," which suggests that this interest in structure existed for me then at the micro-level as well as at the macro-level. I underlined, too, many instances of the phrase *apple tree* and most instances of the words *gold* and *blossom*, by which I once wrote "key word." These markings turn the story into something like a tone poem, a resonant structure of repeated language, of "imagery." *Very* new-critical. The likely source of this approach is another book I've kept since the 1950's: Dorothy Van Ghent's *The English Novel: Form and Function* (1953), a book that approached the interpretation of texts through a formalist analysis of language and structure. Van Ghent represented a received reading style at Princeton in 1954–58, one that I would ten years later push beyond its usefulness in a dissertation on *Tristram Shandy*— a work that does not take New Criticism kindly.

Beside Galsworthy's first mention of the grave at the crossroads is my marginal note, "reflection of situation"—the characters, too, at a crossroad. Beside the description of Stella as one who "played fluently, but without expression," I wrote "key to Stella." I can't imagine how either of these notes could have become a question, or an honest question: This must have been one of those points when the teacher stepped in and said, in one way or another, "See, class—an image!" This, too, would have fit the literary analysis I was exposed to in college: reflector characters and emblematic scenes, presented as tools the writer "used" to make "meaning" but, in retrospect, like the iambs and trochees, a special language that I had available to keep my distance from my student-readers. In this class, I would be better prepared than my students. I would keep my place as the best reader/interpreter in the room.

I seem to have asked my students some rhetorical questions, too—the disguised lecture. I underlined passages that seemed to illuminate character, such as that Ashurst "had learned not to be a philosopher in the bosom of his family." My memory stirs here, and I remember that these underlined passages were to be the meat of a series of "What does X tell us about Ashurst (Stella, Megan)" questions: an apparent discussion, but a disguised lecture. Years later I would find comfortable Stanley Fish's analysis of how a literary work affected a reader progressively as the reader read. In 1958 I was proceeding very much as Fish would later: Here's how Galsworthy forces our judgment of Ashurst here; and here, later in the story, is where he makes us review and revise this judgment. What's interesting, too, is what I left unmarked: the true-to-its-time misogyny—Megan and Stella represented as objects of the hero's choice—and the one not chosen must die! And a phrase that equates *animal* and *Red Indian*.

My markings in a second story in the *Quarto*, Conrad's "Secret Sharer," are a bit more full, because I knew more about Conrad than I did about Galsworthy: I had written my senior thesis on Conrad's *Lord Jim*. There are markings here that seem to be my own musings, not for class: "Like *Lord Jim* here." And at the end of the story I have question marks beside passages that are, still, terminally ambiguous. What is Leggatt's "punishment" to be? And what is he to be punished for? And what does it mean to say that he, or anyone else, is a "free man"? The markings in the text lead me to believe that I conducted an honest discussion here, perhaps because I knew that the world of Conrad scholarship was itself filled with disagreement, and perhaps because I felt more sure of my authority in presenting this author whose work I knew so well. But here too I was principally a formalist reader, teaching structure. Heavy, blue-ink lines mark and bracket an emblematic scene—"The straight line of the flat shore joined to the table sea, edge to edge, with a perfect and unmarked closeness, in one leveled floor half-brown, half-blue . . . "(*Quarto*, p. 26). I mark many occurrences of pairing, doubling, reflecting, including the doubled *g*'s and *t*'s of the hero's name, Leggatt. Later, in Joyce's "Counterparts," I mark all the counterparts—and there are lots of them to be marked.

As I was teaching literature, I was, apparently, teaching writing too. My evidence here is slim but powerful: the words of Chip B., whom I taught in 1959, using this same text, the *Quarto*. After leaving St. George's, Chip went on to Brown University, where he stayed for three months and then left to join the Navy. In 1986 he was named a MacArthur fellow and was interviewed therefore by the St. George's alumni magazine. In the interview, he explained that he left Brown because he didn't think he was learning anything new. "Charlie Moran taught me how to write; 'Spud' taught me Latin . . . and Robin Rogers taught me English." Chip's printed words make me remember: I regularly had one-to-one conferences with students on the writing they did about the literature we were reading.

This teaching of writing was part of "English," but it was entirely disassociated, for me, from the teaching of literature. The teaching of writing went on in my apartment (actually, a room on a dormitory corridor distinguished from student rooms only slightly, and by dimension), at my desk, student and teacher huddled over the emerging essay, during evening study halls. Students who wanted to would come in, ask me to read their work with them, and ask me to comment. After the conference they would revise their work and would, sometimes, return for another round of commentary and revision. The teaching of literature, on the other hand, took place entirely in the classroom, *Dead Poets Society* notwithstanding: one teacher and 25 students, iron-and-oak student desks screwed into the oak floors, the teacher seated behind, or on, a battered, huge oak desk that signalled authority conferred by tradition. Looking back at Chip's words, I need to note that Robin Rogers and I both taught English courses identical in aim and format, differing only in reading list. Chip remembers what he learned with me as *writing*, and what he learned with Rogers as *English*. In 1959, apparently, we all believed that *writing* and *English* were different. And apparently, though I saw myself as teaching English, I was teaching writing as well. But because I saw literature and writing as having no clear relation to one another, there was no way that my writing pedagogy could inform the way in which I taught literature.

Steady as She Goes: 1962–77

After my stint at St. George's School, I went to Brown University where I taught Freshman English, a course that was understood to be a writing course because students could be exempted from it by passing a writing test, but which was really a literature course, designed for what its teachers were training to be: teachers of literature. The course married the teaching of argument with the analysis of prose style. I still have my copies of the texts I taught from at Brown, with marginal notes intact. The notes and markings confirm that I was teaching the subject here much as I had at St. George's. These texts were filled with "literature" in any case. Martin and Ohmann's *Inquiry and Expression: A College Reader*, in the chapter called "Proving," contained a thirty-page section that was headed "What *is* the meaning of Hopkins' 'The Windhover'?" and included Hopkins' poem and criticism by Empson, Winters, et al.—comfortable to me because this poem had been in the *Quarto* I'd taught from at St. George's and was one of the poems that I had, in the process of teaching, read up on and practically memorized.

Another assigned text was Wells's *Prose and the Essay*, subtitled *A Developmental Anthology*. It was not, as the subtitle would suggest today, a book designed to "develop" students' reading/writing abilities. It was a book designed to chronicle and illustrate the "development" of English (and, for two of its seven chapters, American) prose style. It was filled with the prose of such authors as Elyot, Ascham, Samuel Johnson, Hume, Wordsworth, and Coleridge—good preparation for our Qualifying Exams, but an extremely indirect means of improving our students' writing. Next to the paragraph from Carlyle's *Past and Present*, which begins "O sumptuous Merchant Prince, illustrious game-preserving Duke," I had written "rhythm, diction, 'style'—sentence structure, emphasis, paragraph structure." That, presumably, was what I was teaching here—close reading of a certain kind. And, through my graduate training I was becoming a professional New Critic, too, as my note at the end of this selection tells me: "Use of water imagery in Carlyle."

I brought this model with me to the University of Massachusetts where, in 1967, I began teaching "Masterpieces of Western Literature" and "The Eighteenth Century Novel" to classes of thirty-five undergraduates. The Masterpieces course was modeled on the "Great Books" curriculum, which had been brought to the University by Milton Mayer. At its center was the Socratic teaching of thought-to-be timeless issues given artistic expression in the master works. From this period I have chiefly memories of searching for fruitful questions to ask about the *Odyssey*, Sophocles' and Euripides' plays, *The Divine Comedy*, Cervantes' *Don Quixote*, *Hamlet*. Most of the texts I taught from during this period have disappeared, absorbed into our children's education and libraries—but I do have my 1967 copies of the *Odyssey* (Fitzgerald's 1961 translation) and of Sophocles' *Oedipus* cycle. The marginal notes in these texts tell me that I continued to teach from a text, keeping it open before me and having available a kind of script, or set of alternate paths that I might take through the text. They tell me, too, that I continued to teach much as I had learned to teach at St. George's. The marginal note "character of Helen?" suggests that I taught the *Odyssey* as I'd taught Galsworthy: Both texts were verbal structures that produced on the reader an effect that we called "character." Another marginal note, "echo of return to Ithaka," tells me that I was still reading as a formalist. My range of interpretation had expanded to include archetypal criticism, as my "Fisher King" note in *Oedipus* suggests, but this was expansion of range, not change of conceptual or pedagogical frame. As a New Critic I looked for image patterns to lead me to meaning; as an archetypal critic I looked for "archetypes," which could be images or larger structural units, to lead me to meaning. In both cases I saw my teacher function to be the reading and interpretation of the text.

The New Dispensation: 1993–95

This teaching I have described seems alien to me now, entirely different from my present goals and strategies. I feel the difference, yet my feelings and memories are uncertain support for my claim that my teaching has changed. I therefore continue my archaeology, my "dig," and bring forward documents from a recent (Fall 1993) moment when I found myself teaching literature. Under the aegis of the MLA-FIPSE English Programs Curriculum Review Project, I'd been a consultant to the English Department at Northern State University in Aberdeen, South Dakota. I'd visited this department in 1991 and had heard from faculty that the department wanted more students in its literature courses, and I'd read in student course evaluations that students wanted more writing in their English courses—both a national as well as a local situation. So I suggested to the chair that in my Fall 1993 visit to the campus, I give a workshop on ways of integrating writing and the teaching of literature. He agreed, and I found myself on a Thursday afternoon planning a workshop for the following Friday. I had thought about this workshop earlier, and knew that it would be one in which the participants wrote in response to prompts that

I would discover in the literature they were then teaching, following the outlines of a practice I had described in articles published in 1981 and 1990. I therefore asked the teachers for copies of anthologies they taught from, and received three: Guth and Rico's *Discovering Literature: Fiction, Poetry, and Drama*, Kirzner and Mandell's *Literature: Reading, Reacting, Writing*, and Perrine and Arp's *Literature: Structure, Sound, and Sense*. I took these back to my motel and began to prepare, reading from the anthologies during my solo dinner and, captured by what I was reading, continuing long into the night. I wrote about this reaction in my journal:

> As I read through the poetry—I'd determined to use poetry as prompt, because it was manageable, short—I was reminded of how much I love reading poetry. I'm a comp person who loves reading poetry. I read the poems, some quickly and some less so, as I had dinner at the Holiday Inn—what a feast! And then later that night, I dog-eared the pages that looked good and useful—but found myself reading slowly all kinds of poems—concrete poems, sonnets by Shakespeare. I saw a section in one anthology on sestinas and villanelles and vowed to return to that when I had time. I've written a couple of sestinas and found the verse forms as generative as Kenneth Koch has said they would be. It would be fun, I thought, when I had a moment, to see how these other authors had handled some of the problems I had as I wrote mine.
>
> And as I did this, and as I write these notes, I realize that this is now how I approach literature—as a writer, a fan, an amateur who, given another life, might have spent more time writing poetry and prose and who might, at the end of all this time, have had a few good pieces to show for it. No regrets, mind you—but a view of potential, of possibilities still alive.

My journal and my scribbled notes from that night tell me that I was both attracted to the poetry I found in the anthologies and repelled by the anthologies' "machinery." My reading notes taken that night say, "Need, if we want to do this, to work *against* the anthology—e.g., Guth, *Discovering Literature*, 1993—the writing about literature sections, e.g., p. 532; the chapter headings (e.g., 'symbol,') or p. 665, 'The Receptive Reader.'" Retracing these notes, I find that the Guth/Rico anthology has "Writing About Literature" sections in each of its chapters; sections with headings such as "Seeing Symbols in Context" and "Looking at Imagery." On the noted p. 532, where "Seeing Symbols in Context" begins, the anthologists open their "Writing Workshop" section with this advice:

> When you write about symbolic meanings, you soon learn to steer your course between two extremes. Some readers are too *literal minded* to respond to symbolic overtones and associations. To them, water is just water. They need to become more perceptive.... Water, for instance, may become the symbol of spiritual regeneration in a wasteland of dried-up feeling.

At the other extreme, the anthologists write, "Some readers free-associate *too freely*." The anthologists assume that poetry is a vessel that contains "meaning"—and if one follows proper interpretive procedures, in this case a golden mean between being too literal and too associative, one will arrive at that meaning. One needs a guide, a master-interpreter: a teacher or an anthology-writer. "This," I wrote in my journal, "is the enemy."

Thinking about my instinctive and visceral reaction to this section, I wrote this in my journal on the day after the workshop:

> I'd taught from anthologies early in my career and had not minded them. I began my teaching, tenth-grade English, with the *Quarto of Modern Literature*—a book I still have, and whose works I still know. I was thought to be a "good teacher" back then. But now, as I look back on that text—well, it was not really as bad as Guth—but still I wonder, what was it that I was teaching?

Clearly what I was about to do was a radical departure from what I might have done in the same situation in 1958. What I was going to do was so different, and so entirely opposed to the anthology in its assumptions about the nature of literature and the purposes of teaching, that I had become angry at the anthologist for embodying a set of assumptions that I had held myself for practically twenty years of teaching.

After reading steadily in the anthologies from six to eleven P.M., I fixed on a poem by Katharyn Howd Machan in the Perrine anthology, "Leda's Sister and the Geese." It's a *tour de force*, really: "Imagine," the writer seems to say, "What Leda's older sister would say, perhaps to a neighbor, over a back fence or on the telephone or, perhaps, to herself in an interior monologue, about what had happened to her sister." Here was my first prompt for the workshop. To this I added a possible beginning. I could have given Machan's first line, "All the boys always wanted her," but I decided to give the writers a bit more leeway, so I gave them two for-instance beginnings: "You'll never guess what happened to Leda" or "That *Leda. . . .*"

I singled out another poem, too: Josephine Miles's "Oedipus," a poem in which the author imagines that the Chorus has decided to buy Oedipus a going-away present. They choose "a traveling case, fitted, which we personally/ Should have liked to receive." In my journal I wrote, "What a wonderful premise! If I ever teach *Oedipus* again, this will be a text that I bring to the play, and one that I'll think about using as a prompt." And I sketched out a second prompt: "Imagine that the Chorus has decided to buy Oedipus a going-away present—something to take with him as he leaves, banished. Write what the Chorus would say as they announced their decision. What would they buy? And how would they announce their decision?" And I found a third, in case I needed still more ammunition—though this was only a ninety-minute workshop: Margaret Walker's "Lineage." Here was a first line that would serve, all by itself, as a prompt: "My grandmothers were strong."

The workshop began at three in the afternoon, not a good time for our biorhythms. I opened with the "Leda" prompt and we all began to write. We wrote for fifteen minutes or so, and then we read aloud what we had written. The writing was good, we all agreed—full of voice, thoroughly imagined and, given the situation, remarkably fully realized. The teachers have said that I could quote from their writing, so I take advantage of their generosity. Here's Tom Hansen's piece:

> I asked her to slow down and tell me the whole thing over again. She did. It was the same incredible story. Then, having heard it twice, I asked her some questions. . . . A swan? A white swan? Feathers and wings? And it happened where? In Wylie Park? And exactly when? Around nine in the morning? And what was the weather like? Was it nice? Were other people about? Did you see anyone? No one at all? Are you sure? And have you told anyone else?
>
> "Do you know (I asked her) how hard this is to believe?" But I could tell she believed. She absolutely believed it. She wasn't sure how he got her clothes off. She must have been in a shock or a trance. But she does have bruises—from the nape of her neck in his beak. And she offered to show me others, or to go see the doctor to get a pelvic exam.
>
> I absolutely don't. . . . and yet. . . .

And here's Carol Lynch's response to the prompt:

> Dear _____ ,
>
> You won't be surprised to hear this probably—but you'll be horrified. L. just came in and she's had a really weird experience. You know—this happens with her a lot—she seems to *invite* trouble and then wants someone to bail her out. Always so surprised that it happened. But she's always messing around where she shouldn't be—maybe *asking* for trouble.
>
> You'll probably be hearing from her yourself—she said something about calling you. Were you sympathetic to her last crisis? Maybe if you know about it before she calls you you'll be able to deal with it. . . .

All of the writing carried, in some degree, the assumption carried in the prompt and by the voice in Machan's poem: that the rape had been something that Leda somehow deserved, had asked for. As the "teacher" in the room, I then raised the issue: Leda might have been, was really, hurt! And the speaker is glad! Like Browning's "Porphyria's Lover," the unspeakable is made even more unspeakable by the voice of the killer or, in this case, the jealous sister. Perhaps students would be engaged by this issue and would write an antidote, a piece written from the assumption that Leda's rape was an act of criminal violence. Or perhaps a piece *about* rape on campus. And we could bring in Yeats here too—his Leda. How do we react to the question he poses at the end of his poem? Do we care if she put on his knowledge with his power? Is the indifference of the beak now an issue?

By this time we were halfway through the workshop, so I skipped
Miles's "Oedipus" and gave us the first line of Walker's "Lineage" as our
second writing prompt: "My grandmothers were strong." I offered the line,
began writing, and realized that I couldn't say this easily of my grandmothers, both of whom died before I knew them. I wanted to write about my
great-aunt Lucy. So I reported this to the writers, saying that I'd permitted
myself, and therefore all of us, to change the plural of the line to the singular, and to replace "grandmother(s)" with "great aunt." Here's Andrzej
Duszenko's response, the beginning of a poem that I hope he returns to:

> My grandmother was strong
> She survived the movement of the Earth
> When the war ended and the Earth finally stopped trembling
> Three soldiers walked into the house
> And told her they were going to move the Earth
> The house where her grandmother had lived
> And where she had survived another trembling of the Earth,
> The trembling to end all tremblings.
> That house was going to remain
> But it was now in another country
> And my grandmother left Poland
> And went to live in a new house
> In the new Poland. . . .

And Patrick Whiteley gave us this, which seems to me a finished poem:

> My grandmother was strong
> She hung bed sheets in the January wind
> And leaving them to freeze walked across the living room
> Wiping on a matted tissue blood from her cracked fingers
>
> My grandmother was strong
> On her shoulder leaned my one-legged grandfather
> Drunk on Irish whiskey
> Vomiting in the foyer
>
> My grandmother was strong
> She couldn't die when told she would
> She was afraid so she said so
> Afterward dying without describing it

We were stunned by the power of this writing—and I hope that this was
the lesson imparted by the workshop. I said a few teacherly things about the
relation of what we'd done to the Walker poem: that the Walker poem takes
this same first line and goes with it in a direction that none of us had taken,
raising—and we were in farm country—the issue of whether previous generations were stronger, and the further issue of whether there is a strength
from being close to the land. Both huge issues, and important. Do we need
land? When we can synthesize food from all kinds of protein, do we really

need land? Do we need to farm? And if so, why? But this seemed pretty pedantic stuff—the power was in the writing, the activity, and what had been for them would be so for their students.

The Change and its Likely Causes

In 1958, and from then through the early 1970's, I taught literature as "art," the work standing essentially free of the culture and of the reader, an object to be contemplated and interpreted. The student was an apprentice; the teacher was the master-contemplator and master-interpreter. This relation to literary texts derives, given our ecclesiastical ancestry, from the priest's relation to the sacred texts. Writing in these classes was a marginal activity, valuable only as a field in which students practiced the interpretation of literature in the form of the critical essay.

The approach to literature I found myself taking in 1993 was one in which literature is important, not as a focus but as a catalyst, a place to begin a writer's journey, a "prompt." At the center of this approach is not the art object but the activity of writing. The student is assumed to be a writer, one who is different from the professional writer in degree, not kind. The systematic study of literature is now, for me, on the margin: Literature is a special category of writing, a category that our canon wars tell us is constructed, not given.

This change in my teaching has been driven by a number of forces, some of which have acted invisibly, to me, but some of which I can see. One force has been, certainly, the change in my age, position, and perceived status. At St. George's I was a twenty-one-year-old, brand new teacher, working in a system that had its own powerful, long-standing pedagogical tradition. My teaching was largely a reflection of what my students and colleagues expected of me. In 1993, I am a veteran, even, locally, a bit of an authority. I have tenure and can, within limits, teach any way I want. In 1958 I was grateful for the authority that the existing system conferred on me; now I have authority, sometimes more than I need or feel comfortable with.

But aging by itself will not account for the change I have described. What has principally driven this change has been my experience as a writing teacher. I single out two aspects of this experience for particular notice: my introduction to the activity-centered classroom by Roger Garrison and Donald Murray, two writing teachers; and my introduction to thinking-about-teaching as a legitimate activity, which occurred as I entered the field of rhetoric and composition and began to read related books and journals.

My introduction to the model of the activity-based classroom took place in 1973, through my encounter with the work of Garrison and Murray. Both advocated a writing workshop in which students wrote and teachers circulated as in-process editors. Their work was later reinforced by the writings of James Moffett, Janet Emig, Peter Elbow, James Britton, Nancy Martin, and all the writers and scholars who participated in the explosive activity in composition studies during the mid and late 1970's. It has been reinforced, too, by all my colleagues—faculty, staff, and graduate students—in our writing program here at the University of Massachusetts.

This writing pedagogy represented an absolute break with what I had learned and practiced earlier. Indeed, at St. George's in 1958 if I asked students to write in class, it was assumed that I had done so because I had failed to prepare for class. I was punished for this behavior, too, because I then had to correct, that night, more than a hundred pieces of writing. I first tried the Garrison/Murray model in 1973, and found it to my liking—much like the evening tutorial sessions I had held at St. George's. In our advanced writing class I began teaching entirely by tutorial. This activity-based approach gave me access to students as they learned: I could see them making and revising their writing, and their worlds, as they wrote. Between 1973 and 1979, when I taught my last full-scale literature class, I brought writing more and more into the center of my literature classes, causing a few students to object that they'd signed up for a literature course and had found themselves in a writing course—the old, continuing distinction between *English* and *writing*.

What is at least as important as the newness of this pedagogy is the fact that it was consciously held. In 1973 or thereabouts, I became what would now be termed a "reflective practitioner," a person who thought about teaching. Reflecting on our teaching is something that we commonly do in composition studies, and something that we seldom do in literary studies, particularly at four-year research universities. As a new English teacher in 1958, and again at Brown University, I was given no training at all. English teachers (read *literature* teachers) did not, apparently, need to think about teaching. The appropriate pedagogy was assumed to be implicit in works being studied and would, through their influence, be enacted. At the 1988 NCTE Summer Seminar on Teaching Literature to Undergraduates, Janet Emig rose to say that the participants had spent two full days talking about "theory," and not once had there been mention of *pedagogical* theory. NEH seminars in literature still eschew teaching talk; they tend to be "pure" literature. And the MLA conference program, in sharp contrast to the CCCC program, has very little room for pedagogical topics. In 1993 our writing program has a full and comprehensive training program for its teaching assistants, one that includes systematic reflection upon teaching practice; in the literature wing of the department there is no counterpart.

Perhaps this "change" has been, for me, less a change in behavior than a change in my perception of what I'm doing, a change that has been permitted by my move from literature to composition. Recalling Chip's statement that in 1959 "Charlie Moran taught me how to write," it seems likely that even in my first years as a teacher I was an enthusiastic and effective writing teacher. The after-hours tutoring and coaching that I did must have been effective, but I didn't see this as important work because I was a teacher of literature. However gratifying and stimulating this work with student writers might have been, it was a sideline—a low-prestige activity.

Now a member of the community of writing teachers, I am able to move this same once-marginalized activity into the center. Writing, in its fullest sense, is the new center. And so in the faculty workshop I've described, we, the writers in the room, using the work of literature as a catalyst, made our own meanings of aspects of our lives—powerful, important work, as the writings of Carol and Tom and Patrick and Andrzej attest. We turn to literature for its energy, its forms, its history, but at the center of the class is our own writing. As an English teacher, this is the kind of classroom, whether its title be writing or literature, that I try to establish. This is English at its best.

Works Cited

Brown, Leonard, and Porter G. Perrin, eds. 1957. *A Quarto of Modern Literature*, 4th ed. New York: Scribners.

Guth, Hans P., and Gabrielle L. Rico. 1993. *Discovering Literature: Fiction, Poetry, and Drama*. Englewood Cliffs, NJ: Prentice Hall.

Kirzner, Laurie G., and Stephen G. Mandell. 1988. *Literature: Reading, Reacting, Writing*. Harcourt.

Martin, Harold C., and Richard M. Ohmann. 1963. *Inquiry and Expression: A College Reader*. New York: Holt.

Moran, Charles. 1990. "Reading Like A Writer." In *Vital Signs I: Bringing Together Reading and Writing*, edited by James L. Collins. Portsmouth, NH: Boynton/ Cook.

—————. 1981. "Teaching Writing/Teaching Literature." *College Composition and Communication* 32: 21–30.

Perrine, Laurence, and Thomas R. Arp. 1993. *Literature: Structure, Sound, and Sense*, 6th ed. Fort Worth: Harcourt.

Van Ghent, Dorothy. 1953. *The English Novel, Form and Function*. New York: Rinehart.

Wells, Celia T., ed. 1962. *Prose and the Essay: A Developmental Anthology*. Boston: Houghton Mifflin.

I make students write in literature classes to get them to figure out their response to a text. When I say I make them write in literature classes I mean literally, in the class. The writing is simply thoughtful engagement. Although most of my students dutifully read assigned literature, fewer have critically reconsidered the reading. You might reasonably ask, why not just discuss the reading? Cut to the chase. Two reasons come immediately to mind, both fairly mundane, but clear contributors to a more dynamic and interactive class.

A writing prior to discussion allows students who haven't put a real effort into the reading, for whatever reason, to play catch up and join or at least understand the discussion that follows. For those who have done a careful reading, a focused freewriting primes the pump for discussion. It is exploratory writing, an attempt to explain to ourselves what we know in anticipation of having to explain or argue our position to others.

I'm not using the plural pronoun here speciously. I write in response to my own in-class assignments, with students. It's tedious to walk into a class with your response in a bag, yesterday's stale sandwich. I don't mean it's wrong. Just boring—makes the day longer than it ought to be. I rarely complete an in-class writing failing to unpack a new insight, however miniature, or reexamine a former intuition. I employ informal written response in literature classes because it works for me, as a reader. And it cuts down on potential time for pontification. Like many instructors primarily involved in teaching writing, I don't see much point in lecturing. I'm anxious to get involved in a conversation, and writing in class makes conversation more likely to happen.

Tracy Santa
United States Air Force Academy

4

Motivating Writing Differently in a Literary Studies Classroom

James A. Reither
St. Thomas University

Kenneth Burke tells us in *The Philosophy of Literary Form* that "critical and imaginative works are answers to questions posed by the situations in which they arose. They are not merely answers, they are *strategic* answers, *stylized* answers" (1). According to Burke, "every document ... must be treated as a *strategy for encompassing a situation* ... as the *answer* or *rejoinder* to assertions current in the situation in which it arose" (109). Along the same lines, in *A Grammar of Motives* Burke discusses his "scene–act ratio," urging us to understand that a writing scene or situation "is a fit 'container' for the act" (3); and, "from the motivational point of view, there is implicit in the quality of a scene the quality of the action that is to take place within it" (6–7). A scene thus "contains" a determined likelihood that certain symbolic acts—certain stylized texts—will serve as appropriate responses to the situation; others will be inappropriate, even disallowed. Because texts are answers to situations, and because different situations differently motivate, different scenes require different strategies, resulting in different texts. Change the scene, and you change the act (xix).

These notions offer us a powerful way of thinking about the writing scenes constituted by courses in literary studies, leading us to believe that if we ask, "What kinds of 'strategic answers' are appropriate to the scenes that are literary studies classrooms?" the answer will be that they are indeed "fit 'containers'" for exactly the kinds of writing students produce in them. Like everyone else, students compose texts strategically, to encompass the situations in which they find themselves. If they are not doing the kinds of writing we want them to do, and if they are not learning to write the way we want them to write, the likely reason is that our classrooms tend to be "unfit containers" for the kinds of writing that enable students to join us in literary

48

studies discourse. To put this assertion even more bluntly: Chances are good that it is not our students who are misreading the situation; it is we who are misreading it.

Literary studies courses, it seems, are getting precisely the writing they deserve. And it's not that our courses make it difficult for students to write the way we (and I think they) want. It's that our courses render well-nigh unattainable our goal to teach, and our students' goal to learn, the kinds of writing they need to learn if they are to join with us in discourse that is mutually rewarding. If we want students to change why, what, and how they write, we have to bring a whole new set of conditions into our classrooms.[1] We have to change students' writing scenes to motivate their writing differently.

We can get a clearer idea of our students' writing scene if we compare it to our own professional writing scenes. Whereas our writing scenes call for discourse among what Bruffee (after Rorty) calls "knowledgeable peers," students in literary studies courses work in a hierarchically organized situation where they write not to peers but for teachers. While our own professional scenes require us to compose texts to do the work of literary studies, the scenes we organize for our students do not require them to write for this purpose. (We might tell our students that we invite such discourse, but other conditions of the scene send students a message that contradicts and drowns out our invitation.) While our texts are embedded in the give and take of ongoing literary studies conversation, our students' texts are embedded in our assignments, and, located only in the give and take of grades, their texts have no function outside our classrooms. Thus, while our discourse is designed to change the ways our peers think, see, and know, our students' discourse is designed merely to earn their way out of our courses. Our discourse is a way into the system. Our students' discourse is a way out of it.

The clearest thing about this writing scene is that teachers and students are not in classrooms to engage in conversations: Teachers are there to teach students what they know and know how to do; under the best of circumstances, students are there to learn what teachers have to teach. Teachers, the insiders, are knowledgeable and skilled—that's what makes them insiders; that's what positions them as teachers. Students, the outsiders, are uninformed and unskilled—that's what makes them outsiders; that's what positions them as students. In this situation, teachers' questions shape and focus the students' study, thinking, discussion, and writing; the teachers' agenda, not dialogic exigency, controls turn-taking; teachers provide feedback on students' work, so that response is routinized; and, of course, teachers assign grades.

One consequence of this arrangement is that teachers, not students, make almost all of the important choices involved in the students' writing—the conditions that precipitate their writing, their rhetorical goals, their relationship with readers, the issues they will address and how they will address them. In other words, in the writing assignments they give, teachers make most of the choices that enable writers to engage with and make meaning through writing or that enable inexperienced writers to learn how to do those things. When the teacher is making all those choices, it is easy to imagine that the idea of using writing to say something meaningful in honest-to-goodness written discourse might strike most students as an inappropriate strategy. Since this scene does not motivate that kind of relationship, students wisely compose texts that embody strategies to encompass the particulars of the situation; that is, they produce precisely the kinds of texts implied in the motives of instructional feedback and assessment.

Because they understand the function of their writing in this situation, students also understand that their commitment must be to satisfying the carefully controlled and limiting requirements of their teachers' assignments. Nothing in the situation encourages students to imagine that they should write to explore a range of answers and approaches, to discuss, judge, and pool ideas, or to construct knowledge by contributing to one another's understanding. On the contrary, the idea that they should be doing any of those things would strike students as curious, oddly out of place, because any need for real communication or discussion is obviated by the fact that what counts in the situation is right answers and right ways of doing things. Because this scene requires students to compose texts by which their knowing can be judged, not shared, the students' obliging rejoinder is to bequeath us texts designed to show us what they know and can do, with the aim not to "communicate" but to garner positive assessment. When the business is credentialing, the writing that counts is that which is composed for teacher feedback and evaluation. Thus, as Peter Elbow tells us, "every time we give a grade we are speaking through an institutional structure that says our ranking is not just 'one more piece of information'—but rather is *the most important* information, the information that *counts*: It is what appears on the transcript, it is the institution's judgment, it is supposed to stand for how other teachers in the institution judge. Because of these institutional and cultural structures, ranking drives student attitudes and it drives curriculum" (102).

Given their necessary commitment to satisfying others' needs and expectations, and not to exploring, discussing, and evaluating ideas, it is not surprising that this scene leads students into the traps of conceptualizing writing as merely an ability to turn out clear and coherent sentences, paragraphs, and essays, on the one hand, and of trying to write "what the teacher wants," on the other. We know that experienced, competent writers understand that different circumstances and rhetorical goals call for different genres, different rhetorical moves, and different writer–reader relationships; we know that, within the limits of situation and their own sense of who they are and who they want to be, writers can be ironists, testers of ideas, critics, exhorters, advisors, objective reporters of data; and we know that writers write to change what people know, how they think and feel, and who they are. It's difficult to imagine, however, how students can come to understand those things in the circumstances in which they write. Because their situation discourages and pushes from view, even disallows, choices regarding rhetorical goals, writer–reader relationships, and *ethos*, they have little opportunity to see or to practice the profound rhetorical and epistemic functions of writing.

Finally, perhaps the most pervasive and counterproductive condition motivating the writing in most literary studies classrooms is that they are places where people talk and listen, not read and write: Except for the written lectures of teachers and the written notes students take on those lectures, the really important business of a course is conducted orally. Reading and writing are relegated to "homework"—subsidiary activities the students do to prepare for the really important activities of the classroom—and a literary studies classroom in which students spent their time reading and writing would look to many like a classroom in which the teacher was spending her time not teaching. Students rarely find themselves in circumstances that encourage them to see their writing as an opportunity to interact with others to redefine relationships or to change what and how others know, think, and feel. That's simply not what writing is for in a literary studies classroom.

This, then, is the students' predicament. More often than not, their writing scene asks them not to communicate but to offer up texts designed to demonstrate competence and survive assessment. Their teacher-dictated assignments require them to write to enact others' choices about most of the important rhetorical dimensions of writing. Their situation limits their search for meaning to an attempt to give the teacher what she wants, so that writing is demeaned as homework and talk is elevated into the means by which all the truly important activities are carried out.

Changing all that—changing classrooms to motivate writing differently —requires something more like revolution than tinkering. The problem is clearly systemic, not merely individual, and we and our students operate in what Garth Boomer has called "an unnatural, institutionalized setting constrained and molded by forces political, economic, cultural, and historical" (16). We are "socially constructed and positioned" (Boomer 16) so that our range of choices is severely limited. Nevertheless, although I teach only literary studies courses, my reading in composition studies has shown me that, though institutional constraints and a dismal lack of alternative models for both teachers and students make it difficult for us to bring about radical classroom change, there are choices we can make that can help us create scenes that enable students to perceive differently who they are and what their writing can do. In particular, there are choices we can make that do not compromise the traditional course objective of "covering" material that is ordinarily expected in a given English course. There are ways, that is, to organize literary studies courses so that students will learn powerful lessons about writing and the roles of writing without sacrificing the scholarly integrity of the field of study, so that students can come to know and understand what can and must be said—the "sayables"[2]—in an informed discussion of a given area of literary studies.

In outline, my view is that we need to make our classrooms over into scenes where students' writing can count as a contribution to the knowing of others who need or can use what the writer knows. Writing will be motivated differently if students write not to win grades, but to join with their peers (the way we do) to read and write to carry out the work of literary studies by stating, modifying, challenging, and otherwise deliberating and negotiating its sayables. In particular, writing will be motivated differently if students' texts take over at least some of the responsibility for organizing and presenting the information and ideas that are the business of the course—and, of course, if the readers of those texts are people who need and can use the writer's information and ideas to further their own learning and knowing. The main business of writers in literary studies is to write about literature and literary issues so as to change what and how people know. They take part in the enterprise by offering information others do not have and by suggesting ideas others may not have considered. It is in this way that writing is, as I said earlier, a way into something. People take part in the process by immersing themselves in the field's sayables, mastering and using them in disciplined conversation. They contribute most significantly when they add to readers' sayables or when they offer new and better ways to utter those sayables. Literary studies is itself a scene that motivates writing; and what makes a text valuable in such a scene is its ability to contribute to the knowledge-making process.

I teach a course for third- and fourth-year students called, after the title of one of Kenneth Burke's books, Language as Symbolic Action (LSA). My aim in this course is to create a disciplinary scene that will motivate it differently by making student writing matter differently. To that end, I set the scene and "direct" the enterprise almost entirely through two kinds of texts. The first is a written "course description" that I give to students at the beginning of every course I teach. In course descriptions I tell students about course content, methods, requirements, and means of evaluation. The second kind of text I use is one I call a "prompt." Unlike course descriptions, which students see only at the beginning of a course, prompts are ever-present: I write one for every class I teach.[3] In prompts I ordinarily do three things: I survey what occurred in the previous meeting of the class, often using or citing words, questions, and claims used by students in that meeting; based on progress and decisions made in the previous meeting, I lay out a scenario for what the students will be doing in the present meeting; and, finally, I suggest what students should do to prepare for our next meeting.

My texts, however, are ultimately less important in the situation than is a third kind of text—one written entirely by the students. This text, called a "course book," dominates and controls the students' work in ways that my texts cannot. I make writing a course book a central requirement in all my courses. I try to organize things so that, in everything they do, the students' attention is fixed on a need to get their learning down in writing that they can include as a section or chapter in their course book. I stipulate that they must "contribute significantly" to the writing of this book, and I advise them along the way about matters pertaining to accuracy, quality, and completeness, but I give the students responsibility for determining precisely who their audience should be, what should go in the book, and how it should be organized.

In the course description for LSA, I tell students that those

> who enroll in this course will join their professor in a collaborative scholarly project that is based on the assumption that language is action-through-symbols and . . . designed to explore ways people use literary and non-literary language to *do* things—to change the ways people feel, believe, and act; to build and maintain community with others; to forge their own and others' identities; and to construct knowledge and reality itself.

I go on to explain that the course is organized as what I call "collaborative inquiry—disciplined, question-driven inquiry/reading/writing":

> Once the project is underway [I tell students], you will be asked to take the project over by posing your own questions, doing the "textual research" necessary to develop your own answers and (usually in small teams or groups) writing and revising your own claims regarding those questions. . . . Our method, then, will be to read, write, listen, and talk our way to an understanding of as many of the key issues as time allows. Or, to say it another way: Our method will be what Stephen North . . . calls "standard humanist scholarship . . . developing rational arguments founded on textual evidence" (5). . . . [This] method . . . contrasts sharply with the conventional method [you] are accustomed to at university—listening to lectures, reading textbooks, writing term papers, and taking exams. I will not lecture or conduct discussions; neither will I assign term papers or set exams; and the one required text for this course—Burke's *Language as Symbolic Action*—will not function as a textbook that you will be expected to "master." . . . The class will write a "Course Book" addressing (if not answering) questions that emerge as our project moves forward. Specifically, this book will talk about and demonstrate some ways language can usefully be seen as "symbolic action."

When I explain course requirements I say that "the clearest requirement is for full and committed participation in the day-to-day work of the investigation. This will mean . . . coming to class meetings—to learn from and to teach others. It will mean contributing substantively to the course book."

Finally, regarding evaluation, I tell students that they will

> earn a starting grade in the C range simply by coming to class, doing your share of the work of the course, and helping to write the course book. . . . You earn a grade in the B and A ranges by contributing to the learning of the others in the class. If you help others learn—if (even a few times) you

write and say things that help others understand, if you get out front once
in a while to show others the way . . .—you'll earn a grade in the B range.
If you become a leader in the class—if you are persistently . . . helpful to
others . . .—you'll earn a grade in the A range. . . . At the end of the course
I will (1) count up the number of classes you attended and the number of
assignments you took part in (to determine whether your starting grade is
in the C range), and I will (2) ask your peers to acknowledge your contributions to their learning, to ascertain whether your grade should be higher
than the starting grade you've earned by being there and doing your work.

I also explain that I will not comment on or grade anything they write, and
that, in fact, I will not even read much of what they write, because so much
of it will consist of notes, drafts, and revisions of drafts and reports they will
be working on with others to revise into writing for their book. (My primary
function regarding their writing is to organize their activities so that they can
read and use each other's written work.)

I hope that my aims here are reasonably clear: I'm trying to establish
conditions that tell students that the function of their writing is to communicate real information and lay out real claims. Everything I say in this course
description is designed strategically, to position students to think differently
about themselves and the roles of their writing in the process of making
meaning about language as symbolic action. What I want is a scene that
affords students' engagement with the choice-making processes evidenced in
real competence in writing, on the assumption that having students make
those choices will more deeply engage them with the issues the course is
ostensibly about. I am, moreover, trying to provide students with an opportunity to develop expertise—the expertise that comes not from knowing
vastly more than others, but rather from knowing things others don't know
and from seeing issues differently than the ways others see them—so that the
students will know enough about particular issues to have something to say
to which others are apt to give a hearing. (You and I function that way. What
prompts me to write is that, at least in this present situation, we know pretty
much the same things; but, because we see and think differently, we know
differently. In other circumstances, you and I would be positioned differently: I would be reading your writing.) This is photographer David Vestal's
take on this issue:

> There's this to say about expression: We are all alike, so we can understand
> each other; and we are all different, so we have things to tell each other.
> The sameness makes communication possible, and the difference makes it
> worthwhile. (304)

What I'm trying to create, then, is a classroom scene that asks students to
know things others do not know and to know the same things differently—both
of which are powerful motives for writing. On the assumptions that students

can get information and ideas from the same sources we get ours (i.e., not from textbooks but from the books and articles current in the field), that searching out and making sense of information and ideas immerses students in the processes of organizing and explaining what they find, and that these activities teach students not only about content but also about writing, I turn all or most of the responsibility for researching, generating, organizing, and communicating course content over to the students. Thus students take on what are, traditionally, teachers' roles; the "movement" of content is not one-way, teacher-to-students. Instead, because the students are responsible for making knowledge about language and literary studies through pooling, clarifying, and negotiating, content knowledge has multiple sources: It is constructed by those involved in the inquiry. "Expertise" is redefined and relocated, and the course is not a system for delivering information or a training ground: LSA is a venue for investigating the knowledge and know-how of a particular field of practice.

When it works, such a situation puts tremendous pressure on students to learn more and better. Much of the pressure originates with the teacher, the institution, and the discipline, but, of course, the pressure that matters is that which originates in the new responsibilities and new roles (researcher, writer, explainer, persuader) that are implicit in the students' new relationships to their peers and to the field of study. And the pressure is unrelenting: It comes not just at exam and paper-deadline time; it is there as a daily part of the situation, because every meeting requires students to act on their responsibilities to one another by writing and reading.

And that's where three months' worth of prompts comes in. Since, obviously, a single document at the beginning of a course is hardly enough to create the writing situation I want LSA to create, I write prompts to build and maintain a scene in which students take most of the responsibility for generating content and meaning. Prompts make writing a way things get done; they model ways writing can structure inquiry. More practically, prompts keep the investigation going, focused, and on track. Let me again offer a concrete example from the same course.[4] In the first three meetings of LSA we had experienced and sought to make sense of what I called "virtual reality"—the reality created when readers read fiction empathetically, engaging with the virtual reality of the story's characters and events (another name for this is, of course, vicarious experience). I had asked the students to write about the experience and its meaning, trying to come up with an explanation of virtual reality and how it happens. Then, in the fourth prompt (for the fourth meeting), I had asked each student to "write up a list of the questions you think you ought to answer about virtual reality for people who know as much about the concept as you did when you came into this course."

Over the next couple of class meetings the students worked with the list of questions that resulted from my request. Watching for overlap, repetition, and irrelevance, they boiled their lists down to twenty-three questions, which they then grouped into six "larger" questions. Each student "signed up for" a question she was interested in working and writing on, in that way forming teams who would write for the other students in the class. Their six questions: "What is VR?" "Who experiences VR?" "What are the effects/results of VR—i.e., What does VR do to us?" "How does VR happen—i.e., What causes VR?" "What do we learn about language by learning about VR?" and "How is VR different from "real" reality—i.e., What's the relationship between VR and RR?" Finally, in their groups, each student assumed responsibility for one or more of the sub-questions that had been originally posed by the class. At the end of the sixth class meeting, each student left knowing not only what question she—and she alone—was responsible for, but also how her question connected with other questions her colleagues were working on. Her job was to write a report that would complement the reports written by others in her group, so that in the next meeting the members of the group could read what each other had written and merge the various statements into one collaborative text that they could present to the class as a whole. Once every group had written and presented to the class, a revising committee was established to merge the several group-written reports into a chapter for the course book on virtual reality, how it works, and how it stands as an instance of language as symbolic action. The class did additional research designed to help them to clarify and substantiate some of their claims. In particular, they sought out, shared, and tested their ideas against their experience of texts that seemed to them to exemplify sharply the ability of a text to move readers into virtual reality: magazine advertisements, a Cotton Mather sermon and a Daniel Webster speech (two or three of the students were taking an American literature course), a poem by Earl Birney ("The Bull Moose"), and several short stories.

With that project well underway—dropped into the out-of-class background of the course—another project was launched, this time at the instigation of a student who had read a parable demonstrating the power of names to shape people's lives. By the tenth or eleventh meeting of the class, each student had read the parable, found an article in the popular press that she believed illustrated the truth (or lack of truth) of the claims implicit in the parable, and written to explain how the author of the popular-press article had attempted to shape or construct reality for a reader by "naming" reality in a particular way. Again, what they wrote led to a round of questioning, winnowing, revising, and grouping—this time about the power of language to shape one's reality by naming. (Into the mix of the parable, the articles they had read in the light of that parable, and what they had written about how those articles named people's experiences so as to shape the way readers viewed their reality, I had tossed Kenneth Burke's discussion of Bentham's notion of "question-begging appellatives" [*Rhetoric* 90-101] and his essay "Terministic Screens" in *Language as Symbolic Action*.)

This project led to the culminating project of the course, in which the students wrote in answer to this—their own—question: "Can you think of a 'central experience' in your own life where a process of naming or *renaming* changed your world, your life, and you?'' Whereas the students wrote their earlier chapters by merging individual texts into group-written texts that were then merged into single, class-written chapters, this time each student wrote her own chapter. By way of illustration, I quote Kathryn Saunders's brief piece:

Only I Determine Me

One year ago, a trip to the doctor demonstrated to me how powerful an effect language, specifically naming, could have on my life. The appointment was to figure out what to do about an annoying although minor problem. After a referral to another doctor and a battery of high tech tests, a name was applied to this minor nuisance, which by this time had disappeared. Everything confirmed a diagnosis of multiple sclerosis, and from the instant of the naming my reality and my perception of reality changed.

Multiple sclerosis, m.s., is a disease of the central nervous system which is characteristically progressively degenerative. Manifestations can include just about anything—sight and hearing impairment, loss of part or all motor skills. It comes and goes at whim. There is nothing to do (or not do) to avoid it. There is no treatment or cure, and, because of its capricious nature, there is no prognosis.

For several days after the naming I became the disease, and the litany of symptoms and adjectives marched through my head twenty-four hours a day. Minor twitches that wouldn't even have penetrated to consciousness the day before now took on major significance. The evidence mounted that I was falling apart.

Then I got mad; I got furious. I decided that m.s. would never again be my total reality. It would never again determine who or what I am. I knew intellectually that I was the same person with the same strengths and weaknesses, goals, family, and potential that I was before the naming occurred. But even with the conscious decision to ignore the disease until it actually does something, the language, the naming, changed the way I live. For example, a couple of years ago I would have felt obligated to write papers during the March break. This year it was pack up the kids and spend part of the week at my parents' home and the rest of it skating and playing at Mactaquac Park. Now when I look for a house I have to consider how easily it can be made wheelchair-accessible—just in case. The effect of the language was to force me into examining what I really want, what is truly important, what can be put off because it will always be there, and what can't be because the opportunity might disappear.

I couldn't say that having m.s. is a positive thing. Living with a time-bomb in your head can be downright scary. But beyond that, the way in which the disease has made me take stock of myself and my life has created positive changes. I focus more on the things I can do instead of those

I can't. I value my family and friends more than I ever did and I tell them
so. As corny as it sounds, the naming of m.s. has caused me to appreciate
every day, to try to learn something every day. It has given me a stronger
sense of who I am and the m.s. is the smallest part of all.

What strikes me about this is not so much that it is "good" writing, but
rather that it is deeply committed writing. It's not that a student "learned to
write" in LSA, but rather that she had connected emotionally with an idea
she had developed in a literary studies classroom and then wrote to enable
others to make that connection. Other chapters in the book exemplify the
usual academic genres, using institutional forms and voices appropriate to
exposition and analysis—the fruits of scholarly labor. In these chapters, however, the students found places for themselves and their voices in the scholarly conversation about language as symbolic action. They told their own
stories, and those stories demonstrated the truth of an idea that had become
important to them. In this way they created for their readers a set of virtual
experiences that enacted language in symbolic action.

Although the project began with my questions and I "orchestrated" the
inquiry, the students' written answers were the "material" they dealt with,
and these answers almost immediately gave rise to their own significant
questions. They were writing, and others were reading and evaluating that
writing, but in this circumstance "evaluating" meant finding relevance,
meaning, and usefulness in it. Through writing and reading they negotiated
meaning dialectically. In so doing, they changed one another's minds and
ways of seeing, and they developed an understanding of ways language is
symbolic action with the ability to shape readers' realities.

In this classroom, students' texts were strategic answers to needs to
develop and explore ideas and perspectives, to pool knowing so that everyone would learn, and, ultimately, to earn place and status among peers. What
they wrote did not answer to a demand to produce texts for evaluation. In
fact, their texts were not "responded to," commented on, or graded in any
of the usual ways: Their texts were used—or not used—by knowledgeable
peers. Moreover, until quite late in the process, their texts tended to be more
"exploratory" than "presentational" (Barnes). Consisting of notes, freewrites, reports, and drafts, most of what they wrote was used and then set
aside or discarded as the enterprise proceeded. Because one outcome of the
course was a book that presented the findings and implications of their
inquiry, the only writing that was preserved was that which was suitable for
publication in their course book.

While I remained largely responsible for the process, and to some extent
the quality of the content, I did not control the entire agenda. (Teachers cannot control much that really matters on the agenda: As John Gage has shown
us, intentions are not things we can assign; as I have sought to demonstrate
here, intentions are conditions of situations.) I set the initial terms of the

investigation, but the requirement to do the research and writing that would result in a course book enabled the students to organize their thinking and to make their findings available to others. As the students came to see more clearly the options available to them in the situation, they began making more of the decisions about what they needed to investigate, when they should investigate it, and how they should investigate it.

Thus, once the project was underway, the students' questions drove their inquiry. I worked with them to help decide how to go about answering the questions, but, for the most part, they determined what answers would work for their ends. And the usual exigencies began to come into effect: Windows of opportunity opened and closed (as, for example, when the need for a text had passed, the chance to contribute to that stage of the inquiry was no longer available); peer pressures grew as their responsibilities to one another intensified; and so on. At first, the students had to do the research, writing, and pooling, because a teacher required it. Later, however, they discovered (sometimes to everyone's amazement) that they wanted to participate because they did not want to let themselves and one another down.

All the situational changes I've discussed here can be managed by teachers and students working within institutional settings. The aim of such changes is to enable students (and teachers) to make their own choices about their rhetorical goals and the means by which they might achieve them. In so doing, they have a chance of redefining or re-creating themselves as they try out, modify, accept, and reject new roles and relationships, new language and genres. They can take as their own any that "work" for them, refining and reshaping them to suit their propensities and needs. That way, they define and redefine themselves not by what we tell them they ought to be and do and know, but rather out of culturally available and culturally sanctioned language, roles, values, priorities, methods, goals, and plans. The end is to resituate discourse to motivate writing differently. The means is to create writing scenes that allow students to write not for us but to each other. Change the scene, and you change the act.

Appendix: Sample Prompt

LSA-p1
Today

First, for those who have never taken a course from me, a few sentences to explain what you're holding in your hand (if you've seen my prompts before, I'd think you could skip the next paragraph).

> The document you're reading is what I call a "prompt." I write prompts to help organize what we do in this course. Ordinarily, prompts do not come

out of the blue; I write them for almost every class; they develop out of
what we have done in previous meetings; and they move our project forward. Thus I usually talk in prompts about what we'll be doing in the
present and the next class meeting. The code in the upper left-hand
corner—"LSA-p1"—is a computer file name you and I will use to identify
the prompt we're working from. (*LSA* says it's *L*anguage as *S*ymbolic
*A*ction and *p1* says it's *p*rompt #*1*.)

This particular prompt summarizes what I anticipate we will do today. Then
it gives you something to do for our next meeting, on Thursday (when I'll
give you another prompt).

After I passed out and we talked about the Course Description for LSA,
I read aloud a Matt Cohen story called "Keeping Fit" and asked you to write
on these questions:

- Where were you as I read the short story "Keeping Fit?"
- Who was there with you?
- What were you doing? What were you thinking about? What ques-
  tions were you asking?

You handed what you had written around for others to read (silently),
and then some of what got written was read aloud ("What jumps off the
page at you? What seems to you well-stated? What seems to you unexpected,
surprising?"). We talked. I presume we agreed that listening to and engaging with the story "took you somewhere," into a kind of reality that was
"not quite, but next to" what we might ordinarily call "*real* reality." I also
presume that I gave you a name to call "the place" it took you—Virtual
Reality (VR).

For **Thursday's** meeting I'd like you to do some more writing, this time on
these questions:

- What is virtual reality? How do you think virtual reality is best
  defined?
- How does virtual reality work? That is, how does virtual reality
  come about, or how does it happen? Who and what are involved in
  making it occur/happen?
- What are the implications of virtual reality
  - for the reader?
  - for our understanding of what literature is, how it works,
    what it does?
  - for the notion that language is a kind of action-through-
    symbols?

Bring what you write to class, for others to read and for us to work with.

Notes

1. Obviously, many students do bring powerful motives for writing into our classrooms. For whatever reasons, these students already understand the power of written language to shape their worlds and to get things done; they come into our classrooms already skilled and determined writers. Unfortunately, however, large numbers of students are not so motivated. If we can provide these students with classroom scenes that enable them to experience written language as a means of negotiating meaning and place in literate cultures, then they too might have a chance of carrying those motives with them into other courses, other experiences.

2. I presume that everyone reading this chapter has done just what I ask my students to do. We "worked up a field" in this way, coming to know its "sayables," when we studied for our Ph.D. comprehensive exams, for example, and we have done something very similar whenever we have taken on a new course to teach or when we have developed a new scholarly interest. It is this experience that prepares us to take our students through what amounts to the same scholarly process—except that our students have the benefit of our expertise as researchers and their peers' assistance as co-inquirers.

3. While course descriptions (also called course outlines and syllabi) and their content are mandated by St. Thomas University's academic senate, prompts are not. I employ written prompts because I want to strengthen the presence of writing in my classroom and the enterprise, to demonstrate the roles complex written texts can and must serve in the research enterprise. My aim, that is, is to enact the ability of written language to affect and govern people's behavior—to "regulate" what they do, how they think, what they know, and how they relate to others by writing and reading texts.

4. Since space will not allow providing entire prompts, I have appendixed, as a sample, the full text of the first prompt I distributed in one version of the course.

Works Cited

Barnes, Douglas. 1980. "Language Across the Curriculum: The Teacher as Reflective Professional." *The English Quarterly* 13.3: 9–20.

Boomer, Garth. 1993. "How to Make a Teacher." *English Education* 25.1: 3–18.

Bruffee, Kenneth. 1984. "Collaborative Learning and the 'Conversation of Mankind.'" *College English* 46.7: 635–52.

Burke, Kenneth. 1969. *A Grammar of Motives*. Berkeley: University of California Press.

———. 1966. *Language as Symbolic Action: Essays on Life, Literature, and Method*. Berkeley: University of California Press.

———. 1973. *The Philosophy of Literary Form: Studies in Symbolic Action*. 3rd Edition. Berkeley: University of California Press.

———. 1969. *A Rhetoric of Motives*. Berkeley: University of California Press.

Elbow, Peter. 1994. "Peter Elbow Responds." *College English* 56.1(January): 101–105.

Gage, John T. 1981. "Towards an Epistemology of Composition." *Journal of Advanced Composition* 2, 1–2: 1–9.

North, Stephen. 1987. *The Making of Knowledge in Composition: Portrait of an Emerging Field.* Portsmouth, NH: Boynton/Cook.

Rorty, Richard. 1979. *Philosophy and the Mirror of Nature.* Princeton: Princeton University Press.

Saunders, Kathryn. 1992. "Only I Determine Me. In *Making a Name for Ourselves,* written and edited by the students of English 3–494, Language as Symbolic Action. St. Thomas University: Inkshed Press.

Vestal, David. 1975. *The Craft of Photography.* New York: Harper & Row.

II

Student Writing and Teacher Learning

5

We Wrote the Book on That
Excerpts from Our Journals

Joseph F. Trimmer
Ball State University

8/24   I could start this story anywhere. Brainstorm some leads.

College Student: In the middle of the bookstore, I weigh my investment in the assigned text, *Norton's Anthology of English Literature, Volume 1*. Does he really expect us to read two thousand pages? And what about Volume 2?

Assistant Professor: In the back row of the conference room, I grumble about the adoption of St. Martin's *American Literature: The Makers and the Making*. The headnotes are longer than the selections. What am I supposed to teach?

Textbook Author: With my editor from Harcourt Brace, I sort through the responses to my short story anthology, *Fictions*. "Too many oldies. Too many PC's." Are they teaching the same book? Why don't they report what their students like?

All possible . . . , but . . . the defining moment: At the secretary's desk, I inspect the order form for "Intro to Lit." I skip over the five recommended texts, and, on the line reserved for alternatives, I write *NONE*! "But what will your students read?" Don't worry. They're going to write their own textbook.

8/26   That was last spring. Next hour I'll have to explain this alternative to the students in R(obert) B(ell) B(uilding) 107. I have a theory:

> Students don't read literature. They read literature anthologies. Somebody else has packaged the process of reading and selecting. But students need to practice this process to understand the big questions: What is literature? Who writes it? Who reads it? Why study it?

I also have a theory problem. I don't like telling students what they will learn. I prefer to sketch out assignments, encourage students to refine them, and then listen to them talk about what they have learned. I know. It's just another theory. In the writing classroom, teachers coach students to create their own texts. In the literature classroom, teachers judge students by their commentary on other texts. In RBB 107, I'll invite students to create, arrange, and interpret their own textbook—and see what happens.

8/27   Why am I always surprised? Fifteen students. Fifteen responses. We're going to keep journals so we can compare notes. But who knows what they're saying between the lines? **John:** "In most of our classes, we know exactly what we are going to do before we start. But this class makes me nervous. Who knows what will happen?" **Krista:** "The class sounds interesting and challenging. I like the idea of working together to create a final product—our own textbook." **Paul:** "The project is a MONSTER and Trimmer is pretty vague about how we are going to pull it off. Just what I need. A textbook I can't sell."

8/31   *Freewrite about your past experiences with textbooks.* Common complaints (too expensive, too big, too dull) and wonderful stories. **Chris:** "My English teacher made us follow the textbook. You know—by the numbers. If she was discussing question #3, nobody could say anything about #4." **Carrie:** "My English teacher loved to trash our textbook. The selections were terrible. The headnotes were wrong. The best way to earn points was to find typos." **David:** "Some guy named Tony had the book before me. He marked it up with cartoon balloons ('If you want to see how I get out of this mess, check out page 94') or phony footnotes ('For hard copy on Fitzgerald's Honoria, see Clifford Knotes, "The Last Time She Saw Paris." *Essays in Honor of Marion Peters.* Babylon:UPS, 1963:24–26.')." The one-liners raise questions: Why do we remember these books as bad? Why do teachers still use them? How do they present literature to students?

9/7   We form five study groups. Each group selects one of the five recommended texts, and then, using reviewers' questions from a publisher, spends a week researching and writing a "market report." Show and tell. **Shelly:** "I've never read a preface before, but that's where they tell you what they think they've done." **Doug:** "I'm not sure I'm qualified to judge our book. I've read a few selections, but don't recognize most of the authors." **Michael:** "The headnotes in ours drive me crazy. They don't tell you anything you want to know. When I hit the italics—you know, all the other books this guy's written—I just glaze over." **Deanna:** "I've read one story in our text in three other classes, but I have no idea what these study questions are about." **Melinda:** "All these books follow the same rules. Like a sonnet. Preface. T.O.C. Intros. Headnotes. Selection. Apparatus. Glossary. Index. I hope our book breaks some rules."

9/16   We've re-searched our experience with textbooks. We've researched the competition. Now we have to draft our proposal. (Notice the pronoun shift. The class transformed itself into an editorial board. Melinda is chair. I'm a consultant. It's all fiction, of course, but it has changed the purpose of our conversation and the process of our deliberations.) For openers, we decided that our book will exhibit the following features:

1. *Contemporary Authors*: We want to read literature written by all kinds of authors who live in our time.

2. *Student Authors*: We want to contribute our own literature to our textbook.

3. *Contemporary Themes*: We want to read and write about subjects we care about—a sense of humor will help.

4. *Various Forms*: We want to include all kinds of literature—fiction, nonfiction, comic strips.

5. *Lively Headnotes*: We want to know how our writers live, why they write, and how they make a living.

6. *Vivid Art Work*: We want our cover, design, and illustrations to reflect our visual culture.

7. *No Apparatus*: We don't want to write stupid questions and silly exercises.

9/21   **WORDSTRUCK**. The consultant suggests that a four-day literary festival featuring some of the nation's most distinguished writers might be a convenient place to find potential authors. The editorial board looks over the brochure and decides to shop for authors. Four (Chris, David, Steve, and Travis) want to shop on their own. No problem—except the editorial board votes that all headnotes must be based on personal interviews. Chris, David, and Travis start checking phone directories; Steve decides to use e-mail.

9/23   The editorial board sketches out a format and a new schedule of assignments. Each student will edit one twenty-page chapter. It will contain (1) headnote (based on research and an interview), (2) selection (taught to and approved by the class), (3) profile (an analysis of the student as writer), and (4) student text (developed in drafts and "read" to the class). Editors will work on their author until midterm (dates for **WORDSTRUCK**), their own writing up to Thanksgiving, and then publish the text by finals.

9/28   After a weekend in the library, everybody has an author. The board composes three new assignments:

1. Research the library's holdings on your author. You only have twenty pages, so save room for your own work. Look for short stories and essays about ten pages long. Look for a variety of poems. Pick stuff that fits our criteria and that you understand. Remember

you have to teach it to the class.

2. Talk to teachers in the department about how they would teach your selections: Professors Koontz and Peterson (poetry), Professors Dimoplon and Jennings (fiction), Professors Munley and Papper (nonfiction). Trimmer's around—if you're desperate.

3. Xerox biographical info from *Who's Who* and *Contemporary Authors*. Copy headnotes from other anthologies. Check Resource Center for videos and recordings. Interviews. Readings.

9/30   The questions always come from left field. We are reading biographical information. **Steve:** "How come all our authors went to the same schools—Iowa, Hopkins, Harvard? What's an MFA?" **Deanna:** "Do we have to list all these prizes? Is a Guggenheim like an Oscar?" **Jolene:** "What does a writer-in-residence do? Does she stay in her residence and write, or go to school and teach? How can she write poems if she has to teach them? How do you grade a poem?" **Shaun:** "It took David McCullough ten years to write *Truman*. How can anybody spend ten years on one book? How did he pay the bills while he was writing?" **Travis:** "Most of the headnotes on Joyce Carol Oates look like they were cribbed from *Contemporary Authors*. Is that plagiarism?" **Melinda:** "Remember, our headnotes are supposed to be different. Let's make a list of the questions we want to ask our authors. Then we'll do some mock interviews."

10/5   Last week editors circulated copies of headnotes and selections. This week they started teaching. A few performed like little professors—reading notes from biography, summarizing plot, asking questions about *the* theme. Most approached their material tentatively, sketching the life and stumbling over the story. This "approach" encouraged the class to help. Sensing a crack-up, the students coached the teacher to talk about the author's life. Sensing a connection, the teacher asked the students to help interpret problems in the story. Surprises came from non-**WORDSTRUCK** editors. Steve used an overhead to trace the thesis of Chomsky's essay, "The Responsibility of an Intellectual"; Chris asked the class to freewrite on why Jonathan Winters' comic story, "A Well-kept Secret," should be considered a literary text. I don't understand these selections, but the editorial board thought the combination was a real "hoot."

10/7   The teaching will continue for the next three weeks. About three presentations during each two-and-a-half-hour period. But the immediate concern is how to interview authors at **WORDSTRUCK**. Today, Michael taught Louise Erdrich's *The Red Convertible*, Doug taught a chapter from Michael Dorris's *The Broken Cord*, and Carrie taught "Anything," an essay from Dorris's new book, *Working Men*. At the end of their presentation, they showed a video of some Brit interviewing Erdrich and Dorris. **David:** "The interview with Erdrich and Dorris was a good example of what not to do. Do not talk like Robin Leech. Do not make happy talk between questions. Do not ask questions that would take a lifetime to answer.''

10/12   There is no way to capture **WORDSTRUCK**. A four-day literary festival featuring over thirty authors reading and talking about their work at different sites around the city. Some students stayed all day each day. John and Carrie won the prize for hearing seven authors in one day. Major question: What is a *reading*? Everyone had different experiences. **Krista:** ''Alice Friman was terrific. She has this deep, theatrical voice. She really made her poems come alive. What I enjoyed most was listening to her explain how she got the ideas for a particular poem.'' **Paul:** ''James Tate is not a dramatic speaker. He's frail, cautious, confused. He didn't say anything. He simply read a poem, turned a few pages, and then read another poem. His voice is playful. I saw that in the poems. I'm glad the audience laughed when he read the poems I picked for the text.'' **Shelly:** ''The little theater was packed for Lynda Barry. A real Saturday Night Live crowd. I was wondering how she was going to read her work. She projected the cartoons on a screen and read them. They were just as funny as the first time I read them in the *Voice*. I'm coming back next weekend to see her play, *The Good Times Are Killing Me*.'' **Deanna:** ''I couldn't believe Momaday. He's enormous. Big black ten-gallon hat, cowboy boots, sunglasses. He told us about the first reading he went to at the University of Virginia. He got a front row seat to see his idol—William Faulkner—but all he could see was the lectern and some smoke curling up over the mike. Faulkner, who smoked a pipe, was about five feet tall, so the lectern hid him. All Momaday could do was listen to Faulkner's voice and watch the smoke.''

10/14   **WORDSTRUCK** war stories could go on all semester. Today's topic: interviews. More precisely, ''Dumbest Question.'' **Shaun:** ''Some guy asks McCullough, 'In all your research did you ever come across the name of Clyde Penrose? . . . He's my cousin and a policeman. He gave Truman directions through Greenfield when he was driving back to Washington.''' **Doug:** ''How's this? I ask Dorris, 'Mr. Dorris, when you write, do you prefer fiction or non?''' **Michael:** ''I can top that. I corner Erdrich at the reception, but I forget all my questions. So I said, 'Where did you get the idea for that sex scene with the geese?' . . . She looked shocked. Then smiled, 'Well, it certainly didn't happen to me!''' **John:** ''Martone and I are both from Fort Wayne, so I started out with some local stuff. Then I told him, 'I've always dreamed of being a writer, but you stole my best material. Why don't you write about something else?' When he signed my copy of *Fort Wayne is Seventh on Hitler's List*, he wrote, 'To John. Another writer stuck with his subject. Bombs away. Michael.'''

10/19   We need to start writing our own literature. **WORDSTRUCK** lingers. **Jolene:** ''I had never heard of Rosellen Brown before this project, but once I started the research I was hooked. I read her poems, stories, essays. I even read a long interview somebody else did with her. Then my car broke down on the way to her reading. The next week I got her phone number in Houston and called her. She's great! Extremely normal! I asked her about some of the poems and stories I was considering, and she gave me the background for each one. I hope she wasn't just being polite when she said I could call her again if I had questions. When I teach her writing, I'll have a bunch.'' **Melinda:** ''I interviewed Scott Russell Sanders at **WORD-STRUCK,** drove across the state to see him teach a writing class, and talked to him several times on the phone. I want to get some of what I've learned into his headnote. He says his 'family is central to his work'—which probably explains why his favorite essay is one he wrote about his father, 'Under the Influence.' I picked 'Looking at Women' for the textbook. He wants me to call him after I teach it—to hear how the guys respond.''

10/21   We shift into the familiar pattern of the writing class. Groups. Conferences. Readings. But our purpose has shifted. We are writing LITER-ATURE that will appear in a textbook next to the work of people we know. Some remain ''under the influence.'' **Deanna** tells her group that Momaday has inspired her to write about her childhood on the reservation. She circulates the last few lines of a poem, ''Cherokee'':

I raise the pipe to my lips.
I breathe deeply from its red fire.
I close my eyes as the smoke curls
From my mouth to my nose to the air,
Upward to the Great Spirit.
Drums beat.
My spirit is released.
I am the smoke.

Shelly tells her group that she is going to draw her story—á la Barry—in a comic strip. **Doug** can't stop talking about Dorris: ''I couldn't believe it when I heard that his son, Adam, was killed—hit by a car as he was walking home from work. Dorris put Adam's story at the back of *The Broken Cord.* Maybe I'll put Adam's story in our text. As for my story, I think I'll write a little *non* about reading, teaching, and interviewing Dorris. Something about how writers change your life and never know it.''

10/26   Unscheduled conference. The non-**WORDSTRUCK** editors come by my office seeking a reprieve. Chomsky won't answer his e-mail. Winters's phone is unlisted. Oates and Shepherd haven't written back. They still like their choices, but suspect they missed the party. **Steve:** ''I didn't know any of the authors. I studied Chomsky's essay last semester and knew I could teach it.'' **Chris:** ''I really like the stuff we've read. I've got Michael's copy of *Love Medicine,* and he says her new one, *The Bingo Palace,* is even better. But I wanted to make sure we had some humor. Besides, I think the Winters's story is a 'classic.'" What about your own writing? **David:** "I'm working on a great story about crashing the National Cheerleaders Convention. It will play off the Sanders essay Melinda picked. But it's hard to write funny. I'm reading more Shepherd to pick up some tricks." **Travis:** "Mine's unusual. About the problems of computer networking. I'm calling it 'Virtual Friends.' I didn't think about it until just now, but it goes with the Oates I selected. They're both sort of 'hypertexts.'"

10/28   Two weeks of conferences on the way to two increasingly trau-matic deadlines. The Reading. The Publication. **John:** "WORDSTRUCK was a ball. But now—after all my big talk to Martone about being a writer—I can't think of anything to write about. Carrie says I should write about not having anything to write about. But I don't want to read garbage in front of this class. I certainly don't want to appear in print for the first time next to my bud, Michael, as the author of some piece of trash." **Jolene:** "I'm still not sure what I'm going to write about. I used to think literature had to be about something extraordinary. Not after *Street Games*. Brown writes about ordinary people. She told me not to worry about finding something spectac-ular: 'It's not what you write. It's how you write about it.' Amen!"

11/9   Draft, revise. Draft, revise. The readings at **WORDSTRUCK** have upped the ante for the readings in RBB 107. **Michael:** "You've got to real-ize that I'm terrified of speaking in public. In my high school speech class, I grabbed the sides of the lectern so tightly that I cracked it apart." The con-sultant suggests authors practice by reading into a tape recorder: "Play it back to see how you sound. Keep your text in front of you. Mark the spots you have trouble reading. You may want to revise them. Listen for those passages where you want to create a special effect. Score them so you'll remember how you want them to sound. After you listen to yourself read your text several times, you'll stop reading and start performing." **Michael:** "I know I'm ready. If I have to listen to myself read this story one more time, I'll puke."

11/11   There is no way to capture The Readings. A four-day literary fes-tival featuring fifteen authors reading and talking about their writing. The audience has heard the texts in various drafts, but this is the final rehearsal before publication. The texts are extraordinary. Funny. Thoughtful. Poignant. The audience is spellbound. Where did this literature come from? How do the authors feel about the applause? Let the quietest one speak for the rest. **Krista:** "I really worked hard pacing my story about the time my mother took me to see my first musical, *Oklahoma*. The night was magical. But I needed an ending. I kept thinking about Friman's big, theatrical voice, and my little voice. The tape recorder helped. I imagined myself as a little girl, home alone, reliving the previous evening's performance. I put on the record.

Adjusted the gooseneck lamp for a spot. Turned to the audience. And then, together with Curly and the rest of the cast, I stretched out my arms and belted it out: 'We're only sayin', You're doin' fine Oklahoma! Oklahoma, O.K.!' And it was. I couldn't believe I sang in class. But I did. Then everybody applauded. Unbelievable!''

11/22   We are at the bottom of the emotional roller coaster. Profiles. Profiles. We forgot about the profiles. **Carrie:** "What are we supposed to write about? We've hardly had a life: 'In eleventh grade, she worked as a hall monitor.'" **Travis:** "What about influences? I learned about life from Archie Bunker and 'Hawkeye' Pierce." **Steve:** "I could write a profile for somebody else. Shaun's story was incredible. I'd love to write his headnote. Or Michael's. Or Krista's. Anyone else but me." **Paul:** "Is the entire class going to write the profiles in the first or third person? First seems more lively. That's what we said we wanted. But third makes us sound like authors." The editorial board encourages editors to write two drafts—one in first, the other in third. "It's your chapter. Pick the one you like best. Be sure to describe the process you used to create your text."

11/30   Now the roller coaster heads for the finish line. We try to organize fifteen chapters into some kind of sequence. **David:** "I think we ought to organize our chapters by theme, but I haven't the slightest idea what our themes are." **Michael:** "I think we should vary the pace. Some serious. Some funny. Some serious. Shelly's drawing should go in the middle." **Deanna:** "I've done a little math. We have fifteen chapters, but only five women authors—professional authors. There are six women in the class. We have three Native Americans, but no other minorities. Why didn't anybody pick Yusef Komunyakaa? I heard him read and he was great." **Melinda:** "I can't believe we blew it on minority and gender. Somebody should have done Mari Evans's poetry or Susan Neville's story on looking for John Mellencamp. But we got what we got. We need to arrange it, design the cover, copy our chapters, and assemble sixteen copies of the book. Fifteen for us, one for Dr. T." **Chris:** "I'll design the cover if somebody can come up with a title." **John:** "Here's my idea for a cover. Title: *Textbook*. A black and white generic cover with a little barcode and a warning: 'Grade "D" But Readable. Sell Before 12/94.'" **Paul:** "We've got to have a signing party."

12/9   Details. Details. Details. Specs on type size, credit lines, cameraready copy. The assembled book, 371 pages, looks longer than expected and suspiciously like the five tomes on the list of recommended texts. The "master" goes off to the copy center.

12/14   Boxes of manuscript come back from the copy center. The cover looks great. Chris has inserted a signature page so the class can autograph each other's copies and authorize the consultant to quote from their work if he decides to write his own story about the project. Doug, David, Michael, and Melinda bind the copies with black plastic binders.

12/16   The signing party in RBB 107. **Jolene:** "I can't believe we made the whole thing." **Shaun:** "Now I know I'd rather be in print than read somebody else in print." **John:** "I'm signing 'Bombs Away' on every copy." After much yakkin' and congratulatin', the party ends when Melinda announces she is going to perform a ceremonial reading of her preface. When she finishes the last paragraph, the class explodes into cheers:

"So here you have it. A textbook featuring the best contemporary writers— some intellectual, some entertaining, all engaging—combined with the literary efforts of gifted student writers. It meets all our criteria for a textbook. It is written by people we know, concerning subjects we care about, amplified by artwork and enriched by humor. We did it. We like it. It's done. Now it's your turn. Do your own."

12/28   I could end this story anywhere. I probably should have ended it with the last paragraph of Melinda's preface. But here I am in the book exhibit at MLA. Books and books and books about literature. How to read it. How to teach it. How to write about it. As I browse, I compare professional and student choices. Most editors print Erdrich's *The Red Convertible* and Momaday's *A Way to Rainy Mountain,* but none print their poems. Check two for our side. Most print Oates's "Where Are You Going, Where Have You Been?" but none print "How I Contemplated the World from the Detroit House of Correction and Began My Life Over Again." Another check for our side. Nobody seems to know about Michael Martone, Alice Friman, Rosellen Brown, or Lynda Barry. I feel smug. Who needs an offical tome when students can make better choices and contribute their own texts? I pick up a book on "how to write about literature." As I thumb the pages, I imagine the response of the editorial board: "Yeah. We wrote the book on that!"

Appendix

Textbook: Table of Contents

For me, writing is basic to teaching literature. Nearly every day we write for a few minutes in class, and after every reading assignment the students write at home for five minutes in their reading logs. Sharing these informal writings with each other leads to lively discussions of the literature. Sometimes we trade writings, noting marginal responses on the page. Sometimes people volunteer to read to the class. Sometimes I say, "Everybody wearing red share a line from your writing."

Peer-writing techniques become methods for understanding the text. The students make clusters or webs of the ideas in the text. Sometimes, in pairs, one person listens, drawing out the other on the text for five minutes, before trading roles. Sometimes I ask the students to draw a picture of the poem or story. Drawings of open windows, fish dangling from rods, or bedraggled armies can start minds thinking in new directions.

We start our discussion of a new piece of literature with the presentation of a student paper on it. Early in the semester students choose texts on which they will write. We sit in a circle to hear the paper, taking notes on our reactions to the ideas. After reading the paper, the author leads a discussion. The first question is always, "What did you like about the paper?" Next comes, "What questions or comments do you have?" A spirited discussion of the text follows. "How can the road least traveled be the road to sin?" "Why do you see Hamlet as a representative of the proletariat?" The students require solid evidence for assertions. The authors discover that people care about their ideas, that they can influence people's thinking by careful support and presentation.

In a literature class, sharing writing allows students to discover the power of their own ideas.

Elizabeth Finch Hedengren
Brigham Young University

6

Textual Terror, Textual Power
Teaching Literature through Writing Literature

Lynn Z. Bloom
University of Connecticut

Where We've Been: Background and Theory

Revolutionary principles often look like common sense, especially from the familiar comfort of retrospect. In *Textual Power,* Robert Scholes offers the revolutionary, but highly common-sensical principle that the best way to understand a text is to produce a text in response to it: "Our job is not to produce 'readings' for our students, but to give them the tools for producing their own." He amplifies, "Our job is *not* to intimidate students with our own superior textual production," as high priests of literature brilliantly unlocking the "right" readings of poetry before classes of students awed by our interpretations, arcane and esoteric and oh-so-scholarly. We can and should introduce our students to "the codes upon which all textual production depends," and then encourage them to write their own texts in response to the texts they read in a literature course, any literature course (24–25).

Scholes is talking here about encouraging students to write independent criticism of literary works. Critical freedom can—and should—lead to creative freedom, as Scholes illustrates throughout this equally revolutionary common-sensical *Text Book.* Indeed, as I will argue and demonstrate in this paper, why not encourage students to write creative texts in the genres and modes of the works they're studying, in response to and as a way of understanding these works?

Scholes articulates in *Textual Power* and *Text Book* an admirable solution to a problem that has plagued me from my undergraduate days through three decades as a writer, scholar, and teacher: how to help students combine the study of creative literature and the practice of creative writing. The literary critics and scholars who determine, by their own example, the normative, high-priest way we teach literature through critical *explications de texte* have, by and large, relegated these activities to separate spheres. This arbitrary division has the same deleterious effects on critical understanding and critical writing that the racism and sexism of "separate spheres" have had historically on the relations between blacks and whites, men and women.

Indeed, it has taken me twenty years to be able to integrate the critical and the creative successfully in my literature classes. The climate is finally right. Nevertheless, because teaching and learning continue to be dynamic and reciprocal processes, what I say here about teaching literature through writing represents only the current state of a process of continual evolution. Consequently, much of my illustrative material will be drawn from the class I've most recently taught, a graduate course in Fall 1993 at the University of Connecticut in "Autobiography: Telling Secrets, Telling Lies, Telling Lives."

My own behavior as a scholar and writer anticipated Scholes by two decades. To understand as an insider the issues I'd raised, as an arrogant outside explicator, in my critical dissertation on literary biography (1963), I spent seven years writing and publishing *Doctor Spock: Biography of a Conservative Radical* (1972). I could not have learned except by writing a biography myself that this genre has not only a human face, but a human heart and soul (1993). When I first started teaching poetry, I wrote several hundred poems—and published some (see "Definition of Poetry," 1974)— to learn a better way to teach this individualistic, elusive genre.

But the logical next step—as a teacher who would enable and therefore empower students to do the same thing—took another fifteen years. Scholes had to articulate the theory. I had to publish creative nonfiction and personal criticism—and to do that, the critical climate had to change. In "Beyond Literary Darwinism," Frey points out that the adversarial mode of criticism has dominated the most prestigious journal, *PMLA,* for at least the past twenty years. In "The Literary Argument and Its Discursive Conventions," MacDonald demonstrates that such criticism is opaque, elitist, and unutterable inscribed by the unreadable—and the very antithesis of the clear, consise, accessible prose that writing teachers have been advocating during the same time that the Literary Darwinists have dominated professional meetings and journals.

Professional criticism created the prevailing model for how literature should be taught in the classroom, as well. Argumentative models of every sort, whether New Critical, Deconstructionist, or any other intellectual framework, have isolated the primary creative works from the very students eager to enjoy them, as Eudora Welty's mother read Dickens "in the spirit in which she would have eloped with him"(7). Instead, student writers are required to adopt the critical models of their mentors and to write adversarial literary criticism, becoming junior Literary Darwinists closing in for the kill. What sparks of creativity can survive in this critical jungle?

Until recently, there has been little journal space for mavericks such as William H. Gass, whose idiosyncratic wit enlivened the critical wilderness with such works as *The World Within the Word* (1978) and *Habitations of the Word* (1985). Not until 1987 did Jane Tompkins's "Me and My Shadow" appear, followed in 1989 by Susan J. Leonardi's precedent-shattering *PMLA* article, "Recipes for Reading: Summer Pasta, Lobster à la Riseholme, and Key Lime Pie." These and some other feminist theoretical works (see Frey) were harbingers of the far more comfortable climate of the 1990's, now receptive to such works as G. Douglas Atkins's *Estranging the Familiar: Toward a Revitalized Critical Writing* (1992); Michael Kowalewski's collection, *Temperamental Journeys: Essays on the Modern Literature of Travel* (1992); Diane P. Freedman, Olivia Frey, and Frances Murphy Zauhar's *The Intimate Critique: Autobiographical Literary Criticism* (1993); and Raymond Federman's playful *Critifiction: Postmodern Essays* (1993).

In this climate I have finally found editorial encouragement to take the risk, and places to publish the creative nonfiction (1992, 1993) and creative criticism (1990, 1991) that I always wanted to write. If I can do it, I have the right to ask my students to do it too, because I have the credibility to show them how (1991). I also believe that I, and other graduate English faculty, have a particular obligation to teach the literature of creative writing in part through the practice of creative writing, including creative nonfiction. Our students themselves, primarily English M.A. and Ph.D. candidates, will become teachers of literature and, willy-nilly, of writing; they should take the plunge while the water's warming up.

Where We Are Now: Classroom Application

So for the past six years I have been requiring students to try writing in one or more of the literary modes we're studying in the course. By mid-semester in every literature course I teach, all students have to write at least one short paper *of* literature, rather than *about* literature, so that what they've learned about creative writing from the experience of trying it themselves will inform the rest of their semester's work. (Of course, I really want this experience to inform their subsequent reading and teaching and to change the rest of their lives, but I don't confess this extraordinarily demanding—and daunting—goal at the outset.) To encourage freedom and experimentation—and to allow the timid and the terrified to do it at all—students can waive a grade on this paper, if they wish. To date, only one has done so.

The assignments vary depending on the course. In "Women Writers," the students must write in one or another of the genres we study—poetry, creative nonfiction, fiction, or drama. In "Rhetorical Theory and Composition Research," the students write a short paper of stylistic imitation, and another research paper in their own voice rather than in academic discourse. The host of possibilities in "Autobiography" is illustrated below. Initially, these assignments are startling to some, intimidating if not terrifying to others. Their vast, open universe forces students to look beyond the critical boundaries in which they have been comfortably, sometimes complacently, confined. By the time these students are in graduate school, they have become competent ventriloguists in the language of critical jargon, submerging their own voices in the process. They *know* how to write as critics, but many—often most—have never written in any of the literary genres they have been learning to dissect.

"Me? A poet? I've never been asked to write anything creative before," worried Bethany Drews-Javidi, a doctoral student taking her last-course-before-prelims. "I've never written anything except in military language," confessed Steve Ryan, a career army captain returning to grad school to prepare to teach at West Point, his prose as ramrod-straight as his military bearing. "This is the toughest assignment I've ever had, to imitate another's style," but he grinned as he said it.

To be a producer as well as a consumer of texts enables—no, obliges—the writer to understand works of literature from the inside out. In poetry, for instance, nascent poets learn through experience and experimentation why lines scan the way they do, why line breaks come where they do, why certain words are used instead of others for alliteration or for rhyme. In autobiography, as Carol Virostek observed on returning to college to earn a doctorate after twenty-two years of high-school teaching,

> I began to see that one need not have all the answers about some life situation or conflict in order to write about it, that the writing could in fact become part of the resolution. I began to understand that writing about oneself need not be self-promotional or confessional (despite personal admissions) and that the events in the lives of ordinary people such as I and my classmates contain all the elements of drama one could expect to find only in the lives of the famous and infamous people [whose autobiographies] we've read.

Among the variety of obvious and more subtle aspects of imaginative writing the students learn from the experience of doing it are the following, with particular reference to autobiography:

1. The innumerable versions in which a particular experience can be rendered.
2. The relation of style to substance, style to self.
3. The significance of emphasis, de-emphasis, omissions, gaps, erasures.
4. The difficulties, ethical and aesthetic, of dishonesty.
5. The importance of each word, each syntactic structure, each punctuation mark, in every text.

6. The critical rigor that undergirds writing well for an external audience.
7. The necessity, aesthetic and personal, of rewriting.
8. The importance of reading literature as well as writing it, with an understanding of the writer's craft, the writer's art.

Writing literature to learn literature obliges and enables the students to become invested in their own writing, and in the writing of their peers, in ways they would never have imagined before they tried it. The students fret. They stew. They write and rewrite and rewrite again before they're ready to share their work with me and with each other—also part of the requirement.

In every case, sooner or later, when the students have begun to understand what they've done, textual terror gives way to a sense of textual power. "Is this good enough to submit for publication?" asked Bethany, bestowing an elegant, laser-printed, slender volume on each member of our "Women Writers" class. "Well, almost." Steve's account of his experience in a refugee camp during Operation Desert Storm did indeed prove to be a publishable example in a composition textbook.

> The camp seems loudest at night. A huge, dulled murmur flows up from the valleys with hacking, rattling coughs, unending moaning like mantras, mules braying, wails, and shrieks as if a child stepped on a nail. Clank tap-tapping, metal pots clanking and wood chopping sounds, but no sounds of laughter. The footsteps and shifting of thousands make a pressure on the ear just below the level of a sound, and no strong wind whistles close distractions or carries the sounds away. Rising to the hill in the middle of 85,000 Kurdish refugees, the sounds articulate our mission.

The experience of writing these short assignments invariably influences the term papers. Some students in the Rhet/Comp and "Women Writers" courses decide to write their longer papers in the voices and modes with which they've been experimenting. I always allow this alternative, but do not require it, though with Spock as my stylistic mentor I do insist on a clear, readable style—preferably one that is humanly engaging. "Autobiography" engenders the writing of creative nonfiction; reading and writing about others' life stories—a dozen published autobiographies of distinction accompanied by a dozen three-to-seven-page interpretive response papers—inspires the students to tell their own. Although I'd expected these students in a critically oriented graduate program to write critical term papers, seven of the ten chose the option of autobiographical essays. As Carol summed up, "I will have plenty of opportunity to write critical papers in future courses. I couldn't let the opportunity to re-read my own life pass me by."

I am a restless teacher. Just as I'm always pushing my own writing to make it better, and my students' work to make it publishable, I am always tinkering with my teaching; even if something works well in the classroom,

I want to make it better. Although for thirty-five years I have taught writing courses through workshops, not until the fall of 1993 did I do what now seems both obvious and inevitable—incorporate writing workshops into my literature course. To help students write their short autobiographical paper, it seemed logical to embed seventy-five-minute writing workshops into two of the two-and-a-half-hour class sessions. The first one, a preparation for the student writing, would come in the fifth week, a month before the paper's due date; in the follow-up we'd read and analyze student papers.[1]

The preliminary workshop would focus on prize-winning creative nonfiction written in other courses by two students in the class, and—with great trepidation—a draft of my own work-in-progress, "Growing Up with Doctor Spock" (1993). Now I knew why, that although the critical and ped-agogical climate had changed sufficiently during the past six years to allow me to share completed work with students, I had never dared to commit the ultimate act of collegial teaching.

Every word, every sentence, every segment of an autobiography of qual-ity is a rendering of the truth that is at the deep heart's core of both imagi-native literature and creative nonfiction. As Gertrude Stein says, "I write for myself and strangers." But how would it be possible to write such profound, intimate truth for those former strangers, now students, whom I would have to see for the rest of the semester—or for much longer, as advisees, friends, and colleagues? How would I be able to maintain professorial authority when my students understood how vulnerable I, always upbeat in classroom—still remained to the pain and exile, personal and professional, that were inter-twined with my writing of Doctor Spock's biography? What if I cried in class as I cried every time I wrote and rewrote the tough parts? The work-shop sessions, like the writing on which they focused, were to deal with the art of crafting an honest, engaging autobiography, not with confession for therapeutic purposes. It would have been much easier to spill my life to strangers on airplanes.

Nevertheless, I handed the class a draft of "Growing Up with Doctor Spock" a week in advance. And every day, because I was pushing a pub-lisher's deadline as well as the courses's, I slipped ever more condensed revisions of the most difficult material—my parents' anti-Semitic rejection of myself, my husband, our marriage, and ultimately of the Spock biography—into the students' mailboxes, three on the workshop day alone. The sharing of this work changed the dynamics of the course so dramatically that I now not only feel obliged to write this most crucial assignment every semester I require the students to do so, but also to offer it, revision and all, for class critique in a workshop session.

Student evaluations are unanimous in identifying the pivotal importance of this workshop session. It quickly established a "writing community," said TA Jason Hunt, in which "the hierarchical boundaries, student/professor, student/canonical author seemed to disappear." Veteran middle-school teacher Jim Fuller debated whether to write about the recent death of his nine-month-old daughter, Hadley, until, he said, "Your example made me feel comfortable with opening my own life up to the class." He added that the workshop critique was also "an effective teaching device [that] said to us, 'There now, I did it and you can do it too.' The atmosphere changed after that class. You bridged the [arbitrary] division between the critical and the personal, the intellect and the emotions, [and enabled] us all to leap the divides constructed by years of habit."

Moreover, the stream of revisions had other, serendipitous effects. The students saw this exposure of the revising process, as TA Bob Myhal said, "most significant in establishing the link between teaching, writing, and studenting," because it was "more honest, more difficult, and more risky than bringing a published, and thus polished, piece of finished writing into a class." Jason took heart from the "constant revisions appearing in my box. . . . Even though I try to teach writing as a process, I still have to fight the suspicion that for published writers [writing] really isn't as hard as they'd have me believe. To see you struggling"—and publishing the results—"renewed my faith in the process. So we all, professor and students, struggled, and the [distinguished] papers that resulted underscored the value of our effort."

As I increased the pressure on myself as a teacher and as a writer, I did not intend to increase the pressure for excellence on my already hardworking students, but that was the effect. Space limitations allow quotations from only two of the intricate, elegant, tough long papers of both autobiography and criticism that this class wrote, and rewrote, and rewrote—to the point where they are, I believe, worthy of publication and prizes. All of the papers, irrespective of subject, represented a witnessing of powerful life events that in their literate rendering became life-affirming: birth and death, coming of age, coming out, living as a stranger in a strange land, building a house and building a marriage, moving from suicide to an affirmation of life.

Indeed, Elizabeth Bidinger, a professional editor with an M.F.A. in creative writing, titled her paper "Witness." Where in her earlier fiction courses Elizabeth had written with comic detachment about her family uncomfortably transplanted from Appalachia to Michigan, her new understanding of autobiography enabled her to interpret the same people, comic and pathetic, with bittersweet compassion. In "Witness," she depicts her family's complicated disintegration on the Christmas eve of her thirteenth year. Into their house walked

> a thin young woman I'd never seen before. . . . I noticed that not only was
> she pigeon-toed, but she had a wandering eye, too. . . . She was our dad's
> girlfriend, the one he kept threatening to marry as soon as he could afford
> to, even though he still lived at home with us. . . . I had sworn to my mother
> that I would kill Debbie when I had the chance. Because of her, my mother
> had virtually stopped living, and had nearly starved herself to death. But
> here Debbie was, right before me in our very family room, and I was not
> killing her but hoping that she would like me. . . .

"Thank you for coming here," my mom said to her. "Why don't you tell the girls everything you've told me over the phone. . . ."

"I shouldn't be here," [Debbie] said. "I have no business being here. Jim lied to me is all, he told me a bunch of lies."

"No shit, Sherlock," Angela [Elizabeth's fifteen-year-old sister] said. "I'm leaving." My mother yanked her back by the elbow.

"No," my mother said coolly, "You girls are staying. I want you to witness all of this. You're going to witness."

She turned to my father's girlfriend. "Let me see those papers. . . . "Here," she said, handing them over. . . . [My mother] offered the papers to me. "*Witness*," she said.

I had never seen divorce papers in my life . . . but instantly I could see what stupid fakes these were. They were horribly typed on Angela's eras-able paper, with letters out of line and ink smears and a clearly unofficial style. The top sheet identified my dad as a U.S. naval pilot. Far from the truth: He drove a bulldozer at a gravel pit. It said that he had divorced Sharon last year. Also not true. It said that he had no children. . . .

The ensuing class discussion reaffirmed Elizabeth's view that "Doing the personal writing for the class helped me to see that my [own] family history is rich and valuable, rather than something to be ashamed of and to disguise; this . . . is a significant step in my growth as a person and as a writer. . . . This course revived my spirit. I am not overstating it when I say that the class reminded me of how deeply I love literature and writing and scholar-ship and even life. . . ." Indeed, Elizabeth's paper, like those of her col-leagues in class, demonstrates that she had learned the major literary lesson of this course, that through writing, controlled in persona, tone, and detail, she could gain the psychological and aesthetic distance that enabled her to translate life into art. This writing is by no means objective, nor (McGinty's objections to autobiographical student writing notwithstanding) can it be, but it has achieved both insight and rhetorical finesse through a writing and revi-sion process similar to sanding down a piece of beautiful wood, layer by layer, then painstakingly rubbing it to bring up the grain.

Jim Fuller's paper, "A Twist of Fate," bore a more painful witness. He juxtaposed sections of the ever-more-somber account of his daughter's inex-orable death from spinal muscular atrophy (a fatal form of MS)—"she was by far our happiest baby. That she couldn't crawl or turn over didn't frus-trate her. She had a perfect disposition for her disease"—with ironically hilarious vignettes of the death-defying exploits of his robust four-year-old twins and their brother whose "room at home," stockpiled with toy rifles and pirate swords, "already had that quaint early-armory look so popular with today's six-year-olds. . . . I had the eerie feeling that I might be raising a mercenary." Through this comic enjambment of the normal against the abnormal, Jim manages the difficult feat of not succumbing to self-pity or sentimentality. Indeed, his affirmation of life resonates through his daughter's death; he concludes:

> As a teacher, I live for the echo, knowing that if I work hard, some part of me will echo through the adolescents I spend my days with, just as I know that I myself am an echo of the compassion and enthusiasm of my best teachers. Hadley has changed me. My work, my life will now be an echo of her.

This was the one occasion where, as a class, our emotional response was so powerful ("The whole class wept unabashedly," as one student noted) that it had the potential for interfering with critical commentary—always a danger in such courses, but here kept in check by the theoretical and critical commentary on the genre that the students read through the semester.

Elizabeth Bidinger spoke for the class in responding to her classmate's work, read during our final class session of collaborative reading, writing, and eating:

> I was simultaneously aware, while listening to the painful details of her death, that the bereaved father has created an intimate record of the event that is so beautiful in its telling that it makes his listeners love life. It is a death-defying act, magical in its refraction of the pain from a man's worst possible loss into a piece of writing that has the spark of life in itself. . . . Writing autobiography has heightened my awareness as a critic, which in turn has deepened my appreciation of how generous and meaningful a gift a fine autobiographical piece can be.

Notes

1. Actually, there were two follow-up workshop sessions. Three students had written papers that tiptoed genteelly around the edges of their subjects, such as a sweet, conventional commemoration of the peaceful death of the author's aged father. ("A very nice tribute," I commented on it.) In concentrating on the more distinctive hard-edged papers, there wasn't time during the first session to discuss the writings that pulled their punches. The next week I "forgot" to present these papers to the class; spontaneous revisions were appearing in my mailbox. By the third week the revisions reflected stunning transformations, intellectual and technical. Class discussion reflected major changes in the writers, as well as in their work. As the author of the originally sentimental eulogy said, "The long-term effect of this class is my firm, undying resolution never ever to write anything 'nice' again!"

Works Cited

Atkins, G. Douglas. 1992. *Estranging the Familiar: Toward a Revitalized Critical Writing*. Athens, GA: University of Georgia Press.

Bloom, Lynn Z. 1974. "Definition of Poetry."*College Composition and Communication* 25.1 February: 111.

———. 1972. *Doctor Spock: Biography of a Conservative Radical.* New York: Bobbs.

———. 1991. "Finding a Family, Finding a Voice: A Writing Teacher Teaches Writing Teachers." In *Writer's Craft, Teacher's Art,* edited by Mimi Schwartz, pp. 55–68. Portsmouth, NH: Heinemann.

Bloom, Lynn Z. 1993. "Growing Up with Doctor Spock: An Auto/Biography." *A/B: Auto/Biography Studies* 8.2 (Fall): 1–15.

———. 1963. "How Literary Biographers Use Their Subjects' Works: A Study of Biographical Method, 1865–1962." Ph.D. Dissertation, University of Michigan.

———. 1992a. "I Want a Writing Director."*College Composition and Communication* 43.2 (May): 176–78.

———. 1992b. "Teaching College English as a Woman." *College English* 54.7 (November): 818–25.

———. 1990. "Why Don't We Write What We Teach? And Publish It?"*Journal of Advanced Composition* 10.1: 87–100.

Federman, Raymond. 1993. *Critifiction: Postmodern Essays.* Albany: SUNY Press.

Freedman, Diane P., Olivia Frey, and Frances Murphy Zauhar. 1993. *The Intimate Critique: Autobiographical Literary Criticism.* Durham, NC: Duke University Press.

Frey, Olivia. 1990. "Beyond Literary Darwinism: Women's Voices and Critical Discourse." *College English* 52.5 (September): 507–26.

Gass, William H. 1985. "Emerson and the Essay." In William H. Gass, *Habitations of the Word,* pp. 9–49. New York: Simon.

———. 1978. *The World Within the Word.* Boston: Godine.

Kowalewski, Michael, ed. 1992. *Temperamental Journeys: Essays on the Modern Literature of Travel.* Athens, GA: University of Georgia Press.

Leonardi, Susan J. 1989. "Recipes for Reading: Summer Pasta, Lobster à la Riseholme, and Key Lime Pie." *PMLA* 104.3 (May): 340–47.

MacDonald, Susan Peck. 1990. "The Literary Argument and Its Discursive Conventions." In *The Writing Scholar: Studies in Academic Discourse,* edited by Walter Nash, pp. 31–62. Written Communication Annual, v. 3.

McGinty, Sarah Myers. 1994. "Why Are Students Stumped by the Application Essay?" *Chronicle of Higher Education* 5 (January): A64.

Scholes, Robert. 1985. *Textual Power: Literary Theory and the Teacing of English.* New Haven: Yale University Press.

Scholes, Robert, Nancy R. Comley, and Gregory L. Ulmer. 1988. Text Book: *An Introduction to Literary Language.* New York: St. Martin's.

Tompkins, Jane. 1987. "Me and My Shadow."*New Literary History* 19: 169–78.

Welty, Eudora. 1984. *One Writer's Beginnings.* Cambridge, MA: Harvard University Press.

I treat published literature as just another text, like my students' own writing. I stress that there is no correct or incorrect reading, often by giving them a friend's original poem and having them suggest meanings for it. In this different context, students can come up with all kinds of meanings. They're all legitimate, I tell them, because my goal is to get them thinking about their own experiences. Approaching literature as I approach student writing, suggesting different contexts, audiences, and purposes, for example, reduces my students' fear of "great literature" and says to them that it is OK to take from it what they want.

I even share with them a list of "great literature" I don't like and invite them to do the same. I don't ever remember my literature courses being taught this way, but it wasn't until I got over the sense that literature was something above me that I was able to find reading it entertaining and meaningful and not just burdensome. Eventually, I came to love literature, and it's been gratifying to see some of my students come to love it too.

Isabel Buck McEachern
Jefferson Community College
Louisville, KY

7

The Rape of Clarissa
Teaching, Writing, and the Struggles of Interpretation

Richard J. Murphy, Jr.
Radford University

"You mean he *raped* her?" Wendy T. asked one afternoon this past semester. Her question came near the end of a class meeting in which we were discussing Samuel Richardson's *Clarissa,* the book Christopher Hill calls "one of the greatest of the unread novels" (102). Another of the students in the course had just referred to Lovelace's rape of Clarissa as if it were obvious in the text. At first, Wendy was startled into silence by this declaration. When the class hour came to an end, she continued to sit there for a few moments dumbfounded, trying to race back through the book in her mind. Finally she said, as if to herself, "He raped her, and I missed it." And then she added, looking at us all but especially at me, "*Did* he?"

Twenty years ago, I wrote one of the chapters of my dissertation on *Clarissa.* In the past few years, I have returned to the novel, arranging to teach it six times—once in an introductory undergraduate course in fiction, twice in undergraduate survey courses for English majors, twice in graduate courses in eighteenth-century studies, and once in an independent tutorial. Each time I teach the novel, I reread it. These recent encounters with the book have been full of surpirse for me. I hadn't forgotten the story's general outlines; I had forgotten its felt intensity. In rereading, I am struck again with wonder at its tragic intricacy and perplexity. Though I know what's coming through *Clarissa's* mazes, I am still ensnared by its illusions, still writing myself notes in the margins (e.g., "Is this a genuine letter or a fake? There is no hint that it's false."). I am unsettled by another surprise, too: Students are more confused by the novel than I expect, and more resistant to it. Whatever enthusiasms, clarifications, instructions I offer for helping them read, they take what they want, ignore the rest, and make the book—even if they reject it—their own. Wendy's question has helped me see both their experience as readers and mine as teacher in a new light.

When I say I "teach" *Clarissa,* I use the word generically. I mean I assign the novel as one of the required readings and usually allocate about two weeks of the semester syllabus to it. I provide the class with some information about the background of its writing and reception and something about modern criticism and scholarship on it. I facilitate class discussion of the novel and invite students to write about it in any one of a variety of ways.

But whatever I do, students go their own way. Last spring, for instance, a class of English majors effectively refused to read *Clarissa.* I had scheduled it in the syllabus. When the date came around, few students had done the reading. I rescheduled our discussions using the dates the class proposed for reading sections of the book; it still went unread. At the same time, a young woman who had begun auditing the class grew intrigued by my talk about the novel. She had first started coming to the class, she later told me, because she was whimsically following a guy she didn't know into the classroom. As her interest in him waned, however, her interest in the course and in *Clarissa* unexpectedly grew; she went home one weekend and read the novel almost at a sitting.

One semester, in a small honors section of a general education literature course, I assigned *Clarissa* after asking the class to read and discuss selections from *Paradise Lost.* Because the students were taken with Milton's poem, they asked if we could rearrange the course assignments in order to read the whole of it. We did. But when they came to *Clarissa,* they were so alienated by it, so frustrated and disappointed after *Paradise Lost,* so something (they acknowledged that they couldn't say exactly *what* was wrong) that in their end-of-term evaluations, they marked the downturn in the course at the point that we began to talk about *Clarissa.*

Another semester I invited students in a graduate seminar to read the unabridged Penguin edition of the novel. Ordinarily, I assign only the abridged Riverside version, edited by George Sherburn, but this semester three students agreed to substitute the (much) longer unabridged text for most of the other reading in the course, and every Friday afternoon the four of us met at a local sandwich shop for chips and beer and talk about *Clarissa.* At least one of the three students tells me now that he has still (years after graduating) not finished reading the novel.

The question of what I am doing when I "teach" *Clarissa* must have something to do with these refractory responses of students to the book. But the story is more complicated than reader resistance. When I first read it, I was captivated by the conflict between Clarissa and Lovelace. As the story progressed, I insisted on recounting for my patient wife the latest developments in the story. In doing so, I was not too different from Richardson's

first readers in 1748, who could hardly wait for the novel's next installments
to appear and who wrote to each other breathlessly about it.

Some students in my courses—like the woman who read it straight
through—have been as absorbed as I. This semester, for example, one student reported in her journal that she had to leave home to read it. In the midst
of family conflicts of their own at least as wrenching as those that isolate
Clarissa in the novel, Sarah B. moved into a motel room, alone, with the
book. Later she wrote that the irony was clear to her even at the time. There
she was—like Clarissa—in temporary flight from her family, with nowhere
to turn and no clear sense of what to do next, employing the time—unlike
Clarissa, who wrote—by reading.

The three students who worked in the ad hoc group on the unabridged
novel arranged a splendid class presentation as the culmination of their work.
They compared a specific passage from the abridged and unabridged texts
(i.e., a scene in which Lovelace gives himself an emetic to make Clarissa
believe he is ill). They accompanied this central activity of their presentation
with various theatrical elements—a fictional letter from Richardson asking
his friends how to abbreviate the scene, photocopied maps of the London of
Clarissa and Lovelace, a quill pen for each of us to try, a simulated death
certificate for Clarissa, and black armbands they each wore as tokens of
mourning. Their manifest engagement with the book had the ironic effect of
making their fellow students feel, as one of them put it, "cheated" by the
abridged version. Bryan E., one of the three presenters, found the epistolary
form of *Clarissa* compelling enough that he went on to write a master's thesis in which he used that form, with his own embellishments, to tell the
fictional love story of his great-aunt.

But, whatever its satisfactions, the difficulties of reading *Clarissa* persist
for students in my courses. One possible source of the difficulty may be the
version I usually assign, the abridged version edited by George Sherburn.
This text is only one-quarter as long as the unabridged editions. As such, it
may cut too much to make the novel's plot clear or its characters convincing
or its conflicts coherent or profound. Margaret Anne Doody and Florian Stuber have recently (and vigorously) criticized the Sherburn abridgment for just
such failures.

Still, my own experience reading the novel makes me skeptical. Though
I can remember distinctly being deeply moved by my later reading of the
unabridged novel, I believe that my *first* reading, in the Sherburn abridgment,
was in the end both clear and coherent. B. J. Bowman's experience was similar. During a recent graduate independent study of the unabridged novel,
Bowman took up Doody and Stuber's challenge. She agreed with their claim
that in its full-length form, Richardson's book has enormous power. But her
analysis of the specific weaknesses Doody and Stuber raise and of the evidence they point to led her to conclude that, in its own right, though abbre-
viated, the Sherburn text is a complex, dramatic, richly detailed rendering of

Richardson's story. "Like all abridgments," she writes, Sherburn's is necessarily "an adulteration of someone else's original." But in this case, she
concludes, "it is a faithful adulteration" (13).

This past semester, Crystal N.—the student whose mention of the rape
so startled Wendy T.—also read Sherburn and then went on independently
to begin the unabridged Penguin edition. She reported to the class on several
occasions how much "better" the unabridged text is. Her enthusiasm was
irrepressible. It seemed to me that her experience was a strong confirmation
of Doody and Stuber's criticism. But when she mentioned details that the
unabridged novel gave readers that had been omitted from the Sherburn, I
checked the two texts and found them to be exactly the same. This is not to
say that Crystal was not registering a real difference in the aesthetic experience of her reading or that Doody and Stuber are not right about the inferiority of the Sherburn abridgment. It simply seems that the difficulty I have
seen readers encounter with *Clarissa* cannot be explained wholly by attrib-
uting it to their reading a shorter, slighter version of the novel.

In whatever form, *Clarissa* is an epic novel. Its landscape is severely
restricted; almost the whole novel takes place in bedroom or parlor. But its
scope is vast. It is a love story so beautiful in its design, so complicated in
its passions, and so terrible in its consequences that it reflects in ruthless
detail the character of an entire (and corrupted) world. Clarissa Harlowe and
Robert Lovelace become entangled in a love affair that neither of them
desires or wants to admit. Both are young, wealthy, and beautiful. Clarissa
dresses in fabulous garments embroidered with silver. She manages her
mother's great household with consummate skill. She is renowned for mod-
esty, charity, and filial obedience. Lovelace is dashing (the word must have
been invented for him): ebullient and poised, charming, inventive, and
infinitely energetic. He has travelled widely and read subtly. He manages his
estates responsibly and efficiently. As a landlord, he is fair; as a rake, notorious. The brilliance, talent, wit, and intelligence of Clarissa and Lovelace
enable them both to perceive the failures of their society and to find in
each other virtues they admire and love. But at the same time their pride and
integrity doom their relationship, and the closer they come to one another
the more inevitable it becomes that their love can end only in violence
and death.

On Monday night, June 12 of the year in which the novel takes place,
Lovelace rapes Clarissa. Having slipped drugs into her hartshorn and water,
tea, and table beer, he rapes her. He is not alone. At least one other woman
(perhaps more than one) is present to witness that act, possibly to assist in it
by holding the victim. Three weeks later, in recounting the events of that
night for her friend Anna Howe, Clarissa writes: "I was so senseless, that I
dare not aver that the horrible creatures of the house were personally aiding;
but some visionary remembrances I have of female figures flitting before my
sight, the wretched woman's particularly" (354–55).[1]

Lovelace's attack is calculated. For weeks, he has been moving gradually toward the resolve to rape Clarissa. He has imprisoned her (without her knowing it) in an elegant London brothel. He has declared to his friend John Belford on a number of occasions that if his attempted seduction of her is unsuccessful he will resort to darkness, terror, and force: "Night, *midnight, is* necessary, Belford. Surprise, terror, *must* be necessary to the ultimate trial of this charming creature" (236). The women of the brothel have been mocking him for his delay. "How the women urge me on," he writes to Belford; why, they say, "*should I make so long a harvest of so little corn?*" (233). And Anna Howe has warned Clarissa several times to be wary of him, to flee from him if possible. Clarissa herself senses the increasing violence and ugliness of Lovelace's passion: "The man, my dear, looked *quite ugly*—I never saw a man look so ugly as passion made him look" (237). She barely manages to escape one half-hearted attack by him in the early hours of the preceding Thursday morning, June 8. The next day she flees from Lovelace, from the house, from London altogether, but she eludes him only for the weekend. He finds her in Hampstead, tricks her back to town again Monday evening, drugs and then rapes her.

As clear as this sequence of events may seem when detached from the text, summarized, simplified in a sketch such as the one I've given here, it is extremely complex and elusive in the process of reading. It is never extrapolated in the novel. Its elements and chronology, its motives and logic, must be seen as parts of a pattern that the novel only suggests. Even the rape itself requires reader inference to be understood.

At the end of class, Wendy looked up at us all, especially at me, and asked, "*Did* he? *Did* he rape her?" I put off answering the question, and at the beginning of the next class meeting, she announced with chagrin that she found a note she had written right there in the margin of her own book on page 264: "Clarissa begs Lovelace not to rape her." But as soon as she read the note aloud to us, it ceased to satisfy her. All it said, she realized, was that Clarissa had begged him not to rape her; it didn't say he had. So, though she hoped to have settled it once and for all in her mind, the question was still open.

Crystal had sounded certain in announcing the rape in the first place, but even she had difficulty. Her declaration that Lovelace raped Clarissa was based on hearsay about the book. She had not actually read far enough yet to say for herself, but she remembered hearing the novel talked about in another course and had noticed the syllabus description of an upcoming class meeting in our course—"Rape: Law and Literature." "He rapes her," she said, then turned it into a question, "doesn't he?" (I didn't answer her question yet either.) When Crystal had finished the book, she tried to look back over it to pinpoint the precise moment when the rape occurred. She was confident that it had happened on Thursday morning, June 8, when a false fire alarm in the house exposed Clarissa almost naked to Lovelace's forced kisses and caresses, his grasping hands and threats, and his insistence that Clarissa "pardon" him (262–65).

I said that I thought the scene Crystal pointed to certainly depicted a sexual assault and that Richardson rendered the scene quite explicitly. Lovelace admits that he was "kissing (with passion indeed) her inimitable neck, her lips, her cheeks, her forehead, and her streaming eyes," and he says that Clarissa "tore my ruffle, shrunk from my happy hand with amazing force and agility, as with my other arm I would have encircled her waist" (264). But I also said that I thought Lovelace doesn't actually rape Clarissa in that scene, only later after she has escaped, been recaptured, and brought back to London.

Crystal was unconvinced, but she came to agree. Between that class meeting and the next she pored again over the scene and returned with a number of lines that persuaded her that the rape did *not* occur yet: Clarissa's saying "spare me, I beseech you, spare me" (264); her desperate request that he permit her to rise from the floor "innocent" (264); Lovelace's insisting upon a kiss before he would leave and then retiring, in his words, "like a fool" (265); and his immediate regret in reflecting on "the opportunity [he] had lost" (265). Though Crystal had begun by adamantly asserting that Lovelace raped Clarissa in this scene—the same scene during which Wendy had written the note in her book about Clarissa's begging Lovelace not to rape her—on second thought, like Wendy, she decided the text didn't, after all, say what she had first thought.

Wendy recorded some of her feelings about all this confusion in her notes a week after our talk in class:

> I am still *flustered* over that whole rape discussion. It was awesome!
>
> How incredible that we interpret texts so differently! And how odd that everyone who thought she was raped thought it was during the fire scene. I was finally swayed to believe that she had been raped—not necessarily b/c of that scene, but b/c everyone later asks her if she is pregnant—and Lovelace hopes she is. However, Dr. Murphy made an excellent point in showing us another passage (which is where *he thinks* [original emphasis] she was raped). The reason we missed it is b/c Richardson never wrote a scene on it! . . . Dr. Murphy paid strict attention to the dates—I guess that's what did it.
>
> So, I guess I must concede that C. was raped.

The professional critical literature on *Clarissa* that I have seen contains nothing like this note by Wendy, writing to herself about her confusion. Even though much recent Richardson scholarship and criticism focus on the rape in *Clarissa*, there is little or no discussion of the experience of an actual reader trying to make sense of the text. In *Samuel Richardson: Man of Letters*, for example, Carol Houlihan Flynn writes, "Rape is the central action of *Clarissa*" (107). She goes on to elaborate the ways in which the complex

social attitudes toward rape at the time and the contemporary legal response
to it are reflected in Richardson's presentation of Clarissa and Lovelace's
story. But there is no ambiguity for Flynn about its happening: "She was
raped the night of 12 June, escaped from Lovelace on 28 June, and was still
explaining her reasons for *not* prosecuting on 19 August" (111).

William Beatty Warner acknowledges the complexity of experience
Clarissa offers its readers. In *Reading 'Clarissa': The Struggles of Interpretation,* Warner argues that in the formal features that challenge readers,
Clarissa reflects the uncertainties of its characters. The "struggles of interpretation" are as much Clarissa's and Lovelace's (in trying to frame and
control their own stories) as they are ours in trying to read them. But for
Warner, too, the rape is a decisive event; the only question is how the characters interpret it. In "He Could Go No Farther: A Modest Proposal about
Lovelace and Clarissa," Judith Wilt advances an idiosyncratic hypothesis
about the rape. She argues that Lovelace may not have raped Clarissa himself, but that the others—the women who worked in the brothel and especially its fierce madam, Mrs. Sinclair—were the actual perpetrators. As
unusual as her interpretation is, however, Wilt locates the rape quite precisely. For her, as for other critics, it occurred on "Monday night and Tuesday morning, 12–13 June" (28).

Terry Eagleton argues that the rape of Clarissa embodies the class
conflict at the heart of Richardson's novel. In *The Rape of Clarissa: Writing,
Sexuality, and Class Struggle in Samuel Richardson,* Eagleton acknowledges
that the moment of rape is elusively presented in the novel: "... the point
around which this elaborate two-thousand page text pivots—is the rape; yet
the rape goes wholly unrepresented" (61). "In a sense," he says, "nobody
experiences the rape: not the reader, not the comatose Clarissa, not even
Lovelace, for whom the act is purely empty" (83). But at the same time
Eagleton argues that recognition of the rape is essential to readers' understanding of the book's greatness as a radical critique of eighteenth-century
English society. What he does not explain is how this recognition occurs.
Like other critics, he simply takes it for granted.

Perplexity like that reflected in Wendy's reading of *Clarissa* is generally
absent from scholar-teachers' considerations of the novel as well. At the
1993 conference of the American Society of Eighteenth Century Studies, for
example, Helen Deutsch's paper, "Rape and Pedagogy," focused specifically on *Clarissa.* And her concern began explicitly with teaching: "The
more I teach *Clarissa,*" she wrote, "the more ungovernable a text I find it"
(1). But as her paper developed, it came to be less about the actual experience of readers of the novel and more about theoretical questions of "the
function of Clarissa's rape as metaphor and epistemological figure" (6).

Current critical discussions of *Clarissa*—even those that seem to be focused on teaching the novel—tend to veer like Deutsch's toward questions of
theory, background, or content: Richardson's relationships with the women

friends with whom he discussed his novels, for example; the ways in which the social status and roles of women in the mid-eighteenth century were governed by systems of law and property; the novel's representation of class ideology in the intricate hierarchies of its characters and the subtle geographical movements of its plot. But all such topics are assumed to be accessible to readers because the story itself is assumed to be accessible. Nowhere have I seen anyone (except a student in one of my classes) discuss the problem of trying to read this novel after having been herself raped. And nowhere have I heard anyone discuss the difficulty a student like Wendy would have in understanding the novel, the central action of which she seems for a time to have missed.

Two strands of experience come together in this account of teaching *Clarissa:* my long-term fascination as a reader with Richardson's novel, and my wonder as a teacher with how students think about and understand what they are doing. Inspired by Wendy's report of her experience, I have begun to wonder how many other students over the years have puzzled silently, "You mean he raped her?" as I went on blithely unaware. This semester, I asked yet another class of students about the rape. Many of the twenty-four undergraduates expressed surprise; none indicated that they had registered the rape. Sindy M. wrote in her journal, "I can't believe that Clarissa was raped and I didn't know it—this really makes me see the whole story differently—I thought by being ruined she meant being touched—and when Lovelace said the affair was finished I didn't exactly know what to think." April H., who had read the novel before, was more than surprised. She said she felt "really stupid" because she had now read the novel twice and missed the rape both times.

In *Literature as Exploration,* Louise M. Rosenblatt writes that "the reading of a particular work at a particular moment by a particular reader will be a highly complex process" (79). The confusion Wendy felt about the rape of Clarissa is a good example of this complexity. When the class discussion of the rape was over, her independent response to the novel persisted. She "was finally swayed," her note says, but since she had to be "swayed," her language suggests that her change of mind was reluctant. It doesn't sound wholehearted either; "I guess I must concede," she writes. When I explained how my reading of the rape could be corroborated by the date sequence of the letters in the text, Wendy seems to have supposed that in reading I "paid strict attention to the dates." Actually, I didn't; the book is too complicated for me to have done so while trying at the same time to read. I simply reconstructed the chronology after the fact as a way to help clarify for students (and for myself) the sequence of events. But however Wendy supposed I arrived at my interpretation, she seems not to have been convinced by it. In her note to herself she ends her characterization of my explanation of the dates with "I guess." And she was clearly unconvinced by my conclusion about when the rape occurred; she refers to it with emphasis of her own as the passage where "*he thinks*" Clarissa was raped.

Thus the difficulty of reading *Clarissa* entails more than bafflement, disorientation, and self-reproach. It involves resistance as well. Wendy's resistance makes me realize that information is not enough to settle the question of whether and when Lovelace raped Clarissa. The problem of *Clarissa* for me as a teacher is not simply to devise ways to help clarify confusion. It is not enough to develop analytical exercises and focused writing that might help students see and appreciate more fully how this novel's story unfolds. Whatever I focus on as the teacher—the class struggle, the conflicted psychology of Lovelace's and Clarissa's love, the stylistic virtuosity of Richardson's prose, or the rape—students will read the book they make of it. Looking at the dates won't satisfy. Rosenblatt is right: "No one else," she says, "can read a literary work for us" (278), and this is because literature must be "'burned through,' lived through, by the reader" (277).

That's just what Wendy did: lived through it, burned through this book. It "enraged" her, "infuriated" her, she wrote in her notes. When she tried to write an analytical paper about the novel, she found she couldn't do it: "Personal feelings kept [here she crossed out "getting in the way"] overtaking." "What *kind* of a person can violate another?" she wrote to herself, "To get excited off of someone else's screams?" In one of her written characterizations of the novel's aesthetic effect, she wrote emphatically, "We feel C's pain, pain, pain." And when she finally began to settle on a topic for her paper, her notes reflect how deeply personal it was:

I am bitter b/c C. died—
R [Richardson] had her die on purpose—leaves *intensely bitter* principals, moral lesson.
Her death is vengeful.
—bitter b/c C. *had* to die—that the social conditions made (forced) her to die—
Woman has no other way out.

It was Wendy's own identification with that grim conclusion that animated her paper. While I was preoccupied with the teaching problem presented by student uncertainty about the rape, Wendy was focused on Clarissa's death. She felt it certainly and deeply. No religious consolation, no aesthetic justification could satisfy her. Clarissa's "faith was steadfast and powerful," she wrote; "mine is not." And she positively refused to accept a story that seemed to promise women freedom only after death: "Why should males get their rewards on earth, while women receive theirs only in the grave?"

In the grave: If I could trace the lines of thought and feeling that led Wendy to such a stern phrase, I would be closer to knowing how to "teach" *Clarissa.* Her fresh candor about her reading of the rape permitted me to learn something I did not know about the book. But then her paper taught me something else: Teacher knowledge about literary texts is not finally what counts most anyway. With the critics, we can say, metaphorically, that the rape of Clarissa is at the heart of this great novel. But Clarissa's story matters only as it makes its way to the reader's heart. In Wendy's case, she missed the rape, but she was not at all confused about the death. With painful intensity—and with a bitterness that Richardson himself perhaps did not intend—she felt its imaginative truth in her own life.

Indeed to remember this as a teacher of *Clarissa,* as a teacher of any literary text: What a reader misses will always be less important than what passionately remains.

Notes

1. All citations from the novel are from Samuel Richardson, *Clarissa,* abridged by George Sherburn (Boston: Houghton, 1962).

Works Cited

Bowman, B. J. 1993. "The Attack on Sherburn's *Clarissa:* Confusing Censorhsip with Practicality."Unpublished paper.

Deutsch, Helen. 1993. "Rape and Pedagogy." Unpublished paper presented at the American Society for Eighteenth Century Studies. Providence.

Doody, Margaret Anne, and Florian Stuber. 1988. "*Clarissa* Censored."*Modern Language Studies* 18.1: 74–88.

Eagleton, Terry. 1982. *The Rape of Clarissa: Writing, Sexuality, and Class Struggle in Samuel Richardson.* Minneapolis: University of Minnesota Press.

Flynn, Carol Houlihan. 1982. *Samuel Richardson: A Man of Letters.* Princeton: Princeton University Press.

Hill, Christopher. 1969. "Clarissa Harlow and Her Times." In *Samuel Richardson: A Collection of Critical Essays,* edited by John Carroll. Englewood Cliffs, NJ: Prentice-Hall.

Richardson, Samuel. 1962. *Clarissa.* Abridged by George Sherburn. Boston: Houghton.

Rosenblatt, Louise M. 1983. *Literature as Exploration.* 3rd ed. New York: Modern Language Association.

Warner, William Beatty. 1979. *Reading 'Clarissa': The Struggles of Interpretation.* New Haven: Yale University Press.

Wilt, Judith. 1977. "He Could Go No Farther: A Modest Proposal about Lovelace and Clarissa." *PMLA* 92: 19–32.

In African-American Literature, I had students write in the same ways I ask first-year students to write: keeping journals to converse with authors about texts and writing personal responses to what they read or experienced in the course. This writing allowed some students to recognize their own prejudices and consider ways to deal with them. From Jason's personal response paper: "In October, when I arrived in Birmingham to view . . . the museum dedicated to the civil rights movement, I was . . . impressed with a saying on every entrance . . . 'A Place of Revolution and Reconciliation.' I . . . read it over and over. Something inside of me began to click as I stood there in the midst of a chaotic silence, a paradoxical statement, I know, but that is what it was like. It seemed as if all of the cries, screams, pain of a time not long past came together in a . . . chilling hush. . . . My life this semester, my inner journey, slowly came into focus as those words echoed in my head—revolution and reconciliation." From Jean's journal: "This was an overpowering chapter. I think none of us can imagine the . . . results of segregation . . . the effects it has produced on American society. This is a mind-boggling thing when you really think of its ramifications." And from Chris's final exam paper: "I discovered something that I do not know how to deal with . . . I am a racist, which is something that I am going to have to work on undoing in order to become the just man I want to be." On their final exam, I wrote, "Have I told you lately that I love you?" because as I responded to their discoveries over the semester, I made one myself: Writing and literature had changed our lives. Together they are dynamite.

Beth Murray Walker
Belmont University
Nashville, TN

8

The Reading-Writing Connection—What's Process Got to Do with It?

Cheryl Glenn
Oregon State University

What I want chiefly to do is to assure you that you can teach writing by teaching your subject, and that one of the best ways to teach your subject is by teaching writing.

Ann E. Berthoff

January 1: I spent the entire week between Christmas and New Year's working on my syllabus for English 205, "Survey of English Literature: Restoration and Romantic Literature." I spent all that time, and I'm still not sure if I've assigned too much reading and writing. Why is it that we rarely question ourselves about the reading we've assigned—it's the amount of writing we worry about. The teacher in me convinces me that all this writing is *good* for the students: the more they write, the more they talk about their writing, the better writers they'll be. After all, Ann Berthoff has been telling us for thirty years that we should not only "teach writing in the context . . . of other language activities" (in this case, reading, discussing, and interpreting literature) but that "we should teach writing as a matter of making meaning in those other language activities" (24). So I've assigned three summary-responses (which many students will revise and resubmit), seven weeks of journal entries, and one oral presentation. I've promised lots of in-class writing as well. Graded, ungraded, and minimally graded writing is *good*, the teacher in me tells me. But the human in me tells me that whatever work I lay on the students, I'm also laying on myself. After all, this human wants time this term to see a movie, visit my daughter, and take walks. So I strike a "time-being" compromise and print out the syllabus.

January 3: First day of class—Dryden through Shelley: "We will read a sampling of significant texts that exemplify the literary form and content and the imaginative power of these times. Ours will be a writing-intensive, inter- active class." I walk into a room filled with students. The human in me gulps at the thought of all the writing I've assigned. We go through the syllabus, with students asking questions about the "summary-responses" they'll be asked to do. I've appended a description of this assignment to their syllabi, so we turn to it:

> A summary/response is an academic exercise that asks you to *summarize* the main points (or an important section) of an essay or chapter and then to *analyze* (or respond to) that same piece, perhaps focusing on one point in particular. You will want your clear and concise summary to be accurate yet brief, and you'll want your second section, the longer response part, to be critical, supported by the text, and *thoughtful*. This second section can be exploratory, theoretical, even pedagogical in some cases, but most of all, this section should be *yours*: *your* idea, *your* reading of the text. By the time you begin writing this assignment, I hope you have already tried out your ideas in your journals or in conversation with me or with your writing group. Your peer readers and I want to see just what unique read or analy- sis or comparison that you are able to make; for that reason, you'll want to be sure that your point/your argument is *out there*—loud and clear. In fact, you may well want to begin your second section (your response) with your point (your controlling idea, your thesis).

Students who haven't taken a course with me before ask why they have to do so much writing; after all, this isn't a *writing* class. Students who know me, know my answer: "I teach all my classes alike: we read, we write, we talk, we think." Students sign up for their oral reports (which contextualize our texts historically, politically, or socially) and put their phone numbers on the to-be-distributed class list. They'll need these class lists to get their writ- ing groups organized. And they'll need to work in a writing group if they plan to revise, for only work accompanied by rough drafts and peer- responses can be revised.

January 5: Banking on her FHA public speaking experience, Ginger volun- teers for the first oral presentation, a fine description of the political and social situation of London during 1666 that sets up our class discussion on the Great London Fire (1660) as seen through the eyes of poet laureate Dry- den and private diarist Pepys. I ask the students to compare these writers' points-of-view. I tell them to think of their initial ideas as "rough drafts" that can be improved. I want them to share their ideas with one another, the same way I'll ask them to share their writing—to offer their ideas and ask for response. I want them to see that "composing is a method of making meaning" (Berthoff 114), no matter where they are in their writing process. Each time we encourage our students to see their writing as a continuous act—a process—of interpreting, we are "teaching writing as a matter of making meaning" (Berthoff 24). As one student speaks and another responds, they are making meaning—for themselves, not for their teacher. I distribute the class list, and we take the last few minutes of class to break into writing groups of their own choosing.

Weekend: Jon and I have slipped away to Bend, for a retreat with friends. On one of our long hikes into the mountains, Suzanne Clark, Lisa Ede, and I talk about our students, about the significance of their taking risks. If they're willing to take risks by speaking out in class, then they're often able to risk "owning" the material when they read and write about it. The more they own the material, the more "informed" their risks.

If writing teachers value student writing, it follows that writing teachers value student reading. And if students are ever to believe that their writing is important, and just as important pedagogically as what I call the "exalted text" they/we are studying, then they must come to believe that their readings of those texts are just as important pedagogically as our own teacherly, academically more informed, "exalted" readings. And when students believe that, they can begin to read, to write, to improve, to understand and respect their own reads, their reading processes, their writing, their writing processes, and their learning curves. I like walking through the forest, talking about teaching, stopping occasionally to hear Greg, Lisa's artist-environmentalist husband, explain the geography of the area.

January 10: We're reading Aphra Behn's 1688 "Oroonoko, or The Royal Slave." Before we start our discussion, I ask students to (1) copy out, word for word, a complete sentence from "Oroonoko," perhaps one they've already underlined in the text, and then (2) imitate that sentence-structure, writing out a second sentence of their own that summarizes the plot of the story. They look perplexed; we talk a bit—and then they begin writing:

1. "They parted thus, with grief enough, til night, leaving the king in possession of the lovely maid."

2. They stolen were, with wickedness abound, til death, parting the world with dignity of the rightful royalty. (Gretchen)

1. "They have a native justice which knows no fraud, and they understand no vice or cunning, but when they are taught by the white men."

2. He had an unfortunate life which held much misery, but he remained both proud and brave, even when he was suffering through an agonizing death. (Molly)

Some of the students offer to read their sentences and imitations aloud. The students' sentences help direct our discussion of the novel, for their selections focus on issues of slavery, religion and religious hypocrisy, moral values, human beauty, etc. They've paid close attention to style and substance. Good.

January 12: I ask the students to perform another rhetorical-stylistic exercise, to write a paragraph summarizing the plot of "Oroonoko." Taking time to figure out "what's happening" in the story helps us move more easily into what happened and to theorize what it might mean. Then, I ask them to boil down their paragraph into one sentence.

1. Oroonoko is a prince of an African nation. His aged grandfather is king. Both desire the beautiful Imoinda, who loves Oroonoko but is bound to the king's harem and may not be touched by any other. Somehow the lovers meet and are found out, and by some twist of fate both are pressed into slavery. They meet at Surinam and are promised freedom. When they are delayed their freedom, he leads a revolt of the slaves. They are all subdued, and as a result Oroonoko slaughters Imoinda and their unborn child rather than deliver them as slaves. Oroonoko is drawn and quartered for his crime.

2. The tragic romance of royalty turned slaves, Oroonoko and Imoinda, ends in bloodshed when their promised freedom from bondage in Surinam is cruelly denied. (Heather)

1. Oroonoko was in love with Imoinda, who was taken by his grandfather as his **woman** and later sold as a slave. Oroonoko had many adventures and hardships—reminiscent of Voltaire's Candide—preceding his eventual reassociation with Imoinda.

2. Oroonoko loved Imoinda, even though she was taken by his grandfather and later sold into slavery, and after many hardships and adventures he found her again, killed her out of love and lived on to be revengeful. (Angela)

And then to boil down her sentence even further, Angela writes the best summary of the story:

Oh no.

After the students read their summaries, we resume our discussion of "Oroonoko," carrying forward the discussion we had on Wednesday. We are enacting James Moffett's kinds and orders of discourse (47), moving toward evaluations and theories of oppression, conviction, and morality. The class is heating up—and it feels good, though somewhat draining. They're risking all right.

They've got a summary-response due on Friday, so we take some time going over that assignment, going over the handout appended to their syllabus. I talk about the two cognitive abilities I want them to develop, summary and synthesis, hence, the summary-response assignment.

Seems as though Janet Emig wrote about the importance of summarizing, analyzing, and synthesizing in one of her pieces: "Writing . . . connects the three major tenses of our experience to make meaning. And the two major modes by which these three aspects are united are the processes of analysis and synthesis: analysis, the breaking of entities into their constituent parts; and synthesis, combining or fusing these, often into fresh arrangements or amalgams'' (129). This exercise works really well for my students, most of whom cannot remember ever summarizing anything; the limits of this exercise seem comfortable to them. Students met in their writing groups for the last part of the class, setting up their out-of-class meetings.

January 19: Students eye their papers that lie on my desk while Daniel provides a biographical sketch of Lady Mary Montague in terms of her education and literary career. Alison then describes the educational opportunities for women, both upper-class and working-class women. The students are doing the kind of library research and lecture writing that teachers usually do, the kind of work that helps the researcher/writer remember better than anyone else. After the oral presentations, we turn to the "Epistle from Mrs. Younge to Her Husband," a poem from the point-of-view of a wronged wife. I ask the students to perform a rhetorical-stylistic exercise that incorporates several language activities: imitating the style and tone of the poem, translating the poetry into prose, paraphrasing the substance, and adapting the opposite point-of-view. I ask them to generate an "Epistle from Mr. Younge to His Wife."

The former Mrs. Younge,

How dare you accuse me for acts which your coquettish airs have forced upon me. You say that "laws of honor bind/The weak submissive sex of womankind." I need not remind you that it was you who broke these laws. Perhaps now you know why these laws exist! They are designed to guide the weaker sex and keep them from falling out of societal redemption.

Please acknowledge that both England and her laws have proved my innocence; they alone condemn you. Keep your false claims away from me, for my conscience is clear and clean. As I always am

Mr. Younge (Andrew)

Madam,

Your letter, a failed attempt at justifying your filthy betrayal of my honor and respect, was so full of faulty reasoning and wrongful thought that I was amazed that I could be so foolish as to marry you in the first place.

You were bound to me as my servant, a woman's rightful place in relationship to me, and as such, should not yield to other temptations, in

respect for your vow and my honor at court. You have forfeited your honor
and fortune in your lascivious use of it. Therefore, madam, as both God and
man condemn thee, I condemn thee, with their full support.

    I abandon you to your Fate. (David)

The students are getting into this writing about their reading stuff; they laugh
as they share their epistles. The talk about "epistle" is a good way for me
to talk a bit about the rise of the novel. (Emig tells us that "writing can
sponsor learning because it can match its pace" [128]. Ain't that the truth?)

    During my office hours, I have a minute to look through their in-class
writings. Some of the students wrote about our class as well as about their
writing:

> This class seems to follow the literature through. We talk about ideas, read
> the literature, and write about it. We seem to get the maximum exposure
> from the piece. It makes you keep current with the reading, so you can par-
> ticipate in the discussion. (Andrew)

>   Read, write, talk, discuss. I personally prefer to write out of class so I
> suppose this writing in class—exercises—should help to improve my
> uncomfortability. (Angela)

January 21: On Wednesday, students were in my office until five; today,
they came in until after six. I'm both excited and exhausted by this class. My
thoughts turn to Don "Mr. Conference" Murray, and I wonder why *he* never
writes about getting tired. They come in with their one-page response to my
comments and their written-out plans for revisions. They're not combative,
and they're careful not to ask me what *I* want. They simply want to figure
out how to write better. Their responses and plans give us a place to start,
though they all seem to want to talk about the terms *summary* and *response*.
They want to talk about *controlling idea*, too. But mostly they want to talk
about their papers. Fine by me.

    Jason's happy with his *A*, but he's not happy about the grades the folks
in his writing group made. He wants to talk about responding to writing, how
better to help them. He tells me that he doesn't know where his good ideas
about the reading come from; he gets them when he's walking down the
street, when he's eating pizza with his writing group. He likes to try out his
ideas during class discussion in order to get immediate feedback, then go
home and write them up. *Voila*. He hasn't read the summary-response directions carefully; he doesn't do much drafting; he doesn't need more than in-
class response—so what does he need to know to help his friends? We compare the assignment sheet with his paper and try to see where the
expectations and the results overlap. He doesn't know what he's doing: He's
Emig's "magical writer," and his friends do "non-magical writing" (1983).
How can I help him?

    I hear the students outside my door; they've made a serpentine line
down the hallway. As they file in, they tell me that they've been looking over

one another's drafts while they wait. One student tells me that this is the first time she's ever seen a professor's office. And then she tells me that her *D* was also a first for her. Funny how *D*s can bring on student conferences. *D*s brought many of them in—but these students have the chance to revise. That's part of the game plan: work in a group; hand in group work, rough work, and final draft *on time*; help one another write and revise.

January 24: Students arrive early to discuss their drafts and their oral presentations. The oral presentations are terrific—the students are connecting their topics with the day's reading. Gretchen talks about Swift's education and literary career; Roxanne talks about the educational opportunities for men during this time.

Dan comes to my office hours wanting to argue about his controlling idea, for he plans to revise and resubmit his summary-response on Pepys's diaries. He's arguing that Pepys should have helped fight the London Fire instead of writing about it. When I want him to connect his supporting arguments with the controlling idea, he complains that his paper will be too repetitive. I'm stumped. I read on—then I find a sentence that with a bit of niggling could become a good controlling idea. Dan's cautious. He reads it aloud. Tinkers with it. Writes an upward arrow—and tells me that that's what he'd been trying to say all along. Maybe that's true.

January 26: I start off class by asking the students to write a page about their revisions, which are neatly stacked on my desk. I want to know what they did, thought about, considered as they prepared their revisions. Jason (of course) asks, "What do I do if I didn't do a revision?" I tell them that if they didn't submit a revision, they should write about how they can be a better group member.

> I worked mostly on obtaining the correct controlling idea. Throughout my drafts, I had what I thought to be a good controlling idea. However, none of them seemed to say what I ment [sic]. I worked on the controlling idea or the idea of a controlling idea. But, the whole time the real controlling idea was hidden within the text of the summary-response. I tried to make my paper too flowery, so it sounded nice. I finally realized that sounding nice doesn't make a good paper. It (the controlling idea) must always be supported. The most important thing I learned is not to try and write a controlling idea but to let your ideas form a controlling idea. (Dan)

> I have to learn to be a better group member. . . . I looked over Gretchen's re-write and I feel that I did a better job helping her with her ideas. I stopped myself after every sentence and asked myself what the sentence's function was. If it didn't do much, we talked about it. By doing this, I was able to offer more advice. I think that if I slow down . . . instead of just reading through it, I'll be able to help my group more effectively. (Jason)

January 28: I notice they haven't put the chairs in a circle. I ask them why. Marisa, leaning against the back wall, says it's too much like second grade. (Marisa hasn't sat in the circle for a week or so.) I ask her if she had fun in second grade, if she liked second grade, if she learned in second grade. She says yes, yes, yes. And we all laugh.

So I ask them if they want to sit in a circle and share the responsibility of the class, or if they want me to do it all today. I don't (think I) care one way or another. The resistance I'm feeling from them feels OK. They're really working hard, and when they don't make *A*s on their writing, they, no doubt, wonder if their hard work is worth it. Grades can really hurt students' feelings, even if those grades are revisable. I think their resistance is healthy—an indication of intellectual and social activity (and lots of talking in those writing groups).

I see Marisa scooting her desk forward into the circle. She announces that she's doing so *only* because she likes me. I like her, too. And I'm embarrassed, so I tell them we've got to move on to Part IV of *Gulliver's Travels*. I liked second grade, too.

Weekend: As I read through their journals, I see that some students seem to be enjoying the process of our class—despite their grumbling. But I feel uneasy: I'm wondering if their resistance and opposition might not be healthier at this stage than their accommodation, and I think of Geoffrey Chase's article from the late eighties, about resistance and accommodation [Chase passim].

> First, I find this class to be a real load. The first couple of days I countlessly contemplated dropping the course. I thought that the syllabus would be an impossible task. . . . The reason I stayed in the class, besides of it being required, is the reassurance that you gave us on the first day. You said we would become better **readers**, **writers**, and **critical thinkers**, or something to that [e]ffect. I often refer to it as Dr. Glenn's "triple threat" class. I scanned my memory bank and could not remember any one class that gave me all three pieces. It usually comes in separate courses, but along with it comes triple the work. One must truly be dedicated to this course and stay on top of things. However, if you do fall behind, class discussion still plays a vital role and should never be missed. I often find myself cursing your name and mumbling the words, "She can't really expect us to do all that" each time my eyes cross the syllabus. Somehow I find the time to get it done. . . .
>
> The summary response is a good tool for the teacher to evaluate the student. It demands the student to become skilled in both abstract thinking and writing. . . . I find that my biggest problem is to think abstractly. I perform at a greater level in classes with facts, figures, and one correct answer questions. This type of education [our class?] frustrates me and at the same time stimulates my intellectual being. I hope and now I know that at the end

of this course I will have an easier time thinking in an abstract manner. I also think that writing is a good measure of knowledge in an English course. On the other hand, a written test, one in which I personally would excel, would not measure the kinds of skills that are taught within this well-structured course. (Dan)

January 31: Students are to bring to class their response to Gulliver that there is "no greater lover of mankind than myself." I ask for volunteers to read aloud their writing, and I call on the students who are writing *good* summary-responses, who are revising well, but who are not speaking up in class. If they make eye contact with me, I call on them.

> Although Gulliver ... claims "there were few greater lovers of mankind, at that time, than myself," it is apparent from his detailed descriptions that this is not the case. Instead, he thought that the human race as a whole was ugly, barbaric, cruel, foolish, utterly devoid of honor, given to wars and petty arguments, and full of greed. In the first book, Gulliver describes his betrayal by the Lilliputians. These small people, a representation of the English Government, could turn even his most helpful deed into a treasonable act. Gulliver showed human kind's ability to twist anything to fit their point of view.
>
> In the second book, Gulliver points out all the flaws of the human body "so varified with spots, pimples, and freckles that nothing could appear so nauseous." Later human actions were declared by the King to be "the very worst effects that ... hypocrisy, cruelty, rage, madness, hatred, envy, lust, or ambition could produce." In the fourth book, humans are shown to be just another animal, who will do anything to get control of the territory around them. In Chapter 7, Gulliver at last declares all that is wrong with humankind. He has begun to agree with the King ... and decides upon returning home that horses are better company than humans. (David)

> [Gulliver] "loves" mankind, yet uses the skins of Yahoos as clothing. The Yahoos, though primitive, equal Gulliver in appearance almost exactly, but he denies their humanity because he finds them disgusting in comparison to the Houyhnhnms. The Yahoos represent the mean, filthy side of people, while the Houyhnhnms, who do not resemble men at all, are accorded the virtues traditionally belonging to "smart, honorable, and clean" humankind. Perhaps Gulliver's eventual disgust in all of mankind is a representation of Swift's own ideas about people in general. (Heather)

We start off our class with the students' voices, with their risking. We've talked about their oral contributions being another kind of rough draft that someone in the class will help them revise, that class discussion can be a process akin to their writing processes. They are "drafting and revising" in their reading the same way they do in their writing, the same way they negotiate meaning in their writing groups. The "sitting in a circle" issue hasn't arisen again. Most of the time, they all sit in a sloppy circle. Sometimes, Marisa rests against the back wall.

At the end of class, while I pass back their revisions, I ask them, "If you *had* to come up with a controlling idea right now for a summary-response on *Gulliver's Travels*, what would yours be? Take a few minutes and write out/ work out a controlling idea." They seem stumped—but then they write. Pretty soon, they're asking me if I'll return these in-class writings because they're getting some ideas.

> Swift used Gulliver as an interpreter that saw the wrongs of civilization but also as a personal example of these very wrongs. (Gretchen)

> The exploratory nature of *Gulliver's Travels* serves to pique the imagination of the readers in order to provoke us to be more introspective and critical of our own nature and society. (Stirling)

February 2: Today, we discuss Swift's "Modest Proposal," right after Amy provides the political context for that piece. I ask them to respond in writing to Swift's comment that "people are the riches of a nation."

> I kind of chuckled when you wrote this on the board when I knew it was in reference to "A Modest Proposal." It seemed to me that this was satirical in saying that if we eat these kids we will be making money; therefore they, as people, will be the riches of the nation. I think Swift is trying to open some eyes with this quotation. (LaVonne)

> A nation is made up of its population, not its land mass. The people give it economic power with the goods and services they produce. They give it military power by protecting the country. They should not be abused, starved or killed, because this is just like throwing away money. (David)

> Often this idea of people as a resource refers to the productivity of hand and mind. (Heidi)

As we study *Gulliver's Travels*, the students separate what they perceived to be Swift-the-author's opinions from those of Gulliver. But because Swift signed his name to the "Proposal," I want to make sure that the students continue to distinguish between actual author and speaking voice of a piece. I move our discussion toward Wayne Booth's categories of "flesh-and-blood author," "implied author," and "narrator" [71–75], using "Samuel Clemens," "Mark Twain," and "Huck Finn" for explanation. The students "get it" immediately, so we move straight to the "Proposal," in which the speaking voice/narrator initially presents himself as serious, expert, and well meaning—that's why so many of them got "sucked in" (their term) to his argument.

We talk about the ways we get "sucked in" or persuaded; I introduce the three rhetorical appeals of any discourse: *ethos, pathos, logos.* Discussion of *logos* and *lexis* takes us straight to a discussion of *style,* because the style of "Proposal" is purposely the narrator's rather than Swift's. *Style* allows us to discuss irony, metaphor, hyperbole, litotes. We're cooking with our rhetorical terms; that is, until they remind me that Swift is *always* writing behind a persona, so how can we always separate the opinions? Feels like we're on shaky ground, so I turn that idea back to them by asking them to respond in writing to the one passage in "Proposal" that most entertained, shocked, or stunned them—that most "appealed" to them.

> I was really entertained by Swift's paragraph about the Catholic breeding habits. He calls them the "principal breeder" and "most dangerous enemies," which is so . . . silly. They are poor people with empty, poverty-stricken lives, with sex as the only bright spot. The paragraph reminds me of McCarthyism with the "dangerous Catholics" having sex and producing babies. (Alison)

> I am torn between two different passages. The first being . . . the different ways of preparing the child to be eaten. That I find absolutely deplorable. The gross imagery . . . offends me to the very pit of my stomach! The other that I find equally disgusting was the part . . . where he describes the carcass and filleting it for gloves and shoes. I feel that these two passages are the very height of irony yet they are also the most disgusting things I've ever heard. (Anna)

Some of the students read their passages and responses aloud, providing us material for exploring whether they perceive any distinction between the author's opinions and the narrator's. When writing teachers teach literature, reading as well as writing is a process of constructing meaning. That's what we're doing: slowly constructing our meaning of "A Modest Proposal."

February 7: Students are talking more and more about themselves as writers during class and office hours, and I'm relieved to know that they count the work they do on their oral presentations and their journals as "writing."

> I think many people would mistake this class for a WIC Course. There is a lot of writing to do in here! At first I thought, "Oh, cool! No midterm or final!" But now I realize just how much work this class can be. However, I think it's still "cool" because I feel like I'm learning a great deal by keeping weekly journals. Now I have to keep up and know the material all the time instead of only twice a term. (Molly)

> This class . . . has more writing in it than any other survey class that I've ever taken. . . . [Because it fills a core requirement], this class then forces people who are majoring in all sorts of areas to do some writing. Cohesive

writing is not required in a vast amount of college classes. A real advantage to this class is that the majority of weekly writing is not given a letter grade but instead is given completion credit. This gives students the freedom to write in a "brainstorm" style without having to worry about the conventions of writing such as spelling and punctuation. These conventions are important too yet much instruction and practice have been centered on conventions, which are, for all practicality, refining tools. In effect we are taught how to refine and yet never how to do the actual writing, idea creation, etc. I feel with the three critical responses and seven "freewrite" journals that this class does a great job of combining the two.

> Writing is very hard. (Gretchen)

It seemed at first like I was on a road to peril because my fear of writing. I can keep a journal for myself but writing papers for others is difficult. It isn't as painful as it was before this class though. It used to be extremely difficult for me to tear through a work to find backing for an idea I had. I'm not saying it is as easy as riding a bike now, but it isn't as threatening as it was before. . . . All in all, I am enjoying writing in this class, it helps me involve myself with the readings whereas in other classes *Cliff Notes* were my friends; and it helps a lot in my ability to think through pieces of literature. . . . (Patricia)

Their second summary-response paper is due Friday, so I'm not surprised to see so many during office hours (they stay until nearly seven P.M.). They want to *talk*—about their writing, about the drafts, about their writing groups. Assigning papers and then allowing revision seems to be the best way to get students into office hours. They have a prop (their paper) and a specific agenda for being here. I follow Donald Murray's advice and let them do most of the talking ("They come in and tell me what has gone well, what has gone wrong, and what they intend to do about it" [234]).

Marisa continues to have a hard time with writing assignments. She is simply an inexperienced writer, without much confidence. She's already submitted two revisions of her first paper, and she hasn't made the kind of progress she'd hoped for. She's trying to write about the dishonorable state of slavery in "Oroonoko," and she's having a hard time. She's struggling to bring in information from her history classes and from her personal experience (a connection I cannot seem to understand). We talk about slavery and honor, and if slavery is *ever* an honorable state. She leaves to meet her group, a bit embarrassed to be working still on the previous assignment.

Dan and I work together for what seems to be a long time. And although I listen to him talk about his draft and try to guide him toward a plausible variation of his controlling idea ("Jonathan Swift used satire to disguise the fact that he honestly believed in his 'Modest Proposal'"), I'm not having much luck. He thinks he doesn't have to *believe* what he argues, that the secret's in the layout/framework of the argument, not in the substance. Sigh.

Stirling, Phaedra, Martin, Dinah, Molly all come to see me. We talk—or rather, they talk about their work. I'm not sure this course is teaching students to write so much as it is teaching them to think about themselves as writers. If the line of students outside my door signifies anything tonight, it is that they want to talk about their writing.

February 9: We're reading Blake, the Wordsworths, and Wollstonecraft this week. It's fun watching the students make connections between the Wordsworths' writings. I ask them to take a few minutes to write out what their second summary-response is turning out to be about. Some of them volunteer to read theirs aloud—and ask the class for help in refining their ideas. Their classmates respond directly to them, not through me. I like this dynamic. They are working through the process of writing and reading, beginning with their initial interpretations of the text.

> I'm thinking about comparing and contrasting the two poems about the chimney sweeper, but I wasn't sure if I should since we talked about it in class already. I guess I need help from my group, and possibly you on finding out what it is I need to argue. (Phaedra)

> I am going to take on the question of innocence in "The Chimney Sweeper". . . . I intend to argue that innocence does not exist in the work, but that is it only this language and images that Blake uses that give the sense of innocence. Underneath, however, ia a horrific scene that is anything but innocent. (Jason).

> I think my controlling argument will be on Mary's ideas of women being more intelligent than men and not necessarily in need of them. I will argue that her ideas should possibly be taken with a grain of salt due to her dependence on men and her many attempts at suicide because of broken love with the opposite sex. (Patricia)

Weekend: I read their papers, looking to see how they've done in their groups because if they don't work in a group (peer response groups), they cannot revise. Some students are really working, contributing; some are not. I read Dan's paper and cannot understand why he didn't make any changes, why he held fast to a controlling idea he doesn't believe.

February 14: Today, I give them questions to answer about their writing group: (1) What did I contribute to the group project? (2) What did each of the other group members contribute? (3) What more could I have done on this project? (4) What about the group process is working well? (5) What part of the group process is not working well? (6) How do I propose to improve the group process?

Most students say "time to meet" is their biggest problem, but they have a range of responses.

I do think that the other members have brought a great deal to the group. I've only been involved in it "half-assed," and I take full responsibility for that . . . I'm not working well in the group, and it would not shock me if they did not want me any longer. (Christie)

I don't like group work because I do not take criticism, in any form, well. I enjoy writing but don't like having others read my work. I also don't feel that I know enough to be able to critique others' work. It's sort of like I know what "I" like but that may not be what is good. The other members of my group are very helpful. They're all older than me and more experienced; they do provide insights that I didn't catch. (Anna)

In our group, Kasha and Lisa are very helpful. They read my paper and give constructive help as far as where they see a need for improvement. I don't feel that Christie does much. She comes late and doesn't necessarily even read all of our papers. She reads parts and signs and wants us to sign hers even though it isn't really a rough draft, just a couple of ideas. (Dinah)

Dan's slumped down in class, disappointed, he says, because I'm not passing back their papers. I'm wondering about him—and he's wondering about my response to his paper. I'm not sure he *could* change his paper—and, more to the point, I wonder why I couldn't help him see why or how he *should* change his controlling idea. Sigh.

During my office hours, Jill comes to me to see if she can revise her second paper. But she didn't participate in a group. She tells me that Stirling and Anna were in her group but they didn't have drafts. I explain that while she was out of town the previous weekend, Stirling had gotten himself into another group. She is dismayed. She tells me how time-consuming and problematic groups are. And I ask her if she has to work in a group in any other class. "No." I ask her if she has the option of revising in any other class. "No." Well, revision isn't an automatic option in this class.

She wants to revise. So I remind her that she *can* revise next time, but she must submit group work. Otherwise, she's in the same situation as her other classes: she hands in a product and takes a grade. Period. Then I get up on my soapbox and tell her that six months from now, she may not be able to tell, with full certainty, a Coleridge poem from a Wordsworth poem, but she will know more about herself as a reader and a writer. (As I transcribe this, I wonder about my words: their truth, their audacity, their appropriateness; their uppityness.)

February 16: I hand back their papers at the end of class and try to get a show of hands about how many will be coming to see me today during my office hours. Lots. So I tell them that if they're planning to talk with me about their revisions, they must bring to our conference a page of revision plans that include direct responses to what I wrote on their papers. I want them to tell me what they think I'm saying about their papers and how that information informs their revision plans/goals. An hour later, I have a line outside my office door.

Amy comes in looking glassy-eyed and confused. She claims she doesn't know what to do. I see that she hasn't worked in a group, so I tell her that it's all a moot point anyway. But she claims she'll revise to learn. [She did submit an ungraded, much-improved revision, and she worked in a group for her last paper, doing very, very well.] Dan, who'd come to me earlier with his rough drafts and hasn't followed any of my advice (or the advice from his group), wants to complain. He's miffed about his *C;* he deserves a higher grade because he worked really hard on his paper. We've all been trying to tell him that Swift is a satirist, but Dan will not/cannot see it; he insists that Swift's opinions are not transformed by satire. I am stymied; I don't know what to say to Dan to help him see—or if I should say anything. During his conference, we experience moments of absolute silence. Neither of us knows what to say.

Murray says let the students do the talking. I don't think I've consciously (if ever) done this before. Why have I clung to the idea that students were coming to hear me hold forth? (I think back on my telling Jill what she'd get out of our class—?—a sense of herself as a writer.) In theory, if not always in practice, we encourage our students to write the way *they* want to write, to say what *they* want to say, rather than to write for the sole purpose of pleasing us. So why don't I "let" Dan write about Swift in the only way he understands right now? Why doesn't his writing "please" me? Why was our conference pocketed with silences instead of his voice?

March 2: Today we begin *Frankenstein*, a book I began reading for the first time over the weekend. The students are surprised when I tell them that I haven't read the book before, that we'll be doing some "rough reads" as well as rough drafts. And we talk about how much fun it is to read a book for the first time, to be able to experience the delicious suspense. After we know "what happens," our suspense transforms, at best, into an appreciation of the irony in the story, so we agree to talk about just the first part of the book (since most of us have not yet finished it and many of us have never read it). We're using the St. Martin's edition of *Frankenstein* because it has five critical/theoretical essays that I want to go through. The students tell me that they've never had theory before, so I try to comfort them with the idea that a theory is a way of reading. That's all these essays are—five different ways of reading *Frankenstein*.

I ask the students if they'd all be willing to write their last papers on *Frankenstein*. Dinah and Jason yelp. Dinah's already begun her last paper; Jason wants to write about W. Wordsworth. OK.

Our first in-class writing is about the cultural baggage they bring to *Frankenstein*. If I want these students to be able to work their way through the case studies at the end of the book, then I have to prepare them for it. I want to prepare them for reader-response theory, cultural criticism.

> I think that actually I've heard more about the bride of Frankenstein than the monster himself. I've read the book before, and it was surprising that the monster was not actually Frankenstein but the scientist. (Jill)

> I read Frankenstein last term and prior to that knew just a smattering about its real content. All the campy movies and "myth" swirling around it gave me a distorted view as to what it was actually about: a man who takes creation into his own hands and cannot control what he has done, and the consequences for playing "Prometheus." (Alison)

> I expect the basic story that we've all seen/read. The story of a man scientist who gets a body from the grave yard, does all sorts of scientific things to him then takes him up to the lightening when he gets electrocuted and comes to "life." I don't recall what happens after that because I usually flip the channel by then. That's another reason why I actually want to read this book, to find out what happens. (Marisa)

The students read their writings aloud, providing us an opportunity to talk about not only the baggage we bring to the novel, but the expectations we bring as well. Because I want these students to think about composing meaning in yet another way, I ask them to turn to the text itself and respond to Shelley's account of her own "invention" process:

> I busied myself *to think of a story* . . . one which would speak to the mysterious fears of our nature, and awaken a thrilling horror—one to make the reader dread to look round, to curdle the blood, and quicken the beatings of the heart. If I did not accomplish these things, my ghost story would be unworthy of its name. . . .
>
> Every thing must have a beginning . . . and that beginning must be linked to something that went before. . . . Invention, it must be humbly admitted, does not consist in creating out of void, but out of chaos; the materials must, in the first place, be afforded: it can give form to dark, shapeless substances, but cannot bring into being substance itself. . . . Invention consists in the capacity of seizing on the capabilities of a subject, and in the power of moulding and fashioning ideas suggested to it. (21–22)

> I know Mary Shelley wrote this in a chaotic time in her life. She'd recently lost a child and was pregnant (I believe) at the time of this writing. It's somewhat logical for her to create this story about the horror of creation-gone-bad when she herself was so devastated. (Alison)

> Shelley's idea of invention is not creating something entirely new, but reforming what already exists. She is explaining that invention must be worked at and formed; it does not merely come into existence. The creation

is formed not out of void, "but out of chaos." Her notion of creation is lin-
ear. You have to work towards it (there is an evolution). (Andrew)

The students' responses gave way to a discussion of writing "assignments,"
writing groups, and invention, which led naturally into a discussion of what
it takes to compose. The five canons of rhetoric—invention, arrangement,
style, memory, and delivery—seemed to fall into place for them. We applied
the canons to their reading as well as their writing processes, with some success, I think.

Weekend: I like the way our class has been going. They take much responsibility for themselves and for the class. I think about them as I read their
journals, which are supposed to be about their responses to the literature,
how the reading makes them feel, what expectations get raised, what ideas
they're getting for their own writing, etc. But—

> I've always liked the idea of classes structured like this one is. My father,
> who is currently getting his teaching degree in Spanish, thinks that classes
> should be taught not by lecture, but by interaction. I personally believe that
> it is hard to learn in a lecture because it does not require anybody to think.
> The students just dutifully copy down notes as their teacher spells out
> information. This method is also very conducive to sleep.
>
> On the other hand, a class where the students are expected to think and
> actually discuss their opinions and write about them makes it almost impos-
> sible for them not to learn. This way, the students are teaching themselves
> and each other. Tests, especially multiple-choice tests, for subjects such as
> English are ridiculous. All they require is a little good guessing, very little
> thinking, and a lot of BS, especially on any essay questions that might be
> thrown in. (David)

> After [our] discussions, I'd like to formulate my ideas for my next summary
> response—this sort of represents my brainstorming so that I won't forget
> the argument(s) I'd like to discuss.
>
> March 7, the class discussed the meaning of the text. What really
> caught my attention was when we discussed the superego and id of Fran-
> kenstein. We were trying to decide whether the monster represented Fran-
> kenstein's superego or id. In my opinion . . . the creature was NEI-
> THER. . . . Rather . . . the creature himself possessed a combination of
> both. . . .
>
> Okay, it is now Wednesday, and again I've changed my topic. I think
> I'm going to use my first idea. . . . The idea in who was more of a monster:
> Victor or the creature. Like most of the people in our class, I side with the
> creature. I find myself sympathetic towards his character. My argument is
> that he's not the monster. . . .
>
> When Victor was doing his research, he should have taken special care
> to make [the monster] "look" more normal so that the creature wouldn't

have to lead a desolate and lonely life. I think that if you look at the story in that aspect, one feels empathy for the creature. It is not the creature's fault that he becomes the murdering monster Victor vows to kill. The creature tried to bargain with Victor to no avail. All Victor sees is the physical hideousness of his creation instead of being proud to have made such an accomplishment as a living, breathing being!!!

My mind is set. I am not at all impressed by Victor. I don't think he should have been so quick to judge what he did not like without first getting to know the creature. In light of all this, Victor is the true monster because he abandoned and rejected what he so carefully and tediously created—his child that basically wanted love and acceptance from his father as well as from others. (Roxanne)

March 7/Last Week of Class: We're working our way to the ending of *Frankenstein* and, at the same time, discussing the different ways we could read it, in terms of creation, of human limitations, of defining "human," of alienation, etc. Different students are responsible for explaining the different ways of reading *Frankenstein* that are appended to our text. We're sailing smoothly—until we try to make closure on the book. Different students are reading the ending in different ways: some think the monster has destroyed himself; others think he has escaped. I ask them to write a new ending for *Frankenstein*.

Newsflash. Scotland Yard—Three people were reported strangled to death. Alice Webster, neighbor and close family friend of the Saville's, called Scotland Yard and reported disturbance at 3:04 A.M. Police are searching the scene for possible motive. No clues have been found as of yet. Any person with information or clues should notify Scotland Yard immediately.

Newsflash. Ingelstadt—Professors M. Waldman and M. Kempe were murdered in their studies at the university around 7:00 A.M. Classes have been cancelled and a reward is being offered for any information leading to the apprehension of the killer. What appeared to have been a strangulation in both cases is a tragedy for the school and families. Police are searching for possible motives. (Lisa)

The creature drifted on the ice-raft for several days until he became trapped in the ice again. He set off across the ice northward to his destiny. The cold whipped around him as the screams of Clerval and Elizabeth tormented his mind. These thoughts pushed him on. He wanted to end the horrible life he led. His mind kept coming back to Frankenstein and how he had destroyed his father's life. Just as he had made Frankenstein suffer for his abandonment, the creature was now going to extract the revenge of his deeds upon himself. His mind ran through his life deeds over and over as he trudged northward farther and farther. The screams of the past became too much for him and he fell to his knees and slept. But even in sleep he could not accept the death he had caused. Upon waking, the creature went about executing his end as quickly as possible. Once his funeral pyre was built, the creature looked up to the heavens and cried, "Take these agonies from me." He climbed on top of the pyre and dropped the match. The creature lay back and covered his face with his hands. As the flame grew, a faint smile grew under the hands. He would finally find happiness. (Kasha)

The students made their way to an understanding of *Frankenstein* by providing themselves an alternative ending, a resting place in their confusion. They've been a good group; we've all moved toward an understanding this term of what it means to write-to-learn, of what it means to compose meaning as we read and as we write, of what it means to respond to texts.

> The best part about writing in your class is that it makes us very critical and analytical. We can't write (or say) anything unless we support it with textual evidence. This is great because it keeps us from blowing a lot of hot air. We have to think before we speak. . . . I also like the fact that you let us revise. That really ticks me off when a professor slams me with a bad grade and says, "Tough luck." At least you give us a chance to improve. (Molly)

> The problem is that once a writing/English class is finished, I too stop writing. This is bad because usually by the end of a term, I am finally having an easier time and not struggling so much with writing phobias. I would like to join a writing club to prevent myself from this yo-yoing but I don't want to be in a group of wonderful English-major writers. . . . Is there a writing group for people like myself who really have a hard time getting their ingenious thoughts on paper? A support group for people who don't like to write but would like to learn how to? It would be fun to start such a group and to explore what is so difficult for us. It would be nice to have contact with a teacher just as support and encouragement. I am curious to find out what you think. (Colleen)

Final Entry: I'm scheduled to teach English 205 again next year. And as I think about what I'll do differently, I think in terms of different texts, not different pedagogy. When a writing teacher teaches literature, she simply teaches. She wants her students to see their reading as well as their writing as an unfolding, ever-improving process of growth and understanding—each time they write to crystallize their thinking, each time they share and discuss their drafts, each time they revise. Whether they are reading or writing, they'll need to revise until their words take the form that best presents their intended meaning. So what's process got to do with it? It's only and solely everything.

Works Cited

Berthoff, Ann E. 1981. *The Making of Meaning*. Portsmouth, NH: Boynton/Cook.

Booth, Wayne. 1961. *The Rhetoric of Fiction*. 2nd. ed. Chicago: University of Chicago Press.

Chase, Geoffrey. 1988. "Accommodation, Resistance and the Politics of Student Writing." *College Composition and Communication* 39 (February):13–22.

Emig, Janet. 1983. *The Web of Meaning*. Portsmouth, NH: Boynton/Cook.

Moffett, James. 1968. *Teaching the Universe of Discourse*. Boston: Houghton.

Murray, Donald. 1988. "The Listening Eye: Reflections on the Writing Conference." In *The Writing Teacher's Sourcebook*, 2nd ed., by Gary Tate and Edward P. J. Corbett. New York: Oxford University Press.

Shelley, Mary. 1992. *Frankenstein*. Edited by Johanna M. Smith. New York: St. Martin's Press.

III

Writing and Rewriting Literature

9

Canon and Community
Using Literature to Define in the Poetry Writing Classroom

Wendy Bishop
Florida State University

1. What is poetry, you ask, what should I teach in poetry writing class? I
think of the genres of poetry:

song	rap
greeting cards	occasional verse
Elizabethan sonnets	romantic narratives or epics

And contemporary free-verse, free to move into its own genres (or themes)
like:

beat	confessional
L=A=N=G=U=A=G=E poetry	nature poetry
political poetry	urban performance poetry

Since I'm teaching a *writing* class, I can't and don't want to "cover"
four hundred years of English poetry, not to mention lengthier periods of
non-Eurocentric verse—Chinese, Japanese, Indian, Latin American, or Caribbean. But clearly, my students and I need to read poems to write poems,
need to explore themes and genres together. If I choose to introduce only my
favorite poets, I reproduce my own eccentric education; if I choose antholo-
gized masterworks, I risk valorizing professional texts, final products that
deny their own construction, and do this in a course that emphasizes construction and processes of generating poetry. At the same time, when I begin
a course by defining it negatively—not a course about songwriting, not a
course where greeting-card verse is valued, not a course for writing limericks
or hate and love poems to significant others—I deny the real language-love
that has caused students to enroll.

The poetry world I live in? One of writers in creative writing programs who *are* trained to valorize the (supposedly) unteachable, the "high-art" academic poem, because of the language qualities it embodies: generally lyric free verse, full of the commonplace details of contemporary American life, turning on a concrete image, and so on. Creative writing programs—beliefs, textbooks, classroom practices—are largely still craft- and product-based, developing from a perception that "high-art" writing can't be taught, although the "tools" of form, leading to better craftspersonship, can be provided. Traditionally, in the creative writing workshop, we present exemplary poems, analyze the techniques that have been achieved, and send our students home to write like the professionals; that is, like "Artists." Capital A.

2. What students wonder (I was one of these) when they go home: about our assumptions about the genre of *contemporary* academic poetry, about what we think is good and why (it isn't clear and it isn't familiar to them; it isn't Shakespeare and it isn't on the radio). We have our preferences for alliteration and assonance over rhyme, associative or deep images over symbol, personal histories and daily observations over political statement, and so on. The poem of the literary journal and contemporary mainstream academic poetry book is an identifiable genre that is both taught and valued in graduate writing programs. However, it is more often something undergraduates are expected to intuit or affiliate with unquestioningly at some risk of social sanction. ("You like that heavy, sing-song, end-rhyme; go to the back of the class, please!")

At home, in the roommate- and music-tormented sea of the dorm or corner apartment—warm humid Tallahassee spring night, frogs and local bars vying for white-noise primacy—undergraduates, though, if they are reading poetry at all, are generally being introduced to a historical canon that stops short in about 1970. Many textbooks and courses don't highlight this issue or ask by what processes poets achieve their products. When contemporary literary examples are provided, these examples are, more often than not, presented to inculcate an unexamined canon or status quo rather than to offer students knowledge that lets them challenge, investigate, and (re)develop discourse knowledge. That is, of course, a fancy way of saying that they're offered:

AnonymousChaucerWyattSidneySpenserRaleighShakespeareJonsonDonne
HerrickHerbertMilton(maybe Bradstreet)MarvellDryden(Finch, new to the
canon)JohnsonGraySmartBlakeWordsworthETCDickinson(ah!)Hopkins
HousemanYeatsFrostStevensETCeecummingsThomasBishopRoethke
WrightGinsbergKinnellGunnRich(really?)SnyderPlathBaraka(finally!)
Atwood(broadening our definition of NorthAmerica)Heaney(reminding us
of our Irish influences and born in 1939 the most recent poet in *Poetry in
English: An Anthology,* Oxford, 1987, most handy on my shelf at home.)

while their teachers may really prefer or emulate Joy Harjo, Li-Young Lee, Robert Hass, Sharon Olds, Marilyn Hacker, Elizabeth Alexander, Edith Shoemer . . . (fill in your own).

3. As a writer who teaches literature (that is, how to write "literature"), and given my concerns about the traditional and narrow use of the literary canon in traditional poetry writing classes, I can change how poetry writing is taught by:

> introducing students to the language/world of poetry genres; encouraging them to read further in many directions; strengthening our academic pact to explore a particular genre in the universe of poetry genres—that of contemporary academic verse; and, performing this introduction/argument without devaluing the affection for word play in general and poetry in particular that brought students to my classroom in the first place.

Lofty goals. This means I use literature in the poetry writing classroom but do so in a very particular way—to build canon knowledge as a living, expanding principle. Canons are made within and for communities and we create our canon knowledge as we explore definitions, understand the tradition, AND investigate new possibilities for poetic expression. (You: "Ta-da. Sounds good. But how?")

4. Go along with me, through a term or two? To start. Ask students to contribute a poem by a *living* poet to a class anthology, including a paragraph-length statement about why they value this poem. Ask, also, for one of their own poems that embodies their interest in poetry to date, that interest also explored in a paragraph-length statement. (Contribute your own; of course, as a writing teacher teaching literature, you learn by exploring how you make literature, too—whether your last try was in high school or the poem you force out for this classroom "experiment" the night before [like most of us?]. Or, by thinking, "I'm going to teach poetry, I'd better read and write poetry, get a good process guide and dive in all summer before I do.") During the first weeks of the term, read across this class anthology to see who is read and why; to understand what has been written and what influences that writing. (If students say they haven't—can't—previously written a poem at all, ask for a piece of their prose with "poetic qualities.")

The second half of this initial class anthology consists of poems you've chosen that will illuminate writing issues you'll want to cover in class. (If you're looking at poetic form, choose contemporary poets writing in forms—lists, pantoums, villanelles, sestinas, haiku, prose poems; if you want to focus on collaborative writing and poetry as performance, share the work of Native American poets, or Anne Waldman's performance poetry.) In addition, ask class members to bring in poems they like for read-aloud sharing during the first fifteen minutes of each class. Because I'm a writer who teaches literature (and it can work in the same way for readers who teach literature, I think), I begin this read-aloud sharing by contributing poems I'm drawn to in my weekly issue of *The New Yorker* or in literary journals that I receive that term. I explain the ways I "mine" the poems I read for ideas for a poem I write each week to share with my own informal writing group. I write. They write. We write.

Finally, throughout the term, publish work in class books and, in doing this, add to the classroom canon. These activities, undertaken as the term opens, woven into your discussions throughout the term, help define your community and shape your work, illuminating that the world of poetry writing is broad and that in a class, you are, of necessity, going to visit only a small portion of the territory. Still, by exploring class members' preferences, by challenging definitions, by sharing developing "poetic taste," you (we, I, they?) are better able to understand the variety of responses that occur in class workshops. This way, writers and readers learn poetry from the inside out and, I believe, write better poems.

5. Now try it with me. It's two years ago in a linked, senior- and graduate-level poetry writing workshop. Students contribute the following poets to our classroom canon. Juniors and seniors at the 4000 level choose Shel Silverstein's "Where the Sidewalk Ends" (two students choose the same poem), "Untitled" by Jim Morrison, "words" by Sonia Sanchez, "The Lover Remembereth" by Leon Stokesbury, "Dog Poem" by Philip Levine, and "Deadwood Dick" by Elizabeth Alexander. These students are English writing majors. The Sanchez and Stokesbury poems are taken (we suspect) from the textbooks assigned to those students in English courses the previous semester. We know that the Alexander poem comes from a collection of that author's work that we loan to that student the first day of class when he says: "I've never read any poetry. Do you have any I can use?"

Michelle A. and Michelle W. surprise us with their twinned names and twinned choices of Silverstein's work: in statements in our class anthology, they give similar reasons for contributing his poem. Michelle A. says: "Even though it is intended more for children, Silverstein made me realize that poetry didn't have to be so serious and dark all the time, which is what I thought poetry had to be in order to be good." Michelle W. explains: "Shel Silverstein's poetry may be written for children, but the meanings and morals are ones to which I can relate. Mr. Silverstein's poetry gives me comfort when I'm lonely, makes me laugh when I'm sad, and reopens my eyes to simplicities I gawked at in childhood."

Klif G. chooses the Jim Morrison poem because "he [Morrison] has a rhyme like style that is both musical and meaningful . . . freespirited, without being chained by poetic norms." Brad R. chooses Sonia Sanchez for her "realism," explaining, "I relate well to her writing because I like things to be interpretive, while always defining boundaries with which a thought can be carried.'' Tom H. chooses Philip Levine's poetry for ''a certain forcefulness in its language, but [he] manages to convey strength of its sentiment without relying on words that are by themselves overtly compelling. . . . I do not try to write like Levine, but the topics he chooses I, too, find of great importance.''

Tophie M. chooses Alexander's poem, from the book of poetry we loaned him two days ago, since it is based on a photograph: ''I have found it hard to describe a picture of something and still have what I have written be poetic. I hope to one day write as well as she does.'' David C. likes the moment when his expectations about forms are broken: ''Leon Stokesbury's sonnet, 'The Lover Remembereth Such as He Sometimes Enjoyed and Showeth How He Would Like to Enjoy Her Again,' is an interesting sonnet. I read it initially because it had a long title written in traditional sonnet language; that interested me.''

Graduate students in this linked workshop contribute poems by Carolyn Kizer, Leiann Larson Burton (from a regional literary journal), Ntozake Shange, Amy Clampitt, Linda Hogan, Mary Oliver. My contribution is work by a friend, Patrick Lawler, a recent University of Georgia Press poetry award winner. (Your contribution is . . . ?) It's not hard for us to see that the graduate-level class members are clearly more ''schooled'' in canon building; their choices more clearly reflect the genre of contemporary academic poetry. They choose poems from poets' books and from literary journals rather than from English-course-assigned anthologies. Their rationales are far more schooled also: ''This poem [Mary Oliver's] in particular illustrates contemporary ecofeminist theory through the treatment of the two deer'' and ''Linda Hogan is a Chickasaw poet whose work, no matter what her topic, has a compelling physical immediacy.'' Some graduate-level contributors are more interested, of course, in sharing reading pleasure: ''Ntozake Shange's poems appeal to me because, like this one, they are honest and painful and loaded with images that are personal and real.''

6. Reviewing this class anthology outside on a warm spring day under a soon-to-bloom magnolia, we see much that we expected as we planned this class: a very diverse background of taste, reading influences, and investment. You point out spots where traces of students' past training and technical analysis meet present enthusiasms and unexamined responses. The Silverstein and Morrison choices, of course, are always enough to cause us to hold our heads for a moment. How to respect the student's pleasure in those genres (children's verse and song)? (How to remember our own love for those genres? We start to swap stories. I tell you about visiting my four-years-older sister in college and dating an ''older'' man who read me Rod McKuen late into the night, how I walked around my senior year reading all, ALL his books and this has made all the difference and you tell me. . . .)

How to respect our students' pleasure in those genres and at the same time hurry up what feels like a needed reading maturity? We discuss our options: Ignore the choices? Praise lavishly those who chose academic poets? Ignore the poet who exhibits "poor" taste? We've seen each of those strategies in the classes we took ourselves as undergraduates (time out here, to share some of those stories). But we don't like those strategies because they leave too many novice writers outside the community instead of inviting them into the conversation. By talking this through, we learn how *class-compiled* course anthologies might provide clues for our instruction. Deciding graduate students in our class have more sense of academic poetry that they could share, we consider mixing one or two in each peer group to function as an initiate or guide on our journey toward defining and writing contemporary academic poetry this term.

I point out that students' choices of influences show me that they already have a grasp of the technical elements of poetry: alliteration, rhyme, and so on. Why should I reteach what is already known? And you see that they have attitudes about "good" and "bad" contemporary poetry. They know such poems are "dark" though they might like "light." Our instructional time we decide will be better spent on comparing and contrasting these generic expectations than in trying to (re)force technical tools into students' hands.

As we stand up, a little sunburned despite the magnolia's deep shade, we decide to start the next section of this course by classifying types of verse, asking students to bring in "good" examples of greeting card/occasional verse, popular verse, songs, historical verse, contemporary poetry—since the song/contemporary poetry distinction is one that constantly arises. You agree to prepare a sheet that allows us to compare popular songs and contemporary academic verse. I chuckle when I see you've placed "Tears in Heaven" by Eric Clapton beside "A Blessing" by James Wright, and "Traveling Through the Dark" by William Stafford beside "Across the Great Divide" by Kate Smith.

"You must have been born about..." I say, "Your song sense is always hopelessly outdated. Mine too. We'd better invite students to bring their own favorite lyrics to share later in the same class period or we'll exacerbate the generational divide."

That day, in class, I look over Clarissa W.'s shoulder to see her notes. You're orchestrating the class discussion so I have time to observe. She writes:

> We decided that "Traveling Through the Dark" and "Across the Great Divide" are narratives but Stafford uses slant rhyme and unrhymed quatrains, has a turning point in the center of the poem, and relies on prosaic language. Kate Smith uses contractions, a repeating chorus, full rhyme, never becomes as textured or mysterious or evocative in her "story" as Stafford does in his.

7. We're determined to keep the excitement that we see growing in this class; it's NOT like classes we took where we were TOLD who to read and

WHAT to aspire to but not WHY exactly, or HOW, certainly; we find that
something else can be seen in these original class anthologies. Anyhow,
today in the common room I'm shivering and complaining about the overac-
tive air conditioner (next week, you remind me, it will be underactive).
Looking at Klif G.'s anthology poem. "Guess who is Klif's favorite poet?"
"Jim Morrison," we say in unison and smile. We've been here before with
student writers. Klif's poem, in part, runs like this:

Flow

keep it going
keep it moving
don't stop
can you feel the breeze
the river's streaming
my heart's bleeding
the body's needing
whose words you heeding
girl

In his anthology self-analysis, he says: "I like this one because it's free
from poetic norms and 'flows.' Music is a big interest for me, and I feel like
this poem can almost be made into a song, and for that reason, this one is
the one for me." About Morrison, remember, Klif says: "He has a quality in
his poems that is free-spirited, without being chained by poetic norms."
We've been here before, but this time, we're determined to figure out how to
make this understanding work for us.

You put on a second sweater and read on, tracing this reccurring pattern.
Brad R. submitted the Sonia Sanchez poem. The rationale he offers for his own
poem is very similar to his reasons for sharing Sanchez's work. Brad liked
Sanchez because she lets things be "interpretive." He feels his own poem
"offers interpretation but keeps the reader focused on the objects described."
Michele A. does not write her poem in stanzas like her favorite poet Silverstein, but she does use end rhymes with similar full-rhyme force: away, crave,
sun, become, spite, night, pain, gain (Silverstein chooses—begins, white,
bright, flight, wind—in his first stanza). Michelle W. appears to be less
influenced by Silverstein, but her own poem, she says, is a commentary on
Anne Rice's *Vampire Chronicles*. She, like Michelle A., writes out of her
popular, non-academic readings. Conclusions to be drawn? In this first try at
a class-generated anthology, we can see clearly that students are influenced by
their reading. (Initially this supports a creative writing classroom truism that
students should read more, read "exemplary" examples of academic verse.)

"But," you say, "I'm not sure I should start each course with heavy
doses of professional verse. Look. By assigning and highly valuing a type of
verse that Michelle, Klif, and Tophie don't know, I risk leaving them in the
classroom dust. As English/writing majors, they've already been "exposed"

to academic poetry—like a virus—but, when given free choice to name influences, they show the degree to which this exposure hasn't been all that effective or important.''

"We need to figure this out," I insist. "What is the connection between a student poet's reading and her writing?"

"There's clearly an 'imitative' overflow," you say. "Students are echoing assigned academic but they prefer to share self-assigned popular reading. Clearly, we have a canon gap."

"And not only between the canons-forming-in-the-head of the more advanced graduate students and some of these undergraduates, but also between the canons-forming-in-the-head of more and less school-based senior students themselves. You know, it's funny, though," I say. "The undergraduates who chose academic poets that we think came mainly from their class-assigned anthologies? They *might* produce more sophisticated academic verse but their more extensive reading doesn't seem to guarantee this at all. Look at Tom H. who chose Philip Levine as a topical influence while deciding not to imitate Levine's technical effects.''

"I can't take the air conditioning a minute longer," you say. "Besides, we have to experiment with this stuff. We need to learn more."

8. Late one night, at the computer, on e-mail, we brainstorm some more (What else is good teaching, really?), sending suggestions back and forth through the ether:

ME: How to draw the student-generated canon into a working relationship with the contemporary academic canon? I want us to co-contribute to our community, but it IS essential that at the end of the long road we arrive at a particular destination.

YOU: Do we agree that students do need to exit this course understanding more clearly (perhaps even valuing) academic poetry, knowing better how to write it themselves? Well, if so, to do that, we need to invite, explain, and highlight our potentially conflicting definitions of poetry writing so that students can actively "discover" some of these issues themselves.

ME: OK, let's guide them through sequences of meta-analytic writing about poetry and then through poem drafts. This way, they become contemporary poets (this act requiring a little to a lot of instructional nudging).

YOU: Well, nudge away. What's a teacher for? Let's ask students to "read themselves" in the class anthology.

ME: Yes, and better, let's read the anthology, say a minimum of three times across the term. Write a series of "snapshots," first responding to the initial contributions, then at midterm looking back to the initial anthology, and finally at the end of term, describing the course of the semester's work. I've done parts of this before. See how, in this journal entry, Joye responds to poetry by her peers:

> Some of the poetry written by class members really impressed me. Others left me feeling not so alone in my lack of poetic ability. I noticed a lot of "high school" themes coming through. Which is expected. Natasha's poem especially impressed me. I can't stand most of these poems that go on for hours about things I don't grasp or understand. I could read Natasha's piece many times and still enjoy it in a new way each time I read it. My writing is very simple and I don't really want to spend this semester trying to make it complex. I know I will, though. I tend to be like everyone else—I want to just come up with a brilliant creation. It will be interesting to see where this class ends up. I think I'll go back at the end of the class and see how some people changed; how I changed. Should be educational.

YOU: Interesting, so Joye realized for herself that she would learn from observing the way her classroom community of writers changed. There are some problems, though. Joye portrays herself as a student who knows she can work harder but doubts she really much wants to. Did you see this in other journal entries?

ME: Yes. Absolutely. Students remind me that they're not writing in a more invested way not simply because they haven't read enough contemporary poetry—instead, they're simply busy. Paul explains: "My poetry is really poor, but I feel like it could get better if I spend the time I really need. Three writing classes. Two literature. Insane. Insane. This is what it's all about. Where is all of this taking me if not to academia [graduate school]?" Joye's journal entry also points to another common instructional issue in creative writing courses: the myth of brilliance. She suggests she and many others would like to go to sleep one night and wake up the next day as, well, ah, Edgar Allan Poe. . . .

YOU: Or, if not Poe, then at a minimum transformed into a "great" writer. [What are we doing writing e-mail about teaching at 3 A.M.? ;) :)]

ME: Remember how it was for us, too? How declared writing majors so quickly experience the taught competitiveness of "goodness?" They want to be "as good" as the professional poets venerated in our canonical anthologies. They also want to be good students. If they buy into the traditional creative writing truism that "poets may be born and not made," they arrive at the conflicted position of having to admit that maybe they weren't "born" a poet. But as students of poetry they are competing for grades against other writers in their program and workshops. Matthew says:

> In high school, I was always top dog, in English and in writing, and felt unstoppable. Getting into college, I discovered I was surrounded often by people just as talented as I. I was jealous—I wanted to be the only one.

YOU: We included graduate students' work-in-progress in another class anthology to address some of the jealousy quotient the good high school writer like Matthew brings to classes. Readings and talks by campus and local writers help too. It's hard, though, for over-performing students to relax a bit as they consider a writer's processes, and the need for long-term, lifetime-long, work commitment (as opposed to seeing writers as those who have the elusive momentary flash of brilliance). So here's some more of what we need to do. Dip into the initial anthology often; everyone is encouraged to bring in poems to read to class. For the first few weeks the questions we pose during sharing sessions hinge on definition and technique.

ME: Questions are my stock in trade. How about these?

- Where in our categories of genres of poetry does this poem fall?
- Do we know anything about the author; is he or she living or dead; does it matter?
- Does it matter where and when the poem was written?
- What do we think the poet's aims and intentions are?
- What techniques does she or he rely on?
- How can we steal/borrow those for our own poems?
- Has a class member in the anthology already used these techniques?

YOU: The first class poem, like you said, shared in small groups and with us, is always derived from an invention exercise. However, some students didn't produce radically improved imagistic poems from this exercise. But we have to learn to trust this process. Still, how do we best emphasize the qualities of what we judge to be good, contemporary poetry through reading and modeling and imitation? When we try to do this, how do we keep in mind that students are adults with fully formed writing expectations and tastes, even if those tastes differ from the goals of the course as we have set forth those goals in our syllabus?

YOU: And so on?

ME: And so on. I like how we used highlighting pens to show what we found were the most evocative images from each poet's work and then read those images to the class, describing what effects we found and why we find them effective. I sort of understand now what happened that day. Essentially, we can create a mini-lecture on contemporary verse, which begins in their work and moves to samples from the professional poets in our book.

And, in a similar way, let's ask students to respond to an early poem of their own *as if they are the/a teacher,* since we learned that they already know most of the poetic terminology we might choose to teach them. When I tinkered with this, I got fascinating results. For instance, in comments on her own poem, Jodie points out that she uses good images in the third stanza, is too clichéd in the first stanza, and uses hyperbole well in the final stanza, and that she's tried to contrast and juxtapose images. Look, let's face it, student poets already know many of the weak points of their work and have, for some reason, chosen not to address those points in the current draft (BTW. Note to us: This is a discovery we should explore further with other classes—the "why" of resistance to revision, the neglect of known revision opportunities!!!?? ;) !!!).

YOU: Is it OK to be ultra-honest at 3:30 A.M.? This stuff sounds good, is good, but I can be as frustrated as the next teacher with a sheaf of workshop poems that seems to have moved not an inch from the non-academic verse of our initial anthology. In the first half of the term, then, we should draw up a list of general poetry-writing suggestions. When we present our "suggestions," we can differentiate them from "rules" (school being what it is, :) :) this is hard to do). Students may know clichés are anathema to poetry teachers (the problem being of course that what is clichéd to an experienced reader of contemporary poetry is fresh and new, often, to a new writer of poems).

Other rules are the more perplexingly internalized understanding that contemporary poetry is "dark" and serious (rather than "light" like Shel Silverstein's poetry). You know, I'm guessing that sometimes these rules or understandings are based on assumptions that genre expectations are inviolate, eternal qualities of that form, instead of representations of community choice and commitment.

ME: In this case, it's the community of academic poets—a community that is relatively small and esoteric, that prefers serious themes. Aren't we talking here about taste and an acquired taste at that?

ME: I think we should keep doing this. Here are my chalkboard suggestions for writing poetry, generated from class poems, as copied into Kathryn's journal on 9/7/93:

- Use first person everyday voice
- Focus on the particulars you know (try snapshots, photos, paintings) rather than the universals you're guessing at
- Always use metaphors/images or similes in rhymed verse
- I often don't know what you're saying, to whom, and what (why)— try to use your language to be precise, in control of the scene you present to the reader
- Take advantage of titles
- Try to evoke a mood or tell a story; know your point so your reader can too

- Avoid archaic, fairy tale, and sci-fi—damsels in distress and personified concepts—time and all eternity
- Rhythm lives in the regular or disrupted syntax of sentences
- Sing-song patterns eventually bore in their predictability

YOU: But remember, remember, remember, when presenting suggestions like this we should always try to explore the danger of these suggestions becoming rules, to encourage rule-breaking (any enthusiastic activity, in my mind, being better than no engagement), and to illustrate these effects with positive examples from the workshop book.

YOU: OK. More possibilities. They're gonna groan when they see this syllabus, aren't they? But we can't learn to write without writing or learn how literature ticks without writing literature—I believe. That's partly why I see how differently I teach literature because I'm a writer and writing teacher. Anyway, I also choose one canon-building, required report each term. I'm getting quite a set now. Like:

> craft report (defining and offering samples of imagery, alliteration, etc.) or poetic form report (defining and offering samples of contemporary poets writing sonnets, sestinas, etc.); writing an introduction to the work of a contemporary poet, completed after reading a complete volume of that writer's poetry; reading an issue of a local literary journal and reporting on the types of poetry found there; attending a local live poetry reading and reporting on the event.

Always, these reports are shared with the class. They are bound into an additional class anthology. This way, we write one book on poetry writing together, and . . . well, should I go on?

ME: Look. It's 4 A.M.. We need to stop for tonight (for tomorrow?). Do you think my students will believe I pulled an all-nighter? We only got as far as midterm, didn't we? Brainstorming—why, there's so much we can do, it's pretty exciting. For students too. For instance, in a midterm snapshot, Joye says:

> I wrote a lot of poetry in high school—it was all the same—one form—when I started this class, I thought I was a pretty good writer but I was also a very narrow-minded writer. I had a set idea of what poetry should be and what was good poetry—I am now seeing the process of writing poetry. I discovered there are so many ways to create poetry. There are not good or bad choices but different and better choices that depend on the poetry. Poetry itself has also become more interesting for me. I am reading other people's poetry because I am starting to understand not only the rules behind the poetry, but also the technique and the process the poet has utilized. This is helping me become a better poet myself.

What Joye knows, I want all my students to know. And those choices depend on how we're defining contemporary poetry writing, the writing done by published poets, the writing we do in order to become such poets. Look, I can't stop there. You know I'm a collector. Look at Paul's entry:

> The fact that I had made up my own rules [for writing poetry] meant in fact living in an unruled world of poetry that led me to resist real instruction for my writing. It's a difficult thing to give up all that freedom but it's really the only way to get better, to at least learn how things are done by other criteria. I'm understanding better how that other world [of academic poetry] works and when I stand in it. It's making me be a lot more conscious of my writing and far less careless. I realize how many good ideas are out there and how many talented writers and just how far I have to go to consider myself near their level. I'm also realizing my own worth. I wondered if I was really any good at all, or if I was just fooling myself. I can see the potential in myself that might be realized if I put the effort into it. The picture of the poetic world, as it also compares to the fiction world, is beginning to take shape.

I want students new to poetry to negotiate the difficult terrain of ruled and unruled poetic worlds. I want them to develop new understandings, to create new definitions, to try on new beliefs without doing violence to who they are when they begin the course. By building a literary canon together—testing it, questioning it, broadening it—we find that the loss of some freedom can result in needed control and knowledge. We can put together a picture of the poetic world. Carefully. Together. As we enter it with our words.

YOU: A poetry teacher's manifesto?

ME: Oops. Sorry. Nope, just a writing teacher who teaches writing and reading and loves both and . . . yawn!!!!!!. See you tomorrow for coffee?

YOU: Yes, please. Or is it already coffee time?

As a writing teacher, one thing I try to do is take student writing seriously as literature. I believe in that. I'm philosophically committed to it. But I couldn't really do it until I started seeing literature less as Literature, stopped putting it on a pedestal and started seeing it as something that could be messed with, played with, re-imagined the way we try to help our students re-imagine their work.

What would happen, I asked myself, if my Intro to Fiction students tried re-writing the ending of Malamud's "Idiots First"? Tried re-telling *Heart of Darkness* from Kurtz's point of view? Filled in a missing year in Toni Morrison's *Sula?* What if they invented new characters for Louise Erdrich's *Love Medicine* and wrote whole new chapters around them? They did. And then they wrote about what they had done, how it changed the piece they had read, how it changed their reading.

The *Love Medicine* pieces were best—so good that I asked several students' permission to send them to Erdrich, who had just been in town for our Writers Conference a few weeks before. She never replied. We were disappointed. Was she horrified? Pained? Or just busy?

I wonder if those students noticed that five years later she released a new edition with her own added chapters. . . .

Elizabeth Rankin
University of North Dakota

10

Teaching Literature Through Performance

Charles Schuster
University of Wisconsin–Wilwaukee

Did teaching writing change my way of teaching literature? Yes, in multiple ways. But I want to focus in this essay on one theoretical and pedagogical repositioning that occurred as a result of my seeing literature from the perspective of a renegade rhetorician. That repositioning has most of all to do with the nature of the text—its ontological status and negotiability, its site as an interpretive space for students.

Let me begin by briefly outlining the relevant assumptions upon which my teaching of literature initially rested. Conceiving of literature as sacral text, I positioned myself as rabbi or priest and literature as holy writ to be expounded upon from pulpit and podium. Over the years, I found ways to involve my congregation of students more fully, but I persisted in believing that literature was written by the hand of God, that it was beyond mortal apprehension, accessible through divination made accessible by a long and intense semiotic initiation. I still carry some of this assumption with me when I teach. It dovetails into another which I have abandoned—namely, that learning to read literature is a passive activity. If literature is sacred, then it is best understood when placed upon the altar of our minds bathed in the light of soulful contemplation. Thus it was to be consumed the way one devours a soufflé or fine fruit, in silence but with an occasional gentle smacking of the lips.

Initially in my literature classes, I talked and the students listened. When conversation occurred, it was often more monologic than dialogic: in poor imitation of that great ur-teacher, Plato's Socrates, I would enter the classroom with an agenda to be pursued. I would guide, hector, and massage our discussions toward specific points and passages. I had certain lessons I wanted the students to learn, certain "readings" to advocate. The literature classes I taught followed this pattern—and to some extent still do. Reader-response theory notwithstanding, I assume that I am a more acute reader than most of my students, especially my undergraduates; I know more about perspective, irony, tropes, plot, crises (literary and personal)—that whole symbolic complex of aesthetic patterns, strategies, and intuitions which I have built up through intensive reading and scholarship. So my tendency has been to talk through those subjects, to open up texts through close analysis, to become the disembodied voiced that unfortunately positions my students as disembodied ears.

The students' role in this setting was not just to listen and engage in reverential discussion, however, but also to write. In addition to exams, they composed interpretations, appreciations, and explanations. Those writings performed a rhetorical obeisance to the literature; they required students to analyze literature in terms of structure, form, and meaning in typical critical fashion. They were essays in homage, essays whose purpose, in Keith Fort's terms, was "to condition students to think in terms of authority and hierarchy" (178).

Increasingly, such values have little place in the contemporary literature classroom. For one thing, literature is now not only not sacred, it is hardly even literature. It is cultural production, often viewed as an expression of post-colonial, classist, nationalist, racist, sexist, or otherwise suspect sensibilities. It is conflicted, situated, deconstructable. It is "ecrit." Aesthetic distinctions are called into question, and those who persist in defining literature in high formalist terms are in danger of making themselves irrelevant. Much as I may desire those new-critical, formalist days of my youth, I am confronted with a different reality in today's literature classrooms. As Robert Scholes has written, our "loss of faith in the scriptural status of literature has coincided with drastic changes in the needs of our constituents" who, says Scholes, need to learn not literary appreciation but rather "the kind of knowledge and skill that will enable them to make sense of their worlds, to determine through their own interests, both individual and collective, to see through the manipulations of all sorts of texts in all sorts of media, and to express their own views in some appropriate manner" (15–16).

In other words, what our students need is rhetoric. Teaching writing, after all, is precisely about teaching students how to engage critically with the world as text. Unlike the literature classroom, which emphasizes talking, listening, and interpreting, the composition classroom centers on inventing, generating, workshopping, critiquing, revising, and responding. Students there stand in a different relation to texts: expressions of everyday life, they partake of the secular and quotidian and require little interpretive energy. Moreover, in Kenneth Burke's terms, they participate in the psychology of information and not the psychology of form (29–44). Accessible and filled with fact, they are models and stimuli—like a bottle of celery tonic or head of raw broccoli. If there is one primary mission to writing instruction, then, it is to teach students "to see through the manipulations of all sorts of texts in all sorts of media, and to express their own views in some appropriate manner."

But texts in a composition classroom provide other uses as well. Because they have a different status, because they are of the world and not above it, because they are often written by students, columnists, and contemporary pundits distinguished more for their ideas than their aesthetic excellence, texts in a composition classroom can be more readily engaged. In such classrooms, these texts are rigorously critiqued. They are dittoed, discussed, torn apart on the overhead, reshaped, rewritten—frequently with the writer present. True, published essays are often treated with more respect than those written by classmates—but not much. Students have little compunction disagreeing, critiquing, or amending texts in a composition classroom; after all, that is the central role these texts are supposed to play; that is why they are assigned.

This difference in the status of the text can be transferred from the teaching of writing to the teaching of literature. If literature is not sacred and is not of a whole other category than rhetoric, then it is available not just for response and critique but for manipulation, revision, and reinterpretation. It is rewritable—not because it exhibits weakness or lack but because by transforming it we alter its ontological status as text along with the ontological status of the student as passive reader. The primary means by which I try to realize these pedagogical ends is through performance.

By performance I do not mean the cognitive concept of "drama" as articulated by James Moffett in *Teaching the Universe of Discourse,* although Moffett's insights concerning the conceptual richness of drama as a mode of learning are certainly relevant. It was, after all, Moffett who argued that:

> drama and speech are central to a language curriculum, not peripheral. They are base and essence, not specialities. I see drama as the matrix of all language activities, subsuming speech and engendering the varieties of writing and reading. (60–61)

Nor do I intend by the term the dramatic renderings of scenes and passages by Shakespeare, Ibsen, or Hansbury, although clearly such enactments are useful. Instead, I take the term "performance" in the same way that Richard Poirier does when he states that the emphasis in reading should be relocated "from communicated values of a philosophical nature, roughly speaking, to the values of performance, from the idea of the work as a cultural monument in which truths await our apprehension, to the idea of the work as an exemplification of actions" (310). When literature is read rhetorically in terms of performance, it ceases to function as a artifact of high culture that conveys semi-eternal truths; instead, it offers itself as a text that embodies "a struggle with words and not a putting forth of something predigested in the mind" and it assumes "that the most worthy acts of writing and reading are signs of vibrant, creative life . . ." (309). Performance introduces fluidity into

the reading of literature. It creates transformative moments in the classroom
that are simultaneously rhetorical, analytical, hermeneutic, and celebratory.

Performance is nothing new in literature classes where faculty have typically asked students to soliloquize from *Hamlet* or act out a scene from
Ceremonies in Dark Old Men. Certainly enactment enhances the teaching of
drama, but what happens when we make all texts amenable to performance,
texts like Zora Neale Hurston's "How it Feel To Be Colored Me," Flannery
O'Connor's "Revelation," Richard Selzer's "The Corpse," Audre Lorde's
"The Master's Tools Will Never Dismantle the Master's House"? How does
this emphasis on performance alter the basic business of literature classes:
teaching reading, interpretation, and analysis?

In my experience, the results are (pun intended) dramatic. In "The Performing Self," Poirier states that "Performance is an exercise of power," a
curious one because "it is at first so furiously self-consultive, so even nar-
cissistic, and later so eager for publicity, love, and historical dimension"
(87). For Poirier, great literature is written by authors committed to the performative; it infuses their work with qualities that transcend the page. After
all, writers are generative; that is part of the great black joy that lies at the
heart of being a poet, essayist, dramatist, or fictionist. Few of our students
(or their teachers) can realize that same commitment and satisfaction, but a
similar effect is possible through performance. After all, if I am given a literary text and instructed to make it my own, to breathe dramatic life into it
through artistic revision, and then present that performance to an audience of
teacher, classmates, schoolmates, visitors—something akin to creative pride
becomes all but inevitable.

This approach to teaching is quite common in K–12 English/Language
Arts classrooms and has an army of devoted followers with many teachers
and scholars offering spirited testimonials, including Joanna Hawkins
Maclay, Leslie Coger and Melvin White, Jerry Pickering, Shirlee Sloyer, and
Gerald Ratliff, to name just a few. Betty Jane Wagner has written an illumi-
nating account of the uses of drama, filtering her analysis through the
insights of that great guru of classroom performance, Dorothy Heathcote.
Wagner writes:

> If we think of any material stored in books as an unpalatable beef bouillon
> cube, to use Heathcote's metaphor, then some means must be found for
> releasing this dense mass into a savory broth of human experience. . . . In a
> drama, [Heathcote] deliberately immerses a class in the mystery of not
> knowing and shows them that the impulse to research is born of this ten-
> sion . . . [ultimately] the learners have found they have power over material
> rather than its having power over them. (186)

As Wagner, Bruce Robbins, and others make clear, drama reconceptualizes
literature. To create a performance out of a text, especially a non-dramatic
text, students must develop a reading, strive for an effect, reshape meaning

in their own words. They must engage in a hermeneutic that is both public and intertextual. They can't write a five-paragraph theme or thumbnail analysis; instead, they must translate their interpretation into an extension of the text itself. In Poirier's terms, they must become the reader/performer/writer.

Let me offer an example, something short that can be deployed economically in the space of this essay. Here are the first two paragraphs from "Livvie," by Eudora Welty, a story that is not particularly dramatic or performative:

Solomon carried Livvie twenty-one miles away from her home when he married her. He carried her away up on the Old Natchez Trace into the deep country to live in his house. She was sixteen—an only girl, then. Once people said he thought nobody would ever come along there. He told her himself that it had been a long time, and a day she did not know about, since that road was a traveled road with *people* coming and going. He was good to her, but he kept her in the house. She had not thought that she could not get back. Where she came from, people said an old man did not want anybody in the world to ever find his wife, for fear they would steal her back from him. Solomon asked her before he took her, "Would she be happy?"—very dignified, for he was a colored man that owned his land and had it written down in the courthouse; and she said, "Yes, sir," since he was an old man and she was young and just listened and answered. He asked her, if she was choosing winter, would she pine for spring, and she said, "No indeed." Whatever she said, always, was because he was an old man . . . while nine years went by. All the time, he got old, and he got so old he gave out. At least he slept the whole day in bed, and she was young still.

It was a nice house, inside and outside both. In the first place, it had three rooms. The front room was papered in holly paper, with green palmettos from the swamp spaced at careful intervals over the walls. There was fresh newspaper cut with fancy borders on the mantleshelf, on which were propped photographs of old or very young men printed in faint yellow—Solomon's people. Solomon had a houseful of furniture. There was a double settee, a tall scrolled rocker and an organ in the front room, all around a three-legged table with a pink marble top, on which was set a lamp with three gold feet, beside a jelly glass with pretty hen feathers in it. Behind the front room, the other room had the bright iron bed with the polished knobs like a throne, in which Solomon slept all day. There were snow-white curtains of wiry lace at the window, and a lace bedspread belonged on the bed. But what old Solomon slept sound under was a big feather-stitched piece-quilt in the pattern "Trip Around the World," which had twenty-one different colors, four hundred and forty pieces, and a thousand yards of thread, and that was what Solomon's mother made in her life and old age. There was a table holding the Bible, and a trunk with a key. On the wall were two calendars, and a diploma from somewhere in

Solomon's family, and under that Livvie's one possession was nailed, a picture of the little white baby of the family she worked for, back in Natchez before she was married. Going through that room and on to the kitchen, there was a big wood stove and a big round table always with a wet top and with the knives and forks in one jelly glass and the spoons in another, and a cut-glass vinegar bottle between, and going out from those, many shallow dishes of picked peaches, fig preserves, watermelon pickles and blackberry jam always sitting there. The churn sat in the sun, the doors of the safe were always both shut, and there were four baited mouse-traps in the kitchen, one in every corner. (85–86)

Although I have authored the following script myself, I can well imagine that students might come up with something similar that would be performed by four students ("A", "B", "C", and "D").

"Livvie"

A: When he married her, Solomon carried Livvie twenty-one miles away from her home.

B: Twenty-one miles!

A: He carried her away up on the Old Natchez Trace into the deep country to live in his house.

B: She was sixteen—an only girl, then.

C: How was I to know? I was jus' a child.

A: Once people said he thought nobody would ever come along there.

D: "Ms. Livvie, won't nobody come along here."

A: He told her himself:

D: "Girl, it has been along time, and a day you never knowed about, since that road was a traveled road with

A: *people*

D: coming and going. Yes, I tell you girl. This be a house halfway to nowhere."

A: Solomon was good to her, very good to her in his way,

B: But he kept her in the house.

A: She had not thought that she could not get back.

C: How was I to know? I was jus' a child.

A: Where she came from, people said

B: You know how it is—an old man don't want nobody in the world to
ever find his wife, 'cause they'd steal her right out of the house.

A: Solomon asked her before he took her,

D: "Girl, will you be happy?"

A: He asked her very dignified,

B: for he was a colored man that owned his land

A: and had it written down in the courthouse;

B: and she said,

C: "Yes, sir," since he was an old man and I was young, so young.
How was I to know? I was jus' a child.

A: He asked her,

D: If you choosing winter, girl, would you pine for spring,

A: and she said,

C: "No sir, no indeed."

B: Whatever she said,

C: Whatever I said, always, was because he was an old man . . .

D: I know I'm old but I'll treat me a wife well

A: while nine years went by.

B: All the time he got old,

C: so old,

D: so old,

B: so old that he gave out,

A: sleeping the whole day in bed.

C: And I was young still.

A: Now Solomon had a nice house

B: inside and out.

A: It had three rooms, lovely rooms, with holly paper on the walls and
fresh newspaper cut with fancy borders on the mantleshelf

B: and photographs of old or very young men, yellow photographs,
Solomon's people.

A: Solomon had a houseful of furniture:

B: A double settee, a tall scrolled rocker,

A: an organ,

B: a lamp with three gold feet

A: set on a three-legged table with a pink marble top

B: next to a jelly glass with pretty hen feathers in it.

A: Then came the bedroom with snow-white curtains of lace at the window

B: And a lace bedspread atop the bed.

D: I had me a bright iron bed with polished knobs

C: like a throne.

B: Solomon slept there all day

A: under a big feather-stitched quilt made of twenty-one different colors, four hundred forty pieces, a thousand yards of thread.

B: It was what Solomon's mother made in her life and old age.

A: And the rest of house was lovely too—

B: It had a table,

A: a wood stove,

B: a trunk with a key

D: . . . and a Bible.

A: It had

B: A wall hung with two calendars and a diploma,

D: from somewheres in my family,

A: and under that

B: hung Livvie's one possesion:

C: a picture of the little white baby of the family I worked for

B: back in Natchez

C: before I was married.

A: In the kitchen, there was a big wood stove

B: and a big round table

A: with knives and forks in one jelly glass

B: and spoons in another

A: and a cut-glass vinegar bottle between

B: and dishes of

A: pickled peaches,

B: fig preserves,

C: watermelon pickles,

D: and blackberry jam,

B: with a butter churn sitting in the sun

C: and a pie safe . . . with the doors always shut tight.

A: And four baited mouse-traps in the kitchen

D: One trap in every corner.

In drafting this text for readers theatre, I find myself more fully imagining, interpreting, and analyzing the relationship between Solomon and Livvie than I do when simply reading the original. My version emphasizes Solomon's dignified demeanor, his care, his age, his well-furnished and carefully constructed house, Livvie's youth and inexperience and slow surprise at the long loneliness of living with an old man as husband, even in so splendidly and painstakingly furnished a home. Already I have in mind other versions that might take Solomon's point of view more explicitly, or dramatize the interaction between Livvie and Miss Baby Marie or the sexually charged verbal and kinetic dance of courtship between Livvie and Cash McCord (both of which occur later in the story). As I envision performative possibilities, the literature takes on various hues and shapes. As Gavin Bolton explains it:

> Learning in drama is essentially a reframing. What knowledge a pupil already has is placed in a new perspective. To take on a role is to detach oneself from what is implicitly understood and to blur temporarily the edges of a given world. It invites modification, adjustment, reshaping, and realignment . . . (156)

In practical terms, exploring literature through performance demands that we conceive of literary texts to be open to reinterpretation, revision, and reshaping. In a sense, literature becomes essay—essai—a try, an attempt, and the students become co-creators and interpreters rather than passive consumers of an already-commodified object d'art. To build performance into my classroom, I include it now in my syllabus and strongly encourage my students to participate. I find that asking former students to model a performance (preferably one they've authored themselves) motivates my students and tamps down their anxiety. I require all performances to be collaborative group efforts and ask that students choose a text that we have read and discussed in class so that their performance will provide us with another interpretation. Although I stipulate no time limits, I recommend that a group of four or five students plan on presenting a five- to ten-minute performance. Afterwards, the entire class discusses what the group did, why they did it, and whether it succeeded.

Performing texts is so rewarding that instructors will likely want to find other ways to apply it. A useful follow-up is to offer assignments that require students to speak or write in the voice of a character or author; their performance will then consist of responding to issues, questions, and concerns raised by the literary work from fellow classmates. As a way of maintaining interest and reading assignments, this kind of dramatic activity is much preferable to short-answer quizzes or spot-checking journal writes—and student performances can be evaluated as part of class participation. Several years ago, to cite another example, I taught Richard Selzer to introductory literature students. One part of my final exam asked students to put themselves in the role of a hospital personnel director who had to decide whether she/he would hire Selzer as a surgeon based on a reading of *Mortal Lessons*. Those students produced the most memorable final exam responses I've ever read—and they had to form a judgment based on a close reading of the text. I have also asked students to create speculative performances, anticipating what a silent character would say if offered voice, enacting a dialogue between characters from different stories by the same author (or different authors working on similar themes), theorizing alternative beginnings and endings to narrative accounts. The possibilities are limitless.

Introducing performance into literature classes has its difficulties. It can be destabilizing: Students remake the literature according to their own vision. Their interpretations may run counter to the instructor's or may seem entirely counter-intuitive or distressingly perverse. I have experienced fewer difficulties of that kind than I have of another; namely, the perception that performance of any kind in a college classroom is embarrassing, silly, or somehow preadolescent. There is no doubt that this kind of classroom activity is more prevalent K–8 than it is in high school or college. Unfortunately, that is their gain and our loss. Performance produces multiple benefits in any classroom, and its opportunities for creative interpretation and enriched understanding only increase as students mature as readers and thinkers. By working in groups, students develop collaborative skills as they forge a vision of a literary work. To author a readers theatre script is to learn how to edit and revise toward the creation of a performance that is presentational and public. In any case, students and instructor find the results unpredictable and surprising. I think this happens because students, at least in most cases, are able to get inside the text by giving voice to characters, ideas, and interpretive possibilities. They are simultaneously in the text and beyond it, a very useful kind of embodied disembodiment that leads toward metacritical understanding. In most literature classes, instructors attempt to further that kind of understanding through the assignment of essays or journals; in a performance-based class, the literature itself becomes the ground on which and through which interpretive analysis occurs so that students participate in a dialogized relation to a text. Finally there is that most obvious benefit: the introduction into the classroom of risk, play, the ludic. Johann Huizinga has stated that a more appropriate designation for the human race than Homo sapiens may be the term "Homo ludens," man/woman "the player" (1–27).

J. Hillis Miller has written that "Rhetorical reading should be the center of literary study" (297), and by rhetorical reading he means teaching the tropes and strategies that authors deploy as they create stories, dramas, and poems. I too want to teach my students to read—and one important way to do that is to teach that complex, rich, quicksilver category we are calling the literary, although I'm not at all sure anymore what is in it and where to draw its borders. What I do know is that I want students to understand literature as an expression of performance; just as important, however, I want them to be able to participate in a parallel act of creation so that they can experience and enjoy literature as something felt and visceral, so that they can achieve some sovereignty in relation to the text. The alchemic power of performance has allowed me to achieve this goal. In my experience, it is one of the central ways that we can best further the education of our students as readers, writers, speakers, authors, and performers.

Works Cited

Bolton, Gavin. 1985. "Changes in Thinking About Drama in Education." *Theory Into Practice* 24.3:151–157.

Burke, Kenneth [1931] 1968. *Counter-Statement.* Berkeley: California University Press.

Coger, Leslie, and Melvin White. 1967. *Readers Theatre Handbook.* Chicago: Scott, Foresman.

Fort, Keith. 1975. "Form, Authority, and the Critical Essay." In *Contemporary Rhetoric,* edited by Ross Winterowd. New York: Harcourt.

Huizinga, Johann. 1950. *Homo Ludens: A Study of the Play Element in Culture.* Boston: Beacon.

Maclay, Joanna Hawkins. 1971. *Readers Theatre: Toward a Grammar of Practice.* New York: Random House.

Miller, J. Hillis. 1993. "Thinking Like Other People." In *Wild Orchids and Trotsky,* edited by Mark Edmundson. New York: Penguin.

Moffett, James. 1968. *Teaching the Universe of Discourse.* Boston: Houghton Mifflin.

Pickering, Jerry. 1975. *Readers Theatre.* Encino, CA: Dickenson.

Poirier, Richard. 1993. "Pragmatism and the Sentence of Death." In *Wild Orchids and Trotsky,* edited by Mark Edmundson. New York: Penguin.

———. 1971. *The Performing Self.* New York: Oxford University Press.

Ratliff, Gerald. 1981. *Beginning Readers Theatre: A Primer for Classroom Performance.* ERIC Clearinghouse on Reading and Communication Skills. [ED206036]

Robbins, Bruce. 1988. "Creative Dramatics in the Language Arts Classroom." ERIC Digest Number 7. ERIC Clearinghouse on Reading and Communication Skills. [ED297402]

Scholes, Robert. 1985. *Textual Power: Literary Theory and the Teaching of English.* New Haven: Yale University Press.

Selzer, Richard. 1976. *Mortal Lessons.* New York: Simon and Schuster.

Sloyer, Shirlee. 1982. *Readers Theatre: Story Dramatization in the Classroom.* Urbana, IL: National Council of Teachers of English.

Wagner, Betty Jane. 1976. *Dorothy Heathcote: Drama as a Learning Medium.* Washington: National Education Association.

Welty, Eudora. 1993. "Livvie." In *An Introduction to Literature,* edited by Sylvan Barnet et al. New York: HarperCollins.

I have had literature students experience genres by creating similar texts themselves. And I also have had them write short responses to dramatic scenes read aloud in class, writing spontaneously, before we move into general discussion. I want everyone to capture and articulate his or her own passionately felt, personal reactions and ideas before being influenced by others.

For example, when three student volunteers finished their in-class readers'-theater production of Tennessee Williams's short but powerful drama, *Twenty-Seven Wagons Full of Cotton*, I sensed a room electrified by students' thoughts and feelings. I immediately asked them to capture their passion on paper during the remaining ten minutes. These twenty-seven second-semester, first-year students in a small, rural, state university in central Pennsylvania were simply taking a required general-education introduction to the genres of literature course. Yet as I read their responses in my office that evening before I left, I was truly energized, excited, and impressed by the strong feelings aroused and the sensitive insights into the characters—especially in the young women's reactions to Flora, the childish, slightly demented, masochistic wife/victim of Jake.

Wanting to reveal the relation of characterization to meaning in literature, I began the next class period by reading aloud some of their most stirring responses. I introduced this as evidence of both traditional and modern, creative, feminist reactions to the 1945 drama. In my students' expressions I saw that they, too, were impressed. More than any lecture could do, hearing the diverse emotions these characters had aroused in our own readers'-theater audience now opened their eyes to and illustrated Tennessee Williams's "sharply etched and richly detailed" characterizations. Even more importantly, these students now respected each others' abilities. They were eager to engage in readers'-theater and spontaneous writing again, and we did— over and over throughout the semester. Incidentally, my highest student evaluations, over two years, twelve courses, and sixteen sections, came from this class. Could there be a connection?

Mary Ann Rudy
Lock Haven University
Lancester, PA

11

A Merging of Lives
From Self to Other

Brad Peters
Texas Christian University

I. An Autobiographical Link to a Text

We pretend to have the upper hand in guiding our students' development as readers and writers. But students always manage to sneak up on us with their own agenda. Maybe that's why I continue to teach. I thrive on surprises.

Let me offer an example. It was near the end of a recent semester in college freshman composition. A student I'll call Julie turned in an essay on Maya Angelou's *I Know Why the Caged Bird Sings*. She examined the theme of sexual growth and development. Two excerpts from that essay suggest how Julie approached her analysis, and why. She wrote:

> Maya's first encounter with sex came when she was eight years old. She had moved from Stamps, Arkansas, to live with her mother and Mr. Freeman (her mother's live-in boyfriend) in St. Louis. One morning, after Maya's mother left the house, Mr. Freeman began fondling Maya. He proceeded to make her fondle him. He then dragged Maya "... on top of his chest with his left arm, and his right arm was moving so fast and his heart was beating so hard ..." (Angelou 61) she thought he was going to die. When he finished, he took Maya gently into his arms and held her close. . . . She thought she finally found a real father after many years of having one absent. . . . Maya and her brother Bailey had been shipped off by their real parents, due to their divorce, to live with their grandmother and uncle. Throughout their early lives, they never had a strong, loving father figure. So when Maya was held by Mr. Freeman, she was expressing "... a child's Oedipal conflicts and not real events ..." (Finklehor 11).

Thanks to the student writers who granted permission to cite their work pseudonymously.

Her second encounter was worse than the first. Mr. Freeman actually committed the act of rape on Maya this time.

... much of my life has been quite parallel to Maya's. After Maya was raped, she developed a firm hatred for men. ... This happened to me also after I was abused by my boyfriend when I was sixteen. Like Maya, I warded off all men whatsoever. I wouldn't go out with or even talk to men in general. ... I feel that I was trying to avoid getting myself into the same situation once again.

Julie's excerpt is part of what I have come to call a "companion text." By using such a term, I do not mean to identify a particular genre. Rather, I mean to describe the whole or the *corpus* of student writing that can accompany the reading of a literary work. A companion text may include personal notes and observations, pre- or post-discussion meditations, fragments of relevant memoir, wool gathering, or journal entries, as well as more directed assignments in analysis and research. But of specific interest to this study are the parts of a companion text where cognitive shifts of some kind occur— moments of recognition, for example, or formation of new ideas, discovery of unexpected connections, or exploration. Such cognitive shifts emerge in a companion text as the student gets opportunities to locate and enlarge upon issues that cut across the literary work, her own life, and various other sources.

Based on applied theories of reader response, companion texts are likely to appear in classrooms where writing assignments are designed to slow down and encourage multiple, personalized readings of a work. But a companion text also facilitates a student's growth as a critical reader because its composition necessarily draws upon the dynamics of interaction among the student, her peers, and her teacher—all of whom are composing their own companion texts at the same time. Teachers of literature as well as teachers of composition have a vested interest in the concept of a companion text. It suggests a more effective approach toward enabling students to write about what they read.

Julie's companion text to *Caged Bird* began with an earlier class project. She came to a writing conference six weeks into the semester and told me: "I want to do an autobiography about what happened to me at the end of my freshman year in high school. I was raped. I signed up for your class because I'm ready to write about this, and I knew you'd let me do it."

Julie knew as well that the assignment would require workshopping at least one draft and sharing the final revision among her classmates. When I suggested she or her readers might feel uneasy about these activities, she said: "I have no problems with it. If anyone doesn't want to read it, they can go to someone else's essay, can't they?" I assured her they could.

Julie's pre-Angelou autobiography turned out to be a powerfully self-affirming narrative of "... how I gained control of my life after being taken advantage of ... and how I went from a naive girl to a strong, mature woman capable of handling anything." She wrote about the rape, but focused mostly on the two years following her attack. During this period, she also survived a serious auto accident, formed a much closer friendship with her mother, became a dedicated dance instructor of young girls, and eventually found a boyfriend who helped her regain self-trust.

Richard Marius doubts the value of this kind of writing. He feels that composition courses should require students to peruse texts rather than their own lives. He asserts:

> If the texts are interesting and if the students are interested in them, and if the teacher is helpful, they find ideas in those texts and expound on them without having to wade through a demeaning apprenticeship of writing about themselves. . . . Autobiographical writing demeans our profession. (475–76)

Yet the way in which Julie connects her autobiography to her later essay on *Caged Bird* implies that it is not probable—nor even desirable—that students stay at such a remove from interesting texts, especially if those texts help them to rethink what they have written in regard to their own life experiences. It may be that when such rethinking occurs, students like Julie take an important step toward understanding what intertexuality really means: a life-enhancing, "unending conversation" among readers and writers (Burke 110–111). Writing a companion text to a literary work may therefore invite students to engage in more intensive rereading and re-interpretation of many texts—not only the ones they read, but also the ones they write.

Notwithstanding, a nationwide survey indicates that most teachers gravitate toward Marius's perspective (Applebee 166). The majority of freshman college students come from high school English programs that favor formal, text-based essays (75 percent in public schools) over reader-based essays such as Julie's (7 percent). We might ask why the traditional methodology persists. But the answer is all too obvious: The risks that Marius implies are genuine. Unpremeditated use of an autobiographical component in teaching can provoke resistance from students unlike Julie, who may wish to keep personal information to themselves. An autobiographical mindset can encourage students to overgeneralize first-hand experience as the best measure for *all* experience. A misapplication of autobiography as a teaching technique may lead students to romanticize their lives—and the works they read—rather than to sharpen their critical thought. An autobiographical approach can be misinterpreted as a form of therapy, placing the teacher in the inappropriate role of therapist. In any of these instances, the purpose of composing a companion text would be defeated (Graham 1991).

Therefore, integrating an autobiographical component in our efforts to improve the way students read and write about literature requires methods that address or avoid the potential problems.

This study will sketch out methods that I have found useful. In working with *Caged Bird*, Julie and her classmates responded to five shorter assignments that guided them around the hazards I've enumerated, while they moved toward deeper critical thought. The five assignments also fed into a culminating essay on a topic that they would develop from several different perspectives: events in their own lives, Maya Angelou's experiences, incidents that happened to close acquaintances, and reflections upon other texts. Julie's excerpt on sexual growth and development came from this last project.

An important note: Julie and most of her classmates grew up in white, middle- to upper-middle-income families. Three students came from different ethnic backgrounds—one Black, one Vietnamese, and one Thai.

II. The Five Assignments

What expectations do students have when they know they will be reading a book such as *Caged Bird*? How might they benefit from examining magazines or newspapers published during the author's childhood and adolescence? What topics might still be relevant? Julie and her classmates made a foray into the library to find out.

One student, Sharon, discovered an article on the topic of lynchings. She learned that anti-lynching legislation did not seem to be effective in Angelou's time. She speculated that "The lynchers lynched not in spite of the fear of prosecution, but because they had ample reason to know that there would be no prosecution." She then commented: "Lynching no longer occurs today. Blacks have equal rights unlike the 30's and 40's. Government is now in total control and no longer ignores these brutal crimes."

But after a small-group discussion where she presented her findings, she composed this brief reflection: "I couldn't, or at least I didn't want to, believe what I was hearing. . . . I learned of several experiences faced by the Blacks. Some of the stories absolutely brought tears to my eyes." One of her classmates had discovered a news item about ugly attitudes toward Blacks in the sports world of the 30's and 40's. He compared it to what a friend in football had confided about racist attitudes among his teammates. Another classmate looked specifically for stories about the everyday conditions of Blacks' lives. Instead, she ended up collecting demeaning illustrations of Blacks in advertisements. I shared with Sharon's group what Rick, a Black student from another class, had mentioned about lynchings. He wrote: "Events that occurred then do still occur now. It is just kept under the rug. For example, an event that occurred close to the town where I live—another town called F_____ —a Black man was hung for talking or going with a white female."

What Sharon wrote in reflection upon her group's collaboration helped her to see history as a continuity, where the juxtaposition of past and present creates an essential dialectic. Her reading of *Caged Bird* began in the context of an evolving politics of Black experience and culture.

But how often do class discussions or a successful application of sources provide students with a true grasp of complex social issues? What more might students do to join the larger conversation of such issues, which one book can merely represent? The students conducted out-of-class interviews to learn about others' perceptions and experiences.

When Keith—a student who took pride in calling himself non-racist—interviewed a Native American friend of his, he made these observations:

> As I asked her how racism had changed in the last fifty years, she kept telling me that she thought it had changed very little. She said it has just transformed itself. I disagree. . . . From what I have heard and read [in *Caged Bird*], racism was a lot worse years ago. At least in my world, I think racism has declined.
>
> [My friend] grew up in southeastern Oklahoma, but never really ran into racism until she visited an aunt in southern Alabama. There the people hated Blacks and harassed them constantly.
>
> . . . Up until I was in elementary school, I lived next to a Black family. They were good friends of mine. I would like to think I am completely not racist, but I believe I do have a little problem with some Orientals, but I'm working on removing that difficulty.

Keith's sketchy treatment of his friend's observations, and his pointed shift from her perspective to his own, caught my interest. Once he had listened to the results of his small group's interviews, he exchanged his paper with someone from another group. He and his partner commented on each other's interviews and then made connections to the small-group findings. His partner wrote to Keith: "[One woman in my group] wrote about the racism towards Orientals. . . . I have never seen racism towards an Oriental, except in a movie. Besides, one of my best friends is Oriental, and he has never been in a situation where people called him racist names."

In my own written response to Keith, I said, "It's interesting how [your partner] deduces that the problem of racism is improving, whereas your interviewee feels otherwise." I wanted to keep the conversation going, if possible.

In a journal entry, Keith also seemed eager to continue. He wrote: "Ever since we had that discussion on racism last Monday, I have not stopped asking myself if I am racist." He went on to detail the story of the Black family who lived next door to him as he was growing up—and to recount the friendship he had had with another Black fellow, "from fourth grade on." Then he revisited his earlier remarks: "I don't see myself as racist against any race except Orientals. . . . My dad's best friend in the army was Black, so [my parents] raised me not to be racist, but my mother hates Orientals so I probably jump to conclusions on them. . . ."

The conversation that gave rise to Keith's autobiographical reflections and enlivened his reading of *Caged Bird* thereby enabled him to scrutinize his values, where they came from, and how he practiced them. Why had he never recognized his racist attitude toward Orientals? Keith took the initiative to confront this question and to consider how he should deal with it.

Once students realize the larger conversations that surround a topic, once they reflect such conversations in their own texts, and once they see the impact such conversations have upon their own perceptions, how readily might they move on to the intertextuality that academic writing requires? The students returned to Colombo's *Rereading America*—an anthology they had worked with earlier in the semester—to seek texts and topics that would somehow "speak" to Angelou.

Ted, a student from a broken home, decided to explore how divorce alienated children and parents. In an essay, he used Arlene Skolnick's "The Paradox of Perfection" to explain:

> . . . [Angelou's] dad came to take [her and her brother] away from Stamps . . . to go see their real mother in St. Louis. Maya is afraid, and does not want to leave Stamps. As Skolnick says, "they [mothers] have an 'ominous power' to destroy their children's innocence and make them discontented 'for years' or even 'forever'" (408–09). I think Maya's parents have made her feel this way, which shows her mistrust . . . even going to see her mother.

Ted's application of the Skolnick quotation to Angelou's experience actually includes Michael Zuckerman commenting on Benjamin Spock, so that he creates a barbershop quartet of textual voices. Yet a student like Ted may find it hard to imagine an intertextual network as interpersonal conversation, unless an exercise such as this allows room for his own voice and experience to enter. Predictably, a series of subconscious personal associations emerged in Ted's writing as a result of his textual voices essay. During an in-class exercise on the topic of empowerment, he jotted down the story of how he'd felt powerless after having a car wreck. In the margins of his story he scribbled, "My mom? Or dad!" Writing about the car wreck seemed to make him recall the Skolnick comment about mothers and their ominous power. But he was making a crossover from mothers to fathers. Later, Ted wrote about his dad's effect on his life:

> He left us, and therefore I figured he really does not care to see me. Our relationship is like Maya's and her dad's: we do not communicate well. When Maya's father takes her to Mexico, he takes her to a party. [Angelou says:] "Dad must have been beyond my reach in one of the little cabins out back" (200). Maya is alone, and has nobody to talk with. When I go out with my dad, I feel alone. . . . We do not really talk much because I have nothing to say to him.

But Ted did not stop there. He went on to recall his car wreck, and how afterward, his Uncle Joe had helped him to rebuild the car:

> As Joe and I worked on my car, I invited my dad to come and help us, but of course as usual he did not show up. Joe encourages me to go and see my dad, but I would rather go and visit Joe because I know I would have more fun. . . .
>
>   I cannot necessarily relate to Joe as my father, but we have a relationship similar to Maya's and her mother Vivian. I feel comfortable around Joe, and he treats me as though I was his son.

In such an instance, literary analysis becomes a kind of psychoanalysis. I therefore wanted my response to Ted to remain unintrusive. I wrote that his autobiographical reflections on *Caged Bird* showed why ". . . there is not really an impulse for a child to 'choose' a role model in a surrogate parent, unless an original parent fails to provide what the child needs. This idea is played out in the positive in . . . Joe's influence in your life." These essentially descriptive remarks affirmed and dignified Ted's reflections. Meanwhile, the remarks sustained my position as teacher, not counselor.

When students have successfully attempted one kind of intertextual conversation, what others might they try? How can they maintain their participation in the conversation and expand on it? What sorts of texts enable students to experiment, to seek new levels of meaning? *Caged Bird* has a suggestion. Angelou writes: "Oh, Black known and unknown poets, how often have your auctioned pains sustained us? . . . we survive in exact relationship to the dedication of our poets (include preachers, musicians and blues singers)" (156). Pedagogically, I accept this passage as an invitation to introduce students to poetry about Black experience. Is there a need to do so? One student verified as much, noting that she had heard of Langston Hughes—but of anyone else on the list I provided (including Alice Walker, Gwendolyn Brooks, Paul Laurence Dunbar, and even rap artists), she knew nothing.

Nick, another student who felt very unfamiliar with Black poets, chose Hughes's "Mother to Son" to explicate (Hughes 67). He relied upon a theme of self-image to give his explication focus. He developed a system of matching lines from the poem to events in the book. For instance, when the mother who narrates the poem says, "Life for me ain't been no crystal stair . . ./I'se been climbin' on," Nick extracted the line "And turnin' corners . . ." He associated it with an incident when Angelou turns an important corner. She drives her drunk father home to California, after he has had an evening of revelry in Mexico. Nick wrote, "Maya had never driven a car before and the . . . miles down a steep mountainside proved the ultimate challenge." He went on to say, ". . . and, though she wanted attention and approval from her father, that was all she needed to keep 'goin' in the dark/ Where there ain't been no light.'" He then extracted another line "Don't you fall, now . . ." and associated it with Angelou leaving her father, when she:

... ran away from the pain at home but ran to the security of ... making it on her own. Because of her recent experiences, she believed she could make it [among a group of other runaways], and she did.... [Angelou says:] "After a month my thinking processes had so changed that I was hardly recognizable to myself. The unquestioning acceptance by my peers had dislodged the familiar insecurity." (216)

In bringing Hughes's voice and Angelou's together, Nick went on to consider the reasons why his own self-image had developed so differently:

When it was hard for Maya to build a positive self-image, it was easy for me.... My dad says, "It is so important (for both parents and kids) to know the difference between love of a person and the negotiation of issues." Many people believe that love equals total agreement, but many people are wrong.

The paternal voice that affirmed Nick's own experience resonated so tellingly with the maternal voice that narrates Hughes's poem. Maybe this resonance of voices provided the conceptual bridge over which his insights travelled and explains why Nick did not facilely dismiss the formation of self-image as he saw it occurring in Angelou's experiences. Instead, he appreciated and tried to comprehend the otherness of the childhood conflicts Angelou describes, as compared to his own. As a result, Nick avoided generalizing that he couldn't understand Angelou's life because she came from a family background, time, and culture so different from his.

If students benefit from orchestrating intertextual and autobiographical approaches to a literary work, yet if they also continue to practice sharing and assessing their writing collaboratively, what might they learn from participation in a research group? How might they edit and shape their research findings for a group presentation to the rest of the class? To see, student groups took up topics such as homelessness, sexual development, alcohol abuse, divorce, and unwanted pregnancies, with each group member seeking different links between Caged Bird and contemporary concerns.

Tina, the only Black woman in class, worked with the group that examined the topic of unwanted pregnancies. In a preface to her part of the group's panel presentation, she expressed approval of Angelou's own reaction to motherhood at age sixteen. Angelou keeps her child and raises it. But Tina speculated that Angelou did so because she might have had little choice. "Who would adopt a Black baby during those times, when prejudice was such a big thing in people's minds?" she asked. Then she pointed out options in present times and argued: "Personally, I'd rather see adoption before an abortion." She went on to describe her investigation of a home for young, unwed mothers who chose adoption. After talking about the services that the home provided, she observed:

It's more of an upper-class home, so many poor are not there. I think it is because the resources are not there for them. Then another reason could be because the poor are more prone to have "contaminated babies." From my understanding, they do not have any minorities there. . . .

By "contaminated babies," Tina explained that she was referring to infants born addicted to drugs or infected with AIDS and other diseases. She pointed out a common perception that Black mothers frequently had such babies. Then she objected to this perception, saying that most unwed Black mothers tended to keep their babies, as Angelou had done, not because they were "contaminated" and no one else would take them, but because the babies were wanted and loved.

However, Tina did not say that one of her closest friends illustrated the latter option. Instead, in a journal entry, she told the story of how her friend had become sexually active quite early in adolescence—even though her friend continually advised her not to do the same. Tina went on to write:

> Whenever I want to know [answers to] a . . . sex-related question, still to this day I ask [my friend]. . . .
>
> She has taught me how to do certain things without getting hurt, different types of birth prevention, and how to use just about everything on the market. I still never understood why she has three kids if she knows so much. It would seem that she would not only help to protect me, but also protect herself. . . . She seems to know all orally, verbally, and physically. But mentally she is dumb.

Tina probably did not mention her friend's experience during the panel presentation because of a conflict that went far beyond her friend's illogical behavior. Implicitly she was struggling to determine whether her friend was part of, or apart from, the church community whose values her family represented. In the same journal entry, Tina said her family strongly objected to her association with her friend, so she simply didn't make it known that the two of them kept in contact. Tina had begun to realize the multiple and competing perspectives that complicated her own response—let alone her group's response—to this topic in *Caged Bird*.

III. Culminations

More than two decades ago, James Britton said of developing writers:

> I don't believe in setting the written model for their writing. I believe in reading for reading's sake and the kind of internalization that comes from reading for reading's sake will then articulate, interlink with the . . . resources which have in general been recruited at the spoken level. . . . It's a personal job, a personal selection and internalizing in terms of individual needs and interests. . . .

Let me add very briefly, I believe the writing and the reading are complementary processes and we need both. We need to test out in writing what
we can do with written forms, what meaning we can communicate in the
written forms. The written language forms the gateway to most further
learning. (99–100)

Britton, et al., later explained how the writer's personal construct of the
world was altered by the "interaction between people and the cooperative
building of a common world" and "the way individual representations fit
into the jigsaw of a social reality" (79).

So far, I have recounted how the classroom application of Britton's theoretical credo leads to the ripening of a companion text. The five assignments
that I described exposed students to written sources beyond *Caged Bird*.
They considered each other's experiences as well as Angelou's, and reconceptualized their own autobiographical perspectives. They discovered and
assembled tentative critical frameworks: historical, cross-cultural, psychoan-
alytical, post-modern, feminist, Afro-American. Accordingly, the students
arrived at a point where they might make the move from understanding self
to understanding other. This is where the maturation of the companion text
occurs. My remaining discussion will turn to one student who very clearly
demonstrated as much.

Carl had enjoyed autobiographical writing for its own sake, but felt a bit
unsure about incorporating personal commentary or experience when the
assignments or class activities on *Caged Bird* invited him to do so. This tendency became especially apparent when the incident of Angelou's childhood
rape gave rise to a very intense class discussion. In a pre-discussion exercise,
Carl wrote: "I don't pardon rape but I've never had an experience with anybody who has been raped, so I know nothing of its effects personally."

In earlier journal entries, Carl had mentioned a former girlfriend who
attended a university several states away. Unexpectedly, the next week, he
turned in the following entry:

> You know how we were talking about rape that one day in class and I said
> I had no close relationship with anybody who had been raped? Well, [my
> friend] called on Wednesday night and told me she was raped when she was
> in high school. . . . I felt so helpless as to her situation. . . . It made me realize
> I cannot do anything, call or write, that would comfort her unless I was there.

Carl's lengthy entry went on to describe his shock and bewilderment
when a few days later his friend sent him a letter saying she intended to end
their friendship. Although I felt I was trespassing, I replied: "You may be
misperceiving the situation. It's obvious that she called you . . . because you
are important to her and you helped a lot just by listening. Maybe [her let-
ter] is a reaction of insecurity—she told you something that might make
people reject her, so she's doing the rejecting first." I chide myself for not

having indicated that Angelou writes about the same kind of rejection when
she recounts a valentine incident with a would-be beau named Tommy.
Such a tie-in with the text would have anchored my comment in a safer
harbor.

Shortly afterwards, the students received their final major assignment: to
choose a topic from *Caged Bird* and develop it into an essay incorporating
interviews, material from their anthologies, library research, poems, films, or
other sources that might help to make a connection between the book and
their lives. In another journal entry, Carl wrote: "I do not feel depressed
anymore. I had [my friend] blocked out of my mind until the paper in your
class came around. . . ." He had decided to do his essay on the topic of rape.

Carl carefully reread the section of *Caged Bird* that recounted Angelou's
experience of telling her brother about her assailant. Then he telephoned his
friend. He asked her for permission to write about her experience, so that he
could sort through his own confusion about it. He emphasized her right to
refuse. However, if she consented, he guaranteed to give her a pseudonym
and respect her need for privacy in any way she wished.

There are occasions when students startle the breath right out of me. I
want to believe the progression of previous assignments had somehow prepared Carl to think through this situation so his own wisdom would tell him
whether to write about it or not. I do believe such a claim is warranted with
other students I've cited. But once a student like Carl so radically turns a
course into his own, shaping it to meet his genuine needs, all a teacher can
do is accept the role of the guilty bystander and hope for an opportunity to
assist rather than interfere. At the same time, I'd maintain that Carl's choices
to write autobiographically during this period did not demean him. I dare say
instead he was putting his learning to the test. This is perhaps the *modus
operandi* of a companion text.

Carl's friend agreed to the project. Or rather, she agreed to his attempt
to redefine and preserve their friendship. I let Carl know I considered any
writing that issued from his project—other than the resulting essay—to be to
and for himself. Accordingly, I would avoid making comments whenever it
made me feel intrusive.

Carl's first draft described Angelou's experience as a prelude to his
friend's. He narrated the latter story in third person, portraying himself as
buddy to a guy named Adam. He wrote:

Mary's boyfriend, Adam, did not know of this incident until a month ago.
Mary feared that if she told him of her dark past that she would scare him
away . . . that she would change his image of her. . . .

At first Adam was angry at Mary for not telling him this in the first
place and then he was angry at himself for not being able to do anything in
her time of need. . . . to calm himself, Adam took it out on the road as he
came and got me from my room and took me for a drive. . . . We went to
his car and started out of the parking lot like a bat out of hell. . . . I was in

the passenger's seat holding on for dear life with both of my hands on the emergency brake, ready to pull it if the car was to go out of his control.

Students who read and responded to Carl's draft avoided this passage. One focused on the more "researchy" part of the draft and ". . . the way you used all those quotes to help you." Carl's first quotation came from a pamphlet distributed to dorm residents: "Rape is never the victim's fault. No one asks to be degraded, humiliated, and have complete control of their body taken away." The second quotation came from Angelou: "The act of rape on an eight-year-old body is a matter of the needle giving because the camel can't. The child gives, because the body can, and the mind of the violator cannot" (65). The third quotation came from Mary. It reconstructed her immediately personal sense of horror, pain, and loss.

My own response centered upon "Adam's" reaction. "The sense of anger is powerfully described," I wrote. "Yet it may also be useful to point out that once the feelings of anger pass away, the focus must return to the victim—and helping her to make the transition to being a survivor." I suggested he contact the county women's center.

Carl took up the suggestion. He talked to a counselor at the center and asked for any available information. As a result of his efforts, the revised version of his essay contained the following passage:

> Now I know what Bailey (Angelou's brother) was going through because my friend went through the same thing. . . . The anger, the hate, the frustration and the need to let it all out. . . .
>
> Not only are those who are attached to the victim of rape crimes hurt, but the people around them as well. The effect is somewhat similar to a ripple in a pond. Some people feel distanced by the victim because of their unwillingness to talk or interact with the rest of society. Some want to help but do not know how to because they have no experience in the matter. Others just feel utter rage and hatred but cannot do anything because anger will not solve the problem. . . . The [county women's center] was very helpful in helping Adam deal with his frustration. They gave him pamphlets that described methods on how to help the victims of rape cope with themselves and how to help them get back into life.
>
> In Maya Angelou's case, the catalyst that brought her back into society was the push by Mrs. Flowers [a member of Angelou's community]. . . . Mrs. Flowers encouraged Maya not just to read but to speak and . . . to be more receptive of others besides Bailey.

Perhaps Carl did something similar for "Mary."

IV. Concluding Notes

This study illustrates how companion texts remediate the sense of distance and intimidation a student may feel when a course requires her to take up a literary work. I do not favor expressive writing over others, but agree with Janice Lauer when she says that a writing course must show students "... how to move flexibly from expressive to persuasive and expository writing" (127). Such a movement incorporates methods that transform dialogue into dialectic, because students see that their own written work is read and commented upon as attentively and positively as the work of famous authors. Placing this caveat at the heart of teaching literature and composition provides the student with a classroom where the teacher does not impart wisdom and truth, but offers honest, thoughtful reactions that will help the student develop her own wisdom and truth. The student thus comes to see a literary work as something accessible, vis-à-vis the collective experiences and observations of the author, other readers, and herself.

In such an interplay of relationships, no one reader's opinion or interpretation prevails. The student does not try to second-guess the teacher, creating "... an empty dialogue of misrecognition, denial, rationalization, and illusions" (Ragland-Sullivan 162). Rather, they use literature to shape or revise their own knowledge, at the same time they learn to relate to and benefit from other readers' and writers' knowledge.

As teachers of literature and composition, we must trust our students' capacity for learning on the levels that are more intimate and personal to them. Maybe those levels provide the only soil in which the metalingual and theoretical substances of critical thinking can ever really take root. We must devise and share more methods that, as Marius puts it, are helpful rather than demeaning. Accordingly, students can become more aware of their movement "from expressive to persuasive and expository writing" and their movement from self-conscious to multiculturally sensitive reading.

Our students want to learn from methods that are not only intellectually rigorous, but personally useful and empowering. They want to connect critical thinking with the whole blood of human experience. They will tell us as much, if we listen. Here, for instance, is what Julie wrote as she reflected upon the common bonds she found with Angelou in her composition of a companion text to *Caged Bird*:

> I brought together many, many years of memories and incidents. It was amazing how easy it is to write when you write from your heart about things you really care about. This is where I really began to dig deep within myself and write consistently with what you might call "passion." This is where I began to write with *meaning*.

Works Cited

Angelou, Maya. 1970. *I Know Why the Caged Bird Sings*. New York: Bantam Books.

Applebee, Arthur. 1993. *Literature in the Secondary School: Studies of Curriculum and Instruction in the United States*. Urbana, IL: National Council of Teachers of English.

Britton, James. 1982. "Writing to Learn and Learning to Write." In *Prospect and Retrospect*, edited by Gordon Pradl. Portsmouth, NH: Boynton/Cook Publishers, Inc.

Britton, James, et al. 1975. *The Development of Writing Abilities (11–18)*. London: Macmillan Education LTD.

Burke, Kenneth. 1973. *The Philosophy of Literary Form: Studies in Symbolic Action*, 3rd ed. Berkeley: University of California Press.

Colombo, Gary, et al. 1992. *Rereading America: Cultural Contexts for Critical Thinking and Writing*. Boston: Bedford Books of St. Martin's Press.

Finkelhor, David. 1984. *Child Sexual Abuse*. New York: Free Press.

Graham, Robert. 1991. *Reading and Writing the Self: Autobiography in Education and the Curriculum*. New York: Teachers College Press.

Hughes, Langston. 1963. "Mother to Son." In *American Negro Poetry*, edited by Arna Bontemps. New York: Hill and Wang.

Lauer, Janice. 1989. "Interpreting Student Writing." In *Encountering Student Texts: Interpreting Issues in Reading Student Writing*, edited by Bruce Lawson, Susan Sterr Ryan, and W. Ross Winterowd. Urbana, IL: National Council of Teachers of English.

Marius, Richard. 1992. "Composition Studies." In *Redrawing the Boundaries: The Transformation of English and American Studies*, edited by Stephan Greenblatt and Giles Gunn. New York: The Modern Language Association.

Ragland-Sullivan, Ellie. 1986. *Jacques Lacan and the Philosophy of Psychoanalysis*. Chicago: University of Illinois Press.

Skolnick, Arlene. 1992. "The Paradox of Perfection." In *Rereading America: Cultural Contexts for Critical Thinking and Writing*, edited by Gary Colombo, Robert Cullen, and Bonnie Lisle. Boston: Bedford Books of St. Martin's Press.

F rom the *Seinfeld* television series program titled "The Red Dot" comes this intriguing exchange between George and his potential employer, Lipmann:

Lipmann : Who do you read?

George : I like Mike Lupica.

Lipmann : Mike Lupica?

George : Yeah, he's a sportswriter for the *Daily News*. I find him very insightful.

Lipmann : No, no. I mean authors.

Since Lipmann is the senior editor of Pendant Publishing House and George is interviewing for a job as an Assistant Editor, the "real" meaning of the question has to do with George's qualifications as a literary agent. Yet, there is something in this exchange that always gets a laugh from my students, when I show the videotape in class, because they know George has dared to say out loud what he really, truly enjoys reading, which is not, as it is not very often in school, a real matter of interest. But, it could be. Television brings us its written and spoken literature in that medium, scripts and programs we tune into regularly, because we like them. I ask my students to write both about and for *Seinfeld*, for instance, analyzing characters, styles of sitcom humor, and relationships between subplots. Sometimes I ask them to write themselves into a brief *Seinfeld* scene and we read these in class, to learn more together about what makes a script work aloud, dramatically and humorously. Students feel as though they already know Jerry, George, Elaine, and Kramer, so they can just get down to the business of writing them into being once again, authoring and joining them in their fictional world of mishaps, mis-statements, and misadventures. I find them to be, as George says, very insightful about writing for television. The above format works well.

Barbra Morris
University of Michigan

12

Reading and Writing Back to the Future

Diana George,
Michigan Technological University
Saralinda Blanning,
Wright State University

> Here is a seldom mentioned but universally known fact of our profession, bluntly stated: The vast majority of our undergraduate students do not love or appreciate literature as we do.
>
> Dan Morgan

In the popular film *Back to the Future*, Michael J. Fox plays a character who has the chance to go back to the fifties with knowledge of the eighties. His initial confusion about time and place are eventually outweighed by the insight he brings to the past and then back to his present life. In the same way, as writing teachers who teach literature, we begin by abandoning the idea that we can read a text in historical or generic isolation. We acknowledge that we can only read past literature through the lens of the present, and we wish to teach our students what Fox's character learned: The past informs the present and the present re-forms the past.

The distress that is clear in the passage that opens our paper echoes a complaint that has become common these days, and though Dan Morgan clearly does not mean for it to, that complaint intersects well with arguments over core curriculum, multicultural education, and canon formation. In it, we sense a tenor of nostalgia, and yet we would not dismiss Morgan's worry lightly. It is true that like art, classical music, and much of philosophy, literature has become irrelevant and inaccessible to too many students. And yet, contrary to what Morgan suggests, our students are just as susceptible as are their teachers to the pull of literary expression. Any student, for example, might simply find a piece of beauty in something like nineteenth-century fiction, as did the student who, writing for a British novel course in the spring of 1993, found poetry in Wilkie Collins' *The Woman in White*. He added the following comment and poem to his final essay for the course:

> This little part I'm throwing on to the end is something that might interest you. Last spring term I took creative writing; the class dealt strictly with poetry. Randall Freisinger was the instructor. He said that taking prose and turning it into [poetry] was a legal way to make poetry. I think he meant it by using a couple of lines out of a prose as a base for a poem. Anyway, it being spring and all, I wrote a poem by taking some prose out of *The Woman in White*. The prose I took is from Walter's description of Laura when he first sees her.

Love

Think of her,
She will quicken
pulses within you
which none of her sex
had art to stir.

Let kind,
candid blue eyes
meet yours,
feel warmth pound
in your chest.

For whatever reason—the moment, the prose, Collins's story—this student became so engaged with the world of *The Woman in White* he was moved to find his own poetry in it. Neither the note nor the poem had anything to do with the paper he had written for the course. It was simply an opportunity for writing he could not resist sharing. That moment of engagement, the moment when the literature found its way into this student nearly as much as he found his way into the literature, is, we will argue, what can happen when writing teachers teach literature.

It is true, of course, that, in 1985 when Maxine Hairston first declared war on using literature in writing classes, many writing teachers thanked her. She had finally set composition free from the tiresome constraints of so many literature scholars and teachers. With that declaration she had insisted that teaching writing was a valuable task in and of itself that need not be validated by the inclusion of literary study. Her cry was taken up again nearly ten years later by Erika Lindemann who, at 4Cs and in *College English*, made many of the same arguments: Literature teachers do not teach writing, Lindemann proclaimed. They lecture too much. They teach imaginative literature that will not prepare students for writing tasks outside the English classroom. They are using the writing course to train teachers for literature departments.

At the same time, teachers of literature have been concerned that literature has dropped out of the curriculum as something that has any real meaning for our students. Morgan, for example, calls for teachers of literature to make their students *readers*, not *scholars*, and asks that we work at connecting literature with our students' lives. For writing teachers, that urging must have a depressingly familiar ring, for while Morgan does acknowledge that "many of the recent approaches used in composition can be adapted to the literature classroom" (496), he does little to explicate that connection for the study of literature, perhaps because (despite his insistence that individual students provide the only way into most literature) Morgan's focus is still more on the literature itself—the artifact—than it is on the student. The simple fact that Morgan can identify such tools and techniques as journals, collaborative learning, and portfolios as strategies of the *composition* classroom indicates how far apart the goals of writing courses often are from those of the literature course. As teachers of both writing and literature, we would argue that those goals can be more closely connected than they have been in the past. In addition, we believe it is less important to get students to "love or appreciate literature as we do" than it is to teach our students that they do have *access* to that literature; they have knowledge and skills that they can bring to bear on the literature they are reading. Strategies like reading journals, collaborative learning techniques, freewriting, and argument analysis that are common in composition pedagogy are just as crucial in literature classes to give our students their own ways into the literature. Once in, we find that students are quite good at making connections and at navigating the troubled waters of interpretation. They do know about meaningfulness. As well, like the student who made poetry from Wilke Collins's prose, they are touched by what they read. Too often, however, they have been locked out of that literature by courses that make the literary text a kind of icon, and the reader the worshipper of that icon.

During the spring of 1993, we taught the novels *Dr. Jekyll and Mr. Hyde* and *Frankenstein, or The Modern Prometheus* to two different kinds of classes at Michigan Technological University: a first-year writing and literature class and a third-year British novel survey. Because the two of us have backgrounds in literature as well as composition studies, our teaching has been informed by the coalescence of those two disciplines rather than the struggle so often outlined by writing teachers such as Maxine Hairston and Erika Lindemann. We would not say that what we do in a course like British novel changes what students learn about the traditions of British literature. It does, however, change the way we approach the text in this course and others. Our emphasis shifts from the literature itself to our students, the ways they interact with the popular culture texts that are so much a part of their lives, and the ways they might interact with literary texts through both personal and popular texts. Our goal, then, is to provide students with an understanding of literature that is elastic rather than static, a knowledge that can develop along with the students' intellectual growth. Thus, in both courses, we provided our students several kinds of entries into the literature, many of these informed by our practice as teachers of writing.

Back to the Future

By drawing on the lessons of composition studies, we know that students must start with their own knowledge and experience as a way of making literature relevant to their lives and their learning. As modern readers, for example, we are much more familiar with the subsequent distortions of *Dr. Jekyll and Mr. Hyde* than we are with Robert Lewis Stevenson's original story. We cannot have the same experience with that novel as did readers a hundred years ago because, without ever opening the actual book, most of us know that Dr. Jekyll and Mr. Hyde are not two but one—a man obsessed by his experiments concerning the separation of good and evil. We know that Jekyll becomes Hyde by drinking a strange and horrible potion and that Hyde is the evil counterpart of Jekyll. How do we know this? Some of us know it because we have seen any one or more of a number of film versions of the story. Others know it because they have watched Sylvester chase Tweety Bird around a cartoon lab where Tweety drinks a concoction he finds on the scientist's counter. In an instant, the tiny yellow bird turns into a giant, red-eyed, green-tinted, maniacal bird/beast who chases the now trembling Sylvester around and out of the lab. In fact, we can depend on most of our students being more familiar with Tweety than they are with Lon Chaney, Spencer Tracy, or Jack Palance as the misguided doctor. The ways in which they have encountered the Jekyll/Hyde phenomenon are, however, irrelevant. The important fact is that few readers today can pick up a copy of this novel in a classroom and experience the same suspense and surprise Stevenson's narrator Mr. Utterson experiences as he traverses paths of deception, confusion, and slow revelation.

The complications for contemporary students reading *Dr. Jekyll and Mr. Hyde* are straightforward: They know the conclusion of the book before they begin chapter one. With *Frankenstein* the complications of reading back to the future are not quite so straightforward. We have seen the movies, eaten *Frankenberry Crunch*, listened to the monster singing Christmas carols on *Saturday Night Live*—we know the scoop. We know that Frankenstein is a monster of the living-dead type, that he has a dark, ragged mop of hair, a square head, and bolts protruding from his neck. We've seen the moment of his creation: The mad scientist pieces him together, lays him out on a table, and brings him to life with a jolt of lightning or some other source of electricity. What we (and our students) know, of course, is who Frankenstein is in twentieth-century popular culture, but the monster was something quite different when Mary Shelley created him.

What most current readers do not know is that "Frankenstein" is actually Victor Frankenstein, the creator of a creature/monster bearing no name. Because they are so familiar with the twentieth-century Frankenstein monster, many of our students are initially disappointed by their first encounter with Shelley's novel. It is, after all, not what they might imagine it to be. The "creation scene," so glorified in the movies with bubbling vials, electrodes, lightning, and mad-scientist cackling in a dungeon-like laboratory, takes up no more than a single, quiet paragraph in the book. The monster is not a stiff, monolithic, non-verbal vehicle of destruction; rather, he is a lithe, pensive, sentimental, and verbally adept creature seeking love and acceptance. Shelley's book is a horror story and a love story, but it is neither Stephen King nor Danielle Steele. So how, as writing teachers who teach literature, do we help our students find value in a text like *Frankenstein* or experience revelation in a novel like *Dr. Jekyll and Mr. Hyde*, stories that can be simultaneously discovery and disappointment?

Dr. Jekyll Meets Oprah

In both classes, we wanted our students to establish their own knowledge base before they even read the original texts. We began, therefore, with our students as readers rather than with history or genre or biography—any of the more typical openings for literary studies. For *Frankenstein*, process began with in-class freewrites in which students detailed what they knew of or associated with "Frankenstein." They wrote about movies, Halloween, cartoons, all of the things any one of us might write about the monster we grew up knowing. The classes then watched portions of such films as the Boris Karloff version of *Frankenstein*, *Abbot and Costello Meet Frankenstein*, *Young Frankenstein*, *The Rocky Horror Picture Show*, and *Edward Scissorhands* to further remind them that they already know a great deal about the creature and the theme of a mad scientist driven to create life. They have seen this story before, and it can be serious or comic, fascinating or ridiculous.

Our purpose was neither to devalue nor exalt these modern texts. Instead, we acknowledged their fundamental role in any reading of the original work. For students in the upper-division British novel survey course, those early discussions of the Frankenstein myth, as it had been translated into the twentieth century, initiated examinations of how cultural, social, and generic concerns can change a story and the way it is told. British novel students might thereby be able to explain why, in a period of Romanticism surrounded by the most prominent Romantic poets of the age, Mary Shelley's creature would be tormented by alienation and desire and why Victor Frankenstein might urge Captain Walton to keep seeking unknown lands despite the fears of his crew. As well, these same students began to write about the demands of popular film and the fears engendered by modern science that might have led to the movie versions of Shelley's novel.

Both discussions allowed these students to place Shelley's story and Karloff's monster into contexts they could understand and write about. One student, for example, used his experience of watching films and television to explain why Karloff's monster is so different from Shelley's creature. In his analysis, he notes that any novel translated to film must go through what he called "pre-interpretation," a process by which the novel has been "interpreted by a writer, a producer, and a director. All of these interpretations eventually led to a warped version of the original . . . [to] keep the interest of the film audience." He took *Dr. Jekyll and Mr. Hyde* and Forsters' *A Room With a View* through the same discussion, always drawing on his knowledge of the conventions of popular film to support his position.

Throughout the paper, this student did not lose sight of the course's concern with literary history. He tells us, for example, that "The historical significance of [*Frankenstein*] also seems to be lost in the translation onto film. Somewhere in Hollywood, the movie gained a new set of moral lessons and values that correspond to those practiced in society at the time of production. The setting may be eighteenth-century England, but the feel is Twentieth Century Fox." In many ways, it is the confidence with which this student wrote about both novel and film that impresses us here. Without that confidence to make connections and judgments, students often struggle in their attempts to gain the access to literary texts that can make those texts meaningful for them.

For students in the introductory literature and composition course, the third in a series of three introductory writing courses, the discussions and writing were less concerned with locating the literature in a generic or historic context than they generally are in a course like British novel. The university catalog calls HU 103 "continued study of the composing process and of literature as an expression of human values." Thus, this course has the potential to take students beyond the standard composition classroom, as well as beyond the traditional literature classroom. We want our students in HU 103 to become engaged by the literature, but we also want them to be able to identify and articulate intellectual questions and issues embodied in those texts.

As one means of achieving that difficult combination, the instructor and the students created events that forged points of active discourse between the students and the literature they were reading. This discourse combined what we normally consider *composition* strategies (freewrites, response papers, journals, and collaborative learning activities) with typical *literary study* strategies (interpretation, analysis, and historical synthesis) in a way that gave students access to both writing and reading opportunities that connect with "real life." The first of these events (this one designed by the teacher) came to be called the "Monster Debate."

The overarching purpose of the Monster Debate was to explore the ethics of scientific and technological creation with a group of students whose primary academic focus is on science and engineering, one way of making the text relevant to their interests. The questions raised in this debate are common questions for students of science and technology: Who is responsible for development? Who is responsible for application following development? Who is responsible for negative repercussions of development? To introduce some of the complexities of the issues embodied in the text, the instructor urged her students to think seriously about the terrible events of this novel, including incidents of appalling prejudice (largely based on physical appearance), numerous murders, physical and emotional torture, and the abandonment of all responsibility for the creature. Using these offenses as a springboard, the class was given the task of *assigning guilt*—deciding who was responsible for what crime(s). They were then divided into the following five groups (with four students in each group):

1. *The Victor Frankenstein Group*: This group was to defend Victor against charges of neglect, irresponsibility, prejudice, and emotional torture.

2. *The Creature Group*: This group took the position of Frankenstein's creature and defended him against charges of murder and torture.

3. *The Creature's Victims*: This group, consisting of everyone killed by the creature, was to demand explanations for their murders, make accusations, and help decide guilt.

4. *Victor's University Professors*: The professors, having learned about Victor's research, were asked to discuss its importance to the academic community.

5. *The Moderators*: The moderators were asked to assure that the varied arguments, accusations, and defenses would all have a chance to be presented. They were free to call on groups, interrupt speakers, and otherwise control the flow of the debate as they saw fit.

Perhaps because of her own background in drama, the instructor encouraged her students to act the parts they had been assigned. For instance, all four members of the Frankenstein group were to pretend to be Victor Frankenstein, and each person in the "dead people" group was assigned a specific victim. The "dead people" were to think about how they would feel if they came back to life for a day to attend the debate. Although they would probably be angry, they might also be partial to Victor. Because of their relationship to him, they might be confused about whether to blame Victor or his creation. Students were advised to re-read portions of the book carefully to prepare for the debate and to come to class with relevant passages marked and notes detailing their strongest arguments. The groups were entirely responsible for running class on the day of the debate, and the teacher stepped aside to become a silent observer.

There were very few ground rules for this debate except that students were to keep the purpose (i.e., assigning guilt) in mind. Since this was to be a debate, it was not necessary (or even desirable) for groups to reach final conclusions, but they could push for conclusions if they wanted them. Perhaps the most difficult part of the debate for each group was that, though they were to put together the strongest arguments they could for the positions they were assigned, they would not necessarily be arguing for their own personal opinions. They were asked to try to understand the characters and their situations, and they had to use what they knew about human nature and the ethics of scientific research to help them argue their position.

On the day of the debate, students did, in fact, come well-prepared. They sat in a pentagon, with one group on each side. As the debate proceeded, groups asked wide-ranging questions: Was the creature supposed to be physically attractive? Who was responsible for the creature? Should Frankenstein have gone public with his research? Would people have thought Victor was crazy? Why couldn't Victor have made the creature a companion dog instead of a companion woman? For that matter, why did Victor start so big? Why didn't he create a mouse first? Some accused Victor of not adequately taking the implications of his research into account. Others countered by saying that knowledge in and of itself is not evil, but the use of it can be. Many suggested that, at the very least, Victor should have taken responsibility for educating and raising the creature, explaining that *nobody* grows up entirely alone. Still others dismissed the creature's murders as a "minor design flaw." It was clear that most students found support for their arguments in their academic disciplines and their personal lives, as well as in the text. One particularly amusing exchange occurred when the moderators asked the professors if they would advocate further research along these lines. One of the professors leaned back in his chair and with a crack of his knuckles explained that, before he could comment on the advisability of such actions, he and his colleagues would have to form a committee to examine the situation.

By the end of the fifty-minute debate, all but three students had contributed to the discussion (two of whom had very recently added the course.) Without any intervention from their teacher, these students had raised and begun to explore a number of sophisticated ideas and issues from multiple perspectives. Many of the students pursued the ideas raised in the debate more thoroughly in their response papers, as we will demonstrate later in our discussion. The kinds of connections they made and that exercises like the Monster Debate can encourage are connections that can make literature relevant to the lives of the students—connections that give students new ways to approach both their fields of study and their personal beliefs.

After the instructor-designed Monster Debate, students began finding contemporary avenues into this literature by designing their own events. One group, later in the term, used an Oprah Winfrey-like talk show they called *True Confessions* to examine *Dr. Jekyll and Mr. Hyde* in relation to the phenomenon of split personalities. A host began by introducing the show to the class and explaining that today's topic was "People with Multiple Personalities." Then she gave a concise (and well-researched) clinical explanation of what a multiple personality disorder involves. The co-host of *True Confessions* proceeded to introduce and interview the guests: Don Starling, a Ph.D. in electrical engineering, and Bedilia Jekyll, a college student. Don, an avid bowler, was involved in a court case where he was accused of hitting someone with his bowling bag. He explained that he was two different people, a sweet, kind person at home and at work but a vicious, violent person in the bowling alley. Bedilia, too, was two people, a studious, responsible student during the day, and a wild, out-of-control partygoer at night. Don claimed that his dual personality stemmed from his passionate love of bowling. Bedilia explained that she created her second personality with a potion that had been passed down in her family. She claimed she only used the potion to try to rid herself of evil.

After the two guests introduced themselves, the co-host turned to the class: "We go now to a classroom in the Walker Arts and Humanities Center for a discussion." As a vehicle for discussion, the cast of characters asked the class several questions: What are the characteristics of modern monster movies? What types of monsters are there? Which can't you kill? Which are classics? What frightens us now? How many of these monsters have "split personalities?" Is there realism in these monsters? Is "crazy" the same as "split personalities"? The co-hosts asked everyone in the class for answers to several of these questions, then wrote all of the answers on the board. These questions then became springboards for discussions about how Hollywood movies simplify the issues of good and evil, how we are all both good and evil, and how books and movies can reflect human nature in both exaggerated and simplified ways. The discussion even raised questions about what we consider "sane," how we define "crazy," and the difficulty of being "different" without being classified as crazy. The final question was about contemporary Jekylls and Hydes, and where we find them. One student called on contemporary news and entertainment for the answer: PeeWee Herman, child entertainer/porn moviegoer.

Making Connections

It is simply not the case that interpreting texts will help students gain confidence in interpreting the results of a chemistry experiment, a field experience in a psychology class, or a sculpture. (Lindemann 315)

Dan Morgan, whose remarks open this paper, argues that students need to "make thoughtful connections to their lives and concerns" (495) with the literature they are reading. We would agree, but emphasize here that there are multiple ways of making "thoughtful connections." For many of our students, the connections they make are less personal than they are academic- or discipline-based. At Michigan Tech, at least, students do seem to take much of their identity from the fields of study they have chosen. Our engineering students, for example, call themselves "engineers" and participate in professional activities such as industrial co-ops long before they graduate. Many identify themselves with science and math rather than with literature and art. As one student in a first-year writing class said, "They [engineering students] can *talk* math and science. I can't do that. For me when I finish my problems, the book goes on the shelf." In other words, students make connections on many levels and in many arenas of their lives, not solely the personal.

We would even go so far as to say that Lindemann might be wrong when she says, in the passage we quoted previously, that learning to interpret texts does not prepare students for work outside the humanities or literature classroom. One student from an earlier composition and literature class, in fact, argued just the opposite. He claimed that learning to read poetry had helped him solve college chemistry problems. According to this student, his high school chemistry had been easy but different from college work. In high school, he ran experiments and then wrote up what he saw happening in the experiments. In college, however, all of the problems were "word problems," which were extremely difficult for him to understand. When he saw how language worked in poetry, he was able to transfer that knowledge to chemistry and learned to pay more particular attention to the language in those word problems. According to this student's account, he was then able to solve problems that had baffled him earlier in the term. We would not argue that most students can make that kind of transfer. We suspect it is rather rare. Students do, however, make connections between what they know from one discipline to another, and that is something we can take advantage of in a literature course. Sean, for example, is majoring in nuclear physics. He included the following comment in the cover letter with his final portfolio:

> To be honest, as far as the question of what I've learned this term, there really hasn't been any bolt of lightning that said "hey—this is new." This doesn't mean that the class wasn't interesting and even, dare I say, fun. It's just hard for me to look at a literature/writing class and feel I really learned anything because the instructor is more of a guide than a teacher. They just help us to see things we already know.

While these comments might sometimes be discouraging for a teacher— "What do you *mean* you had no epiphanies in my class!"—they are rewarding for a teacher whose goal was to create a bond between the student and the text rather than to make students feel as if they are able to glimpse or grasp the teacher's bond with the text. Sean's comments are those of a student who is a confident and competent reader, a student who can apply the universally valuable tenets of critical inquiry to both *Frankenstein* and nuclear physics, as he demonstrates in the following excerpt from his response paper, "The Atomic Frankenstein":

> The government gathered the greatest scientific minds in the world and sent them off to New Mexico with the sole purpose of constructing this device [the atomic bomb]. . . These scientists were all much like Victor was. Consumed with the passion of discovery for its own sake, and also seeing possible good implications from their work as well. The only difference was that Victor had no intention of creating a weapon, the scientists did. Both were driven by their work in spite of its questionable morals and methods. Victor was forced to rob graves in order to create his creature, while the scientists in Los Alamos were creating what they knew was a weapon to destroy thousands of people at a time.
>
> At this point, many people may be easing up on their criticisms of Victor and putting them on the creators of the "bomb," which is not my purpose. The point that must be discussed is exactly what must be considered in science, and what scientists should be held liable for. Victor had good as well as greedy reasons for his work, as did the scientists. Both succeed in it; however, Victor hid his creation from the world and realized its potential for destruction. Many of the creators of the atom bomb petitioned the government to make their intention to actually use the bomb public knowledge in hopes of pressuring the government into taking their views into consideration. There were some, however, who felt as Victor did that the truth would only scare people. The end result was that both creations caused other people to be killed and all creators involved eventually tried to stop their creations in some way.

Although Sean says he had no dramatic revelations in this class, it is apparent from "The Atomic Frankenstein," as it was in many of his papers, that he connected to the literature. For Sean, *Frankenstein* became a text that commented on his academic and anticipated professional life despite the fact that the novel was written by a woman in the nineteenth century who knew little about science and nothing about nuclear physics. He was able to read this book back (back into Mary Shelley's world) and then into the future (his future): "They [literature/writing teachers] just help us to see things we already know." Yes, as teachers of literature enriched by composition pedagogy, that is what we aspire to do, to help students see the things they already know using literature as a magnifying glass. If, after that class, Sean has one more window through which he can view his life and career, one more way to address and process the complexities that he will face, then we can be satisfied.

But Sean is only one student, and we would like to convey some concept of the scope of the kinds of connections that students can and do make in literature classrooms informed by composition studies. Another student, who explained in her cover letter that she has "a tough time when it comes

to putting on paper what it is that I'm trying to say" wrote a response paper
she called "Cell Division of Dr. Jekyll and Mr. Hyde." In her response she
worked through some of the major events in *Dr. Jekyll and Mr. Hyde* by
comparing the story to cell division, specifically mitosis. Here her experience
with biology, a field where she feels comfortable and competent, helped her
feel more comfortable and competent as a reader and a writer.

Students in the British novel course, as well, extended their discussions
of the history of the British novel into their own worlds in whatever ways
they could make those connections. One (a student who had a special interest in psychology) connected the novels *Frankenstein, The Woman in White*,
and *Dr. Jekyll and Mr. Hyde* with the way we use darkness in this culture to
signify fear of the unknown. Another wrote about our need to pay attention
to the complexities of human nature as we read and judge the character representations depicted in novels like *Moll Flanders, The Woman in White*, and
Dr. Jekyll and Mr. Hyde. Many students worked to place novels and characters in their time and to explain why the actions and motivations of characters change depending on the cultural values of the times in which they were
written. In other words, our students always were aware that they did have a
way into these works even though the literature may have been written as
much as two centuries earlier.

We close with an HU 103 student whose portfolio cover letter asserts
what we have been struggling to illustrate in these many pages. Willie writes,

> I feel I have learned to write about a whole range of things. I came into this
> class thinking and writing about only nonfiction but after going through this
> class I have learned to appreciate fiction. At first I felt fiction had nothing
> to do with life and how we live, I have since found this to be wrong.

Willie's final essay demonstrates how he forged connections and how
others might do the same. In an essay that compares Stevenson's *Dr. Jekyll
and Mr. Hyde* (assigned in the class) to John Howard Griffen's autobiographical documentary *Black Like Me* (reading that Willie did independently),
Willie explores stereotyping, prejudices, and issues of masked identity.
Though the first two are not necessarily the themes most readers would identify as primary ones in *Dr. Jekyll and Mr. Hyde*, Willie located those themes
and used them to construct parallels between the world of fiction, in which
he discovered new promise, and the force of nonfiction, his original interest.

Perhaps it is true that, as Dan Morgan worries, "our students do not love
or appreciate literature as we do." Still, as writing teachers who teach literature, we would say that probably isn't something to worry over at all. Our
students love and appreciate literature as *they* do; it is *their* way of loving
and appreciating and connecting that we want them to discover. When we
teach literature, our goal does not change much from the goal we have in a
writing class: to allow our students to find the confidence to articulate what
they know. We want them to teach us what they know and how they see the

connections fitting with their lives, their chosen disciplines, their ways of understanding how people live together or not.

Works Cited

Collins, Wilkie. 1992. *The Woman in White*. Oxford Univeristy Press.

Hairston, Maxine. 1985. "Breaking Our Bonds and Reaffirming Our Connections." *College Composition and Communication* 36 (October): 272–82.

Lindemann, Erika. 1993. "Freshman Composition: No Place for Literature." *College English* 55 (March): 311–16.

Morgan, Dan. 1993. "Connecting Literature to Students' Lives." *College English* (September): 491–500.

Non-English majors often complain that literature and composition have no personal relevance. I wanted to change that perception by relating to my students that because literature reflects life in one way, it has relevancy to them. To achieve my goal, I decided to combine literature, composition, and interdisciplinary studies in my fiction course, and I chose Mary Shelley's *Frankenstein* as my tool. I proposed to show my students that some of Shelley's concerns of the early nineteenth century are also concerns of the 1990's. I assigned my students research essays that related one of the novel's issues or themes to issues in their particular area of interest (science, education, psychology, or sociology). The topics were inherently controversial and required the students to adequately substantiate their positions and to clearly connect their topical issue with the novel's issue.

Several students approached the Frankenstein monster as a modern-day social outcast: the disabled, the AIDS victim, the homeless. Other students took a modern psychological approach to examine the probable causes of the monster's change in behavior. Another interesting approach was an examination of Victor Frankenstein as a modern scientist, focusing on topics like cloning and *in vitro* fertilization.

The students were grouped by similar interests and issues for discussions and peer editing. The assignment, which lasted about four weeks, was a process of critical thinking, synthesizing, writing, and rewriting. The students were engaged in continuous writing and sharing of insights and ideas about the novel and their topics, and, most importantly, they were motivated by their personal area of interest.

Betsy Head
Texas Women's University
Denton, TX

13

Reinventing the Literary Text
Student Writers at Work

Brenda M. Greene
Medgar Evers College CUNY

Ah! too much things, Mr. Gentleman, too much things. First, there was Emancipation; then she husband, Cosway, dead—the plantation run over by bush like flies over dead carcass, then the lies, the gossip, the hatred of the colored people; then, after she get married, she son, Pierre, dead because of the fire. After he dead she turn like zombie.

—William

William, a student in my introductory composition and literature class, created this text for the character Christophine, the servant in Jean Rhys's *Wide Sargasso Sea*. Through the reinvention of this text, William is able to provide another dimension to the character. He is able to go beyond the surface level of Christophine's language in the novel and provides an imaginative description of what the underlying discourse would reveal. In other words, his response reveals what Christophine overtly and subtly articulates in the novel. William's effective depiction (through Christophine's eyes) of the plight of Annette, a white, widowed West Indian woman without land in postcolonial Jamaica, indicates that he is able to engage in a close reading of the text and "resee" the text from the perspective of the people who are silenced in the novel.

One of the challenges that has confronted me as a teacher of a composition and introductory literature course is how to help students write about literature from a critical standpoint—how to help them connect with a text and yet create enough distance from it to discuss the text analytically. Most of the writing I require from students who enroll in my composition/literature course involves responding to a theme generated from a poem, short story, or novel. Initially, many students write personal essays that illustrate the theme; others write plot summaries. They are not experienced in writing essays that incorporate the text and focus on its literary elements. It is very difficult for my students to move along the continuum from the personal to the analytical essay, and even more challenging for them to develop a voice to discuss the text analytically.

The reinvention of literary texts is a strategy that I have used in my course to assist students with the interpretation of literature. In this approach, I ask students to "resee" the literary text and to discuss or rewrite certain incidents in the text from the perspective of an underprivileged character or the hidden agenda of the major characters. This enables students to analyze literary elements and to examine the text from multiple perspectives. As students try on the voices of different characters, they gain a more thorough understanding of point of view, tone, mood, setting, style, and character development, and they evaluate how the writer's manipulation of these literary elements helps to heighten conflicts and develop specific themes.

The strategy of reinventing the literary text is not new. Historically, students have always attempted to create literary texts. Wayne Booth (1983) remarks:

> I do not see how any professor of "literature" can be satisfied at any level, but especially in the early years of college, with instruction that leaves the students passively observing techniques and effects in what they read without practicing those techniques and seeking effects of their own. (67)

As students in my classes reinvent literary texts, they actively participate in the reading process and thus practice those techniques that writers use as they create literature. They also expand on these techniques and attempt to analyze the themes that are not stated. In other words, as they reinvent the text from the perspective of different characters, they deconstruct the text; they try to discover what is not being explicitly stated. Their concern is to discover if the writer has a hidden agenda and to expose the contradictions, ambiguities, and ironies in the text.

The concept of creating enough distance to resee the text is drawn from composition research on revision strategies that writers use when they revise the texts of their peers. Research shows that writers find it easier to revise their peers' text than their own because they do not have the privileged information that prohibits them from "reseeing" these texts (Greene 1992); when writers revise their own texts, they have difficulty inhibiting their privileged information and therefore may not be able to see the problems inherent in their work. Since it is easier to "resee" the text of their peers, it is easier to make recommendations for revision. This research provides a premise for having students create the distance for the literary text that enables them to resee or reinvent the text from the perspective of a privileged or underprivileged character. In revising from another point of view, students have to uncover the subtext of the text. They have to determine what is not explicitly stated and use this knowledge to discuss or develop a scenario that reveals the subtext.

Research from post-structuralism also provides a premise for evaluating a text from a deconstructionist point of view. In "Composition and Decomposition," Miller (1983) notes that deconstruction is not a new activity:

> I speak of deconstruction as if it were one special technique of reading, but in fact deconstruction is a currently fashionable or notorious name for good reading as such. All good readers are and always have been deconstructionists. (43)

If we accept the observation that all good readers deconstruct the text, then providing students with opportunities to recreate an incident in a text from different points of view or from the perspective of different characters gives students a strategy for deconstructing the text. This allows students to reconceptualize the text and thus to view it from the perspective of the other.

William's adaptation and reinvention of Christophine's voice and language were created in a course in which students read novels and wrote essays and a major research paper. I used novels from a range of ethnic groups and periods and asked students to write essays and to create or revise literary passages from the perspective of different characters in the texts. As they composed or reconstructed, students reconceptualized dialogue, point of view, conflict, and theme. They manipulated setting, tone, and language to achieve their goals. The following provides a discussion of selected excerpts that illustrate students' reinvention of Rhys's *Wide Sargasso Sea*, Conrad's *Heart of Darkness*, and Chopin's *The Awakening*.

Wide Sargasso Sea, written from the perspective of a white Caribbean woman who wrote the novel as an imaginary depiction of the origin and plight of Bronte's mad woman in the attic, easily lends itself to reinvention. Students read the novel after reading Bronte's *Jane Eyre* and had a critical framework for interpreting the actions of the characters, the conflicts, and the themes.

The majority of students in the class were from some part of the Caribbean, and their discussion and reinvention of certain scenes reveal that they interpreted the novel as a depiction of the effects of slavery and colonialism during the period of post-emancipation in Jamaica, and as an illustration of the status of the white Creole woman in the West Indies. Students were asked to discuss the text from the perspectives of at least two characters by using an essay format or a written script. One of the most creative and interesting texts that emerged was one in which William adopted the voice of a

British reporter to conduct an interview with Christophine. The reporter has gotten Christophine to tell the story about the origins of another character, Annette (Mrs. Cosway).

William: Christophine, what was your opinion of Mrs. Cosway, Mrs. Mason, if you like?

Christophine: Mrs. Cosway, she a proud, pretty woman, that is the Mrs. Cosway I like to remember, before she mind crumple, and she fall apart.

William: You said she fell apart. What caused it?

Christophine: Well, Emancipation change everything. All the white people who used to own slaves feel the pinch. Nobody work particular: colored people walking round like big shots. A . . . few white people kill themselves very well. Mrs. Lutrell, Cosway neighbor, drown herself. Coulibri plantation when to ruin. Mistress had to sell of valuable things to stay alive. . . . She became like white cockroach.

William: White cockroach?

Christophine: Lordie, for she nothing in this world or the next worse than white cockroach. White cockroach worse than a knife in she heart . . . add to that the lies, the gossip, the slyness. She used to tell me: "Pheena, even when them people face serious, they laugh at you with their eyes."

In this excerpt, William captures the language of Christophine as she reflects on the status of the white Creole woman after emancipation. Through Christophine's language, the reader can empathize with the frustration, alienation, and anger felt by the white West Indian woman. One of the prevailing themes in Rhys's novel is that the white West Indian woman was oppressed because of her status in black society. A white woman with no money was belittled and treated as an outcast by blacks and whites. Through the use of dialect and sarcasm, Christophine reveals that underlying reason for the ostracism of the white West Indian woman. She can arouse these feelings because as a black woman who has survived slavery and who has witnessed its effects closehand, she is in a position to describe what it feels like to be oppressed, to be a "white cockroach."

William's dialogue also illustrates the extent of the negative and stereotyped perceptions that whites had for the blacks with whom they lived. After the slaves were emancipated, white West Indians were forced to address the fact that they no longer had a free source of labor to exploit, and they had to face economic hardships and the consequences of depending on people whom they had exploited for years. William's portrayal of Christophine reveals some of the conflicts, fears, and anxieties that accompanied the situations in which white West Indians found themselves.

For this assignment, several students used the following passage to discuss the relationship between the characters Annette and Mr. Mason, Annette and the natives of Jamaica, and/or the effects of slavery on colonial Jamaica. In this passage, Annette informs Mr. Mason that she wants to leave Coulibri. She states:

An agent could look after this place. For the time being. The people here hate us. They certainly hate me.

Mr. Mason responds:

Annette be reasonable. You were the widow of a slave-owner, the daughter of a slave-owner, and you had been living here alone, with two children, for nearly five years when we met. Things were at their worst then. But you were never molested, never harmed.

Mason continues with:

They're too damn lazy to be dangerous. . . . I know that.

Annette responds:

They are more alive than you are, lazy or not, and they can be dangerous and cruel for reasons you wouldn't understand. (32-33)

The following skit by Geri uses the character of Christophine to illuminate why Annette appears to be frightened of the blacks around her and why she wishes to leave Coulibri.

Christophine: You married Annette after five years of bad times here at Coulibri. After Mr. Cosway died dey nearly died. You knew she were poor. She called white cockroach. You knew she were hated by the whites here and jeered at by blacks of this island behind they backs. How jealous dey were.

Mr. Mason: I know she was poor and penniless after her husband's death. I think she was very beautiful and very lovely. She should have made the workers work the land.

Christophine: When she come to Coulibri, the white closed ranks cause she young and pretty. . . . They would have died without help. I help. Me, Godfrey and Sass. You say she not harmed before you come. How you know? Me tell you. They poisoned her horse so she couldn't ride about. Before that, the doctor come see Pierre and never returned again. That child he sick. He can't walk or talk straight. What doctor tell she, tore her apart.

Mr. Mason: Annette thinks leaving Coulibri will solve her problems. She thinks we should go to my estate in Trinidad or Antigua. That will not stop the talking. It's her imagination playing games. She

has been alone too long. Far from people of her kind. "Black people" as I must say are lazy. You people never molested her. She has
no real fear, but fear of being poor.

Christophine: The women here fear me. Dey think me obeah woman.

In this scene, Geri's tone and language reveal why Christophine is angry
and feels empowered to protect Annette and her daughter Antoinette. This
reinvented text refers to the spirit of obeah and its presence in the lives of
the island women. Annette, either intuitively or consciously, is aware of this
spiritual presence and recognizes the power of the island people. She, unlike
Mason, understands her place and her plight as a white West Indian woman.
Annette represents the institutionalization of slavery and is faced with inner
conflicts concerning her status. By providing this perspective of Christophine, Geri assists the reader in more easily seeing how slavery and colonialism have affected both the whites and blacks on this island. Rhys's novel
addresses this issue in a more subtle way, but Geri's reinvented text suggests
that this may be a major theme.

Lloyd, another student, refers to the theme of colonialization from a different perspective. He uses the passage between Annette and Mason to depict
black people's attitudes toward slavery and then emancipation in Jamaica.
His revision of the scene creates a hypothetical account of Christophine's
response to the conversation between Annette and Mason. In it, he supports
Annette's assertion that she is hated by the black people. Lloyd writes:

Christophine: Annette, you not hated by black people here for no reason. . . . You don't have to be fraid, Annette, all you have to do, is
change, you and other white people. And you Mister Mason, you
don't understand black people, cause you used to doing thing, white
people way. You fraid to understand them cause you don't want to
know them. You like other white people, you judge thing your own
way. If it ain't right to you, it no good. You people don't want to
like black people or even recognize them. That's always been the
problem with your kind. You don't want to recognize blacks as
human people. They never did nothing to you. Your people did
something to them. You say they no good, you say they lazy, cause
you see things your way, not they way. they can be understood if
you look at them as people and not as animal. You say: they too
damn lazy to be dangerous. I say you are wrong. What you see ain't
always there. What you believe ain't always true.

Lloyd dramatically captures the feelings experienced by the former
blacks of Jamaica. In Lloyd's passage, Christophine is protective of Annette,
but she still holds her accountable for the atrocities that she and her people
have bestowed on the blacks of Jamaica. Lloyd reveals Christophine's anger
at the whites' perception of the blacks around them. As a result of Lloyd's

reinvention of this scene, the reader is provided with a deconstructive reading of this text, with an alternative framework for analyzing the novel's theme, and, consequently, with the ability to gain insight into the view not explicitly stated.

Another student, Marie, also provides the reader with the black West Indians' feelings about slavery and post-emancipation. She writes:

> Christophine glares at Mr. Mason from across the room. She has no respect for him.
>
> "Yes, you tink we lazy, but we just sitting back and watch you mek fools of you selfs. No one has to invent stories bout you, we know weh you stand."
>
> Mr. Mason standing in the doorway, arms folded and legs crossed, right over left, raised his eyebrows and says: "You Christophine and the rest of the slaves need me more than I need you."
>
> "What gives you the right to enslave us and in the same breath demand respect?"
>
> Mason still in the same position at the door says without feelings: "You and your people are incapable of doing anything constructive without help."
>
> Through her blue-black skin you could see the fire flared within her, the muscles of her jaws move and her lips tighten, then slowly she said: "True, help, meaning the whip, that's because we allow it to happen and don't never say nothing, but things going to change."

Here we witness Christophine's anger and her resolve to change the situation. We also get a foreboding of the tragic events that follow: the destruction of the house by fire and the death of Annette's son.

Student's creation of dialects to deconstruct the text and provide for an alternative reading also helps them create complex characters and examine how language affects the meaning of the text. In creating dialect in the voice of a character, students must first create enough distance to examine critically the multiple meanings in the text. They can then go on to illustrate how the use of dialect reveals subtle themes in the text and forcefully and vividly captures the emotions and tensions felt by those characters who are not in the foreground of the novel. In constructing such dialect, students are also able to depict characters who are not merely one-dimensional representatives of a race of people. In Lloyd's text, Christophine is not simply a loyal servant who feels compelled to protect Annette. Christophine's character is symbolic—she is the embodiment of those blacks who were enslaved in Jamaica. Marie's use of dialect to portray Christophine's anger toward Mr. Mason also reveals a woman who is angry and has no qualms about conveying that anger. By using dialect, both students develop an in-depth portrayal of her character and a way for her voice to be heard loudly and clearly.

The use of dialect also encourages students to respond creatively and imaginatively to a text and to connect to a text that may initially appear to be distant from them. In depicting the language and views of various characters, students are able to explore ways of manipulating styles of language in order to create certain points of view. They can also explore ways in which the language of fiction is created, as well as create their own fictions.

Providing these students with opportunities to reinvent *Wide Sargasso Sea* gave them alternative frameworks for interpreting this text and for reading it more closely. Upon initially reading the novel, they saw it primarily as an extension of *Jane Eyre*. However, their analysis of the language and behavior exhibited by Annette and Mason helped them to reinvent texts that dramatically highlighted the psychological tensions inherent in the novel's characters. After analyzing the novel from varying perspectives, they posited that is was also about alienation, exploitation, and colonialism. Their analysis reiterated the value that "reseeing" a novel from a different perspective has for enabling students to read it more critically.

Conrad's *Heart of Darkness* is another novel that I used to help students interpret a text from the perspective of the underprivileged characters. Students were asked to write essays discussing how *Heart of Darkness* reveals the effects of colonialism from the perspective of either the Europeans, the character of Kurtz, or the native Africans. After giving a historical framework for the existence of colonialism, Mary wrote the following response:

> Colonialism was a traumatic experience, changing the course of history and generating what has been called a "colonial mentality," consciousness of defeat and inferiority. *Heart of Darkness* reveals in many ways the effects of colonialism on both the part of the colonizer and those being colonized.
>
> As seen from the perspective of the Europeans, colonialism facilitates and justifies the practice of racism. The colonizers have little regard for the people they are exploiting. For instance, the statement: "When one has got to make correct entries, one comes to hate those savages—hate them to death" reveals the colonizer's disregard for the Africans. This statement is made as one of the colonizers refers to a group of natives that has just arrived on a caravan. Degradation of the natives is favored by the colonizers because it gives them a sense of control and superiority. The natives are called niggers, ugly, and cannibals. They are not humans.
>
> The Africans see the effects of colonialism as a system designed for their destruction and for the betterment of their "white superiors." Colonialism makes them into subservient beings incapable of deciding their own future and faith. It also makes them become grossly dependent on their colonizers. The starvation and ultimately the death of the Africans is evidence of their new dependency on the colonizers. . . . The Africans after being deprived of their usual diet become sick and infected with disease. Now they are dependent on their colonizer for treatment, which of course is

never given to them. The Africans also see colonialism as a system that indoctrinates them into believing that the white group is superior or better than they are.

This excerpt from Mary's text suggests an important perspective for reading Conrad's novel, which is often read as an exposé and condemnation of colonialism. Mary's reading, however, also suggests that it reveals the racism inherent in colonialism. She illustrates that the colonizers have a contemptuous, superior attitude toward those whom they have colonized. In providing the Africans' perspective, Mary gives the reader an alternative reading of the novel, one that reminds us of the suffering and dehumanization endured by many Africans during colonialism. As readers, we receive the perspective of the other, of those characters who are not privileged. We gain insight into those voices we do not hear—voices that are invisible but audible to readers of Conrad.

James's essay on this assignment further illustrates how providing students with opportunities to explore alternative readings of a text enables them to examine it more closely and critically. The following text from James reveals how the actions of Kurtz and the Europeans offer insight into the minds of the colonizer and the colonized of Africa:

Colonialism is that economic system in which one country exploits the resources of another country primarily for the benefit of the exploiter country. This process generates a particular relationship between the two societies and it affects the lives of all the people involved. Individuals and groups may envisage these effects in some very unique ways.

The *Heart of Darkness* tells of the European colonization of the Congo region in Africa during the dawn of the twentieth century. The Europeans are conditioned to perceive the Africans as being primitive, uncivilized, and an inferior species of human. Armed with these preconceived fixations, they practice racism in its broadest form. The colonizers develop and establish institutions to promote their educational, religious, and economic systems. However, there are individuals who view the colonial experience from very personal standpoints.

Kurtz is one such colonizer. He is an ardent explorer who developed an obsession for venturing into unknown territories. His European education, in conjunction with his love for travel, make him the ideal candidate to serve the International Society for the Suppression of Savage Customs. Kurtz initially perceives the colonial service in a twofold manner. Firstly, the economic objective of securing as much ivory as possible and secondly, to compile a report on the appropriate methods to be employed in the suppression of the lifestyle of the Africans. This exercise provides Kurtz with the opportunity to practice racism in its most brutal form. The primary objective that he recommends in his report reads:

> We whites, from the point of development we had arrived at, must necessarily appear to them [savages] in the nature of supernatural beings, we approach them with the might of a deity. . . . By the simple exercise of our will we can exert a power for good practically unbounded . . . (45)

Kurtz uses his advanced weapons of war to subdue the tribes as he encounters them. He then creates an army of the vanquished to penetrate and plunder deep into the heart of Africa. His success in subduing the Africans creates in him a paternalistic attitude toward the Africans. He continues his plunder for the ivory but he no longer sees himself in the employment of the Society. He isolates himself from the world of the Europeans and cherishes his new god-like image.

His employers do not approve of his one-man crusade. They want his report so as to plan their long-term strategies to colonize, indoctrinate, and maintain total control over the new territories. Kurtz is aware of this, but his newly found prominence has become paramount. He now perceives Europeans as invaders into his empire and he mounts attacks against them to protect his world. The colonial experience has transformed Kurtz from an employee within the process to that of a ruler of the process.

While all this is happening, the lives of the Africans are experiencing many drastic changes. There are established African societies prior to the arrival of the Europeans. The large expanses of land and highly forested areas guarantee peaceful development of these various societies. Each tribe functions as a unit. It works as a self-sustaining community with its unique form of food-gathering, religion, government, and other cultural traits.

The Europeans initially lure the Africans with a peaceful attitude and inexpensive gifts of cloth and trinkets. The Africans provide the labor to secure the ivory for the Europeans who were unable to withstand the climate and new strains of diseases. Subsequently, the Africans are beaten into submission and are used in the conquering of other tribes. This certainly balloons into great animosity among the tribes. These expeditions for ivory and for plunder cause many villages to be abandoned, their people and culture ofttimes destroyed. The Africans become subservient and develop a sense of inferiority. Their material well being is no longer supported by the self-sufficiency of their tribe. They are now appendages to the new economic system of greed of the colonists. The negative effects of colonization permeate the African psyche throughout the world.

In discussing this novel from the perspective of Kurtz and from the perspective of the European, James provides the documentation for and expands upon a major them in the novel. He discusses the interrelationship of colonialism, paternalism, and racism, and he illustrates how all three "isms" assist the reader in interpreting the personal conflicts of Kurtz, one of the major characters of the novel. The narrator Marlow's descent into the Congo provides the reader with the evidence to support Kurtz's character change; however, James expands upon Marlow's account and gives the reader an account of the internal struggles and conflicts encountered by Kurtz. By creating a reinvented text—by imagining what is not written—James provides an alternative interpretation to the events of the novel, one that is not provided by either Kurtz or Marlow. I believe that asking students to reinvent an aspect of this text assisted them in more thoroughly understanding the effects of racism, colonialism, and paternalism in the novel.

Thus far, I have discussed how literary texts can be reinvented by rewriting a passage from the perspective of another character or by discussing the text from the point of view of an underprivileged or minor character. These reinventions involved using characters who were in the text. I applied a slightly different strategy when I used Kate Chopin's *The Awakening* to provide students with ways to interpret a text from multiple points of view. In responding to this novel, I asked students to create a description of what the story might have been like if it had been written by a male. The novel centers on a woman's search for a unified self in a male-dominated society. The major character, Edna Pontellier (a mother and the wife of Leonce) , is involved in a loveless marriage. She recounts her feelings of trying to understand the emptiness she feels and find meaning in her life. Unable to come to terms with her dilemma, she commits a tragic "selfish" act. Larry wrote the following in response to this assignment:

> *The Awakening* was written in 1899 during the time that women were not permitted to voice their thoughts about secret passions or emotions publicly as the author Kate Chopin discovered when she became a victim of that society's shocked and angry response. Her book was considered unacceptable and was taken off the shelves in the Mercantile Library in St. Louis, and she was barred from the Fine Arts Club.
>
> From a male perspective, this action was undertaken to teach those women that the time had not arrived when a patriarchal society would tolerate disrespect of the male image, or even that of a wife and mother who displayed reckless and wanton behavior publicly, or by using frankness of speech, whether written or spoken, or anything else that meant that a woman was acting out of place.
>
> Thus, from a male point of view, Edna's character would be toned down to the point that at the very beginning of the story, Mr. Pontellier (Edna's husband) would not have been made to be a push-over. Leonce might have pursued Edna's hand with ardor, but not to the point of absolute devotion. It would have gone against the grain of his manhood to permit Robert Lebrun, a male younger than himself, to spend so much time alone with his young wife, and not think that something was between them. He would not be as liberal as the author makes him.

A male writer perhaps would have been piqued with a pang of jealousy and would not have allowed Leonce later to say to his wife when he was going out: "Well, send him about his business when he bores you, Edna." (21)

A male writer, early on, would have led Mr. Pontellier to speak out against Edna's behavior. Leonce, rather than speaking out against his wife's behavior ". . . thought it very discouraging that his wife, who was the sole object of his existence, evinced so little interest in things which conerned him, and valued so little his conversation." (23)

The male writer would not have not let Edna get away with these flimsy excuses for her impulsive actions of infidelity with Robert Lebrun and Alcee Arobin when her husband was out of town. Throwing parties and inviting a man over to the house were not the order of the day for a woman of her financial stuatus, which Mr. Pontellier held in such high esteem that he had to lie about her moving out of the house. He stated that the house was being renovated, and that they were going abroad for the summer to wait until the house was ready to move into.

Furthermore, a male writer would not have let Leonce go away for such long periods of time, especially in the summer. . . . Edna would have to be with him wherever he was, because of their age difference and his fear that she would become bored and seek the attentions of a younger lover.

In conclusion, a male writer would not have allowed Edna to escape the wrath of a husband who in his eyes had been made a spectacle in public, whose wife had defied all the rules of society as far as what a "real woman" was supposed to be like, and had done just as she pleased, whenever she pleased, and with whomever she pleased.

In reconceptualizing this novel from what he views as a traditional male perspective, Larry reveals that powerful statement that Chopin made in writing a novel in which a woman defies all social norms and chooses personal freedom over conformity. Rather than address the reasons for Edna's personal conflicts, Larry suggests that because of cultural conditioning, a male writer would not have been able to write such a story of a woman's inability to resolve her inner conflicts. He posits that a male writer would find it difficult to create a situation in which Edna has the freedom and the "space" to reflect on her inner conflicts and to spend time in the company of another man. According to Larry, a male writer would portray Edna as a woman who conforms to the traditional norm in spite of her conflicts. He would ensure that Edna's attempt to defy the traditional norm would be met with scorn and criticism. He would not depict Edna's husband as liberal and would make her pay the consequences for choosing freedom over conformity. Larry's reinvention of this novel indicates what he believes would happen in the patriarchal society of 1899 to women who were more concerned with self than society.

Reinventing provides my students with an important "way into a literary text." It enables them to connect with the text and to read it more closely in order to uncover its multiple meanings, ambiguities, assumptions, and contradictions. It also helps to demystify the literary reading process. My students come to realize that there are many readings of a text and that careful readers take this into account and learn to base their responses in informed readings. As they become proficient in reading and responding to literary texts, they begin to see the validity of their responses and interpretations. The process of taking on the voice of characters and creating an imaginative dialogue connects students to the text, instills them with confidence in their writing ability, and provides them with further validation of their ability to respond to texts in a critical way.

Because many of the texts that my students create do not typify traditional academic writing, I do not evaluate these texts in the same way in which I evaluate their formal texts. The more formal texts, in which students write essays analyzing the points of view of two or more characters, are evaluated in a traditional way. I determine whether there is evidence that the student has responded to the question, presented and sustained an interesting coherent argument, and written a text that is relatively free of grammatical and mechanical errors. The imaginative literary texts that students create, on the other hand, may be written as response papers or as in-class writing assignments after we discuss a text together. I evaluate them in terms of a student's ability to capture a character's language in order to create a dialogue that incorporates what has been left out. I want to see whether adding other dimensions of characters enables students to deepen their critical response to a novel.

Before I respond to students' work, they read their texts in peer groups and select those texts they want to share with the entire class. I then become the next audience. This process of reading, responding to, and sharing papers in the class provides a way for students to socially construct their interpretations of the novel. In this way, students build upon and expand their interpretations and come to understand and appreciate the value of multiple levels of reading.

If reading is a way of writing and writing a way of reading (Miller 1983, 4), or if, as Scholes reveals, as writers we are always reading and as readers we are always writing, then providing students with opportunities to rewrite literary texts from varying perspectives or points of view is a natural way of sustaining the dialectical relationship between reading and writing. Writing teachers who teach literature can draw from research and pedagogy in composition to create a setting and learning environment that encourages the reseeing, revising, and reinvention of varying texts. Providing students with opportunities to reinvent literary texts from varying perspectives is a way of giving them strategies they need to "read like a writer"—to anticipate the reader's response and to uncover the writer's hidden text.

Works Cited

Booth, Wayne C. 1983. "LITCOMP: Some Rhetoric Addressed to Cryptorhetoricians About a Rhetorical Solution to a Rhetorical Problem." In *Composition and Literature*, edited by Winifred Bryan Horner. Chicago: University of Chicago Press.

Chopin, Kate. [1899] 1993. *The Awakening*. Boston: Bedford Books.

Conrad, Joseph. 1989. *The Heart of Darkness*. New York: St. Martin's Press.

Greene, Brenda M. 1992. "Empowerment and Problem Identification and Resolution Strategies of Basic Writers." *Journal of Basic Writing* (Fall).

Miller, Hillis J. 1983. "Composition and Decomposition: Deconstruction and the Teaching of Writing." In *Composition and Literature*, edited by Winifred Bryan Horner. Chicago: University of Chicago Press.

Rhys, Jean. [1966] 1982. *Wide Sargasso Sea*. New York: Norton.

Scholes, Robert. 1991. Speech delivered at NCTE Summer Institute for Teachers of Literature.

IV

Writing for Personal
Knowledge

14

Breathing Life into the Text

Peter Elbow
University of Massachusetts
at Amherst

For a long time after college, I thought that "holding a discussion" was the most noble and useful way to deal with a literary text. I got this attitude, I think, from attending an "excellent," high-toned college, Williams College, where discussions were taken with enormous seriousness. They were powerfully conducted, led, induced, orchestrated by dedicated and often brilliant teachers. These teachers usually had a plan for their discussions, but they didn't bulldoze; they worked with subtle finesse so that these discussions often led to lively eruptions of energy and interesting, surprising insights. (One other thing: I've been left with a kind of subliminal sense that a good discussion always starts with a particular word, intoned either with gravity or irony: "Gentlemen, . . . ")

Maybe if I could pull off with my students what they did with us, I'd still think of discussions as the ideal—though I doubt it. Anyway, since I've been involved in writing and teaching writing, my sense of an ideal classroom has changed. I've come to want some kind of *workshop*. That is, my ideal act of teaching is to get people to have an experience, not just talk. In a sense, of course, I've just made a false dichotomy: Talking *is* an experience; everything we do is an experience—even listening to a lecture. But that's a theoretical point and it involves taking the concept of experience in its broadest sense. As we normally talk and feel things, most students in most lectures and discussions don't in fact experience much: What is said doesn't matter or doesn't affect them much. I want a classroom where more happens, more matters—and where, in a literature class, the texts we read make a difference to students.

I'm grateful to people I've worked with in using and playing with these approaches: most of all to my students, but also to Nona Feinberg, Charles Moran, Jane Tompkins, and Betsy Wallace.

Having come to this pass, I now consider the following four activities as central in the teaching of any text—literary or not. I can't do all four in a fifty-minute class (but I could in a two-and-a-half-hour seminar). And I don't intend for these activities to *replace* discussions, just augment them. (I guess I do want to replace lectures.)

I. Helping students take possession of the territory before they read the text.

The usual pattern in literature classes—indeed, in almost any kind of class in any kind of school—is to read a text first and then write afterwards in response to it. And even if the text we read is imaginative, the writing is usually expository and critical. I hear two messages in this conventional arrangement. First, "The role of writing is to serve reading." Second, "*We* cannot enter the same discursive territory that the 'literary artist' occupies." I want to jostle these assumptions and I think I can do so—can make subtle but profound changes in the spirit of the teaching situation—if I put writing *before* reading and give ourselves permission to write imaginatively. (I'm indebted to Jane Tompkins for the apt phrase, "taking possession of the territory." For more on this argument and this approach to texts, see my "Questioning Two Assumptions of the Profession" and "The War Between Reading and Writing—and How to End It.")

Before I ask students to read the text, I like to ask them to write on the *theme* or *issue* that is central to the text. I try to give students a choice between a broad invitation to the general terrain ("Write about a time of being in love"), and something more narrowly focused on the particular approach of the poem or story we are going to read: "Write a declaration of love"; "Write a complaint about rejection"; "Write a 'Dear John/Jane' poem"; "Write a persuasion to bed." Some students benefit from a broad choice, but others have an easier time getting going if there is a narrower constraint. (Sometimes the constraint helps by providing something to resist. I seem to need the narrower constraint to get going—but then once going, I often need to violate it.) I *invite* students to write from their own experience, but also invite them equally to make something up: "Feel free to take on another voice and *imagine* someone persuading someone else." If we're reading a poem, I invite but don't push students to use some kind of verse: "Try writing in some kind of verse form—perhaps free-floating lines. But it's okay to use prose, too." (I learned this whole approach from Charles Moran, who pioneered using writing in this way.)

Once when I was teaching *The Tempest* I was struck with how the students couldn't enter into the play at all. In particular, I could tell that they were irritated at Prospero, but because they felt he was the "hero" of a "great work," they tended either to defer to him and point out "virtues" in him that they didn't really believe— or else just rail against him. The next time I taught the play, I asked students, before we turned to the play at all, to write two or three pages at home about the longest grudge they have been holding: "With whom? About what? What does it feel like? Can you imagine being over it? What would it take?" This led to interesting and satisfying pieces of writing; students got involved and enjoyed hearing some of each others' pieces. When we turned to *The Tempest*, suddenly they took Prospero much more seriously; they had a much more complex relation to him. They saw what they didn't like, but they also identified with him. Obviously, this writing activity didn't bring out all the important things in the play, but I didn't try to pretend that this issue was *the* central one (though it seems to me what James would call the *donnée*). I was simply trying to *open the door* to the play so that students would *experience* the text in a way that they didn't before. Having done this, I could move on to other issues in the play.

Sometimes I'm completely frank about what I'm doing and why. "Before we turn to _____ by _____ , I want us all to do a piece of writing on a theme in that work. I'm doing this because I've discovered in my past teaching that students sometimes treat literary texts as 'objects under glass'—as 'museumified'—and then you don't get much from them. I think you get the most out of literary texts when you come to them as fellow writers—when you can turn to Shakespeare's play and say, 'Oh, I see you are writing about jealousy. I know something about being jealous—and even writing about being jealous. I may not have experienced it as Othello did or written about it as well as you did, but we are working in the same world here.'"

But sometimes I'll just jump in with no explanation. Perhaps even start off the semester writing on a theme of a work that won't come up for a number of weeks. That is, I think it helps their reading and discussion most if they write about it without being under the shadow of the "great writer"— without a sense that some "author" "owns" this territory. I'm trying to send the message that it's everyone's territory. I find this particularly useful when we are dealing with canonical texts—texts that the culture has in fact already put under glass. But this kind of writing is also very gratifying with unknown and unhallowed texts: Students sometimes feel more on their own footing with them.

"But their writing is so paltry compared to Shakespeare!" I don't find it a problem that young students are not great writers. I'm not asking for fine works of art. Indeed, I usually ask for fast first drafts—even uncompleted sketches. In short, no one is pretending here. We're trying to get the feel of a territory. I'm also—and perhaps this is more important—trying to set up the conditions where students will risk *having* an experience. (Thus it's important that I take the risk of writing my sketch, too—and sharing it.) What's striking to me and to students in the room is not that they have failed to turn out great literature, but that many of the pieces are remarkably satisfying to hear or read, and even effective informal pieces of writing in their own right.

Because these assignments can seem intimidating to some students, I tend to start them in class—sometimes spending as long as twenty minutes writing. It often helps to ask three or four students to share just a few lines or snatches of what they have written after five or ten minutes. Hearing these rough bits of writing serves to prime the pump for others. "Oh, I see. That's not great writing, but it's fun. I could do that." I've learned that people are braver about jumping in if the spirit is playful and we are often settling for short, incomplete pieces. But it's nice to ask people, by the end of the semester, to choose a couple of these sketches to revise into something more finished.

Of course, I can't grade these pieces, but I can insist that students *do* them under heavy penalty of downgrading. I usually find some class time to hear at least a few of them, and I encourage but don't require students to share their pieces with at least one other student in pairs or small groups. I find it a pedagogically helpful enterprise to *require* things that I don't *grade*.

II. Helping students notice and articulate their perceptions, reactions, and responses to a text.

Because of the emphasis on process in composition over the last twenty years, it's become much easier to dispel the myth that texts are magically produced by means of genius or "knack"—the myth that real writers find or create great meanings in their head and then clothe these meanings into text. We've been able to show how most writers engage in a process that students too can participate in: starting with incomplete pieces of feeling, impulse, meaning, and intention—and gradually building them into completed texts; letting the process of writing itself lead them to ideas and structures they hadn't planned at the start. And there's always negotiation with oneself—and often with others.

But it's still difficult to see this process in *reading*: to see how readers, too, actively create and negotiate meanings in texts; how the meanings of texts are not just found as inert right answers sitting there hidden in the text or in teachers' minds or in works of authoritative criticism. The reading process seems more hidden and magic—and sometimes *seems* instantaneous. When we pass our eyes over easy and unambiguous words and phrases, their meanings seem to appear instantly in mind. Students often feel that teachers and critics can engage in this same instantaneous process with hard literary texts, that "good" or "authoritative" readers have a genius or a "knack" for "finding" the right meanings in hard texts—while they themselves as students can't find the meanings because they haven't got this genius or knack.

Reading may look passive: We sit quietly and let the image of the words print itself on our retina and thus pass inwards to our brain. But of course reading—indeed all meaning-making—is a deeply active process of exploration. In fact, when students have trouble reading it's often because they've been mistakenly *trying* to be passive—trying to make themselves like good cameras, that is, trying to become perfect little photographic plates on which the meanings on the page *print themselves* with photographic accuracy. Because reading doesn't work that way, their performance suffers when they try to operate on that model. "Hold still. Don't jiggle." Good advice for old cameras; not good for seeing or reading. The more jiggling, the better.

It's fun to point out the findings of cognitive psychologists: Any act of seeing or "making sense" of what is around us is always a process that occurs in stages—through the passage of time—not instantaneously like an image passing through a lens. In the first stage, our mind takes in the first pieces of information—the first trickles of electrical impulses—and quickly makes a guess, a hypothesis, or a "schema" about what we might be looking at. Then the mind repeatedly checks this guess against further information that comes in. Often we have to change our guess or hypothesis as new information comes in—before we "see what's really there." If plain seeing and hearing are such time-bound, exploratory processes, so much the more so for reading. It's obvious that we cannot take in any text all at once. When we read words or hear them, we *understand what we expect to understand*—till evidence forces us to revise our expectation. Thus the huge effect of culture, gender, race, class, sexual orientation, and so forth. (For example, male and female readers often have different reactions to the same passage.)

I used to make this case conceptually to students. I thought I was convincing, but I gradually saw otherwise. What I've discovered (or rather rediscovered from my writing workshops where I stress "movies of the reader's mind" [see *Writing with Power* 255ff]) is a way to help students *experience* this crucial bedrock fact about reading. I can help students abandon their magical model of the reading process by actually demonstrating to them experientially how all readers gradually construct the meaning of the text over time—just as writers do.

I create a laboratory in the reading process. I present a text to students one position at a time and ask them to pay attention to the process by which they gradually construct the meaning. In effect, I am using a slow-motion camera to show how we all tend to make hypotheses and then change our mind in the act of reading further. That is, if we only see the first few lines or paragraphs of a text and we take the trouble to articulate what reactions, meanings, and expectations occured in us, and if we go on to succeeding pieces of the text and do the same thing, we notice that later pieces of text force us to change our reactions and interpretations for earlier bits. Unless we go through this admittedly artificial, slow motion exercise, we often forget about those earlier reactions, meanings, and expectations because we revised them so quickly. Indeed, those earlier responses were often subliminal.

Therefore, I often cut up a text and pass it out, one section at a time. I ask students to take a few minutes to write out as full and accurate an account as they can of *what was happening* in their mind as they read each fragment—to "give movies of the mind." I need to encourage them not to leave out mental events that might seem stray or irrelevant; otherwise, they may only write down things they associate with English classes—and leave out odd memories and associations or even daydreams. The point is not to worry about the relevance or usefulness of the reaction: If it happened, write it down. *Nihil humanum.* . . .

This exercise helps students come into better possession of their own perceptions and responses—before there is much discussion and conclusion-drawing. Sometimes we have some sharing and discussion of reactions before students have seen the whole text—especially in pairs or small groups; sometimes I hold off any sharing or discussion till the end. I love seeing the play of divergence and convergence: Sometimes it seems like all idiosyncrasy—as though no one is reading the same text; sometimes there is amazing commonality. Usually there's an interesting mixture of the two.

Obviously certain students are better than others at making sense of hard texts (and of seeing rich implications in easy texts), but what less experienced students see is that the *process* used by skilled students is not magic. Movies of skilled students' minds are usually movies of people making multiple starts, multiple hypotheses, being playful, and being flexible about changing their earlier ideas on the basis of later input. In a sense, skilled readers usually have more "wrong answers" in that they have more associations, more hypotheses to start with, and therefore end up abandoning more. And it's palpably obvious that when skilled readers engage a text, they do not enter some "other" "literary" world or "artificial space"; they attend to and consider *lots* of feelings and reactions and memories that unskilled readers often push away as "inappropriate" for "literature."

I'm trying to inject a spirit of *charitable empiricism* into the process of responding to literature (as I've been trying to inject it into the process of responding to the writing of colleagues in writing workshops). "We are not looking for what's right but for what happens. Eventually we can talk about which larger interpretations seem more persuasive or plausible. But for now we're trying to learn to attend better. This is all about paying better attention." I'm trying to help students see that the human mind is never stupid or random. Every reaction, response, and interpretation that occurs makes perfect sense in the light of whatever else is in our mind (and *not* in our mind). I try to help students see how all their reactions make sense—however idiosyncratic they are.

This process leads to interesting discussions about cultural issues. When students pay better attention to their actual responses at what we might call the micro level, they can see more vividly the powerful influences on their minds. Not just the influence of media and common cultural conventions and clichés, though these are important. The same image may trigger very different responses according to gender, class, race, or sexual orientation.

Obviously, this process enriches the discussion. It gives enormous particularity to responses and gets us beyond *global* responses like, "It was scary/ironic/beautiful/sad." Or, to get down to a crass but nitty gritty reality of teaching, it gives students too much to talk about rather than too little— for any subsequent discussion or writing assignment. It helps students and the class become awash in very particulate literary data.

Someone might object, "You are inviting students to drift completely away from the text and attend only to their own reactions. This is not practice in reading, only in self-absorption." I suppose this is a danger, but it's not hard to avoid. I need to remind students to keep reading: "Read it again. See what happens when you read it again." Someone might also object, "You are sending the message that it's fine to be lazy about reading; that there's no need to work, think, struggle, analyze; that it's enough to relax and just notice what happens." It's true that I'm happy to help students not to *clench* as they read and not to feel they should go into some special or artificial "interpretive gear." I want to teach them that the process of responding and interpreting is built out of the everyday operations of the mind. But the process does not militate against thinking and work. The noticings *lead to* thinking—especially in the discussion where people compare responses. And I'm not saying, "Notice what happens when you relax lazily with a text," but rather, "Notice what happens when you struggle to figure it out." Actually, one of the issues that often surfaces is talk between students as to whether they experience this as "school thinking" or "regular thinking"—and the mental differences involved.

Sometimes students themselves object, "But this is so artificial! It makes me think of things in reaction to the text that I never would have thought of if I'd read it normally." I love to respond to this. "Reflect," I say, "on those things you thought of that you wouldn't 'normally' think of. Did I or the exercise *put* anything in your head that wasn't there already? I didn't add anything. Any 'new' or 'odd' reactions, feelings, thoughts, or memories were already in your mind anyway. I merely interrupted you and made you pause so that more of what was in your mind came to conscious awareness. The whole point of the exercise is to notice things that were already influencing your 'normal' fast reading—but doing so in ways that are below the level of awareness. What's new are not those odd reactions, feelings, thoughts and memories; only your awareness of them. There are no meanings *in* words, only meanings people bring *to* them. And the meanings people bring are their own meanings—amalgams of their own individual experiences."

I find it helpful to go through this process with a text that *I* haven't yet seen (having a student choose a text, divide it into sections, and bring in copies for all of us to work on). This lets students see me having initial reactions, responses, and interpretations that later turn out to be inappropriate or

plain wrong. It is important to engage in this exercise a number of times—
starting early in the semester. Students get better at it.[1]

III. Asking students to render, enact, or perform the text.

What do we mean by skill in reading? At one level, we mean skill in getting
meanings from the text. But at another level, we mean more—we mean
experiencing those meanings or feeling some relationship or involvement
with the meanings. To put it negatively, there are two problems in reading,
not getting it and not "getting it." No doubt, the first problem of not figuring
out the literal meaning is more serious than the second one. When we suffer
only from the second problem, we can understand the text, we know what it
says, we can summarize it and perhaps even answer some analytic questions
about it; but we are not making any contact with it or letting it make contact
with us, not getting a felt experience from the words, not being able to feel
any sense in which the words make a difference.

Interestingly enough, those students who tend to have difficulty with the
first problem often do fine with the second one. That is, once they manage to
understand the text, they naturally make contact, they let the text touch them,
they can invest. But students who have *no* difficulty with the first problem of
merely understanding meanings often suffer badly from the second one. This
is not really surprising. For the fact is that the best way to understand lots of
meanings as quickly and efficiently as possible is to remain relatively unin-
vested and untouched by them. In short, sometimes students find that they do
better in school if they don't take texts too seriously or feel their impact too
strongly. Experiencing texts often slows them down and makes it harder for
them to "cover" everything the teacher wants them to cover—and sometimes even leads them to resist the interpretations that the teacher wants them
to make. But when some students don't get the meanings at all and others
don't experience or invest in the meanings, discussions and essays can be
pretty dull and unprofitable.

We've long understood in writing classes that students often get more
benefit from feedback when they read their text out loud than when they just
hand it to readers on paper. It's a simple fact that when we read a text out
loud we almost inevitably *experience* more richly and fully the meanings of
the words we ourselves wrote. Indeed, the act of reading a sentence out loud
(unless we are repeating the words in a rote, meaningless way) tends to make
the mind *create* meaning and coherence. Reading out loud helps with *both*
the first and the second problems in reading. Many poets have long insisted
that poems ought to be heard, not just read silently.

For many years, then, I have stressed the reading out loud of texts in
writing—and literature classes too. But in the last few years, since I've

become particularly interested in the role of the human voice in language, my goal has escalated. I can't help thinking about the voice as physical and part of the body. I've come to think that the ideal classroom somehow involves some kind of embodying and enacting. I've come to find it profitable to set students the task in small groups of finding a way to present or render or enact or embody the text (or part of the text if it is longer than a page or two). I steer away from the word "perform"—not just because it often makes students feel more nervous, but also because it stresses the theatrical more than I care to.

It helps when I lay out for students a range of concrete possibilities or options. "If you want to cop out, you can just persuade one member to read it—or just do a choral reading. If you want to be really adventuresome, you can give a completely wordless version in movement or dance or gesture. After all, it's not really necessary to utter the words; the audience already knows the text. Between these extremes there is a rich assortment of other possibilities: Use different speakers for different parts—perhaps to enact a kind of dialogue between different parts of the text so as to show how different sections or dimensions or voices in it are responding to each other; 'double' certain words, lines, or sections of the text with extra voices in order to produce certain emphases; repeat certain words or sections over and over as a kind of 'ground base' underneath a reading of the whole; read the text so that certain lines or sections overlap or are heard against other parts, as when singing a round."

I make it clear that it's perfectly fine to rearrange the words—creating different orders among words or sections. (What do we notice if someone reads it backwards?!) It's alright to add or weave in other pieces of language that are *not* part of the text: bits of translation or adaptation, bits of other texts or pieces of one's own responses to the text that somehow seem illuminating or interesting, bits of discourse or language that this text might be responding to (*à la* Bakhtin).

I invite a loose and playful approach. I want to allay nervousness and I actually enjoy getting away from a reverent stance—from an attempt to "do justice" to the text. Students throw themselves into these renderings with gusto. It's true that this approach opens the door to the parodic. (I learned that most of Emily Dickinson's lyrics can be sung to "The Yellow Rose of Texas"!) But in fact I don't mind an element of parody, especially when texts are "high literature." In a sense, I want students to "domesticate" these high works, take them off the pedestal, treat them familiarly. But I know some drama teachers who make performance central to their teaching and give a somewhat more serious air to the enterprise. They get excellent results. (They have theater training and I do not.) Sometimes I give students just fifteen minutes of class time to prepare a quick version of something short. But when I give groups more time—for example, asking them to meet outside of class—they often achieve something more ambitious.

I like to ask everyone in the class to work in groups on the same text—
or different parts of the same text. I want us to see multiple renderings of the
same text. (If the class is too large, I can have groups present their renderings to only a few other groups, or I can enlist only three or four groups on
a given day and use other groups on another day.) The process shows in the
most concrete and experiential way how texts naturally yield different
emphases, different centers, different interpretations, different voices or
tones. Even though performances can be playful, they are sometimes moving
as well. And throughout, it is enjoyable and creates community.

This approach often brings out the literary and creative skill of certain
students who didn't look strong before—students who are good at banter,
speech, gesture, and the performative—who seemed unskilled when bare
silent textuality was the only medium in the room. And those very students
often become more skilled at silent textuality when they see that they have
more literary sophistication than some of the students who *looked* more
sophisticated on paper.

I love the way text-rendering makes the text more "felt" and memorable to students. In addition to gaining richer reactions and more developed
feelings about the text, students often end up with a kind of physical or
kinetic sensation of the text in their limbs or body.

IV. Helping students respond as writers: helping them write their own piece of imaginative writing—using the text as a kind of "springboard."

After we've worked on a text I like to ask students to do a piece of *imaginative* writing. The request would be too difficult or intimidating for many
students if I made it at the start, but at this point we have internalized some
of the *spirit* or *energy* of the piece. In addition, the other activities have given
students practice at being both brave and playful.

I ask students to use the work we have studied as a kind of *springboard*
for writing a work of their own. I pick out a few formal or structural features
or some linguistic details in the work that could serve as germs or incentives
to write—to help us *bounce off of* the work or to *take a ride on* it. In short,
I'm inviting students at this point—after having put energy into trying to
hear and understand Shakespeare or whomever—to turn away from
Shakespeare and write their *own* piece. Students can write about the same
theme or even reply to the work, but I specifically invite students to concen-
trate entirely on the structural or linguistic features I've chosen and allow the
topic to be entirely different.

For example, if we had been studying Shakespeare's Sonnet 73, "That
time of year," I might say, "Try writing a poem that starts out mentioning
a season or time of year, and that also mentions a time of day and some
common everyday process (the poem's fire glowing on its ashes). You might

want to restrict yourself further with some of the following features: Use the first word or phrase of each quatrain and of the couplet ('That time . . . , In me . . . , In me . . . , This . . . '); start each line with the first word in each of Shakespeare's lines; try sonnet form; make it some kind of love poem.''

The possibilities for this kind of thing are endless. And it's fun playing with different "extracts" from works of prose or poetry. For some reason, helpful generative and creative energy seems to derive from the borrowing of certain initial *words* or *syntactical features* (e.g., "Get a list of four adjectives in the first sentence"; "End with a question"; "Start with a quotation"). I enjoy using James Wright's poem "Lying in a Hammock at William Duffy's Farm in Pine Island, Minnesota" and asking students to pick a moment where they were at the home of some particular person and describe everything they can see and hear at that moment (as Wright does), then end with a final line that is a large generalization that *seems* unrelated to the preceding lines (Wright ends with "I have wasted my life"). Frost's invitation poem is another natural—where each stanza ends, "You come too." We can similarly borrow formal features from fiction: "Write about an event in flashback form"; "Tell something through the eyes of someone who doesn't quite understand what really happened"; "Tell a story using almost entirely dialogue.''

In borrowing certain features of structure or voice or architecture as aids in getting going, I've learned from the suggestions of poets like Kenneth Koch and Theodore Roethke. Koch, for example, suggests springboards as simple as this: After having students read and work on Blake's "Tyger, tyger," ask them simply to choose an animal and write a kind of poem of direct address—starting by twice repeating the name of the animal. Roethke made much more complicated problems for students, such as laying out a long list of seemingly random words they must use and fit into a tightly defined stanza pattern. He insisted that we make better poems if our minds are so occupied with craft problems that we don't have much attention left for our "theme or message." (On Roethke, see Balaban and Hugo.) What's pleasing about this approach to writing imaginative pieces is that somehow the prior text we worked on and the artificial constraints seem to lead us to write pieces that say things we didn't know we were going to say—but that it turns out we seem to want to say.

In effect I am asking students to borrow or take a ride on some of the imaginative energy or the linguistic and even syntactical juice of what we've been working on. To many of us teachers, this sounds like a scary enterprise, but it turns out that students are willing and able to do this better than most of us are, and usually they are grateful for the chance.

But it's not just presumption and playfulness that I am after. This kind of writing functions as an act of "interpretation"—an act of "replying" or "answering" the text—which is really the most natural and human way to "study" a work of literature. Students understand the work better after this writing.[2]

From Harold Bloom I take this lesson: that one of the most natural and instinctive ways to produce our own writing is to "bounce off of" the works of other writers; to misread them. In short, in this stage of the game, I'm inviting students to function like writers—which means caring more about their own writing than about the writing of the "great figure"—and taking whatever liberties they might like. Using it, borrowing, stealing. I like to invoke Eliot's dictum that amateurs borrow, professionals steal. I believe that proceeding in this way—taking these liberties and insisting on space for their own writing—leads in the end to their being *better* readers and critics. They come back to the texts of others as more interesting, interested, and invested readers.[3]

Notes

1. Numerous important voices are telling us how important it is for students to understand the actual particulars of what happens when we read a text—to see in some detail the phenomenological experience of the *process* of reading. Linda Flower and her colleagues have gone on from their talk-aloud writing protocols (to tell as much as possible about what goes on as someone engages in writing) to get equally useful insights from talk-aloud protocols of the reading process (38–41). Sometimes she interrupts readers at various points in their reading—especially if they stop giving "movies of their mind." She cites a classic experiment by Asch to illustrate how deeply our processing and understanding of a text is influenced by whatever expectations and prior knowledge we might have. Asch had two groups read the same essay that began with the words, "I hold it that a little rebellion, now and then, is a good thing." But one group was told that the essay was by Jefferson, the other by Lenin. Readers had strikingly different responses to the same text. Deborah Brandt, in her impressive book about literacy, argues that "the key to becoming literate is finding out how other people read and write and how print relates to what people do when they read and write" (9):

> But writing (or reading) is a here-and-now enterprise, always occurring in the present tense. It unfolds as a cognitive process as evanescent as speech, erased and usually forgotten in the act of being accomplished. While research indicates that readers have somewhat better recall of "the very words" of a text than listeners do of "the very words" of conversation, process research shows how writers and readers easily forget the routes they have taken to arrive at "the very words" and their meaning. (35–36)

2. Nowadays we tend to assume that the goal of translation is to get present readers to enter the language and culture and world of the original text: to be "true" to the original. But for most of the history of our culture (for example, in the eras of Chaucer, Shakespeare, and Pope)—and for many more cultures than ours—the goal of translation was quite opposite: to *transform* the language and culture and world of the original text into those of our own.

3. Many of the activities I've described here are spelled out in more pedagogical detail in "Workshop II: Interpretation as Response" in Elbow and Belanoff.

Works Cited

Asch, Solomon. 1952. *Social Psychology*. New York: Prentice Hall.

Balaban, John. 1977. "South of Pompeii the Helmsman Balked." *College English* 39.4 (December): 437–41.

Bloom, Harold. 1973. *Anxiety of Influence*. New York: Oxford University Press.

Brandt, Deborah. 1990. *Literacy as Involvement: The Acts of Writers, Readers, and Texts*. Carbondale, IL: Southern Illinois University Press.

Elbow, Peter. 1990. "Questioning Two Assumptions of the Profession." *What is English?* New York: MLA and Urbana, IL:NCTE. 179–94.

———. 1993. "The War Between Reading and Writing—and How to End It." *Rhetoric Review* 12.1 (Fall): 5–24.

———. 1981. *Writing with Power: Techniques for Mastering the Writing Process*, New York: Oxford University Press.

Elbow, Peter, and Pat Belanoff. 1995. *A Community of Writers: A Workshop Course in Writing* (2nd ed.). New York: McGraw Hill.

Flower, Linda. 1988. "The Construction of Purpose in Writing and Reading." *College English* 50.5: 528–44.

Hugo, Richard. 1974. "Stray Thoughts on Roethke and Teaching." *American Poetry Review* 3.1: 50–51.

Koch, Kenneth. 1973. *Rose, Where Did You Get that Red? Teaching Great Poetry to Children*. New York: Random House.

———. 1970. *Wishes, Lies, and Dreams: Teaching Children to Write Poetry*. New York: Chelsea House.

Moran, Charles. 1989. "Reading Like a Writer." In *Vital Signs*, edited by James. L. Collins. Portsmouth, NH: Boynton/Cook. Earlier version: 1981. "Teaching Writing/Teaching Literature." *College Composition and Communication* 32 (February): 21–30.

Wright, James. 1970. "Lying in a Hammock at William Duffy's Farm in Pine Island, Minnesota." In *Collected Poems*. Middletown, CT: Wesleyan University Press.

We often start with ten-minute focused freewrites about literature passages selected by my students or me. The writing is a point of departure, of getting going. So we write about passages we notice, and often this leads to more noticing until no time remains. This is in sharp contrast to the lecturing I did when I first taught literature.

Thomas Boghosian
Atlantic Community College
Mays Landing, NJ

I believe you understand literature differently after you yourself write about it. I require my students to write reactions constantly now—logs, papers, group paragraphs—every day in class and for all assignments outside of class. Gordon Pradl, Lil Brannon, and Peter Elbow taught me this.

Nancy VanArsdale
East Stroudsburg State College
Pennsylvania

15

Reading People
The Pragmatic Use of Common Sense

Thomas Newkirk
University of New Hampshire

We can never know what to want, because, living only one life,
we can never compare it with our previous lives nor perfect it in
our lives to come.

Milan Kundera in *The Unbearable Lightness of Being*

The "unbearable lightness" in Kundera's title refers to the imperfect and
incomplete information we have available when we make decisions. Unlike
the main character in the movie *Groundhog Day*, who wakes up every morning to the same day (to Sonny and Cher's "I Got You Babe" on the clock
radio), and moves through that day until he gets it right, we cannot test our
decisions or return to the original situation. We can never "*know* what to
want" because we can never bring the weight of certain predictive knowledge. Yet despite the provisional information we have at the time of
decision-making, we rarely feel, in Kundera's words, like "an actor going on
cold" (8). Why can we appear so decisive, feel so sure of ourselves, given
the unbearable lightness of the information at hand?

The answer has to do with the confidence we have in our powers of
inference. We do not "go on cold" because we possess predictive theories
that allow us to make use of the incomplete knowledge at hand, a process

207

described by the social psychologist, Erving Goffman. Like Kundera, Goffman notes that the full information we need to define a situation is rarely available. But he goes on:

> . . . in its absence, the individual tends to employ substitutes—cues, tests, hints, expressive gestures, status symbols, etc.—as predictive devices. In short, since the reality that the individual is concerned with is unperceivable at the moment, appearances must be relied on in its stead. And, paradoxically, the more the individual is concerned with the reality that is not available to perception, the more must he concentrate his attention on appearances. (1959, 249)

We try to escape Kundera's dilemma by using behavior and appearance as indices, as cues, that allow us to evaluate or predict that which we can't observe. Someone is late for a job interview and we very likely make a set of inferences—about future behavior (she'll be late to work frequently), about his attitude toward the position (if it were important to him he'd be on time), about his capacity to order his life (he can't plan his time well). In every human encounter we make inferences—about states of mind, aspects of character, and the tenor of our relationships—from the gestures, appearance, and language of others.

Students new to literary analysis run into difficulty when they come to distrust their own capacity for drawing inferences from behavior. Literature becomes mystified, overabstracted, filled with symbolism. They come to distrust the surfaces themselves, having been taught that the meaning that counts is cleverly *hidden* some distance away from these surfaces. They are intimidated by established literary theory and subtly conditioned to think that these established terminologies are the key to academic success. Some strategically disconnect the human act of reading from the analysis they must perform to write papers.

Yet the act of reading, and the primary analysis we do as readers, is making sense of the surfaces, attending to the human gestures of the characters. By stressing the *continuity* between everyday inference-making and the process of reading, we can begin to demystify the process of interpretation. Students can see the reading of literature, not as a special and specialized activity, but as another application of the social and behavioral theories they have developed in their encounters with others. And paradoxically, the same students who plead ignorance when asked to analyze literature are often astute readers (and deadly mimics) of their classmates and their teachers.

I will describe a short reading/writing assignment I developed for my Freshman English class in which I called on some of this social knowledge. I asked students to write a short fictional sketch in which they *revealed* a character through some combination of behavior, talk, and interior monologue. I decided to begin by focusing very simply on gestures, and, with some trepidation, chose to start with creative dramatics.

My class began at 9:40, the middle of the morning to me, but early to my students, still new to the freedom of dorm life. I began by modelling what I was after; in this case, classifying and acting out the forms their sleepiness took (indicating, also, which students favored which technique). There was "stare into nowhere." The student sits erect, looks straight ahead, but doesn't seem to focus on anything. In many cases their mouths are a little more open than usual, and one eye is usually more open than the other. Then there is "the sprawl." Here the right arm is usually stretched out over the pitifully small writing surface of the chair, as he or she cushions the ear on the inside elbow joint. Lastly, there are variations on prying motions, as if the eyes can be held open or massaged open by rubbing the space between the nose and each eye—all of this varied behavior to show sleepiness.

Next it was their turn. I paired them up and gave them a choice of several situations to act out (the most popular being to engage a reluctant fellow passenger in conversation). I gave each pair a few minutes to plan what they might do, and then each took a minute or two to present. Easily the most dramatic occurred when Bean Wright, fresh from boot camp, circled menacingly around Andrew Hussey:

Bean: Give me five, Soldier. [Andrew drops to push-up position.] What are you doing down there, Soldier? That wasn't me, that was someone else. Need to get your ears cleaned. Get up. [Bean closes in to within six inches of his face.] What do you take me for, Soldier, stupid?

Andrew: No sir.

Bean: I didn't hear you, Soldier.

Andrew: [louder] No sir.

Bean: Give me five, Soldier.

By the end of the short skit, Andrew has done about forty push-ups.

I explained that fiction writing involved a similar kind of improvisation—getting inside a character and imagining the ways he or she would talk, act, and think. But before setting up the writing assignment, I wanted students to look at some excerpts of fiction in which characters are revealed through what they do. Fortunately we had an example written by Andie Mitchell, a class member, as her response to Irwin Yalom's *Love's Executioner*. Many of Yalom's case studies involved depression, something Andie had seen firsthand. In her story, "In Living Color," she imagines a young woman, whose mother had gone mad, slipping over the edge herself. Here is how the main character imagines her own suicide:

> I stand on the bridge and put my hands down flat on the dark corroded wood. If I lean forward far enough the blood starts to rush to my head, and

this effect, combined with the sight of the water swirling below, is enough to give me a bit of a high. It's a dreamy, spacey sort of trance. I feel like I'm not really there, not completely, like when you get up from a sitting position too quickly and everything gets gray and spotty for a moment. I love these spots.

When we discussed this paper, Andie said that the clue to developing this character was imagining her obsession with the colors of personalities (the main character is a gray). At the end of the story, she cuts the colored circles out of a Wonderbread wrapper and tapes them to her face. Do we read this act as a descent into madness or a revolt against her grayness?

We also read the opening to Flannery O'Connor's short story, "Revelation," in which the main character, Mrs. Turpin, surveys the waiting room of a doctor's office where she has taken her husband, Claud:

> The only man in the room besides Claud was a lean stringy old fellow with a rusty hand spread out on each knee, whose eyes were closed as if he were asleep or dead or pretending to be so as not to get up and offer her a seat. Her gaze settled agreeably on a well-dressed gray-haired woman whose eyes met hers and whose expression said: if that child belonged to me, he would have some manners and move over—there's plenty of room for you and him too.
>
> Claud looked up with a sigh and made as if to rise.
>
> "Sit down," Mrs. Turpin said. "You're not supposed to stand on that leg. He has an ulcer on his leg," she explained. (488–489)

I asked students what words they would use to describe her personality, based on this opening. "Bossy," "arrogant," "domineering." We talked about the differences in these words. Then I asked how Mrs. Turpin would describe herself: "proper," "a lady," "well-mannered," even "thoughtful." She knew the code of proper behavior; the "white trash" in the room didn't. At the end of the story she sees herself and Claud, marching to heaven, behind the "niggers" and these white trash, and, shockingly, her virtues that had set her apart "were slowly being burned away" (508).

My colleague, Tom Carnicelli, has argued that the words that categorize character are among the most important in the language for us. Words like "arrogant" serve as lenses, what Kenneth Burke called "terministic screens," that enable us to make judgments about character, mood, attitude, and relationship. The diversity and subtlety of the terms—for example, the difference between "arrogant" and "obnoxious"—can provide a rich repertoire of frames for interpreting behavior, and much of what we do when we gossip (and read) is argue over which term fits best.

To help students consider this repertoire, we listed about forty terms we use to describe what people "are like" ("flirtatious," "boring," "crude," "lazy," "patient," etc.). After this list was on the board, I explained the writing assignment. They were to write a two- to three-page sketch in which they reveal a character (who must be named) through action, dialogue, or interior reflection. I had done the assignment myself prior to asking them to try it, and I read to them my attempt.

I have always been fascinated by my own indecisiveness, particularly on small matters. So I created a character, William, who reached a point of paralysis as he tried to choose ties:

> William looked at the ties in his closet. A blue one with red stripes, and an old paisley one from the '70s that had gone in and out of fashion a couple of times. Both would work with his tan shirt, he thought. It was as if the balance was so level, the choice so meaningless, that he couldn't make it. He couldn't shift the scales either way. He was paralyzed by the pure insignificance of what he was doing.

I would like to report that this assignment was a thorough success, but for many it was not. Too many students picked characters distant from their own experience, creating stock figures that, at best, called up a stock response. Others simply did not get to know their characters well enough. But in many of the sketches there were moments when the writer took on the character. Here is Bob Guillou's opening:

> "Where the hell am I?" he thought. His head was pounding, and the buzzing of a neon sign was repeating in his head. The sweet smell of a bakery was quickly washed away by the stink of his own breath.

I like the image of the repeating buzz of the neon sign. Later he effectively captures the drunk man's lack of physical control:

> His own body weight was giving him problems, and he grasped at the banister for support. The world around him began to rotate as it had many times before. Dean was used to the feeling and took pleasure in it.

Andrew Hussey (recovered from his push-ups) was also able to develop a believable picture of Harry, a hard-drinking, rural New Englander, whose wife has just left him:

> Harry had just finished hauling wood for the day. His back ached with pain and his right bicep was bulging with pressurized blood from holding the big Johnson chainsaw. His red and white flannel jacket was coated with chainsaw dust and woodchips. He smelled like oil and gas mixed with sweat.

Michelle Doucette began with a short sketch of Mikah, and developed it into a full short story that describes her infatuation with a college student, Jim, and his brutal date-rape of her. I will quote the scene that describes the immediate aftermath of the rape:

Once home, Mikah felt uncomfortable in her own house. She felt like she had betrayed her own family and that she didn't belong. How could her parents love something so impure? They would be so disappointed if they only knew what happened to her. She quickly threw away her shredded clothing and jumped into the shower. She used the hottest water that would come out of the faucet and tried to burn away Jim's germs. Her body was numb and the water felt cold. She washed her hair six times and scrubbed her body continuously for half an hour until she rubbed skin away. She scrubbed her throbbing genitals hard to wash away the feeling of Jim's penis stabbing her. She hated her genitals; she didn't care if she hurt them more. She hated her body. She wanted to scrub away her fat. Maybe if she was prettier Jim wouldn't have thought he could rape her and would have respected her.

In one paragraph she has captured the swirl of conflicting emotions—shame, anger, self-disgust, uncleanliness—that a rape victim feels (one of Michelle's goals is to be a rape crisis counselor). She is aware that the victim, though terribly abused, can still shift the blame to herself. I would argue that Michelle is enacting a theory of victimization in this section of her paper; we are asked to see Mikah's obsession with cleanliness as a plausible response to her rape. Both writer and reader must draw on behavioral and not literary theory.

I suspect that some literature teachers would claim that the approach I've outlined ignores the various critical theories that might be used to provide a fuller reading. My intent is not to devalue these theories, but to suggest that, as readers, we approach texts with a rich set of theories drawn from life experience. They rarely take the form of explicit generalizations; in fact, they are often not explicit at all. They are representative of what Michael Polanyi called the "tacit" dimension of our knowing, though we clearly can make them less invisible.

These theories, or what cognitive psychologists call "schemata," serve as translators, or generalizers: They allow us to move from specific observations to more global judgments. Without this capacity we would be lost in a sea of particulars. Even a simple act of identifying a letter of the alphabet written in cursive (important for post-office scanners) requires a movement from identification of distinctive features that lead to a reliable judgment (this is an "a"). The scanning we do for personal behavior is, of course, considerably more complex.

One of the most intricate and invisible systems we use concerns what was once called "manners." These inferences usually involve our judgments about the generally accepted ways in which people cooperatively handle the more routine social encounters. As Erving Goffman (1971) has detailed, our face-to-face encounters are governed by a complex set of conventions that determine who we can engage in conversation, how close we can come to the person spoken to, how we can sit when speaking, how we disagree, how long we can take for a speaking turn, whether we can engage in any side activity (e.g., doodling) when spoken to, and how we disengage from a conversation. Goffman argues that individuals "belong to gatherings" (1963, 248) and that, while we may think these social rituals and routines are trivial, when we or someone around us does not act properly, "the embarrassment can be surprisingly deep."

When we read literature, we note ruptures in this code of conduct. In *The Accidental Tourist* (Tyler), Macon Leary, recently separated from his wife, must leave his poorly trained dog at a kennel run by Muriel Pritchard. He must get a plane immediately, but is slowed and thrown off balance by Muriel's questioning:

> "Please," Macon said. "I'm about to catch a plane. I'm leaving for a week, and I don't have a soul to look after him. I'm desperate, I tell you."
>
> From the glance she shot at him he sensed he had surprised her in some way. "Can't you leave him home with your wife?" she asked.
>
> He wondered how her mind worked.
>
> "If I could do that," he said, "why would I be standing here?"
>
> "Oh," she said. "You're not married?"
>
> "Well, I am, but she's ... living elsewhere. They don't allow pets." (28)

Muriel then comes out from behind the counter and tells him that she knows what he is going through because she's a "divorsy" herself.

She crosses the line of conversational convention, probing more deeply in his personal life than her position as kennel manager or her familiarity with Macon would seem to warrant. Her offer of sympathy is not at all what Macon wants or expects, particularly from someone he has just met. She seems to lack standing to offer sympathy. And, as Deborah Tannen has shown, men often resist sympathy even from intimate acquaintances because it seems to put them in a one-down position.

We also see a comment on manners in Andie Mitchell's account of her mother's breakdown:

> That blue-haired woman who lives across the street and never seems to take her neck brace off heard Mom through the open window when she took out her garbage. She came to the window to see if everything was all right and that is when she found my mother on the floor. They took her to the hospital right away, but the blue-haired lady stayed in the kitchen to wait for me. She even helped herself to some coffee.

I read Andie's last sentence as a comment on manners; the blue-haired woman made herself a bit too comfortable waiting. Goffman would call her act a "territorial offense" (1971, 49) in many middle-class communities.

In addition to issues of etiquette, readers draw on their social knowledge to make other types of judgments:

- *Ethical judgments*. How can we judge the moral quality of the character's actions? Does our judgment differ from that of the character? The narrator? The implied author?

- *Psychological judgments*. Is the character's reaction to his or her situation plausible? Is it consistent with our beliefs about how individuals respond?

- *Attractional judgments*. Do we find the character appealing or repulsive in some way—sexually, physically, temperamentally?

In addition, there are schemata that rely less on social knowledge and deal with such things as literary form—does this piece of writing match previous literature I have read so that I can make productive predictions? And even this skeletal listing can only hint at the complexity, the marvelous specificity, of each system. In sum, our students come to class with social knowledge that they act on and refine in virtually every social encounter they have. They are not naive or atheoretical—they are drenched in theory.

Until working on this chapter, I had never bothered to consider whether this view of reading had anything to do with the fact that I am a writing teacher, working out of composition theories rather than literary theories. It seems almost blatantly self-evident to see the student's set of beliefs, funded and revised by experiences with other people, as the primary theoretical tool for shaping writing. When we ask students to use detail or dialogue, we expect that those details will work as cues to the reader for interpreting behavior. The writing is an enactment of their tacit social theories.

But recently, as I reread James Britton's classic, *Language and Learning*, I realized the extent of my indebtedness to him and to other neopragmatists who conceived of reading and writing as experimental tests of our network of tacit and explicit theories, which Britton called our "world representation." Britton writes:

In the experience of any given moment—in any confrontation with the real world—what we make of the occasion will depend a good deal upon the appropriateness and subtlety and complexity of the expectations we bring to it: These in turn, for most of us, are largely the fruits of past thinking, reading, writing, and talking—in other words, they reflect the degree to which we are able to use language as an organizing principle in our accumulated picture of the world. Moreover, what we make of that confrontation is likely to depend further upon the fresh language activity, an exchange of talk, perhaps, and our internal "exchange," our meditation upon what is presented to us. (276)

This statement, with its echoes of John Dewey and William James, is a credo for me. It suggests my opening move as a composition teacher—and as a literature teacher in disguise. I try to convince my students, in whatever way I can, that the theories that matter most are the ones they have constructed and will construct, their accumulated and accumulating picture of the world. This picture will become increasingly complicated as it is put to the experimental test of dialogue with various texts and with other students who bring different sets of expectations.

These evolving social theories help us draw inferences; they enable us to make something of the inevitably incomplete, the "unbearably light" human cues about us.

Works Cited

Britton, James. 1970. *Language and Learning*. London: Macmillan.

Burke, Kenneth. 1966. *Language as Symbolic Action*. Berkeley: University of California Press.

Goffman, Erving. 1963. *Behavior in Public Places: Notes on the Social Organization of Gatherings*. New York: Free Press.

———. 1959. *The Presentation of Self in Everyday Life*. New York: Doubleday.

———. 1971. *Relations in Public Places*. New York: Harper.

Kundera, Milan. 1984. *The Unbearable Lightness of Being*. New York: Harper and Row.

O'Connor, Flannery. 1973. *The Complete Stories*. New York: Farar, Straus, and Giroux.

Polanyi, Michael. 1958. *Personal Knowledge: Toward a Post-critical Philosophy*. Chicago: University of Chicago Press.

Tannen, Deborah. 1990. *You Just Don't Understand*. New York: Morrow.

Tyler, Anne. 1985. *The Accidental Tourist*. New York: Knopf.

Yalom, Irwin. 1989. *Love's Executioner: Tales of Psychotherapy*. New York: Free Press.

As a writing instructor, I know that writing is a means toward clarity and understanding. So throughout my Introduction to Fiction class, students were encouraged to step inside the pages of literature through writing—to more fully understand the authors' intentions—and to carry the characters, plots, and settings off the page into their lives—to create a context for the themes.

Before discussing *The Joy Luck Club* by Amy Tan, students wove tales about their parents' lives, which lead to an understanding of why Tan parallels mothers and daughters. After writing these "oral" stories, the importance of lessons passed from generation to generation was more accessible to them. Similarly, while discussing *Like Water for Chocolate* by Laura Esquivel, students wrote family recipes and gave the food magical properties. Sharing and discussing their foods enabled them to see why Tita's powerful emotions are transferred to the food and into others.

Students also placed themselves within the fiction, becoming characters, recasting stories in different places and times, combining characters from two or three pieces. They became Phoenix Jackson ("A Worn Path") and the mothers in "Everything That Rises Must Converge." They wrote letters from Pilate to Milkman (*Song of Solomon*). They transformed the forest into a city in "Young Goodman Brown." And they created dialogues between Emily ("A Rose for Emily") and Phoenix Jackson. Students were more fully able to understand issues of plot, setting, and character because they were writing the stories themselves. And because their voices were heard and appreciated, the literature became less daunting and inaccessible to them.

These "connecting" and pretending sessions enabled students to analyze and dip more easily into a realm that they began the semester thinking was only the property of "experts." They became the experts through writing, and better writers by becoming experts.

Ida Ferdman
Loyola-Marymount University

16

Journal Writing and the Study of Poetry

Douglas M. Tedards
University of the Pacific

William Carlos Williams

In some ways Williams is the best poet I've read this semester. In other ways I really don't like his poetry either. To me his poetry is just as you hear it; it is what he saw. It's not full of symbolic meanings and messages like other poets. . . . In "The Young Housewife" I just picture a woman that just woke up and is getting ready to start the day. It seems pretty straightforward and to the point. The one thing that really bothers me about this poem is the aspect of another person viewing her and the young woman doesn't seem to know it. It seems kind of disturbing to me that he (Williams) was able to invade a person's privacy like that even if it is only a poem. In all his poems I feel like we the readers are viewing something. We actually aren't in the poem's reality; we are on the outside looking in. Even with "The Red Wheelbarrow" being so simple and to the point, I still only feel like I am viewing a scene in a different world.

Rick M., Journal Entry 3/16/94

e.e. cummings

What an amazing man. I love his poetry, who wouldn't? I love to just sit and look at his poems before I read them. It is always a challenge to figure out why he used a certain space or dash. Very enjoyable. . . . "anyone lived in a pretty how town"—after reading this a few times I discovered that "anyone" and "noone" are people. At first I could only see social comments on this town. Then I began to discover the couple. I began to see that although these two weren't anybody special they found each other, happiness. I really liked these two levels and what the poem had to say.

Sarah D., Journal Entry 3/23/94

Rick and Sarah are first-year undergraduates taking my course in Major American Authors II. Their journal entries were written in response to a selection of modern American poets. At the beginning of the course I explain that a required journal will, in effect, create a parallel text for them—as important as the other writing they will do for the course and as significant in some ways as the 125 years of American literature they will read from 1865 to about 1990. They are understandably skeptical, even though I ask that the journals be brought to class every day along with their anthologies, even though I will design three essay writing assignments that depend on their journal entries, and even though I will collect, read, and comment on their journals three times during the semester.

Of the fifty-five students in this semester's course (two sections), a few have taken the activity of writing in their journals lightly, making only cursory entries. Others resist the requirement outright (two had shown me nothing by the tenth week of the course). And some—nine students to date—have handed in their journals late, composing a bunch of entries in a short span of time despite the guideline that entries parallel the readings and discussions in class and be dated accordingly. Even among the majority who approach their journals with genuine resolve and interest, there are inevitable questions: "How much should we write? Do we have to write about every selection on the syllabus? How will you grade them?" and, most basic, "What do you mean by a journal?" Their level of anxiety is not lessened when I tell them there will be no exams, no tests, no quizzes—none. The essays count fifty percent, journals thirty percent, and class participation twenty percent. So the journals matter; their writing matters. And even though this is a literature class, only about one in four is an English major, with most taking the class to meet an all-university general education requirement. Some will have taken other general education courses where the writing assignments are either formal, lengthy research papers (often coming at the end) or so-called essay exams where the prize goes to the short-term memorizers and facile writers of argumentative prose. If they've had a writing course at the university oriented toward process, draft workshops, and composition-based reading and discussion, they are less alarmed by the emphasis on writing.

I do not take their trepidations lightly, however, for many, if not most, have never kept academic journals of this sort in university courses. Bret, a sophomore, didn't turn in his journal the first time (Week Five) and wrote the following at Week Ten: "This is, as you see (or rather what you do not) . . . incomplete—I'm sending it along anyway, and ask for no clemency—it could have been better, certainly worse—Bye." After reading Bret's journal, I wrote back to him: "Glad you turned in the journal. Despite your disclaimer, it is *exactly* the sort of writing, reflecting, and pondering on poems and prose I intended it to be—for you and, only secondarily, for me." The truism in teaching that praise is just as fundamental to a student's progress as what we criticize seemed to apply in Bret's case. That notion, at least, is reflected in my response to Bret's diffidence about his journal writing. And I believe it worked; for example, here are three of Bret's shorter entries on Wallace Stevens and William Carlos Williams, not the simplest poets for any of us to read and write about cogently:

> *Wallace Stevens's "The Snow Man"*
> It's a cold poem—it uses cold words—in addition to the more plain description, there are words like *crusted, shagged, glitter, misery, bare*—as far as goes my grasp of the philosophy here—well—it's zenny [Zen-like].

> *Stevens's "Disillusionment of Ten O'Clock"*
> I share Stevens's disappointment with society—we are a bunch of dullards in a way that's frightening. We're boring so much of the time—it's not surprising that our dreams would be the same—my dreams are dull—nothing the least surreal—nothing spiced.

> *William Carlos Williams's "This Is Just to Say"*
> I love the tone—the cool words—the luscious words—they're edible. It's a little like the child who lifts from the cookie jar and disarms the mother with her keen smile—lovely.
>
> Bret F., Journal Entries 3/15/94

Like Bret, I value the words, thoughts, and emotions of these poets, but my enthusiasm can be intimidating to students, especially non-English majors. Having students write continuously in a journal to which I respond, in writing, communicates in a powerful way that I also value *their* words, *their* thoughts, and *their* imaginations. As these initial samples of student writing show, the rewards to them and us in terms of imaginative and thoughtful expression are not so far removed from the satisfactions of reading and responding to the poets themselves. Sarah's exclamations about Cummings, for example, echo my first exposure to his poems in college. And Bret's discovery of Stevens's diction—a fascination of mine since Gordon Bigelow introduced me to Stevens at the University of Florida in the late '60s—is especially satisfying for me now as a teacher of these poems.

But the journals must do more than encourage thoughtful free writing and impressionistic reactions to unfamiliar literature. If, that is, they are to serve the principles of writing to learn and learning to write in the context of our studying American poetry *as a community* of readers and writers.

This semester I devised three strands of journal writing to stimulate more breadth and depth to the experience. At the outset of the course, I distinguish three ways of making journal entries: expressive, analytical, and creative. Expressive entries are avowedly personal, anecdotal, and writer-based: I tell them to write these entries with the attitude of "I'm writing to and for myself and can ignore what anyone else thinks about it." Analytical

pieces are necessarily a bit more topical and reader-based, focusing on articulating some interpretation about a given poem or set of poems. Creative
writing takes the form of imitations, parodies, or genre "conversions" (a
story into a poem or vice versa) and new, original poems or fragments of
poems unrelated, ostensibly, to the poetry being read in the course.

In practice, even though I spell out these theoretical differences in
expressive/reflective, analytical/comparative, and creative/imaginative entries,
I don't require that students label their entries or worry about distribution. In
this course, expressive entries ranked first, followed closely by analytical
pieces, yet the two strands were often blurred. Creative writing was a distant
third. In fact, to counterbalance the emphasis on expressive and analytical
entries (this is not, after all, a poetry writing course), I do assign a number of
poetry-writing activities. For example, after we had read a selection of Wallace
Stevens's poems in class, I asked them to write a poem in imitation of
"Thirteen Ways of Looking at a Blackbird"—entitled "Three Ways of Looking at _____." They filled in the blank with their own subjects. The variety
of topics was astounding to me, in part because the last time I gave this
assignment it was a summer session class with, to my great fortune, *thirteen*
students, and I made it part of an in-class writing exercise titled "Thirteen
Ways of Looking at Our Classroom" and published the resulting poem for
them. Here is a partial list of topics my current students used in their journal
imitations of Wallace Stevens just a few weeks ago:

Elvis	leaves	cats	cocker spaniels
the sun	feet	poetry	an open field
Denny's	friendship	a woman	a four-year-old boy
hands	a lizard	a hooker	winter
ivy	lust	scotch tape	a drunkard

And here are parts of the more original, well composed takeoffs on
Stevens's "Thirteen Ways of looking at a Blackbird":

   Six Ways of Looking at J.R.

I
Among the multitudes of mannequins
The sole living thing
Was the winking eye of J.R.
A cool breeze is blowing.
J.R. must be exhaling.

III
O miserable remote-control jockeys!
Why do you fantasize about SI swimsuit models?
Do you not see how J.R.

Turns the heads
Of those about you?

IV
I know comedy and lust,
Distrust, and inescapable blush;
But I know too
That J.R. knows that
Which I know.
—*Chris S.*

Ways of Looking at a Cat

I
A cat, in itself, is one.
A cat, with a human, is one
As long as it's on
The cat's terms.

II
A cat and a dog are one
But the cat has the
upper hand.

III
A cat is God in its
Own eyes and is the
Only one.
—*Michelle D.*

Heaped like a dropped towel
in feline slumber. They—oh—
do they sleep? They start like
switches at a moment's distraction.
—*Bret F.*

Three Ways of Looking at a Woman

I
Behind the snot-nosed child,
In back of the peanut butter & jelly,
There runs the woman.
Barefoot.

II
Baseball, bars, & beer.
Bimbos, Bonds, & beards.
Boys→Woman running.

III
Revlon, Max Factor, Cover Girl.
Behind those mascara-stained eyes,

In the dark,
There lies a woman running.
She screams.
Voiceless.
—*Leisha C.*

3 ways of looking at a . . . Hooker

I
Young child
lost and deceived
hoping to find
love

II
She-wolf of the night
catches her prey
and seduces them into
oblivion

III
Tired and cold
she casually walks
down the longest cement
tombstone
—*Regina G.*

3 Ways to Look at Poetry

I
Take a magnifying glass
   and search between the lines,
Finding only that which
   suits the mind.

Wrinkled eyebrows
Twisted tongue
Cramped brain
There must be some other way
To understand this jumble!
—*Jennifer R.*

I wish I had the space to include all the best imitations of Wallace
Stevens, but these examples show the simple power of asking students to
delve into the craft of poetry firsthand. Exercising our imaginations and agonizing over choices in diction, syntax, and lineation *like the poets we study*
helps us pull these well-known poets down from their lofty pedestals into the
classroom for a more human encounter with their poetry.

Edgar Lee Masters's *Spoon River Anthology* provided an earlier occasion
for a creative-writing assignment, but unlike the imagist, haiku-like imitations

of Stevens, these attempts were less successful. Next time I may reverse the order, having them write like Stevens first and Masters second. Having completed an eight-week segment on the fiction of Clemens, James, Crane, Chopin, and other realists, I made the false assumption that writing a narrative lyric might go better as the first assignment than the more modernist and cryptic form of Stevens's poems. After reading about six of the *Spoon River* poems, I ended class that day with "OK, you seemed to like these narrative lyrics written from the grave, so to speak. Now, I want each of you to work on writing a contribution to our own *Calaveras River Anthology* in your journals—à la Edgar Lee Masters." Since the Calaveras River runs along the northern edge of our campus, I asked them to imagine a cemetery along one of its levees overlooking both the river and the university.

Questions I got on this first, formal request for poetic writing in the journals went as follows: "Who do I write about? Are we really supposed to imagine ourselves dead? What's the point of doing this anyway?" I encouraged experimentation within the framework of Masters's approach and suggested they might pretend to be anyone—not just themselves—speaking from the Calaveras River Cemetery. The question "What's the point of doing this?" is, of course, a harder question to answer and I don't remember exactly what I said on this occasion in class, but here's what I hope I said in substance: "As a professor of literature and a teacher of writing, I've come to learn over the years that specific kinds of writing—free writing, journal writing, and creative writing, for example—give to the writer a certain kind of confidence about engaging the writing of others, even published writing. It gives, over time, the apprentice writer an insider's appreciation for how a piece of writing—an essay, a story, a poem—comes into being on the page. These attempts at a variety of writing tasks, including creative writing, reveal to us a complicated web of thinking and writing, re-thinking and re-writing, in an emotionally charged atmosphere. That activity of writing and rewriting, once experienced earnestly, can be shown to parallel the very same effort that a Wordsworth, a Whitman, or an Edgar Lee Masters engaged in repeatedly throughout his life.

Expressive, reader-response entries and analytical, interpretive entries, as I've said, comprise the bulk of the writing in these journals. At their best, they preview or parallel the reading, thinking, and talking we do collectively in class. Journal-based discussion, either in small groups or with the whole class, is a strategy for getting students to talk more, and more substantively. And thus I find myself turning to them with increasing frequency. "Talk less and teach more" might be the motto, which of course has its origins in the workshop approach to the teaching of writing that I bring to literature courses. There the focus is on what students contribute to class by writing and responding to the writing of others, and I'm discovering that journal writing and journal-based discussion is a way to enliven and open up the teaching-learning process with literature—making the students' own writing the crucial starting point for in-class discussion, analysis, and interpretation of poetry.

For instance, I'll come into class and say, "Today, as you know, we'll be hearing presentations from Regina on H.D.'s "Mid-day" and "Helen," Allyson on Marianne Moore's "Poetry," and Chris and Tien on the Cummings's poems—but first I'd like you to form small groups of no more than three or four and share your journal entries on these poets. While you're doing that, I'll meet with the presenters for today and after fifteen minutes or so, we'll get back together to hear these poems read aloud and to talk about them based on our small-group discussions."

Often what comes up in class will lead to additional journal entries. One student even devised a double-entry pattern using the left-hand pages of his journal to indicate entries written after class discussion. Or others will simply introduce after-class entries with language like "In class yesterday . . ." or "After we talked about this poem in class. . . ." John K.'s entry on T.S. Eliot's "The Love Song of J. Alfred Prufrock" is fairly representative: "This poem was very difficult for me to understand. My first interpretation of the poem was so farfetched I found myself 'reaching' to make sense of it. I began over-analyzing ever sentence, word, period. . . . After we (Tabitha and I) shared in the class discussion, I started to see that this was a really great poem. Although it took some 'spoon-feeding,' I finally got the essence of the poem. The scary part is, many of the characteristics Prufrock suffers from are also a part of my past. I can remember many times debating the question, 'Do I dare?'"

Here's another example from Christa O.'s journal: "We had discussed Ransom's 'Bells for John Whiteside's Daughter' in class, and some people were coming up with some really wild theories about insane women chasing geese and things like that. But to me it didn't seem that hard to understand. Of course, it's easy for me to say that now, after having heard a discussion about it in class, but I really believe I understood the poem!" Christa goes on to write another page and prove to me she does understand the poem, offering new insights along the way that were not discovered in class: "And we talked in class about why it [the poem's title] was '. . . for John Whiteside's Daughter' and there was no mention of the mother. I think that in the days when women stayed primarily in the home, it was the man who made the living and was known in the community. . . . It just shows how far we've come that now the lack of a female influence in the title makes us think twice, where years ago, when the poem was written, they probably didn't give it a second thought." Christa's commentary here on this well-known Ransom poem will enrich my teaching of the poem next time.

I also pay careful attention to students who have a hard time with poetry, as Kimberly admits in this entry: "I will begin this section of my journal by stating—'I hate poetry!' Actually, it is not that I truly hate it but rather that I struggle to find meaning/understanding of the work. There is a song in 'The Chorus Line' titled 'I Felt Nothing'—that sums up poetry for me. But in an effort to 'broaden my horizons' I will proceed with an open mind." And indeed Kim does explore some difficult poems with an open mind but without compromising her initial reservations. On Stevens, she begins, "Wallace Stevens perplexes me—many of the poems have a very dark, heavy tone to them, but I search to find some deep meaning to them." And on William Carlos Williams she writes, "Here we go again—what is Williams trying to say to me the reader? I am beginning to feel like I am missing a 'poetry' brain cell or two." But when the poet Li-Young Lee visited our class to read a few of his poems, answer student questions, and talk about poetry, Kim was effusive in saying that she could have listened to Lee read and talk about poetry for another hour or so.

The journals offer a safe haven for students like Kim to express some fairly negative experiences and emotions about their encounters with poetry in the classroom, but if we are diligent and lucky, they may experience an emotional and intellectual reversal at some point in the course. By periodically collecting, reading, and responding to the journals, I'm given the chance to understand these negative reactions to the study of poetry and to reply personally. I wrote the following to this student about his struggles with American poetry: "Dan—You probably think (or fear) otherwise, but I *thoroughly* enjoyed reading your journal this time. The irony (for me) is that you are so expressive—almost poetic—in voicing your frustrations with the poetic and some of the poems. And your own poems are nothing to sneeze at! DMT 4/9/94."

Finally, to illustrate the usefulness of more analytical, interpretive entries, let's revisit Rick's remarks on William Carlos Williams's "The Young Housewife" with which I began this chapter. First, here's the text of the poem:

The Young Housewife

At ten a.m. the young housewife
moves about in a negligee behind
the wooden walls of her husband's house.
I pass solitary in my car.

Then again she comes to the curb
to call the ice-man, fish-man, and stands
shy, uncorseted, tucking in
stray ends of hair, and I compare her
to a fallen leaf.

The noiseless wheels of my car
rush with a crackling sound over
dried leaves as I bow and pass smiling.
—WCW, 1916/1917

Rick admires the realism and simplicity of this poem, but he is bothered by the notion that Williams's point of view is somewhat voyeuristic and invades "a person's privacy." And indeed, it seems to be more than just a simple observation of a woman by Williams from his car, perhaps as he was making rounds as a doctor in Rutherford, New Jersey. Discussion of this poem appears in a number of journal entries and provides a sustained look at the kind of serious thinking that can occur among students working independently on a single piece of literature. The students quoted here are divided in their interpretations of this poem—nothing new, of course, to teachers of modernist poetry. Some were generally sympathetic toward the poem and others, like Rick, voiced some criticism or discontent. The poem, by the way, was not read or discussed in class prior to these journal entries:

The Sympathizers

This is how one man sees a young housewife as he passes her in his car. Maybe he sees her as being somewhat of a prisoner in her own home, always doing what her husband asks. . . . She hasn't experienced anything about the world outside her home and the driver probably realizes this and decides to smile at her to make her feel a bit more comfortable and relaxed about her obligations.

—Russell G. 3/16/94

I like Williams's comparison of the housewife to a leaf. I'm unclear if the comparison is negative or positive. To me, a fallen leaf seems so solitary and alone. Also, Williams is running over all kinds of fallen leaves with his car. That could be interpreted as the housewife being left somewhere while life kept on moving.

—Michelle D. 3/15/94

I think the speaker is talking about a daily routine that has developed, perhaps on his way to work, where he catches a glimpse of the young housewife a few times everyday. I think the speaker and the housewife are aware of each other's presence; a polite acknowledgment from a distance, but almost flirtatious in the eyes of the speaker. The comparison with a fallen leaf is to tell us he treasures these instances.

—John K. 3/16/94

This poem really turns me on, in a strange sort of way. Williams's small observation of everyday life is not dramatic, not about the rich and famous, just an ordinary housewife. He doesn't even tell me what she looks like— I think it's the "tucking in stray ends of hair" that does it for me. . . "again" she comes to the curb. Did she come before? Has he been watching regularly? "Shy . . . uncorseted . . . tucking in stray ends of hair." It's a vulnerable image—she is shy about her appearance. Maybe that's why he likes watching. It is little wonder, then, that he compares this delicate woman to a fallen leaf. . . . I really like this poem—I identify with his voyeurism to a certain extent.

—Chris S. 3/14/94

As examples of serious student work—careful reading, critical thinking, analytical writing—these entries stand out for me as the best that journal writing can offer by way of encouraging a thoughtful engagement with poetry. But let's hear from the critics of William Carlos Williams:

The Critics

Is it just me, or does Williams seem kind of like a peeping Tom in this poem? It seems like he's luring out the housewife instead of just looking at her. Maybe it's just me!

—Michelle D. 3/15/94

I did not read into this poem at all, I took it for face value. The poem was simply about a young housewife standing on the curb being watched by a strange man from his car. He seems to think she's beautiful, but it rather disgusts me how he watched her each day, almost like a peeping Tom. He obviously feels some sexual desire for her. But on the other hand, I don't think it is appropriate how she comes to the curb in a 'negligee' and 'uncorseted.'

—Jennifer K. 3/17/94

I read this poem with absolutely no idea what to expect. Well, it gave me bad vibes. I don't like WCW already, and this is the first poem I have read of his. Who does he think he is, writing about women and treating women like that? Is WCW chauvinistic? Or is he portraying what it was like during those times? That women were subservient to men. It upset me when it said "I compare her to a fallen leaf" and then he proceeds to say the "noiseless wheels of my car rush with a crackling sound over dried leaves as I bow and pass smiling." Is this supposed to mean that men just walk all over women and enjoy it? Is this really matter-of-fact poetry?

—Allyson W. 3/17/94

Here again, the journals reveal three students of poetry hard at work trying to articulate their psychological discomfort with Williams's poem—its sexual connotations and possible sexism.

The experience of reading this back-and-forth set of journal entries began to feel like a tennis or ping-pong match where the opponents are not sure if anyone is across the net or on the other side of the table. And I, the spectator, didn't know exactly what to expect either or how the "match" would turn out in the end. I was in the enviable position of being able to applaud both sides and set aside my own views of the poem and relish the discoveries being made.

Making this discovery of a sustained "journalistic dialogue" or "debate" about meaning, point of view, and the play of poetic language in Williams's little poem written some seventy-five years ago highlights for me the value of using journals in the course from beginnning to end. I placed on reserve in our library a draft of this chapter for my students to review and comment on near the end of the semester, and Rick—who opened this journalistic dialiogue about "The Young Housewife"—commented as follows: "After reading what you thought about my analysis of WCW, it made me realize my own interpretation of literature is just as important as someone else's who may be an expert" (Rick M., 5/13/94). Just so, Rick—just so!

As students read articles for research in literature or read assignments for my Eighteenth and Nineteenth Century American Literature or Introduction to Literature course, I often ask them to keep a journal in which they reflect on their readings. If they are planning for a research paper, they record ideas for tentative thesis statements, annotate individual sources, or brainstorm informally. Periodic checks of these allow me to know their progress or problems in this process. Commenting on these journals establishes a dialogue with the students and encourages them to stay on schedule with their readings.

I also use focused writing both in and out of class. For example, in American Literature, I often begin class by asking students to compare/contrast writing styles or periods or ask them to summarize a passage such as Thoreau's *Civil Disobedience* to determine whether they are reading for the main ideas with understanding or to use as basis of class discussion. Of course, this prepares them for essay exams as well.

In Introduction to Literature, I ask students to write about a favorite short story, poem, or play and to explain why it is meaningful to them. This gives me insight into their interests and the kinds of literature they have read or like to read. Besides letting me get to know the student, I often use this in revising the course syllabi so they feel part of the process of writing the course. In both courses, students respond to each other at each step of the writing process, thus making the class more interactive and teaching students how to read and revise their own and others' drafts.

Linda Thomas
Midway College
Kentucky

17

Using Journals to Redefine Public and Private Domains in the Literature Classroom

Carl R. Lovitt
Clemson University

I confess that I have always been disappointed with the results of assigning journals in literature courses. Admittedly, there were always some students—interestingly, not always the best—whose journal entries so far exceeded my expectations that I hesitated to drop the assignment from the syllabus; but, on the whole, journals seldom lived up to their advertised potential of fostering writing that was qualitatively different from the other writing students produced for the course. Instead of engaging students in alternative modes of reflection, even the best journal entries consistently revealed the same kind of thinking about literature that I encountered in their formal writing. Perhaps more troubling was the lackluster quality of many students' journal entries: the tendency to summarize plot or to comment superficially on recurring themes, which suggested that they considered the assignment little more than another onerous academic obligation. And there were always those students who defeated the purpose of the assignment by frantically and transparently writing two weeks' worth of entries on the night before they were due; I suspect there are other teachers who understand that different dates and different colored inks can be used on the same day. In time, I reluctantly stopped assigning journals. I concluded that the journals were not important enough to my students to justify the time it took me to read them.

I was never satisfied with the decision to stop assigning journals. Sharing with many colleagues a fundamental belief in the importance of providing academic opportunities for students to express their personal responses to literature, abandoning journals meant depriving my students of the medium presumably best suited to such expression. I could not understand how an assignment that was intended to encourage such responses, *prior to any formal academic experience of the text*, generally failed to engage their interest. Since the premise for assigning journals seemed theoretically sound, I suspected that the problem had less to do with the medium than with the way that journals were being integrated into my literature courses. My frustration with the failure of journal assignments eventually led to my experimenting with a different approach to using journals in literature courses. This essay describes that experiment and examines some of its implications for the teaching of literature.

The Inherently Social Nature of Journals

Journal assignments in my literature courses failed because most of my students had had no previous experience of producing the kind of writing I expected in their journals. Whereas I had assumed that providing a context where students could explore connections between literature and their own lives would elicit their unmediated responses to literature, I had apparently underestimated the extent to which students had already internalized an alternative conception of what teachers mean when they ask students to "respond personally" to literature. Through years of participation in literature classes, students have been socialized to understand the protocols of reading literature in an academic setting. They have been taught to identify themes and patterns, to recognize symbols, to look for "deep" or "hidden" meaning—in short, literature courses have largely equated literary study with analysis and interpretation. An important, implicit aim of many literature courses is precisely to teach students how to move beyond their tendency to identify with or respond emotionally to literature in favor of their learning how to generate more intellectually sophisticated "readings." Since, for many students, responding to literature had become synonymous with interpretation, my asking them to respond personally to literature in their journals was generally understood as a request for them to provide their "personal" interpretations of the texts—not to explore connections between their lives and those texts.

Such a response to my earlier journal assignments suggests that the students did not perceive a qualitative difference between the writing in their journals and the other discourses in which they participated in the classroom: informal writing, classroom discussion, essay tests, formal papers, and so on. What these discourses have in common is that they are inherently social: they all enjoin students to talk or write about literature in a way that can be shared with others. The possibility of such exchange, however, depends on a common "language" for talking about literature—which can only be the official language of the literature classroom. Thus, by writing about literature in their journals in the same way that they were expected to write and speak in other classroom contexts, my students were responding to the perception that their journal writing was intended to contribute to that classroom discourse.

The fact that my students were correct in their perceptions about the ultimately social intentions of their journals exposes the problem with my earlier journal assignments and the contradiction of any journal assignment that anticipates integrating students' entries into the discourse of the classroom. Teachers cannot "empower" students to write about literature as they choose in their journals and, at the same time, reasonably expect those entries to conform to a prescribed model of literary discourse. Yet this is precisely what many journal assignments presume to do. Although teachers generally agree that having students make personal connections to literature is one of the desired effects of assigning journals, this effect is often subsumed by the perception of journal writing as a tendentially social activity. For example, Pat Belanoff, who promotes the use of journals in literature classes "as a way to help students stay connected to direct expression in writing of their free interaction with a text" (101), also anticipates how her students "can begin using their entries as a way of talking to others about what they read" (105). The widespread practice of having students respond to specific prompts in their journals constitutes a particularly explicit approach to ensuring that journal entries conform to the social discourse of the classroom.

My purpose is not to question the validity of envisioning student journals as social documents. Having encouraged students to record their personal responses to classroom material in their journals, there is a pedagogical logic to providing a subsequent opportunity for students to test those responses in the public marketplace of ideas. Yet, considering student journals, in the words of Geoffrey Summerfield, as "ways of preparing for conversation, . . . fragments of work in progress, accountable and answerable" (37), has unmistakable consequences for the role journals play in students' learning experiences.

However integral such activities to the teaching of literature, it would be a mistake not to recognize them as a social construction designed to supplant other models of reading. By equating "response" with "interpretation," we are not making a neutral request for students to perform a natural activity, but instead are asking them to practice a highly socialized, context-specific form of discourse. The ostensibly empowering gesture of designating a site, the journal, where students are encouraged to explore their own interpretations of literature may, therefore, fall short of authorizing their private discourse. By legitimizing students' interpretations, such a structure clearly improves on the traditional model of treating the teacher's interpretation as definitive, but the very proposition of designating the journal as a locus of interpretation necessarily constrains the student writer to engage, in the privacy of her journal, in a type of discourse validated by the literary discourse community. Thus, instead of encouraging fundamentally different writing and thinking from students, journals may implicitly serve the same analytic and interpretive functions as other writing assignments in the course.

The more teachers emphasize the social nature of journals by influencing what students write in their journals or by treating journal writing as a rehearsal for social discourse, the more those journal entries—however

informal—will resemble the discourse of the classroom community. Whatever the gains, exploiting the continuity between the private discourse of the
journal and the public discourses of the classroom will certainly restrict students' freedom to explore the kind of writing journals are intended to foster.
Expecting students to address in their journals the kinds of questions we treat
in our courses denies them the opportunity to explore alternative modes of
response. In fact, I would argue that journals risk discouraging students from
exploring what may potentially be their most significant "personal responses" to literature.

Reaffirming Student Journals as Private Discourse

The alternative is to recognize the inherently social nature of journals as an
obstacle that inhibits students' personal response to literature and to design
assignments that counteract the impetus toward integrating journals within
the social discourse of the classroom. Peter Elbow and Jennifer Clarke offer
a theoretical rationale for such initiatives, when they insist that the possibility of using writing "to make meaning to oneself, not just to others"
depends on the ability "to free oneself (to some extent anyway) from the
enormous power exerted by society and others: to unhook oneself from
external prompts and social stimuli" (32). Empowering students to use their
journals to record their personal responses to literature would therefore seem
to require explicitly freeing them from the expectation that their journal
writing will be governed by the aims of academic literary study. Such a
proposition does not challenge the pedagogical aims of most literature
courses, but argues for expanding those aims to include opportunities for
students to discover how literature relates to their lives.

Many of our students—including most of our English majors—will not
devote their lives to literary study or become teachers of literature. Acquiring
skills in literary interpretation or analysis will certainly enhance their effectiveness as readers, but if they don't, more fundamentally, internalize the
activity of reading as essential or even relevant to their lives, they are unlikely
to become lifelong readers, no matter how successfully they perform in our
courses. Regardless of the other aims we pursue in our courses, we need to
develop strategies in our courses that will allow students to explore, discover,
and establish how literature addresses their personal experiences and concerns.

The model I propose envisions the journal as a separate space where
students can explore their private connections to literature without engaging
in the socialized practice of interpreting literature. At the very least, I hope
to dramatize the tension between public and private discourse about literature
and to suggest the benefits of creating contexts for students to define the
terms of their own response.

To experiment with the possibility of creating a space in the classroom
that privileges private investigation, I developed an assignment for a
sophomore-level contemporary literature course in which students were to

devote their entire journal to writing about a single novel (Barbara Kingsolver's *Animal Dreams*) that was not going to be discussed in class. The assignment called for them to read twenty-five pages of the novel per week and to complete a weekly journal entry on those pages; the novel is long enough for them to complete fourteen entries during the semester. Beyond specifying that the entries were to be informal, my only instructions were that students should use the journal to explore and speculate about "connections" between the novel and their personal lives; I left it up to them to determine the kinds of connections they would write about but suggested that they might focus on academic and cultural, as well as personal, experiences. Of course, by specifying that journals were to explore "personal connections," this assignment also technically restricts students' freedom to write what they want, but this restriction clarifies the intention that the journals did not have to conform to academic models of literary response.

In keeping with the spirit of the assignment, I intervened as little as possible in the process. To see how they were responding to the assignment and to make sure they were doing the writing, I collected the journals only once before they were due at the end of the term. The students also appended a candid analysis and evaluation of the assignment to the completed journal. The following discussion of the assignment will be based primarily on the students' evaluations of the journal assignment. But, first, a few words about the book I asked them to write about in their journals.

Those readers who are familiar with Barbara Kingsolver's *Animal Dreams* will surely agree that I did not expressly select a book to which a relatively homogeneous population of predominantly conservative white students at an agrarian university in the southeast would immediately be expected to relate. In the first place, the novel focuses on the lives and customs of Native and Mexican Americans in rural Arizona—both a region and cultures to which my students are unlikely to have been exposed. In the second place, the novel features the structural complexity of two narrators, neither of whom would appear to have much in common with any of my students: Codi, the first narrator, is a well-educated but under-employed drifter in her mid-twenties who is coping with a serious identity crisis, and her father, the second narrator, is a doctor afflicted with Alzheimer's disease, whose grasp on reality progressively deteriorates throughout the novel. Thus, both structurally and thematically, the novel was more likely to disorient my students than to suggest familiar reference points.

Despite the unfamiliarity of the subject matter and the book's challenging structure, the students consistently found opportunities in their journals to establish and explore connections between the novel and their own personal experiences. They identified diverse and often astonishing connections not only between aspects of their own lives and those of the characters but also between the novel and other books, movies, TV shows, and songs, as well as between issues raised in the book and subjects they were studying or had studied in other courses. Associations ranged from the canonical (MacLeish's *JB*, Rand's *The Fountainhead*) to the improbable (*The Goonies*, "Days of Our Lives," "Groovy Kind of Love"). The journal assignment enabled some students to articulate a connection between official reports about the Nicaraguan conflict in *Animal Dreams* and the government's disinformation in *The Andromeda Strain*. Others commented on parallels between a character's responses to losing a parent in both *Animal Dreams* and *Bright Lights, Big City;* two students wrote about their own experiences of losing a parent. Where one saw a parallel between the Navajo dances described in *Animal Dreams* and the rituals depicted in *Dances with Wolves*, another was reminded by Codi's visit to the Navajo reservation of the confrontation with alien cultures in *Brave New World*. One student commented on the parallels between Codi's relations with her father and sister and those that organize Pat Conroy's *The Prince of Tides*, while another was reminded by Codi's experiences as a teacher in Grace, Arizona, of Conroy's narrative, *The Water is Wide*, about a teacher at a coastal South Carolina school. Several students wrote about the memorable influences of specific teachers on their lives. For one student, *Animal Dreams* raised many of the same issues as *Cold Sassy Tree* about a community's gradual acceptance of an unconventional relationship. Some entries were prompted by such superficial connections as the coincidence of a graveyard picnic in both *Animal Dreams* and the recent *Addams Family* movie or the startling realization that an earlier avatar of the dog with a bandanna in *Animal Dreams* had appeared in a childhood movie the student thought was called *The Golden Monkey*. Other responses were more highbrow, invoking Dante and Beatrice as a model for Codi's bond with Hallie or Faulkner's *As I Lay Dying* as a comparable experiment in multiple narration.

The fact that *Animal Dreams* is both culturally rich and a remarkably sensitive and deeply humane novel would certainly help explain why students would find so many ways to relate to it on a personal level, but I would argue that, for most students, such responses would have remained implicit and incompletely understood had the journal assignment not provided both a context and a pretext for them to become self-conscious about how they were responding to the work. Based on this experience, I am convinced that *Animal Dreams* is an ideal text for such an assignment, but I also believe that this type of assignment not only can help students discover personal connections to any work of literature but also can enhance their appreciation of how literature relates to their lives.

Challenging Preconceived Notions about Teaching Literature

I make such a strong claim for the assignment, in part, based on the discovery that—for my students, at least—identifying personal connections to literature was by no means a simple or straightforward proposition. As I suggested at the beginning of this essay, teachers cannot complacently assume that students intuitively respond affectively to literature and that their more critical and analytical responses require conscious intellectual distance from those initial reactions. My experience with these students suggests instead that they are generally oblivious to those personal responses—assuming they even experience them. Several of my students explicitly referred to the difficulty they initially experienced in completing the journal assignment. Tom, for example, wrote that he "often found it hard to make the types of connections in the journal entries that you asked for." However, as several students explained, the difficulty reflected less the challenge of finding connections than the unfamiliarity of being asked to do so. For Leilani, making connections between the book and her own life was "probably one of the hardest tasks because I don't feel I've ever been asked to do that before." Megan, likewise, found that "the first few entries were hard for me mostly because it was something I had never done before." Angela confirmed that "the *Animal Dreams* journal was a unique assignment, unlike any I've ever had in my college English courses. . . . It allowed me to take a work I've read and apply it to my life."

Since I had naively envisioned the assignment as a liberating experience that would validate students' authentic responses to the novel by creating a private space where they could explore them, I was astonished to discover that students initially resisted and even resented the assignment. "At first," wrote Jennifer, "this assignment seemed tedious and pointless. I love to read books, but as far as relating my own life to one, I did not even want to try. Usually I read to escape reality, not rub my face in it." Thus, far from being a natural consequence of reading, making personal connections to literature was not even a desirable effect for her. As other students confirmed, the problem reflected their skepticism about the very possibility of relating personally to a novel. Laura, for example, wrote that she had to "admit that, at the beginning of the course when we were given this assignment, I thought it was a joke. I couldn't see how my life could possibly relate to this book." In remarkably similar terms, Eric would also "admit that, at first, I was a bit apprehensive about the concept. I wondered how students could be expected to write a series of journals relating what they read in *Animal Dreams* to their own lives."

Yet, the students who experienced initial difficulty with the assignment consistently described how they had overcome their resistance and managed to establish deep personal connections with the book:

> I found the more I read *Animal Dreams* and wrote in the journal the more
> I could connect with Codi and the adjustments she had to make in her life.
>
> Megan

> As I got deeper into the novel, I put more time into my journal entries. . . .
> The more open the characters became, the more open I felt I could be in
> my journal.
>
> Laura

As I progressed through the assignment, the entries became easier for me to write. I actually even started to enjoy them. I felt like the more journal entries I wrote, the easier the next one came for me, especially when discussing something that I am so familiar with, my own life.

Jennifer

As the previous comments reveal, the journal assignment gradually awakened them to the possibility of relating to the novel. As other students confirmed, the fundamental value of the assignment was precisely to teach them that it was possible for them to connect with the book on a personal level. Such a possibility, for example, had never occurred to Christie: "I never knew my life could be put into a character's life in a book." For Jen, this revelation amounted to a general insight into the relation between literature and life: "I learned from this assignment that literature can be related to my life, or the world in general." Moreover, as Susan suggested, students were unlikely to have made such a discovery about the relation between literature and life without the experience of exploring these connections in the journal:

> I like the way we did *Animal Dreams* because it is a novel which deals with a lot of complex issues. I feel if *Animal Dreams* were just read and discussed in class then the students would not necessarily see how those complex issues affect their life.

By encouraging the students to focus on the intersections between the book and their own lives, this journal assignment reduced the distance between the students and the book. The students repeatedly experienced their readings as a catalyst that triggered associations and memories from their own experience. As Jen explained, "Going through the book, I found certain phrases or concepts to trigger my memory of childhood events, dreams, everyday happenings, movies I have seen, or just deep thoughts." Keri wrote that "these journals . . . sparked old memories of my life"; Marc "related to many of the characters in this book, recalling some of them as memories"; and Robert found that the characters "made me think of a time in my life they made me remember." In fundamental ways, the journal put many students in touch not just with themselves and their immediate responses but also with parts of themselves they had forgotten or blocked out.

By shifting the primary focus of the writing from the book to the self— as it related to the book—the journals increasingly approximated the private kind of writing that Elbow and Clarke describe, the kind that is more conventionally associated with diaries than with academic journals. In fact, Robert specifically stated that "the assignment to me was almost like writing an entry in your personal diary."

Likening these journals to diaries, however, by no means implies that the students' writing was confined nor even primarily devoted to recounting personal experiences recalled by events in the novel. For most of the students, the value of the experience was that it stimulated reflection about the book and about themselves. Echoing the experience of many of her classmates, Megan found that "this journal really made me think about things rather than just reading the book." Students consistently characterized the journal assignment as a learning experience, which, because of its explicit focus on the self, helped many of them make important discoveries about themselves:

> My experience with the book *Animal Dreams* has been a learning one. The book taught me a lot about myself through Codi.
>
>   Travis

> One thing that this assignment did was make me understand myself a little better. This sounds very cliché, but it forced me to look into my own life and bring it out on paper.
>
>   Jennifer

> In reading *Animal Dreams* and writing journal entries, I have learned a lot about myself, analyzing literature, and making correlations to other books and events.
>
>   Christie

Christie went on to explain the deeply personal nature of the learning experience she had while keeping the journal, which illustrates that, beyond learning, this kind of writing can serve a therapeutic function in some students' lives:

> Codi and I have a lot of similarities and emotions in common. Her mother died when she was young, and my father died when I was young. We share the same types of emotions from this. By seeing how she reacted to it over the years, I have realized that I still haven't accepted my father's death. I know it happened, but I have never tried to sit down and figure out how I feel. Through these journal entries, I've started confronting it.

Uncannily, Quiantina, who also wrote in her journal about the loss of her father, described how the journal had made her "think about things I had forgotten or tried to shut out because it was difficult to handle at the time." Jen had a similar experience with the journal: "By doing this journal, I feel that it has made me look deeper into myself, and brought me to terms with some of my feelings and thoughts that I normally would have overlooked or taken for granted."

It could easily be objected that this is precisely the kind of writing students would do in a personal—as opposed to an academic—journal and that, if we wanted students to do this kind of writing, why wouldn't we simply ask them to keep a personal journal? In other words, assuming we are willing to discount the evidence that this type of assignment actually helps students understand how literature relates to their lives, how can encouraging students to produce this kind of personal writing be justified in the context of a literature class? The answer my students consistently provided is that this journal assignment not only fostered self-knowledge but also enhanced their understanding of literature.

Personal Understanding as a Prelude to Social Knowledge

The students repeatedly intuited a correlation between relating to the book on a personal level and understanding it more thoroughly. Susan, for example, "felt if we could relate the book to our own lives then we could get more out of it," and Brad wrote that the journal "gave me a better understanding of the book because I could relate to it so well." Leilani also believed that "creating my own personal journal has helped me understand the problems Kingsolver presents in a more educated way." And, for several students, the intellectual benefits of keeping the journal went beyond gaining a fuller appreciation of that one novel.

Tracy, for example, described how the kind of reading required for the journal had transformed the way she read books:

> I felt that I learned a lot about evaluating books through this experience. I noticed that when I was reading other books, I found myself relating different things in those books to my own life. The journals helped me to read more intensely and pay more attention to what I was reading because I knew that I had to write about that section of the book. Even when I was reading the other books that I did not have to write a journal for I found myself paying more attention to those books also.

Even the necessary contrivance of having students read only twenty-five pages per week had the unexpected benefit of enhancing some students' reading experience:

> I'm glad I had to stop and write about it in sections. It helped me get a better understanding out of the book, instead of letting the book explain everything in the end.
>
> Christie

> This project made me look at books in a different light. I am accustomed, like most people, to read an entire novel and then proceed to develop an opinion about it. With this book, however, I formed different opinions almost every time I picked up my pen. I think this also helped me understand the novel better. With this method you are actively reading and can make more inferences throughout the book.
>
> Laura

Some students in this class also validated the widely held belief that having students keep journals will improve their writing; but, whereas such claims are conventionally based on the assumption that the more students write the better they will write, these students offered an alternative explanation for the beneficial effects of this particular assignment on their writing. Tom, for example, who admitted having difficulty making the kinds of connections the assignment called for, found that he had to rely increasingly on his imagination to complete his entries: "I tried my best to make connections and to use my imagination. This exercised my imagination and creativity in writing. I honestly believe I needed that exercise. Hopefully it will carry over into other writing I do and improve my writing skills." Eric, who stated that his journal "evoked my thinking of the situations in my life in new and different ways," made the same point that "journals can be an effective outlet for creativity when the time and effort necessary are put in." The students suggest that it was not just the fact of having to write but the demands this assignment placed on their creativity and imagination that led to consistently richer writing.

The students make a strong case for the heuristic value of this type of assignment. Jennifer summed up the benefits of keeping the journal in these terms: "This way, I was doing constructive work for school, learning new literature, and improving my writing skills all in one assignment. This is what I call a learning experience." Sharing Jennifer's opinion about the value of keeping the journal, Chad helped locate the singular power of this type of exercise: "The journal assignment proved to be one of the most expanding aspects of the course. . . . This new medium of thought is one that should not be abandoned; teaching oneself is a very important tool in today's society."

By proposing the concept of "teaching oneself" as central to the experience of keeping this journal, Chad perceptively identifies the pedagogical rationale for this assignment, but he also touches on the feature of the assignment that may most concern some teachers, namely that it isolates student writing about literature from the social process of constructing meaning in the classroom. If the book is not to be discussed in class, students never have a chance to find out how others have responded to it and how their own ideas will be received. Some students, of course, were perfectly content to experience the freedom of an unmediated response to the text. Jennifer, for example, "felt like it was an excellent assignment because it allowed me to read a book on my own, and draw my own conclusions from it. It also allowed me to discuss freely my opinions and thoughts on the book without any outside prejudices." Revealing a remarkable sensitivity to the implications of socializing knowledge, Jeff, likewise, "enjoyed writing about a book we never discussed in class because this gave our own true opinion about the book. When it is discussed in class you tend to agree with your classmates on some points and it alters your opinion about it." Still, a significant number of students expressed disappointment that the book had not been discussed in class; having developed strong opinions about the novel, they wished they had had a chance to discuss those ideas with their classmates.

Obstacles to Reconciling the Private with the Public

The experience of using this same journal assignment in two consecutive semesters, however, has raised doubts about the feasibility of having the class discuss the novel each student has been reading and writing about privately. In fact, the first time I used the assignment, I did set aside two days near the end of the semester to discuss the book. Although the quality of the journal entries about the book was largely responsible for my repeating the assignment the following semester, the classroom discussion about the novel generated few insights and provoked little enthusiasm. The students gave me two explanations for the uninspired discussion: (1) the personal nature of their insights into the novel provided no common ground for sharing ideas, and (2) it had been so long since they had started the novel that many had only a dim recollection of the earlier sections. In other words, some of the features of the assignment that account for its strengths as a journal exercise ironically inhibit its translation into the public forum of the classroom. Having had such success with the journal, I was reluctant to change the assignment in the hope of improving a subsequent discussion. I was concerned that guiding students toward developing in their journals a common ground for discussing the novel might inhibit the kind of writing I hoped to foster. I opted instead to drop the scheduled discussion the second time I used the assignment, but I substituted another assignment that was designed to encourage students to talk to each other about this novel.

Early in the semester, I divided the class into groups of six students, each of which was responsible for developing a multimedia presentation on an aspect of *Animal Dreams* that I had identified as having broad implications for an understanding of contemporary culture: Ecology, Gender, Multiculturalism, History, Voice, and Form. Each group was to investigate some of the other cultural manifestations of their assigned topic: films, TV, books, architecture, music, etc. During their half-hour presentations at the end of the semester, the groups discussed the relevance of their assigned topic for *Animal Dreams* and then illustrated its ramifications for contemporary culture. For their presentations, the students prepared video- and audiotapes, collages, overhead transparencies, handouts, skits, and dramatized readings. Considered a separate assignment, this collaborative project was successful to the extent that it engaged students in wide-ranging research, provided them with meaningful learning experiences, and evidently allowed them sufficient creative freedom to produce entertaining and informative presentations. But, as several students remarked on their evaluations of the group project, they saw no connection between their journals and the presentations; others noted only tenuous connections between the presentations and the novel. Thus, this

second attempt had also failed to bring students' experience of *Animal
Dreams* into the classroom.

   Although I plan to try a variation of this collaborative project the next
time I teach the course that will allow groups to develop topics of their own
choosing—and theoretically create a context for students to negotiate a topic
by talking to one another about their responses to the novel—the failure of
two previous attempts to bring their journal experiences into the classroom
may suggest that the aims of this particular journal assignment may be
inherently incompatible with conventional models for having students collectively construct meaning. In other words, I am suggesting that the reflection
and writing produced by this type of assignment call for students to engage
in a fundamentally different kind of activity that neither anticipates nor lends
itself to open discussion. This does not imply, however, that such writing
amounts to privileging private learning in an environment that relies on collectively negotiated knowledge.

Reconceptualizing Journal Writing as Interpersonal Communication

However much we may define journal writing as private writing, the necessity of having teachers read and evaluate journals has the potential to add a
communicative dimension to the writing situation. In most journal assignments, however, the presence of this reader is generally downplayed as an
incidental but inevitable concession to the requirements of writing in an academic setting. In other words, students are conventionally enjoined to write
journals as if they were writing for themselves, even though they know the
teacher must ultimately read what they have written. That knowledge may—
and should—impose constraints on what they write, but they are not
expected to write as if they were communicating with an outside reader; the
teacher as journal reader is more of an eavesdropper on a private discourse
than the intended recipient of a communication. The frequent injunction for
teachers not to grade journals underscores the attempt to minimize the
impression that students are writing for the teacher. As several of my students revealed, however, this was not the way they viewed their journal
writing. By encouraging students to relate to literature in a different way, this
journal assignment also transformed their relation to the teacher as reader.

   Asking students to relate to literature on a human level added a social
dimension to the study of literature that is different from what we conventionally understand as the social construction of meaning in the classroom.
The challenge of exploring "connections" between themselves and the text
required students to identify their lives with those of the characters and, in
the process, to portray themselves and recount their histories in their writing.
When Marc wrote that this journal "says something about me," he reflected

his awareness that his journal represented a statement about his identity. Other students were even more explicit not only about their journals being a statement about who they were, but also about the communicative intentions underlying those revelations:

> This assignment also gave you, the teacher, an opportunity to get to know your students, including myself. This is because this journal offers very detailed insights into my life and feelings.
>
> Jennifer

> I think that this assignment helped Dr. Lovitt get to know me better as a person. As he reads my entries, I hope that he can gain a better understanding of how I feel about the issues that the book brings up.
>
> Jim

As these examples suggest, the process of showing how they identified with the text had the effect of making them self-conscious about having presented an image of themselves, hence the awareness that their writing would help the teacher understand who they were. But the social implications of their writing went beyond the intention to communicate with the teacher. Far from being private or expressive, their journal writing was predicated on imagining a more abstract sense of community with other humans, whom they perceived as having shared some of their experiences and concerns. Having helped many students discover that they could relate their lives to literature, the journal assignment introduced them to literature as a form of communication through which humans seek to establish community by sharing insights about the experience of living.

However small a place we may reserve for such understanding in our literature classes, it seems almost a cliché to recall that this is one of the most fundamental reasons we read literature and surely the way it most immediately engages readers. This is the lesson, for example, that Mr. Antolini tries to teach Holden Caulfield in a memorable and climactic scene in *The Catcher in the Rye:*

> Among other things, you'll find that you're not the first person who was ever confused and frightened and even sickened by human behavior. You're by no means alone on that score, you'll be excited and stimulated to know. Many, many men have been just as troubled morally and spiritually as you are right now. Happily, some of them kept records of their troubles. You'll learn from them if you want to. (189)

Although the fact of discovering personal connections to the novel confirmed that many students had grasped this lesson, Angela intuited the implications of such a discovery: "It made me realize that the problems and experiences I have are like those many other people have. It also made me look at the way I deal with problems and compare them to the way others deal with them.''

Thus, by providing students with greater freedom to engage privately with a text, this journal assignment had the unexpected effect of helping them discover that literature could relate to their lives in a way that they were comfortable about sharing with a reader. The fact that so many individuals could have and were willing to share such a fundamentally similar reading experience suggests that such assignments have the potential to help students experience an alternative model of community in a literature classroom. The results of this experiment also suggest that supplementing the pursuit of formal academic objectives in literature courses with opportunities that encourage students to explore on their own the personal relevance of texts can provide different and potentially enduring learning experiences, the kind of experiences that support the goal of transforming students into lifelong readers.

Works Cited

Belanoff, Pat. 1987. "The Role of Journals in the Interpretive Community." In *The Journal Book*, edited by Toby Fulwiler. Portsmouth, NH: Boynton/Cook.

Elbow, Peter, and Jennifer Clarke. 1987. "Desert Island Discourse: The Benefits Ignoring Audience." In *The Journal Book*, edited by Toby Fulwiler. Portsmouth, NH: Boynton/Cook.

Kingsolver, Barbara. 1990. *Animal Dreams*. New York: HarperCollins.

Salinger, J. D. 1964. *The Catcher in the Rye*. New York: Bantam.

Summerfield, Geoffrey. 1987. "Not in Utopia: Reflections on Journal Writing." In *The Journal Book*, edited by Toby Fulwiler. Portsmouth, NH: Boynton/Cook.

My thirty-member evening American Literature class, which meets once a week for three hours, has a built-in limitation: the third hour, after a short break, is often heavy with somnolent students. Using the poems of Anne Bradstreet and Edward Taylor, Jonathan Edwards's "Sinners in the Hands of an Angry God," and Benjamin Franklin's "The Way to Wealth," I broke the class up into groups of three. To each group I gave an assignment: Collaboratively write a letter from one writer to another, from Bradstreet to Edwards, from Taylor to Franklin, etc. After about twenty minutes, I delivered the letters from one group to another, with the direction: In about ten minutes, write an answer.

Lively discussion ensued, letters of varying kinds were sent. Bradstreet asked for comfort on the burning of her house and the death of her grandchildren, Edwards, in return, remonstrated that she should fear hell for herself and not think of the things of this world. Franklin insisted that Edwards turn his thoughts to how to get ahead in this world; Edwards thundered that Franklin, as not a member of Edwards's congregation and therefore of the elect, would burn in hell. Bradstreet asked how she could think less of the things of this world, such as her comfortable home that burned to the ground, and more comfortably accept the next world, then Edwards asked Bradstreet for her recipe for sugar cake to demonstrate to his congregation the sweetness of heaven.

I asked the students to read their letters and replies. I did not expect what happened: One student read the original letter, another the reply. Not only did we learn something about the voice and interaction between authors, we also had dramatic interaction.

Sidney Poger
University of Vermont

18

New Technologies for New Majority Students of Literature

Helen J. Schwartz
Indiana University–Purdue University, Indianpolis

Messages on e-mail

I am totally confused on what I am reading. Can anyone understand what I am talking about? I haven't read much Shakespeare.

—Brandy

About 2 weeks ago, i learned that my aunt had inoperable cancer of the liver.... She died last wednesday. Then today, i ahd to go into the hospital, the baby that i am the associate nurse on was being taken off of his ventilator, avery difficult decision for mom and dad, but one that they made, becuase it would be what is best for Alan . . . but [he] is still at the writing of this message, breathing on his own . . . who could figure . . . A person . . . who looked fit as a fiddle is now dead from liver cancer and one who we thought would go very quickly is still here.

—Barbara

HI EVERYONE, CLASS WAS REALLY SAD TO ME TODAY. I'M NOT SURE IF IT'S BECAUSE I FELT REAL PAIN FROM THE POEM WE DISCUSSED TODAY [Denise Levertov's poem on Vietnam, "What Were They Like?"] OR IF IT'S JUST LIFE.... WHEN HELEN READ THE POEM IT MADE ME FEEL EMPTY INSIDE, LIKE FOR SOME REASON I'VE BEEN WERE THE AUTHOR HAS BEEN.

—Patti

I'd like my motto to be from Theodore Roethke's poem, "The Waking": "I learn by going where I have to go." That means 2 things to me—that I learn from the situation I find myself in ("have to") but also that I see that I "have" opportunities if I will only look out for them.

—Hannah

What would happen if all students and teachers had access both in and out of class to computers, with the ability to communicate with class members and the world at large? This is the situation journalists have predicted for years, and now it looks like the hardware might be arriving. But in 1989 I wondered where the pedagogy would come from and how resources would be made available equitably. I had been working with computers in the humanities since 1979, first in literature classes and then in writing classes as I gained a methodology and revised value system from studies of writing. Since 1979, new computer programs had been developed, pushed and pulled by the astonishing growth of computer capacity and capability. But it seemed to me that the integration of computers into education depended on communication—getting ideas into machine-readable form and then sharing them for analysis.

E-mail systems already connected many universities in the United States and a growing number abroad. Could this new technology serve the New Majority students where I taught—at Indiana University-Purdue University at Indianapolis (IUPUI)? (I'm defining New Majority students as being over twenty-five years of age, attending part-time, having substantial responsibilities at a job or in a family. In short, my commuter students are not like I was, a seventeen- to twenty-one-year-old full-time student at a residential campus, absorbing knowledge and also attitudes and teaching methods that it has taken me years to rethink.) Bent on "re-inventing the university," I led a group of IUPUI faculty working with a Partnership Grant from IBM and the support of our Office of Integrated Technologies (OIT) to create a new pedagogy that stressed active learning with new technologies.

Actually, as with most opportunities, I discovered meaning as I became involved. You see, I am Hannah (quoted above), who learned by going. I was team-teaching with the new Vice Chancellor at IUPUI, J. Herman Blake, and since he had numerous engagements nationwide and had an office halfway across the campus, I insisted we coordinate with the use of e-mail. When I learned through the grapevine that some computers might be unused for a semester, I wondered what would happen if our students got loaner computers for home use to supplement our class meetings and to communicate with class members. Herman had taught me the importance of community and of seeing the whole student, not just the face turned toward the front of the class. His semester-long example inspired a new joy in teaching and clarified my goals in light of the students in my classes. It just so happened that I was also a computer nut. And from that combination came the idea of the Interactive Learning Community (ILC).

This combination of goals, joy, and technology (as well as Herman, OIT, and then IBM's grant of additional computers) led to the ILC loaning up to twenty computers a semester to students in small- and medium-sized classes over a period of three years. I'd taught small classes before the "Introduction to Literature" class (L115) reported on here, but in Fall 1991 this class was the first medium-sized, computer-supplemented class I'd taught. Although lack of external funding eventually halted the loaner program, several classes have continued the option (or requirement) of e-mail contact.

By reviewing my experience in this experimental course, I want to give you a sense of what it was like to teach this class. My point is not only to illustrate the teaching capabilities of computers, but also to narrate how I came to be Hannah—who learns "by going where I have [two meanings] to go." As I have struggled to integrate reflection and revision into writing assignments, I too have learned to be comfortable with revision, saving the omniscient tone for (most) articles and grant proposals. This essay, however, is a process narrative about how the willingness to improvise with computers keeps me open, learning to walk that talk, learning by going where I have to go.

E-Mail

My Intro to Lit class using loaner computers met twice a week in a regular classroom, but students could always be "in touch" by dialing up our mainframe computer, reading messages left via a distribution list (also called a "listserv"), responding to or initiating discussion. Our system did not allow "synchronous" or real-time exchanges (similar to a phone conversation by notes passed back and forth), but it did allow "asynchronous" discussion— like an exchange of voice-mail messages, but left in electronic text. (The slowness or rapidity of response is indicated in examples below by inclusion of the date and time the message was sent.)

From the beginning, one goal was to support "active learning" (whatever that meant) with the technology, but it took a while to understand how the new medium worked—in itself and in particular assignments. The listserv became a playground—for exploration, but not for harsh or rigorous criticism—*by my design*. It is important to note that a listserv is "naturally" neither a playground nor a firing line. A primary responsibility of a teacher using e-mail is to design the electronic meeting place in a way that meets learning goals.[1] For my beginning literature students, I modeled an environment in which mention of work or home was not out-of-bounds (though not required either). Students could write as much as they wanted, and four to five of the eighteen students were heavy contributors, with three to four doing only the minimum. The minimum included one or two postings per week.

I came to know their situations in a way I can only palely duplicate in non-listserv classes with a self-introduction sheet. One student said she had been out of school for fifteen years, another excused her absence from class because her babysitter went into labor early, another talked about hating the authority structure of school. One especially helpful student became the ILC director, two others joined the project's Steering Committee, yet others I saw seldom or not at all after the course ended. As the following discussion shows, however, my knowledge of their working and home conditions not only helped me know better how to teach New Majority students, but also became a part of their learning.

Several factors may have influenced the following interchange in ways that I could not observe or influence very much. First, private e-mail messages went back and forth without class-wide distribution: I wrote personal messages of support or instruction, students worked in sub-groups, and a number wrote private messages to which I had no access. Second, of the eighteen students, only one was male—and this probably heavily influenced the tone and content of messages. (Even though the exchanges in this class resembled those in other ILC classes, no ILC class had more than thirty percent male enrollment, so the influence of gender may be crucial.)

Time out of class became a rich asset, helpful to teacher and students alike. I asked students to respond before class to a set question. Their answers showed me what they did and did not understand, thus helping me tailor my class notes to their needs. (I could also save the best examples for use the next semester.) Building the next assignment on the best outcomes of the previous one also allowed students time to process ideas in different ways, incorporating what they had learned. The ephemeral nature of e-mail also supported what John Holt identifies in *How Children Fail* as the "minimax" strategy often employed in discussions: We preface our remarks with a disclaimer—"I don't think this is right, but . . ."—so that we minimize loss of face if we're wrong; then we state our views, taking maximum credit if we are right. E-mail allows us to keep and claim our ideas in a text that can later be saved, printed, or downloaded. But for a reasonable typist, e-mail feels like talk—informal, evolving, tolerant of spelling and grammatical mistakes, like a discussion in which a student can enter without permission at any time, have as much time to talk/write as he or she wishes, and then send it to others knowing that it most likely will be trashed after it is read.

Students could use time to their advantage, being the first to "publish" if they were the type of student who liked to "help" or have their hand up first. But if they felt unsure or marginalized, as one African-American student in another class reported, they could wait to see how others would respond to the assignment and gain guidance and self-confidence from peer models (Floyd).

In addition, students also saw a greater variety of opinions and models than possible in class discussion or even with peer review. I had explained that our goal was not "convergent thinking" but "divergent thinking," as long as students could support their views with evidence from the text.

Students began early to take "active learning" seriously—by answering each other's technical questions (if they got to the problem before a consultant or I did) or by the spontaneous peer mentoring that also appeared in other ILC classes (Speckman). Brandy, the student quoted above who later proclaimed

her confusion about "Midsummer Night's Dream," early in the semester
bewailed her inability to get her ideas on paper; within minutes of Brandy's
posting, Mary responded:

> Brandy, I, too have a hard time, sometimes, expressing what's upstairs on
> paper. A lot of times I find my drafts get better by doing just that—making
> more drafts, rewriting the danged thang, and expounding on already present
> themes. It's hard and frustrating (and pays off better sometimes more than
> others), but it works. (16 Sep 1991, 21:38)

Later, I praised Brandy as an outstanding listserv citizen because she asked
questions, while also mentioning others as outstanding helpers or astute thinkers. And often students delivered advice with greater authority—as successful
students—than I had as a teacher. When Brandy asked for help with "Midsummer," (Tues., 15 Oct 1991, 21:28), she got it electronically before I even
logged on to read her call for help—from the summaries some students posted
as well as advice from classmates, like the following from Barbara:

> I read this play about three years ago. It always takes me a while to adjust
> to his style of writing, but eventually my brain falls into a Shakespeare
> mode and I can understand. It helps me if I don't read every footnote. When
> I do that, my eyes are forced to keep looking down and then having to find
> my place again. It makes it more confusing and most of the works cited can
> be figured out in context without a second thought. (Barbara, Thurs., 17 Oct
> 1991, 19:02)

Active learning also meant that students felt free to share continuing
reflection on literary works when the syllabus had inexorably moved on. Jill
raised an apparent discrepancy in August Wilson's "Fences" about the dog
Old Blue and the song about him on 26 Sep 1991, 16:56. A reply from Barbara (along with a complaint about hosting Tupperware parties!) was available four minutes later (26 Sep 1991, 17:00). Over a month later (3 Nov
1991), Rhoda posted a long response specifically directed to Jill's question
as she reconsidered "Fences" for a paper. In this way, the ILC functioned
like a residential community.

Here and in many of the following examples, we can see students realizing
the potential of integrating course materials into their world view and value
systems. New Majority students, whose involvement in work or family responsibilities gives them a richer matrix than those in the ivory tower, often
experience their learning as inferior to residential instruction because it seems
fragmented, at odds with the other tasks in their life; the ILC gave students a
place to reflect on their studies and to integrate their learning with their
experience. Again, the medium was designed to foster such exchange, and not
all students took advantage of this "place"—at least not on-line, but the tenor
of the class changed because of the community continuing out of class.

To give a sense of the rich give-and-take and the learning woven through the interchanges, I'll quote a number of messages on Sharon Olds' poem "Sex Without Love," the work in the "love poems" cluster that elicited the most negative as well as substantial positive reaction. (The other most frequently mentioned poems included Marlowe's "The Passionate Shepherd" and Ralegh's "Nymph's Reply," Anne Bradstreet's poem to her husband, and Galway Kinnell's "After Making Love We Hear Footsteps.") After reading the cluster, each student was to post a response on two poems found to be interesting. Then, after reading each other's postings and class discussion, they were to identify the poem they liked best and least along with a criterion for liking or disliking. Both the assignments for the love-poem cluster were posted within a nine-day period (October 7–16).

Susan posted a moderately full response to "Sex Without Love" on October 7. A response by Brandy clearly referred to Susan's earlier message. (Remember that Brandy is the student who seemed to specialize in asking for help.) In addition to agreeing with Susan, Brandy commented honestly about her discomfort with Olds' skillfully chosen word choice, a hint useful to me in guiding subsequent class discussion:

> I DIDN'T LIKE THE WAY SOME OF THE WORDS WERE USED. . . .
> "HOOKED" SEEMS TOO HARSH FOR THE INTRO. OF THE POEM.
> I ALSO DIDN'T LIKE HOW SHE USED THE COMPARISON OF A
> WET CHILD AT BIRTH WITH THE WAY YOU ARE WHEN YOU
> ARE HAVING SEX. MY MIND ALL OF A SUDDEN WENT ON THE
> SCENE OF A MOTHER GIVING BIRTH. (8 Oct 1991 22:40)

Another student, Beth, agreed in disliking the same word choice three days later, but she commented with greater understanding and explanation. Her posting fulfilled the second assignment on criteria for liking or disliking poetry. She explained,

> I also didn't like the analogy between the sweat on their faces and "wet as the children at birth whose mothers are ging [sic] to give them away." It seems sick to me. The speaker begins with a question and she begins to answer it nicely, "Beautiful as dancers, gliding over each other like ice-skaters over the ice." Immediately after that she starts her severeness. (11 Oct 1991 11:57)

Brandy, only four days after her first posting and shortly after Beth's, referred to "Sex Without Love" again in discussing the poem she liked best. Here she revealed how deeply and directly the poem had spoken to her experience, so that, she reported, she even sent a copy of the poem to the ex-boyfriend the poem "explained" to her:

> MY FAVORITE OF THE POEMS WAS: "SEX WITHOUT LOVE"
> SHARON OLDS AFTER MY BOYFRIEND HAD CHEATED ON

ME..., I ALWAYS ASKED MYSELF THE QUESTION THAT
STARTS OFF THIS POEM "HOW DO THEY DO IT, THE ONES WHO
MAKE LOVE WITHOUT LOVE?" I NEVER COULD GET AN
ANSWER. WHILE I WAS READING THIS POEM, EVERYTHING
BEGAN TO COME CLEAR TO ME. "THEY DO NOT MISTAKE THE
LOVER FOR THEIR OWN PLEASURE, THEY ARE LIKE GREAT
RUNNERS: THEY KNOW THEY ARE ALONE WITH THE ROAD
SURFACE, THE COLD, THE WIND, THE FI[t] OF THEIR SHOES,..."
I'VE NEVER READ A POEM THAT HAS ANSWERED A QUESTION
THAT HAS DWELLED IN MY MIND LIKE THIS. I FEEL ALSO BY
READING THIS THAT MAYBE THE POET MIGHT HAVE INSIGHT,
AND THESE ARE FEELINGS SPEAKING OUT TO SOMEONE THAT
HAS HURT HER. (11 Oct 1991, 20:39)

Brandy clearly understood the poem and wove specific quotations in with her observations, her best writing of the semester from the person who earlier felt frustrated by not being able to express her thoughts. Her response pays tribute to the power of poetry to speak the ineffable, a point I could pick up on later in reflecting on poetry and then invite students to write their own poems.

Some of the students clearly disliked poems such as "Sex Without Love," whose experience seemed alien to their world view. For example, Mary later dismissed "Sex Without Love," saying it just did not appeal to her at all (13 Oct 1991, 19:00). But Rochelle commented favorably on the poem as a moral warning (13 Oct 1991, 20:14:) from the viewpoint of someone raised in a close, religious family, and Rhoda liked the poem because it helped her explain her own moral stand on "sex without love" (14 Oct 1991, 06:21).

The most sophisticated literary response to the Olds poem came from Sybil:

> I'd like to talk about "Sex Without Love" for a minute. Alive and raw.... Ironically, it made me understand something about a guy I once knew. He had sex with other females ... alot! And usually claimed to hate himself or at least be dissatisfied with himself over it. I couldn't understand that, or believe it then, but now I can see where he was coming from. I also liked the word choice. "Hooked inside each other" was just so ... graphic and vulgar, yet emotional and real. I think that that one phrase set the act described apart from the act of making love. It helped me visualize this couple, or should I say, two people, scrogging in some alley, or in a bedroom at a party, together physically, but not in the heart or soul. I wrote a poem very simular to this a couple of years ago, but didn't feel it really painted the picture the way it should. This does. (13 Oct 1991, 00:55)

The listserv gave students a chance to hear more views than in discussion or even with peer review of responses, thus supporting our quest for divergent rather than convergent thinking.

In general, I stayed out of the conversations since I had many opportunities to direct discussion in face-to-face class meetings. But it is important to note Susan Romano's caveat about the monitors of listservs who then report on such exchanges: "I counter with textual silence certain student opinions and affirm with textual attention others. . . . Each exemplary success story suppresses alternative stories and knowledges about interactive, electronic discourse"(21, 26–7). The dynamic on our listserv gave scope and support to students like Mary, Jill, and Brandy (perhaps typecasting her as the Questioner), but it tended to exclude the bright but unconventional Sybil and the private and nondisclosing Jackie.

The nonsequential nature of postings on the listserv gave us all time for processing class content as a community in a manner seldom possible outside residential campuses. One standing assignment asked student volunteers to summarize what had happened in class—with modifications by other students or me. The task was accepted faithfully by the students only after reconceiving of the summary as a report to students who had missed the class. In fact, Rochelle, who had initially resisted the computer component of the class, became a heavy user and enthusiast after she broke her leg and "kept up" with us mainly via the listserv. One moderately involved student described these exchanges within a community setting, as follows:

> No kidding guys I got such a great feeling reading about everyone's lives, their feeling on the LOVE poems and how everyone seems to know just a little something about everyone. It like the whole gang is looking out for each other, with Jackie's welcoming party [after trouble getting on-line] and Rochelle's concern messages [when she broke her leg] I feel really good about the direction this project is taking us. (SherriB, 14 Oct 1991, 14:46)

The student experiences the community as primarily social, with a concomitant danger of groupthink developing, but the design of the listserv made it a "place" for integrating learning and life. When "Magic" Johnson announced he had AIDS, that news was discussed on the listserv although it had no relation to our syllabus; later, when students were asked to write a modern beast fable, one student adapted this topic, writing about a champion race car infected with the metallic equivalent of AIDS. (Remember, IUPUI is in the home of the Indianapolis 500.) In the fable, the ailing car was saluted and mourned by colleagues and fans as he circled the track for the last time. The listserv allowed for a process of review, addition of new issues, and reshaping motifs to form new questions.

The assignment to write a modern beast fable or fairy tale grew out of the segment of the class studying the power and flexibility of literary conventions. As we analyzed fairy tales and beast fables in reading and class discussion, students prepared to post a "modern" fairy tale or beast fable. SherriB on the listserv asked me to define "modern"—an excellent question and one that would have remained unanswered until after the assignment was

turned in had it not been for our listserv. My answer acknowledged a broader
scope engendered by her question:

> SherriB, you raise an interesting question about what makes a "modern
> fairy tale" "modern." I had thought that it would be the moral that was
> modern, but I see that you thought of the modern as being the setting. How
> interesting. Would it be a modern fairy tale if you changed ANY of the ele-
> ments we discussed . . . : story, characters, moral, world? (Hannah, 2 Nov
> 1991, 15:54)

After students posted their stories, I then asked each student to comment
on two stories—showing for each what was conventional and what was
"modern." I could write private notes to students who had important mis-
conceptions or problems with the assignment, but on the listserv the students'
responses conveyed only praise by selecting a fable or tale for comment—a
perfect follow-up for the mini-max nature of e-mail. The best work included,
predictably, the good students, but also weaker students. Rochelle, the one
with the broken leg, spun an imaginative, Tolkienesque tale (a skill developed, she conjectured, from telling elaborate stories to her younger siblings).
Her story about the growth and sacrifice of a "king" tree in the forest was
sophisticated in sentence structure and consistently elevated in tone:

> The Great Council [of Oaks] feared him [the promising seedling], and plot-
> ted against him. But, having that foundation of rock, wisdom and knowl-
> edge, he thwarted off any harm. The Great Oaks realized that this was no
> ordinary tree, that they would have to use great powers to overcome him.
> They turned their leaves bitter, hoping that all the creatures would feed on
> him. They stretched forth their arms to try and steal his sunlight to no avial.
> As the great winds and rains came forth, they withdrew their limbs and
> kneeled over to let the young oak take the full force of nature. But the crea-
> tures of the forest clung to his clothing and hung on even to risk their own
> lives, for they knew this would one day be the Great Oak Tree. (Sun., 3
> Nov 1991, 21:28)

Numerous students responded to Rochelle with genuine and well-deserved
praise. In ILC classes, students not only learned each other's names but
seemed to become friends. I know that for myself I learned to relate better to
students as whole individuals and not just as students earning grades: A student (good person; I must be a good teacher) or C-student (lazy? disinterested? or what have I done wrong?).

The students were not alone in being able to process ideas recursively.
I too had the chance to "repeat" what had been said (in class or in our text)
or to spell out important ideas left implicit or given short shrift. Because we
shared information about our lives and our values, I could include in these
mini-lectures much that felt like shared experience. On poetry, the section I

normally am most dissatisfied teaching, I felt great satisfaction in posting the following, an excerpt from a rare, multi-screen message:

> Poetry tries to say the "ineffable" (that is, something which can't be said directly, as in an essay), and it often uses indirection rather than spelling things out. How can you describe what it feels like to love someone? So we need to trust our emotional responses and hold on to them, even when we put our minds in gear. Patti's reaction [about Levertov's poem] is a powerful one, and let us remember it and use it as a touchstone to go back to.... So we read poetry because it says what we can't say. Barbara calls up her mother and reads the poem [Pastan's "To a Daughter Leaving Home"], and I get the impression that what that accomplishes is to say lots of things: I love you, I understand what you have been doing as a mother, I feel at one with you, thank you. That's a lot to do with one poem of less than a page. (Hannah, 14 Nov 1991, 08:47)

Students then had the option of posting their own poems. One responder, Barbara, reflected on her aunt's death and the infant Alan's lingering (quoted previously) as the brainstorming for her poem. The listserv gave students a chance to share with each other their responses, and this gave me a window I had never had before. I don't know if other classes have felt poetry to be such a vital part of their lives, but with this class I became sure that many of the students clearly felt poetry speaking to them and for them.

Current Conclusions; or, Learnings from Going

Active learning was the goal, literary texts were the subject matter, composition studies was my theoretical perspective. What hypotheses emerged from this experience? I hope you will agree that our experience, analyzed by students and faculty alike, has provided a powerful argument and model for using technology despite the remaining problems of equitable access and the continuing problem of training.

With my New Majority commuter students, I learned to overlay the "old verities" with some "new verities" in composition pedagogy delivered with new technology. The old verities of teaching literature involve the teacher in

* lecturing to deliver information and to model an analytic process
* assigning reading
* conducting discussion to involve students
* perhaps giving quizzes or content-based exams, and grading papers on the assumption that students will learn from their strengths and weaknesses for their next paper (perhaps later that semester, perhaps next semester).

The new verities that I have learned from composition studies stress the need
for students learning actively in a developmental setting:

- processing information in different forms, with room for growth
  over time and reflection for integrating new ideas into one's value
  system
- experiencing writing as part of communication or an ongoing conversation about developing knowledge or theories (not just exhibit-
  ing mastery of static knowledge that grows only by accretion)
- taking responsibility for learning by teaching others and asking for
  help with learning
- presenting multiple interpretations that illustrate the logic and richness of divergent thinking

These goals seem especially suitable for an introductory literature course
in which students are primarily non-majors, trying to gain a general education. I find myself striving to give them "cultural literacy," not of the Hirsch
variety stressing "mastery" of a body of knowledge, but of the kind stressing "competency," defined by Shirley Brice Heath as follows: "Being literate means being able to talk with and listen with others to interpret texts, say
what they mean, link them to personal experience and with other texts, argue
with them and make predictions from them, develop future scenarios, compare and evaluate related situations, and know that the practice of all these
literate abilities is practical" (298).

Computers help me achieve my instructional goals. Their amazing and
growing capacities have helped me put the new verities to work in the literature classroom for both traditional and New Majority students. Computers
as a medium of communication have turned the diversity of the student population into a sharable asset that helps me reach my goals for the particular
syllabus and for a larger "literacy" agenda. Working with computers has
kept my role complex, involving me with students as guide and friend and,
yes, authority, too, but also as a fellow learner. I am Hannah, who learns by
going where I have to go.

Notes

1. For example, one teacher I met at a conference required his students to do
peer critique on a conference for a grade; he then wondered why students were vicous
in criticism whereas ILC students were friendly and supportive. In a graduate English
writing class at Michigan Technological University, the teacher decided that all students had to write, but the teacher could only read messages (Selfe and Meyer); when
students are already socialized in the discipline and doing advanced work, it is appropriate that they "own" their listserv.

Works Cited

Floyd, Mary Ellen. 1991. *On-line Conferencing: An Autobiographical Analysis.* Unpublished manuscript submitted for English W411.

Heath, Shirley Brice. 1990. "The Fourth Vision: Literate Language at Work." *The Right to Literacy*, edited by Andrea A. Lunsford, Helene Moglen, and James Slevin. New York: Modern Language Association of America.

Olds, Sharon. 1992. "Sex Without Love." *The Dead and the Living.* New York: Knopf.

Romano, Susan. 1993. "The Egalitarianism Narrative: Whose Story? Which Yardsticks?" *Computers and Composition* 10.3: 5–28.

Selfe, Cynthia L., and Paul R. Meyer. 1991. "Testing Claims for On-Line Conferences." *Written Communication* 8: 163–192.

Speckman, V. 1991. *The Emergence of Peer Mentoring Phenomena in a Computer-supplemented University Classroom.* Unpublished manuscript submitted for English W411.

V

Writing for Critical Literacy

19

The English Literature Seminar as Writing Across the Curriculum

Linda H. Peterson
Yale University

Leslie Moore, one of my colleagues known for her excellence in teaching both literature and composition, used to say to beginning instructors: "You can always tell a syllabus for a literature course from a syllabus designed for composition. The former is dominated by a list of books; the latter is motivated by a sequence of writing assignments."[1] Her antithesis—one she formulated as much for rhetorical effect as for conceptual clarity—was meant to startle graduate students out of their tendency to plan composition courses by first heading for a reader and then choosing essays they wanted to discuss in class. She wanted them instead to think about the writing they meant their students to do and about how a teacher might best encourage such writing, whether through reading, informal or pre-writing, collaborative activities, or formal assignments.

My colleague's words stayed with me this fall as I planned my syllabus for a senior literature seminar, English 429: "The English *Bildungsroman*, Dickens to Woolf"; they prompted me to wonder whether I could do justice in the course to both literature and writing or whether the two would remain in antithesis. The course catalogue, known familiarly as the *Bluebook*, states that senior seminars, with their required senior essays, should "help to provide an appropriate intellectual culmination to the student's work in the major." My department interprets this statement to mean, among other things, that each student should write a long (twenty-page) essay that represents not only original thinking but also a mature integration of historical, theoretical, and/or critical materials. Senior majors have a choice between writing an independent project, undertaken with the guidance of a faculty advisor, or electing a senior seminar with its requirement of a long critical essay. My course was to provide the latter option, and in it I wanted to test the extent to which composition pedagogy could be integrated with literary study—at least within the limits of a semester.

In a sense, what I was proposing to teach was a writing-across-the-curriculum course within the English Department—on what Susan McLeod would call the "rhetorical" model, in that it would emphasize a discourse community and its rhetorical conventions.[2] For the past fifteen years many colleges and universities have offered such courses and designated them "Writing Intensive." By definition, "Writing Intensive" courses integrate reading and writing, the study of a subject with writing about the subject, the methodological premises of the discipline with its written conventions. But such courses, at least at my institution, have always been offered in departments other than English—on the assumption (mistaken, I think) that all English courses are *de facto* "Writing Intensive." I wanted my seminar to be self-consciously "Writing Intensive," to incorporate literary study with pedagogical practices derived from recent composition studies, including a flexible approach to students' writing processes, a focus on revision, and a regular use of peer collaboration and response.

Planning: Prospect Visions

As I planned my syllabus, I found myself reverting to the tendencies of Leslie Moore's mythical literary instructor: My tendency was first and foremost to list a series of books. I could design a sequence of reading assignments and a sequence of writing assignments, but I found it difficult to integrate *on paper* my pedagogy as a writing teacher with my practices as a literature teacher.[3] In my own mind, I saw important connections between the two: that students would begin to read various *bildungsromane* (novels of self-development) and that they would, through informal as well as formal writing activities, develop their own ideas about the genre. These reading and writing activities would eventually result in the draft of a senior paper. Still, despite my good intentions, my syllabus looked as if it had separate tracks rather than a single integrated plan.

As I reflected on the problem, two pedagogical issues emerged—one familiar to writing-across-the-curriculum directors, the other rarely discussed. Both will confront the literature teacher who intends to integrate composition pedagogy within his or her course.

> *How does a teacher allow adequate time for writing without*
> *shortchanging the reading (the "content") of the course?*

This is a question writing directors frequently get asked—and one I, as a director, have frequently answered. For a freshman English seminar, it is easy to respond that the process of writing is as important as—indeed, more important than—the content; writing often *is* the content. Even for an upper-level, disciplinary-based course, it is possible to argue—and, in fact, it has become a standard argument in the writing-across-the-curriculum movement—that a "cognitivist perspective" that uses "writing to learn" can "improve on . . . the 'banking model' of education in which students passively receive, record, and return the teacher's deposits of knowledge."[4] Yet these responses, however compelling they may sound, skirt the very practical issues that face teachers of advanced seminars for majors. They rely on too-simple dichotomies between "banking" models of education (bad) versus a "cognitivist" model (good)—as if these poles represented the only pedagogies that a teacher might choose.

In my own case, I wanted to acknowledge the importance of disciplinary knowledge while incorporating practices associated with "cognitive models" or "writing to learn." Given the very different classes that my students had taken prior to mine, I felt that they needed a common grounding in the Victorian novel and in the *bildungsroman* form in particular. Without that grounding, they could not participate in the collaborative activities I had planned or write the mature papers that the course demanded. I eventually decided to compromise: to cut one book from the syllabus, but also to use class time only for collaborative activities—whether discussion of novels or peer-group work—and leave all other writing-to-learn activities for the students to pursue outside of class.

The decision was not just a matter of time management or professional compromise but my response to a larger pedagogical concern.

How does a teacher respect the writing processes that advanced students—in this case seniors, twenty-one-year-old adults—have developed during their undergraduate education?

Most of the critical literature on writing across the curriculum assumes that all students can (or should) engage in the same kinds of activities in all their classes, whatever their level of sophistication as writers; it suggests that it's appropriate to assign freewriting, journal writing, informal in-class writing, *or whatever else the teacher chooses*—no matter what strategies or processes the students may have developed as (or on) their own for writing and learning. I wanted to teach with a different assumption—that advanced students have already developed their writing processes and should be free to enact them as they choose. It seems to me appropriate to introduce beginning students to a variety of writing-to-learn strategies and to reinforce them through practice within a general education program. But it does not seem necessary to require seniors to enact all such strategies. Presumably, if the writing-across-the-curriculum program has worked, advanced students will already have recognized the value of—and adopted—writing practices effective for themselves.

Naive? Idealistic? Potentially disastrous? Perhaps. But I wanted my seniors to use whatever writing process worked best for them. To guard against the disaster of producing no writing (and failing to graduate), I established a series of deadlines by which writing assignments of various sorts—chosen in part by the students themselves—were due:

First four weeks: A short paper on a topic the student might like to explore further *or* an idea draft on a novel the student might like to analyze for the senior essay *or* an annotated bibliography on critical or historical readings relevant to a topic in which the student might be interested.

Second four weeks: A draft of a section of the senior essay *or* a draft of the introduction to the essay *or* an annotated bibliography of secondary criticism or historical material potentially useful for writing the essay.

Eleventh week: A draft of the essay for discussion in peer groups and for the instructor's comments.

Fourteenth week: The final draft of the senior essay.

Students made their choices in conferences and set up a sequence suited to their individual personalities and projects.[5]

It may seem that, by leaving decisions about the writing process up to the student, I merely avoided the issue of "content" versus "writing process" and that I partially acceded to the banking model of education by devoting most of my class time to the discussion of literature. Not necessarily. If senior majors are to write critical essays at their best, then they need class time to discuss readings, theoretical and critical essays, and their historical discoveries with the instructor and other students. Learning and discussing "content" is an important part of advanced writing in the disciplines, especially if the writing is to be a mature piece of literary criticism.

Moreover, some of the class activities—most notably, the exchanges within peer groups—depended on exchanges of content as part of (or on the way to) discussions about writing. Unlike my practice in freshman English classes, where peer groups are more or less arbitrarily constructed, in this seminar I constructed peer groups around complementary projects. I wanted students to collaborate as scholars might: to exchange historical or bibliographical information, to discuss existing criticism and their own new ideas, to read each others' drafts, and to offer suggestions for expansion and revision. I wanted to suggest, in other words, that exchanging and discussing information is part of the process of writing.

To put it in other terms: I tried to imitate the practices of the profession. In English studies, we don't all begin our research projects in the same ways: Some of us begin with ideas from class preparation or discussion, others by reading existing scholarship and criticism, still others by thinking about a conference paper we have heard or by extending a professional conversation in which we have engaged. Nor do we, in English studies, mandate the way that scholars undertake their research and writing: We do not require idea drafts or journal writing or freewriting or any other pre-writing activity. We do, however, regulate the later stages of scholarly and critical production: We ask colleagues to read a draft, we submit manuscripts to journals or presses for their opinions, we respond to peer critiques or the suggestions of our editors, we negotiate details of style with the copyeditor. In a similar way, I wanted to encourage the seniors in my seminar to use writing throughout the semester and to enact collaborative practices they already knew, but I wanted to formalize only those activities that accord with professional practice.

Teaching: In Medias Res

For most of my students, the opportunity to choose their own sequence of writing assignments and put into practice their most comfortable writing processes was a welcome invitation—and they took it. In the course evaluations one student noted, "I liked the flexibility on the assignments. It allowed us to tailor the semester to our best working patterns while ensuring that we got started on the essays relatively early in the semester."[6]

This kind of positive response tended to come from students who understood their own writing processes and were comfortable with them. Sarah, a double major in English and philosophy, told me without hesitation that she wanted to work out her ideas *first* in a short essay or two before looking at *any* secondary material; for her, writing a critical essay involved a process of thinking and drafting without the "interference" of someone else's ideas. Another student, Elizabeth, a double major in English and history, took an almost antithetical approach; she wanted first to read a great deal of secondary criticism and then to formulate her position within the field. She chose to construct an annotated bibliography for her first assignment and later to draft an introduction to her paper. This was the method she had learned as a history major, and it was one with which she was comfortable.

Students less self-assured—and less practiced in strategies writing specialists associate with early stages of composing—tended not to know how to plan their own writing sequences and to feel, as one put it, that "the first deadline came too early in the course for me to have any idea what I wanted to write my final paper on." Implicit in such a response is a sense that a first writing assignment ought to be a *paper*, that it *ought* to contribute *directly* to the final essay. Absent is a sense that one might use writing to generate ideas and get one's bearings.

The contrasts between confident and uncertain writers, and especially the contrast between the English-philosophy and the English-history majors, led me to rethink my assumption that all students will have naturalized a writing process by the senior year, as well as to speculate how different disciplines encourage different processes for critical thinking and writing, particularly in the early stages. For "strong" disciplines like history, the process becomes "natural" or "comfortable" by the senior year—so much so that it dominates the student's work in other fields.[7] What about the writing processes of English majors not under the influence of another discipline?

For my students as a group, there was no single process for working on a long seminar paper. Some began with a topic they knew they wanted to pursue—say, the role of reading in the female *bildungsroman* or the function of formal education in *David Copperfield* and *The Mill on the Floss*—and they worked out their ideas in a series of drafts that ultimately contributed to the final essay. Others began with a short paper that turned out *not* to be what they wanted to pursue—and they started over. Still others began by constructing a bibliography of secondary criticism with annotations that recorded their responses or key ideas. Most had a sense of how they wanted to work once they got to the stage of writing a rough draft. But there was no uniform approach to invention: to how one "got" ideas, how one related one's own ideas to those of others, or what to do when ideas didn't come. One student confessed, as if it were his fault, that he had never written an English paper integrating historical or theoretical or *any* secondary materials with his own ideas—not at least since high school. All of Kevin's English professors had assigned original "close readings." What he thought was his unique plight turned out to be true for about a third of the students in the seminar (and the next time I teach, I'll need to be more conscious of the needs of this group).

In a sense, the varied responses of my students reflect the state of English studies today. Within English departments and the courses they offer, formalist paradigms for reading and writing exist side by side with other critical approaches—from reader response to feminist to New Historicist and cultural studies. Students encounter these paradigms randomly, depending on the courses they take and the professors they choose. At Yale especially, a long tradition of formalist criticism—from the New Criticism of Brooks and Warren to the deconstruction of Yale school critics like de Man, Miller, and Hartman—has emphasized "close reading" and has privileged writing assignments that position the student as a solitary, original reader of a literary text. This tradition has produced—and still produces—English majors who read and write with intensity, subtlety, and sophistication. But it also creates some confusion when students are introduced to more recent, and particularly historical, approaches to literary study by professors who occupy a different critical camp. Not every English major has sorted it out by the senior year.

One response to the current state of English studies has been to "teach the conflicts," in Gerald Graff's phrase.[8] "Teaching the conflicts" does not, however, clarify—or even address—crucial issues about writing that English majors face.[9] It is a very different thing for students to write a long essay using a New Critical approach to reading and writing than it is for them to treat a literary text in a New Historicist mode. And it would be a very different thing still for them to write senior essays on the "conflicts" within English studies. My colleagues and I resolve this issue in different ways: some by making the essays in their senior seminars essentially an extended formalist reading of a text; others by focusing their senior seminars on a single critical mode (e.g., New Historicist or psychoanalytic or feminist) and teaching students how to write papers in that mode; still others by allowing students as much freedom and giving them as much guidance as possible to allow for diverse critical approaches. I tried the last approach, knowing that the first two might produce a more coherent seminar but hoping that students would profit from the diversity of approaches.

To make that diversity more visible, I used a practice common in "rhetorical" approaches to writing across the curriculum: that of discussing professional essays and the discourse conventions they enact. For one novel, Thomas Hardy's *Far from the Madding Crowd*, we discussed a set of critical essays that included New Critical, "old" and "new" historical, and feminist approaches. We discussed the essays not so much as a springboard for our own ideas, nor even as illustrations of diverse critical approaches, but more importantly for the writing strategies that they suggested. We asked: How did the essayists construct a critical problem? How did they assemble and present evidence? What constituted evidence within each approach? What strategies might students want to try? This discussion of rhetorical strategies helped students anticipate strategies they might use in their own essays or recommend to their peers in revision.

Revising: In Retrospect

However successful my plan to encourage individual writing processes, to stress invention and revision, or to clarify discourse conventions may (or may not) have been, the best integration of composition pedagogy with literary study came in the collaborative activities at the end of the semester. At two or three earlier points, I had encouraged exchanges of ideas, information, and resources among students working on similar projects. These exchanges were helpful; in some cases, they initiated conversations among students that continued throughout the semester and that encouraged informal collaboration. But the final peer-group evaluations were, by far, the best part of the course.

At the end of the semester, each student participated in a collaborative workshop prior to revising his or her essay. Students photocopied and exchanged their drafts with other group members; the group members read and made suggestions for revisions; then each group met for a discussion of the drafts. These collaborative workshops were popular and highly successful —perhaps the most commented-on aspect of the course. Allen, for example, told me that he hadn't read another student's paper since his freshman English class and that it was really interesting to see the work other students had done. Alexia made a special point of visiting me during the next semester to say how much she learned from the workshops. She also suggested that I find other ways to encourage collaboration. She told me that before she began revising, she went over all the suggestions made by me and her peer readers. Page by page, she tried to figure out what evidence she needed to supply, what argument she needed to clarify, what alternate interpretations she needed to anticipate.

Alexia wanted to argue, for instance, that the happy marriage at the end of *Jane Eyre* was pure fairy tale, that it projected the illusory possibility of both independence and union but that in fact it undercut the quest for autonomy that had marked Jane Eyre's progress throughout the rest of the novel. In her draft, Alexia quoted one of the culminating sentences of the novel— "to be together is for us to be at once as free as in solitude, as gay as in company"—and then went on to write:

> How ideal! Although she [Jane] has sacrificed her autonomy, their unification even allows for her freedom and solitude; so she does not miss her independence because she has the best of both worlds. But how can this be? How can Jane experience freedom and solitude when she is completely merged, in both an emotional and physical sense, with her husband? The only resolution I can find is in remembering that I am dealing with fantasy which, by nature, is going to be idealistic and therefore unrealistic.

In peer-group discussion, Alexia's readers had many responses to this argument: They told her that it "put an interesting spin on things," but they also questioned whether Jane ever had, in fact, desired independence or autonomy; they commented that they themselves hadn't found the ending so problematic; they asked whether Alexia wasn't projecting twentieth-century standards onto the novel. In the margins of her paper, they wrote comments and suggestions such as:

- I remember finding this line somewhat disturbing when I read *JE*.
- Tone a little too sarcastic here.
- Doesn't Rochester miss his independence too?
- Why is this in itself problematic? (I'm thinking of some of Shakespeare's "perfect couples," like Beatrice-Benedick of *Much Ado*).

Alexia's peers responded to her paper as engaged readers of the novel *and* of her paper. They took her argument seriously even as they disagreed; they reinforced some of her analysis and questioned other parts of it; they signaled points where her rhetorical strategies failed, others where she convinced them. I think our comments altogether—that is, the students' and mine—gave Alexia a far better sense of what to revise than mine alone could have done. She took us all seriously—mapping out four pages of notes to herself on "topics of what I have to fix" and "solutions!" Her final paper was the best revision *qua revision* that I received, a remarkable improvement in terms of argument and a mature piece of critical analysis.

Why were peer workshops so successful? In freshman courses, peer review can be a mixed blessing: It often helps students locate areas of weakness or strength, but it frequently leaves them confused about what to revise—and how. Perhaps because freshmen are still novice readers and writers, knowledgeable about some aspects of writing but not others, they are not always able to comment wisely and constructively. Senior English majors, however, are by and large mature readers and writers. And, when they have spent a semester working on the same novels and secondary criticism, they are fairly close to "professional" in what they know. In the workshops they were able to tell a fellow student what was successful and original, where an argument was unclear or untenable, what additional passages might bolster it, where secondary criticism or a historical fact might be cited, or, more broadly, why the writer might want to rethink an argument or approach at a certain point in the paper. They were, in short, peers—that is, equals with approximately the same knowledge, critical sophistication, and rhetorical skills.

If I teach the course again, I will take Alexia's suggestion that I incorporate more peer workshops. I'll still use the self-determined sequence of writing assignments, and I'll keep the focus on drafts and revisions. But instead of the informal exchanges early in the semester, I'll try to put my students' critical knowledge to work with a wider impact and clearer focus. In peer exchanges I'll ask students to discuss not only their topics but also, more importantly, the approach they plan to take, the evidence they plan to collect, the critical model(s) they identify with and plan to use. Such exchanges may turn out to be more uneven than the final peer workshops— in that students with stronger training from the sophomore and junior years will understand the issues more readily and perhaps dominate discussion. But I'm willing to run the risk. The early exchanges will help them to help each other—in the same way that we receive help by going to conventions and learning from the research of others, or by reading professional articles and imitating the methodology of others, or by participating in local staff meetings and trying what worked for somebody else.

Notes/Works Cited

1. Leslie Moore made this distinction most recently at a staff meeting for new instructors, held 5 May 1994 at Yale University. I wish to thank Leslie for her continuing advice on being a writer and teaching writing.

2. Susan H. McLeod. 1992. "Writing Across the Curriculum: An Introduction," in *Writing Across the Curriculum: A Guide to Developing Programs,* edited by Susan H. McLeod and Margot Soven. Newbury Park, CA: Sage. 5. In current composition terminology, a "rhetorical" approach emphasizes the discourse community and its conventions—in contrast to a "cognitive" approach, which emphasizes writing to learn. As McLeod points out, writing-across-the-curriculum programs often combine both approaches.

3. In a sense, the problem was the two-dimensional paper itself; a hypertext version of the syllabus, initiated by me and completed by my students, would have better represented my intentions for the course.

4. Christine Farris and Raymond Smith. 1992. "Writing-Intensive Courses: Tools for Curricular Change." In McLeod and Soven, editors. 72.

5. In designing this sequence of deadlines, I was modifying a schedule suggested by the Undergraduate Studies Committee for the senior essay. The schedule reflects a shared assumption that writers need to produce at least a rough draft, on which the advisor can comment, and that revision should represent a process of rethinking and thoroughly rewriting.

6. All course evaluations at Yale are anonymous. If a student's comment was made in class or in conference with me, I use a fictitious name in my essay.

7. I have never taught a double major in English and history who did not want to begin by doing research. The prescription of writing process in that discipline must be so strong that it molds—or attracts—students early.

8. Gerald Graff. 1990. "Teach the Conflicts." In *The South Atlantic Quarterly* 89: 51–67.

9. Indeed, as Richard E. Miller has recently pointed out ("Composing English Studies: Towards a Social History of the Discipline." 1994. *CCC* 45: 164–66), Graff's approach to English studies omits any significant engagement with composition studies, either as it has shaped or currently shapes the profession. On the issue of students' writing, I would add that it is no solution to suggest that all writing should be a kind of meta-critical discourse *about* the conflicts. Surely senior majors should *do* literary criticism rather than just write about how others do it.

While teaching an upper-level survey course in Victorian literature, I read Gerald Graff's book *The Culture Wars* (Norton, 1992). In Chapter 3, "How to Save 'Dover Beach,'" Graff describes how Matthew Arnold's canonical poem might be read differently by an older male professor and a young female professor—a wonderful example of how one might identify specific texts in order to teach the conflicts within the literary profession. But, at that moment, halfway through my course, I had little time and inclination to teach that particular conflict. Yet, I was struck by the gender issues that Graff raised and how such issues made a familiar poem new again, made a Victorian poem somehow contemporary. How would my students respond to this poem if given a reading in which gender was a prominent issue?

To find out how my students would respond, I designed the following ungraded assignment: For homework tonight, after you have finished reading "Dover Beach," take about twenty minutes and write a personal response to Matthew Arnold. Assume that the speaker in this dramatic monologue is Arnold and further assume that you are the woman in the room to whom he is speaking. You have come to Dover Beach together on a romantic holiday.

This is what Felicia, a young woman in the class, wrote in response to that prompt:

The sea is calm tonight
My lips are full, my skin is fair
Why must he stare at the moonlight?
I, a new love, and there he does stand
Watching the cliffs, glimmering in the tranquil bay.
"Come to the window, sweet is the night air!"
What of me? What's that you say?
So, the sea meets the moon-blanched land?
Ignore the grating roar
Of pebbles which the waves draw back, and fling
At their return, up the high strand.
Your words begin, and cease, and then again begin
With tremulous cadence slow, and bring
An eternal note of drowsiness in.

The Sea of Love
Was once, too, at the full, and round my bosom
Lay like the folds of a bright girdle furled
But now I only hear
You long, melancholy voice, an annoying hum
Beating it to death,
Upon the vast cliff edges drear
And naked shingles of the world.
Ah, love, can we be true
To one another? for the world, which seemed

To lie before us like a land of dreams
So various, so beautiful, so new
Hath been darkened by your light.
There is no love to ease your pain.
I cannot dwell on this darkling plain
Swept with confused alarms of struggle and flight
When I had higher hopes for this night.

Art Young
Clemson University

20

Multiple Literacies and Inquiry-based Teaching
The Two-year Campus Literature Course

Jeffrey Sommers
Miami University–Middletown

This essay is the story of my journey as a teacher of composition and literature and my discovery that those paths I had been traveling had converged into a single one. Although I will focus on a specific course I taught in 1993, that course is offered as a case study illustrating the convergence of the two paths. Of course, I did not travel alone, and my story needs to begin with a description of the students I have taught over the past dozen years.

In 1981, I moved to a new teaching position at Miami University–Middletown, a two-year branch campus. While the average ACT score for new students at the university's main campus is 26, at Middletown the average ACT score is 17. The campus operates on a open-admissions policy, requiring a high school diploma or GED for admission, and most of the students are the first generation of their families to attend college. Our student population's median age is twenty-seven. Among the many adjustments these two-year campus students must make to college, they often must overcome their unpreparedness to participate in academic discourse. For most Middletown students, adademic discourse requires a new kind of literacy very unfamiliar to them; in this regard, they resemble basic writers.

Richard Courage describes two positions in the debate over teaching academic discourse to basic writers: one views it as threatening; one sees it beckoning to them (485). He advocates a teaching position that acknowledges both positions by focusing on the multiple literacies of basic writers (490). Patricia Bizzell has argued that teaching students to be literate in the academy should be a "process of constructing academic literacy, creating it

273

anew in each class through the interaction of the professor's and the students' cultural resources'' (150). And Joseph Harris observes that students do not move "cleanly and wholly from one community to another." They get "caught instead in an always changing mix of dominant, residual, and emerging discourses"(17).

My colleague Cynthia Lewiecki-Wilson and I have been developing a two-year college reader that endorses the idea that composition courses on the two-year campus need to take advantage of students' multiple literacies, instead of trying to squelch all but one—the academic kind. Certainly, all college students to some degree face the problem of becoming initiated into academic literacy; however, my argument is that the kinds of students we encounter on two-year campuses face that problem in unique ways. Populated by large numbers of culturally and linguistically diverse students, the two-year writing classroom is at an intersection of many cultures. Using Mary Louise Pratt's description of "contact zones," those "social spaces where cultures meet, clash, and grapple with each other (33)," the two-year college composition course needs to emphasize the multiple literacies students bring into the classroom. Affirming the unique backgrounds two-year students bring with them, the composition course should be broadly conceived to allow students freedom to move across forms of literacy and experience cultural mediation. And implicit in the metaphor of movement, I think, is the assumption that writing is not a static moment but a dynamic process that takes place, often recursively, over time.

Writing Assessment and Multiple Literacies

With the intention of stressing multiple kinds of discourses, risk-taking, and experimentation comes the need for re-thinking assessment of the writing produced by the students. Sandra Murphy, writing about linguistically diverse students, argues that the best reason to assess students is to teach them to self-assess (151), and the first step in making assessment a learning process is to "give students a voice in the assessment process, so that they have some kind of stake in it, a stake for the decisions they are *empowered* to make, not just a stake for the consequences of failure" (151). Inevitably, she advocates portfolio assessment as a means of accomplishing these goals.

In my writing courses, I encourage students to create a portfolio that not only assesses learning, but promotes it by asking writers to perform four kinds of writing tasks that cut across genres, levels of formality, kinds of discourse:

- writing that models the text (this includes imitation, the personal essay, profiles, humor pieces, satires, oral histories, poetry, fiction)
- writing that engages the text (this includes summaries, reports, textual analysis, evaluations, reviews, arguments)

- writing that connects the text (this includes applying the text to personal experience, and observation, writing about themes across several texts and/or media)
- writing that extends the text (this includes further research, investigation, community-based applications or projects)

These writing tasks work at both the individual and collaborative levels. Individually, journal writing serves as a heuristic to generate ideas for further development. Toby Fulwiler has observed that journal writing individualizes learning and encourages students to take an active role in their own education (16); it thus becomes a vital tool in the kind of composition course I teach. Collaboratively, students brainstorm, research, draft, and edit papers—depending on the specific project—with their peers in small groups. My role is to facilitate, respond, and, at times, work along with the students in their composing. I would describe the writing courses I teach as "inquiry-based," in that the course itself develops and changes as the students pursue an inquiry, conducted through their writing, into the "contact zone" in which they find themselves. Thus, each student shapes the course, to a large extent, through her developing portfolio of writing.

Teaching Jewish-American Writers (English 210)

While I have been developing the kind of composition course I have described, my teaching load has also included one lower-division literature course each term, and, inevitably, the thinking I have done in teaching composition has influenced how I teach those literature courses. In teaching Jewish-American Writers (English 210), I wanted to create a course that would enable students to draw upon the multiple literacies they brought with them to the course. These students had already completed our two-course college composition sequence, but that did not offer any guarantee that they would be entirely immersed in academic discourse. Yet I knew that they were indeed literate in a number of ways, not only upon their entering the university but as a result of their prior success at our campus.

English 210, like my composition courses, would be inquiry-based because the students—and I—would construct the course collaboratively in the process of inquiring into the culture of Jewish-American writers. We would use writing as a primary vehicle for that inquiry; writing would thus serve not merely as a means of assessment but as the driving force by which the entire course would move. If the students were willing to risk writing in a variety of ways, using the multiple literacies they brought with them, my anticipation was collaboratively and individually that we would find the necessary direction to make the course a worthwhile learning experience. That direction is quite different from where I began as a teacher of literature.

A Tale of Two Syllabuses

Twelve years earlier, in the spring of 1981, I taught a three-credit course entitled Major American Writers at a four-year university. The course is shown in Figure 20–1. (The calendar continues for an additional twenty-three class meetings, stipulating a midterm exam on May 1 and a final exam on June 8.) My course syllabus for English 210, taught in the fall of 1993, is shown in Figure 20–2.

Figure 20–1

Major American Writers, Spring 1981

Texts	*Anthology of American Literature* (2nd ed.)—McMichael *The Sound and the Fury*—Faulkner
Required work	approximately 1,000 pages of reading two 4-5 page papers two exams class participation
Grading	papers: 40% exams: 40% class participation: 20%
Course rules	1. All written work must be completed or a failing grade will be issued. 2. All assignments must be typewritten. 3. No late assignments will be accepted without penalty of one grade per class late. 4. No make-ups of exams will be offered without a doctor's note establishing the student's inability to attend the regularly scheduled test. 5. Students absent for three consecutive classes will be dropped from the class roster. 6. Departmental policies on plagiarism will be enforced. 7. Assignments not judged to be written at a sophomore level will be returned ungraded for revision. Upon satisfactory revision, a grade will be assigned. A paper with excessive usage, spelling, and punctuation errors is not a paper written at a sophomore level. 8. These rules are my attempt to answer usual questions before they arise. I intend to abide by these rules and request that you do so too.
Course calendar	March 30: Intro to course. April 1: Read "Almost a Man." April 3: Read "Barn Burning." April 6: Read "My Papa's Waltz" and "How I Contemplated the World." April 8: Read "Just as I Used to Say" and "Lucifer on the Train." April 10: Read "old age sticks" and "Flight"

Figure 20–2

English 210 Syllabus (Jewish-American Writers)

Required text	*The Shawl* by Cynthia Ozick

Course calendar	M Aug 30	Introductory
	M Sept 6	Ozick
	M Sept 13	To be determined
	M Sept 20	To be determined
	M Sept 27	To be determined
	M Oct 4	To be determined
	M Oct 11	To be determined
	M Oct 18	To be determined
	M Oct 25	To be determined
	M Nov 1	To be determined
	M Nov 8	To be determined
	M Nov 15	To be determined
	M Nov 22	To be determined
	M Nov 29	To be determined
	M Dec 6	To be determined

Course grades   Due to the nature of the course, I would like to use a contract grading system. A contract grading system means that you and I agree upon a number of activities/tasks that you will complete satisfactorily in order to pass the course or earn a higher than passing grade. The following possibilities seem useful activities to me:

Leading a class discussion
Keeping a reading response journal
Writing a "research paper"
Producing a portfolio of writing
Other

While I am not opposed to including a number of short-answer-type quizzes as part of the contract, I do not wish to give short-answer exams. I want the primary activities to consist of writing, thinking, talking, questioning, and reflecting. See my attached course description for more information about the course.

Final comment: As you can see, this course doesn't really exist yet! We're going to create it together as we go. Let's see what happens.

    I see three noteworthy differences in the two syllabuses: The older one stipulates all of the major texts for the course while the newer one lists just a single text; the calendar on the older syllabus is quite detailed and specific while the newer one remains blank; and the 1981 syllabus outlines required work and grading breakdowns for the students while the 1993 syllabus leaves those details to be negotiated. The two syllabuses construct not only very different courses, but very different relationships between the students and the teacher and between the class and the subject matter to be studied. My own rhetoric in the two syllabuses has clearly changed from a legalistic, distant prose based on an overtly one-sided power relationship in 1981 to a less-formal, more conversational prose based on a conception of negotiation between student and teacher.

By 1993, having reconceived the literature course as based on inquiry, I no longer see as appropriate selecting the texts in advance on my own. In 1981, my course in Major American Writers was in no sense an inquiry; the inquiring had all been completed by me long in advance of the course. The "journey" was not to be an exploration but a guided tour, one I had selected for the class based on my own judgment of what "they" needed. While I expected to learn more about the literature through interaction with the students, that was going to be an indirect result of the course activity rather than a primary objective for me.

Since the 1981 course was a "guided tour," it was not only appropriate but necessary to provide the "guests" with an itinerary. Thus, the course calendar spelled out due dates for all reading assignments and written work. I provided on the first day the complete schedule for the course. My recollection is that I was rather adept at sticking to the schedule, so I can only assume that we "visited" each site on the tour as planned. More importantly, I cannot imagine why I would have changed the plans unless bad weather forced a class cancellation. In fact, had I changed plans, I would have had to notify the class and perhaps answered a question about why things had changed. More likely, I would have decided to make a change, announced the decision, and watched the students silently "correct" their schedules.

But in English 210, I was unable to provide the schedule in advance. Together, the students and I determined the direction the course would take. In fact, it became customary to devote the opening fifteen minutes of each weekly class to reviewing, revising, and developing our plans for upcoming weeks. We not only needed to decide what to read but also who would be responsible for conducting the discussion. In fact, we actually decided on two occasions not to read anything at all but to screen films instead.

In terms of the required work, in 1981 I decided what the students needed to do and outlined it for them on the syllabus. There was an emphasis on writing in that course, yet the writing was intended solely as a means of evaluating the students. The two papers were standard, formal literary analyses. The two exams were essay exams. For example, on the midterm exam, I asked students to complete the following task:

Midterm Exam

Ralph Waldo Emerson wrote, "Whom would be a man must be a noncon-formist." Using three of the works listed below, examine the validity of Emerson's observation. (In our more 'enlightened' times, it seems fair to reinterpret Emerson's use of 'a man' to mean 'human.') You may use your notebooks and textbooks if you wish.

While the exam was designed to stimulate the students to learn more about the reading rather than test their recall—it was an open-book exam— it adhered to the usual academic concern with plagiarism by only providing the topic to the students at the actual exam site and allowing them only the class period to complete the task.

I not only allowed ''revision'' on the midterm, but required it. Remember Rule 7: ''Assignments not judged to be written at a sophomore level will be returned ungraded for revision. Upon satisfactory revision, a grade will be assigned. A paper with excessive usage, spelling, and punctuation errors is not a paper written at a sophomore level.'' Revision here was narrowly conceived of as addressing issues of surface convention, the intention being to bring the papers ''up to'' acceptable levels of ''correctness'' for academic discourse.

Once again, by conceiving the 1993 course as inquiry-based, I was compelled to move away from the approach to required work outlined twelve years earlier. Since I would not know where each student's inquiry would lead, I could not make decisions in advance about the work he or she would have to do. In English 210, the ''required'' work was implicit—reading and writing (and rereading and rewriting)—but the forms it would take were unspecified. I indicated that grading would be individually negotiated based on contracts devised by each student and me, giving some suggested activities, but not requiring specific tasks. The contract grading system allowed me to merge assessment procedures with the notion of an inquiry-based course.

The Contract Grading System

The contract grading system was essential to the course. After our first class meeting when we went over the syllabus and the idea of developing the course collaboratively, I wrote the class a letter discussing our next move: drawing up individually negotiated contracts for the work each student would complete that term.

To illustrate how the contract system worked, I want to focus on one student, Phoebe. Phoebe's proposal specified three goals for the course: ''1. To learn about Jewish people, Judaism, and Jewish history; 2. To further develop my writing skills; 3. To understand and care about Jewish literature.'' In a section of her proposal entitled ''How I Plan to Reach My Goals,'' Phoebe sketched out a plan of reading (which included reading papers written by her classmates) and writing (which included a proposal to keep a journal and write a research paper as well). She wrote, ''I will know that I have reached my goal of developing my writing skills by comparing finished products that I have done rewrites on to first drafts. I will also produce a mini-portfolio of my best papers and do a self-evaluation on them.''

To reach her third goal, Phoebe proposed more journal writing and research. Her concluding paragraph is important in light of what she actually wrote during the term. She wrote,

> I will know I have reached my goal when I am free of any kind of prejudice that I have been taught about these people. I will know I have reached my goal when I can look at the contributions of these people instead of only their struggles and look at them with admiration instead of pity. I would like to look at them as people who have beliefs that are different than mine rather than wrong.

I wrote a contract for each student to examine, based on what each had written to me in their proposals. The first half of each contract was standardized:

> I've read your proposed contract and would like to respond.
> I think your proposed goals are fine, and your plans to achieve the goals seem concrete and worthwhile. I've also read the proposals from the rest of the class and would like to coordinate their interests and yours to some extent, so here's what I'd like to agree on with you:
> a. You'll read five novels this semester, some of them chosen by the class and some by you individually.
> b. You'll do additional reading of short stories, poetry, drama, as agreed upon by the class.
> c. You'll lead class discussions twice.
> As far as your proposed writing activities, here's what I'd like to see you do:

At this point each contract was individualized. Phoebe's read as follows:

> a. Write a reflective piece now about your impressions of the subject material and course and your own abilities as a reader of literature and writer about literary subjects; write a reflective piece at the end of the course that discusses any changes you've observed in those abilities and impressions.
> b. Write a reading response journal that includes at least one page of writing about each selection we read (or view in the case of films). You'll submit this journal three times this semester, each time accompanied by a letter to me reflecting on the batch of entries included. Your final journal entry will focus on the contribution of Jewish-American writers to American literature.
> c. Write one research paper (five to seven pages?) on a suitable topic.
> d. Write a reflective piece after you have conducted class discussion in which you discuss how the class went and what you learned as a product of preparing the class.
> e. Write papers on two of the assigned novels.

    f. Assemble a mini-portfolio (ten to twelve pages?) consisting of your best writing selected from your journals, your reflective pieces, your short papers, and/or your research paper.

Phoebe's and her classmates' contracts illustrated the four different writing tasks used in my composition courses to emphasize multiple literacy. Writing that models the text included short stories in several contracts. (Phoebe "modeled" a text the second time she led class discussion when she selected a one-act play and asked the class to act it out before discussing it.) Writing that engages the text appeared in Phoebe's contract in (b), where she contracted to evaluate the contributions of the writers, and potentially in (e), her papers on two novels, depending on what she chose to write. Writing that connects the text appeared in both her before-and-after papers (a) and her reading response journal (b). Another student identified two kinds of journals she wanted to keep, one a reading response journal and the other a more personal journal about the literature. (For example, she wrote a page of analytical response to the characters' friendships in Chaim Potok's *The Promise* in her reading journal and a page about the burdens borne by children of famous, or infamous, parents in her personal journal entry about the same book.) Another student, an education major, chose to write a curriculum paper spelling out her own plans and rationale for a course on Jewish-American literature, connecting the writing to her own purposes. Writing that extends the text outward most frequently took the form of research projects, like Phoebe's (c). The important point is that the contract permitted students a voice in assessment, a voice that reflected their own literacies and their own goals.

Three Journeys of Exploration

As I described earlier, the course was designed to be an exploration, not a guided tour. Three of those journeys illustrate the nature of the inquiry the students undertook. The portion of Phoebe's journey I'd like to examine began the night she led the class discussion of Philip Roth's short story "Defender of the Faith." In the story, a Jewish army sergeant experiences difficulties in dealing with several Jewish conscripts during basic training. One of the conscripts tries to take advantage of the sergeant by appealing to their common bond as Jews; he is an unsavory and dislikable character. In her preparation for class, Phoebe had learned that some critics have accused Roth of being anti-Semitic, presumably because of his depiction of characters like the conscript. Phoebe raised the point in class. Reflecting on that discussion, she wrote, "I asked the question, 'Do you think that this story and its characters contribute to the feelings of critics who say Roth's anti-Semitic?' I feel that Roth is proud to be Jewish, but is able to write about the struggles that Jewish people go through in a realistic way that appeals to all religions."

Her interest in Roth was piqued. She chose as her first novel for the course his *Portnoy's Complaint*. After reporting on the novel to the class, her interest in Roth intensified, and she decided to write her contracted research paper on his career. Through consultation with me, she chose to write an I-Search Paper, Ken Macrorie's informal research paper, rather than a more formal research project. In the introductory section of her paper, she explained what she wished to learn about Roth: "I would like to find out more about Philip Roth's family life, his education, his awards, his personality, and his reactions to the critics who call him anti-Semitic. I would also like to find out about some of his other famous works and what they are and what prompted him to write the stories that he wrote."

The I-Search Paper continued with a narrative about Phoebe's research and findings. She consulted a book entitled *Conversations with Philip Roth* and discovered that Roth was aware of having been labeled anti-Semitic. She quoted Roth's response:

> The fact is (and I think there's even a clue to this in my fiction) that I have always been far more pleased by my good fortune in being born Jewish than my critics may begin to imagine. It's a complicated, interesting, morally demanding, and very singular experience, and I like that. I find myself in the historic predicament of being Jewish, with all its implications. Who could ask for more? But as for those charges you mentioned—yes, they will probably be leveled at me. (Plimpton 38)

In the conclusion of her paper about Roth, Phoebe observed, "Philip Roth doesn't write for an audience, or to please the critics; he writes what he is feeling and thinking at the time. I admire that about him." This particular journey of inquiry shows Phoebe reaching part of one of her stated goals. She had expressed a desire to rid herself of her prejudices about Jews, whom she referred to as "these people" and "them" repeatedly in her proposal. Although she did not articulate a direct connection, we can see how her interest in Roth and charges of anti-Semitism relates to her concerns about her own latent prejudice. The conclusion she reaches about Roth is a very specific and concrete one; she doesn't judge the entire group of Jewish-American writers based on her study of Roth, nor does she generalize about Jews after researching a single Jew. Instead, "these people" have become a single individual who has interested her enough to involve her actively over a period of weeks. She concludes that she can admire him and articulates her reasons cogently. Her inquiry into Roth has allowed her to begin the process of dealing with her own prejudice by learning about why he has been accused of the same prejudice.

Tamara's journey of inquiry was also focused on prejudice. We viewed *Gentleman's Agreement*, the classic Hollywood film starring Gregory Peck as a Christian magazine reporter who assumes the role of a Jew in post-war New York City so that he can write an exposé of anti-Semitism. In the film

Peck's personal relationships are affected almost immediately, most notice-
ably with his fianceé, Cathy, who breaks off their engagement when she tires
of his judgments of her behavior toward Jews. In her journal entry, Tamara
noted that the film made a very strong impact on her, reminding her of a situation in her own life. One of her girlfriends had been dating an African-
American man, and Tamara's parents were strenuously opposed to the relationship, coercing Tamara into promising not to spend any time with the
couple. Tamara concluded the journal entry by writing, "My parents remind
me of Cathy." Then she returns to her own situation: "I'm not quite sure
what to do.... It's this kind of attitude that helped slaughter the Jews.
Would I be strong enough to stand up to my family? I hope so. It's certainly
something to think about."

Tamara, unlike Phoebe, is not specifically concerned with anti-Semitism;
her interest is in prejudice itself. But Tamara is willing to examine her own
stance on the issue while Phoebe explores anti-Semitism more obliquely
through her research into Roth. Tamara had contracted to write two papers
on the assigned readings/films, so she next developed her journal entry on
Gentleman's Agreement into a fascinating character analysis of Cathy and
the female lead in the 1993 film *School Ties*, which focuses on anti-Semitism
at a private prep school in the 1950s. Tamara begins the paper with an
expanded discussion of the interrracial couple she had befriended and her
own conflicts with her parents. She wrote,

> When I think about the promises I've made I feel ashamed. What I've done
> is exchange a part of my freedom for a little peace and quiet. Am I myself
> prejudiced? Giving in so easily, trying to avoid fighting about it; am I not
> contributing to racial injustice in this country by doing nothing? Questions
> like these keep me awake at night. Is my situation not similar to those in
> the time of Nazi-controlled Germany?

Her reading of *Gentleman's Agreement* was a very sensitive one since
the film focuses on the subtle forms of anti-Semitism of characters like
Cathy, who acquiesce to the status quo although they themselves never
overtly discriminate against Jews. Tamara extrapolated that idea and applied
it to her own life in a situation based on race rather than religion.

In her paper, she next moved into traditional literary character analysis.

> To oppose opposite views and take action against persecution itself requires
> much more courage, independence, and self-confidence. *School Ties* char-
> acter Sally Wheeler and Cathy from *Gentleman's Agreement* are both faced
> with similar issues, and each must decide whether to stand up to the oppo-
> sition or back down and lose the men they care about.

Tamara then did a wonderful job of analyzing the two characters but
always in light of what truly mattered to her: her own dilemma. She had
concluded her journal entry by asking herself whether she would be capable

of standing up to her family, unsure of her answer but certain that the question was worth asking. Her paper reaches the same point of asking that question:

> Were Sally and Cathy anti-Semitic? My opinion is yes, and maybe I am a little prejudiced. I try not to be, but then again that's what Cathy said. Like her I'm not really standing up for my beliefs because that would mean standing up to my family, something I haven't been prepared to do in the past. Next time the subject comes up, though, I think I'll be more aggressive and less likely to back down. When I think about it, what's wrong with a little arguing? It's about time to clear the air.

In this remarkable conclusion, Tamara's inquiry into anti-Semitism and racism led her to some important answers. Her journal entry had compared Tamara's parents to the character of Cathy. Through writing her essay, she had now come to a better understanding of Cathy, a character who is never as overtly prejudiced as her family and who thus resembles Tamara herself. She also determined a tentative answer to her earlier question: She hoped to be "more aggressive" so that she would be "less likely to back down." She hoped the results would be "a little arguing." In other words, the inquiry she conducted into the fictional characters allowed her to begin to understand herself and what she might have to do.

The third journey of inquiry I want to sketch out was a collaborative one taken by the entire class. Early in the term, we all read novels we had selected individually, providing each other with summaries, excerpts, and responses to discuss. I read Daniel Fuchs' novel *Summer in Williamsburg* and concluded my response, "This is the first reading of the term . . . that didn't resonate for me because of its Jewish background. These characters were Jewish, but they could have been any ethnic minority really. We didn't learn much about their culture directly; we did get a full picture of life in Williamsburg at that time, however." One of the students, Betty, noted my concern here and selected a Mark Halprin short story entitled "Leaving the Church" for a subsequent class discussion. The story was about a Roman Catholic priest's crisis of faith and had nothing to do with Jews or Judaism. Of course, the class wanted to discuss in what sense the story was "Jewish-American literature." Betty wrote, "I liked the idea that everyone saw the big difference between Jewish writers that write about being Jewish and ones that don't. I felt that was a strong point: that not always are you going to find things that are just about Jewish life."

The issue that we engaged was one appropriate to any literature course: What should we read? In our specific context, we raised questions such as "If a work were written by a Jewish-American writer, would that automatically make it 'acceptable' reading?" "What if that work were not about Jews?" "Could we 'legitimately' read literature about Jews written by non-Jews?" As we discussed these questions, I mentioned that as a Jewish-American writer, I had published both fiction with no Jewish content and fiction that focused on questions of Jewish identity. But would it be suitable to read anything I had written or only fiction about Jewish issues and topics? At that point, the theoretical discussion took a very practical turn. The student responsible for selecting the next set of readings turned to me and said, "Why can't we read one of your stories and discuss it?" The class quickly agreed. I am used to using my own writing in composition classes, so I didn't hesitate to agree. The class decided to read a story I had written about Jewish identity and the Holocaust. I myself thus became part of the class inquiry into Jewish-American literature.

We never resolved the issue of what might or might not be included in the course reading, but the student who designed her own curriculum only selected literature by Jewish-American writers who traditionally focused on Jewish subjects. And Tamara's final journal letter offered this comment: "Some of the material we read I would keep [in the course], such as "Rosa," *The Promise*, etc. Other items, like the stuff which had nothing at all to do with Jewishness, well, we only had so many weeks, and I feel we could have read or seen something more worthwhile."

Conclusion

I don't believe my 1981 syllabus was bad or wrong-headed. It was right for me at that time, but it would no longer be suitable. I can enumerate many more changes between that syllabus and the 1993 one than I've already emphasized: The newer one includes the possibility of multiple drafts; it includes journals and written dialogue with students; it includes reflective writing; it allows for multiple types of formal writing ranging from a curriculum paper through short fiction to reaction papers, research papers, and literary analyses. However, the truly important differences are not in the pedagogical strategies and techniques so much as in the underlying philosophical changes.

Perhaps, more than any other development, the line of inquiry that led to using my own fiction in class symbolized how very far my literature teaching had moved in twelve years. Not only was this course collaboratively inquiring into the literature by calling upon the students' multiple literacies, but it eventually called upon *my* multiple literacies as well. The students themselves, in pursuit of their own inquiries, asked me to be not just the teacher but a colleague and a subject of study as well. While I wrote academic discourse in the class (the syllabus materials), I also worked in other kinds of discourse: reflective prose (about *Summer in Williamsburg*), letters to students, marginal comments in journals, and fiction.

I began my essay by saying that it would be the story of my journey as a teacher. I ended the narrative of my journey, however, by focusing on the students. Their journeys in that literature course could not have occurred in the literature course I used to teach. That was a course that did not acknowledge that individual students might be different; it sketched out a course "experience" that would be identical for every student. I can no longer teach that way. Between 1981 and 1993, I learned to value the multiple literacies of my students and the significance of their own agendas for their education. I learned to trust the students and to work with them in a genuinely collaborative way to explore the subject of literature. Perhaps most significantly, I came to see that writing could serve a more central, a more informing, a more powerful role than merely as an assessment tool. I learned all of that through teaching composition on a two-year campus to a diverse and diversely prepared group of students.

Certainly, my journey parallels similar narratives that could be related by the other contributors to this volume, many of whose professional lives are situated on four-year campuses where students, of course, are also diverse and possess multiple literacies. Nevertheless, the two-year campus remains a site where the convergence of composition and literature teaching is not only particularly fruitful, but also urgently needed. My own journey of inquiry continues, influenced most recently by Phoebe, Tamara, and the Jewish-American Writers class I have described, but influenced most powerfully by taking place at a two-year campus, the contact zone where my students "clash" and "grapple" so meaningfully with the academic culture.

Works Cited

Bizzell, Patricia. 1988. "Arguing about Literacy." *College English* 50 (February): 141–153.

Courage, Richard. 1993. "The Intersection of Public and Private Literacies." *College Composition and Communication* 44 (December): 484–496.

Fulwiler, Toby. 1982. "The Personal Connection: Journal Writing Across the Curriculum." In *Language Connections: Writing and Reading Across the Curriculum*, edited by Toby Fulwiler and Art Young. Urbana, IL: NCTE.

Harris, Joseph. 1989. "The Idea of Community in the Study of Writing." *College Composition and Communication* 40 (February): 11–22.

Macrorie, Ken. 1980. *Searching Writing: A Contextbook*. Rochelle Park, NJ: Hayden Book Co.

Murphy, Sandra. 1994. "Writing Portfolios in K–12 Schools: Implications for Linguistically Diverse Students." In *New Directions in Portfolio Assessment: Reflective Practice, Critical Theory, and Large-scale Scoring*, edited by Laurel Black, Donald Daiker, Jeffrey Sommers, and Gail Stygall. Portsmouth, NH: Heinemann/Boynton-Cook.

Plimpton, George. 1992. "Philip Roth's Exact Intent." In *Conversations with Philip Roth*, edited by George J. Searles. Oxford, MS: The University Press of Mississippi.

Pratt, Mary Louise. 1991. "Arts of the Contact Zone." *Profession* 91: 33–40.

I 'm most influenced by creative writing as a way into literary study, "transforming" activities as a way into texts. My students represent the rich ethnic and cultural diversity of Hawai'i; as locals, they share the value of oral tradition, bringing literacies to college that "school" literacies resist. I believe that for my students, "transforming activities" lead to analysis and interpretation.

I've learned the painful way that although they are insiders to the Hawai'ian literature used in my writing or literature classes, my students generally are unfamiliar with reader responses and analytical modes. When they've written the more standard "analysis and interpretation" essays, their discoveries, although fascinating, are usually underdeveloped and seemingly unconnected to the textual evidence they struggle to offer. As one of my local colleagues puts it, it's almost as if the students' essays ask, "I've made my discovery —what more do I need to write?"

But when we've approached texts using transforming activities first, the students almost inevitably produce rich analysis and interpretation. For example, when they've translated the local voice (Hawai'ian Creole English) into "Standard American English," students have made cogent statements about the losses and gains in character, setting, emotionality, and meaning. They are also very sensitive to the differences in Hawai'ian Creole as it is rendered in text and in speaking, and to the different generations of Hawai'ian Creole appearing in the stories. These perceptions lead to discussions about the evolving nature of language and the differences between oral and written literature. In turn, some students often develop greater respect for the home language that has influenced them, and they begin to experiment with Hawai'ian Creole in their own writing.

For most of my students, "transforming the text" is the prerequisite for analysis and interpretation. They must own the literature somehow before they can analyze and interpret it. For example, when students invented diary entries of a character from one of the stories, and then explained their choices shaping the entries, their writing revealed coherent and well-supported character analysis. When they shifted the story to a new setting (usually somewhere visited on the U.S. continent), the importance of place and its relationship to local and universal arises.

On the suggestion of my colleague Jill Makagon, students and I have substituted local Hawai'ian fruit for the fig metaphor in Kate Chopin's "Ripe Figs." Some students decide that the use of papaya, for instance, harvested year-round in Hawai'i, would significantly alter the theme of the story, the growing seasons from childhood to adulthood. Other students wonder if mango, a seasonal fruit, is an appropriate substitute for the rare and costly fig. These sorts of judgments lead to further exploration of metaphor and other devices in literature.

Irena M. Levy
University of Hawaii
Kapiolani Community College

21

Portfolios, Literature, and Learning
Story as a Way of Constructing the World

Kathleen Blake Yancey
University of North Carolina at Charlotte

It's Christmas time (a holiday I do keep), and I have yet to pull out the orna-ments from the attic, to wind evergreens and burgundy ribbon down the staircase, to remember with each decoration the stories of past Christmases we bring to this one. I can't do that until I do this: Read the mass of portfo-lios scattered on the floor around me, some in anonymous manila folders, others in good-school-form three-ring binders.

> I began the semester in 1103 with three main goals: (1) to learn to write in many disciplines and to a variety of audiences, (2) to learn to improve syn-tax in my writing, and (3) to learn to type without looking at the keyboard. Now these goals seem somewhat banal compared to what I actually learned and discovered about myself and my writing.

I've read some of the portfolios and decided a grade; others await. It takes me a long time to read these, even with several years of experience reading them and—as important—even with a scoring guide to direct my reading. Inside each one, however, is the story of a single student, one I saw in progress, but only finally narrated in the portfolio. Before now, I saw stu-dents relative to each other and, given that I have a stack of portfolios, I still do. But I also see students relative to their own development and their claims

This work was supported in part by funds from the Foundation of the University of North Caro-lina at Charlotte and from the State of North Carolina.

about what they have learned. Seeing them both ways—relative to their peers and relative to their own history—is seeing them more fully.

> Both the formal and the informal writing that comprises this portfolio express the ideas and discoveries I feel were most important to my development as a writer this semester. This extended beyond 1103 to other classes such as biology and history.

In the portfolio, I have the "evidence" of the student's work against which to measure the claims. In that evidence students include informal writing—the stuff of journals and writers' notebooks—as well as the more formal work, since both foster learning, and learning is, after all, what matters.

Learning is in fact the stuff of teaching.

In the fall of 1993, I taught an experimental course in first-year composition—English 1103, Accelerated Freshman Composition—a single course that, when completed, delivered the six hours of freshman writing credit required for graduation. For a metaphor to ground the course, I turned to literature, and specifically to the metaphor of story, for several reasons. First, since "story" is familiar to students, it doesn't require jargon or special theory or lengthy explanations to be of both value and use. Second, since the notion of "story" invites students to participate—as story readers and storytellers and storymakers—it provides a place and a role for the students as makers of meaning. Third, and most important, through the metaphor of story I could help students understand that ultimately, telling stories is what we do in both text and life—in our personal lives, in our disciplinary lives, in our professional and civic lives. So being able to plot story, to interpret it, and to critique it as we write and re-write our own stories is a primary means of knowing and of being.

The Plot

I divided the course into four parts.

- The first focused on place, included pieces like E.B. White's "Once More to the Lake" and Joan Didion's "Letter from California" (a sociological essay on the home of the Spur Posse published in the July 26, 1993 *New Yorker*), and asked students to write about a place—real or fictional—in any way they chose: memoir, travel brochure, sociological analysis.

- In the second part of the course we read, interpreted, and wrote about *The Great Gatsby*: the stories of *Gatsby*.

- The third part of the course moved us to think about other disciplines and the stories they tell, specifically those in history and biology, and to examine closely two or three stories in a discipline.

- The fourth part of the course required students to construct the story of their own writing through the metaphor of voice.

Throughout the semester, students submitted the four major papers corresponding to the four sections of the course; I read them and commented upon them and then returned them, but without attaching grades. Students were told to archive everything—their formal papers, their notes, their peer review responses—so that they could choose from these materials when they composed their portfolio at the term's end. Generally, I said, portfolios are *collections* of work, based on some principles of *selection* from the larger collection (often called the working portfolio), that include *reflection*, and that involve both *communication* and *evaluation*; communication because the portfolio speaks about the portfolio composer, evaluation because the selection process involves valuing. The portfolio would also, I said, be used to award them a grade for the term.

About two weeks before the end of the term, we decided together the portfolio contents: one formal paper that wasn't text-based, one that was, several informal writings, and a piece they had completed before they entered UNC Charlotte, a selection that allowed students to link the writers/ readers they were with the ones they have become. Together, we also created the criteria that would govern the evaluation of the portfolio:

1. Shows development as a writer;
2. shows ability to manage all writing processes (invention, drafting, sharing, revising, editing);
3. shows ability to write to and from text, to write multiple interpretations of text;
4. shows ability to write for different audiences and purposes; and
5. shows creativity.

The first four relate directly to the course as I had designed it; "creativity" was their value. In class and as individuals and in groups, students worked to make choices that met the established criteria and drafted the final reflection that was to conclude the portfolio.

I collected the portfolios during exam week, I read them, I graded them, and the course ended. I had time, finally, to make a Christmas holiday.

The Story of the Class: Take One

But this scaffolding doesn't tell the story of the class; it doesn't show—the students, the writing, the reading, the learning. Every Tuesday and Thursday we gather in our IBM classroom, a large windowed room with computers standing guard around the perimeter of the class and six more holding court in the center. It's lunchtime, so Melissa, sweaty in her track clothes, sneaks in her yogurt. Amanda giggles as she updates us on her triathlon class and her new job at Hooters and her latest soccer game. About the time she loses the class's attention, Wayne staggers in, faded red baseball cap turned around on his head, eyes glassy, still trying to figure out what happened to last night.

As the bell rings, I remind everyone to turn the computer games off (thinking, "Now, please"), click Word Perfect on, and write to the daily computer prompt that begins each class. As directed, students sometimes work together, sometimes alone, but they always start with the prompt.

Today's prompt asks students to think about the role that the narrator plays in any story. Specifically, they are asked what the article on Lakewood would be like if someone other than Didion had narrated it, and Stephanie replies:

> "Trouble in Lakewood" was narrated by Joan Didion her self. I think that if you chose another narrator the story would have quite a different tone. Where as Didion tends to be pityiful and somewhat condasending, I think that a narrator who lived in Lakewood would tell the story with a ferice pride, and just a hint of being ashamed for what their once great city has transformed in to.
>
> Let's take your average joe, residing in Lakewood. In fact let's call him "Joe." First of all his writing would be more of a plain speak then Didion's. Joe would avoid words such as "amorphous" and "vertiginous" since he comes from a blue colar town in which athletics are stressed insted of education. Since Joe's father had resided in Lakewood, he would probably skip over the history which he now finds boring having heard it repeated again and again. He would also probably not make the connection between the factories closing down and the corruption of morals that led to the Spur Posse insident. It is possible that he would not think of the "Spurs" as an incident, more as a thing that in happening at the high school.

On another day, students are asked about what happens when a well-known story is used as the text for another. What happens to the original story? Is the later story the same story? Our exemplars are Disney's Cinderella and Anne Sexton's version. Working collaboratively at a single terminal, Melissa, Andrea, and Stephanie gloss Sexton's version:

> In essence Anne Sexton did tell the same story with a twist of cynicism. She points to several "real" life Cinderella stories, that have the basic plot of the poor and good become wealthy. Then she goes on to tell the true Grime's version, with all the blood and guts that go along with it. The fact that our group knew only of the watered down Disney version points to the way today's society protects (or shelters) it's children. Sexton writes in her last paragraph ". . . their darling smiles pasted on for eternity", illustrates that reality does not touch fairy tales.

Unlike my students, I read Sexton as a piece of personal history more than
as a fairy tale—**that story.** But I like the women's take on it, their sense of
how children today are (over)protected. I suppose that's true; I hadn't
thought of it that way before. Which is the point: I'm glad to read the poem
in a new way myself, through their eyes.

On still another day, we look at Gatsby, and connect him with our lives.
I think that the novel doesn't really have much to do with mine; mostly, it
reminds me of the all-nighters I pulled writing papers on Fitzgerald in graduate school. I hope my students will do better than I, but I'm dubious. And
the first prompts aren't promising: one young man writes of parties and of
Gatsby as a great party-thrower, while another writes of unrequited love and
of not being a Gatsby again himself. (**That story**?, I think to myself.)

Other responses reflect a more vital link between novel and life. Andrea
talks of the adjustment required of moving that she shares with Nick.

> The only thing that I can find in the *Great Gatsby* remotely similar to my
> life is that the main characters are from a Western society trying to make it
> in an Eastern society. This relates to my life because up until the fifth grade
> my family and I moved at least once a year. . . . I think that Nick feels the
> way I did each time I moved. He made friends or associates but I don't
> think that he really felt like he ever exactly fit in.

Other students connect in more substantial ways, in ways I haven't
anticipated, sharing more of themselves than perhaps I am ready for. One
student talks quite explicitly about how her own family situation is reflected
in the Buchanans' marriage; she conveys her pain well, and I am both honored and a little afraid that she has told me so much. Another writes of herself with accuracy, I suspect, and with acuity.

> Although I hate to admit it, the things that are simliar in the *Great Gatsby*
> as to my own life are the personality traits that I despise in the characters.
>
> Like Daisy I am a manipulator, especially of the opposite sex. I use my
> looks combined with my intelligence to get what I want. (I don't particu-
> larly think this is a "bad" trait, maybe an unmoral one, but it's useful.) I
> also let people take the blame for things I have done. This shows my cow-
> ardice, and this is some thing I constantly strive to correct. I also find a trait
> that I share with Gatsby. I do try to impress people. I've dropped my Phil-
> adelphia accent because that is looked down upon in the suburb in which I
> live. My clothing is that of the current "in" because I come from a
> "wanna-be chic" area.

Computer-generated writings like these help us understand how we construct the stories we read, help us appreciate that we undertake such constructions with more than the cognitive or intellectual material of the story,
with the values and beliefs and experiences that we bring to it as well.

The Story of the Class: Take Two

Such constructions often find their beginnings in a plot, typically a basic plot we hold in common. Cinderella, most readers agree, did sweep ashes, did go to a dance, did meet a prince who assured her happiness ever after. My students, however, don't plot very well. They tend to leap over plot in a rush to interpret, to see the agent of the action as the recipient of it, to omit key pieces of information but to include trivial ones, to get lost in the details, to abstract vaguely. Alas, my review of their summaries confirms this expectation. Joe, for instance, thinks that

> Didion's piece on California is a reflective essay about the past, the present, and the question of the future. She recollects her childhood, the building of her home, and the different experiences she had as a child. She then does a brief recall of what has become of the town that she grew up in. She tells of the differences, mostly the situation revolving around the search for, and lack thereof, of jobs. Jobs related to the aeronautical field being the backbone of the community in which she grew up. She tells the story of the [Spur] Posse, the way they displayed themselves, and their effect on the community. . . .

After the summaries are completed, each student reads a colleague's summary and then comments on whether it is accurate. To do this, we play a version of computer musical chairs called "SneakerNet." Each student moves to the next terminal on the right, reads the classmate's summary displayed on the screen, and critiques it, agreeing and disagreeing as necessary. Jamie, for instance, tells Joe—correctly—that

> This is a fairly accurate summary except for the fact that I didn't know that Didion lived in Lakewood. This summary is concentrating on the historical and industrial side of the Lakewood story, but there wasn't much said about the Spur Posse. . . .

Upon returning to his terminal, Joe responds:

> I totally agree on the fact that I didn't include enough facts about the Posse, however I didn't consider them to be the prime focus of the article. I considered the focus of the article to be more relative to the employment aspect, and how that aspect had changed the community into what it had become, i.e., the Posse presence. Forgot Lakewood was the name of the town, you got me there.

I'm reminded here of what William Perry says about the cognitive development of eighteen-year-olds: they see the world polemically, as an either/or place, a place where the Didion piece is about the town or about the Spur Posse.

We summarize *Gatsby*, too, and the pattern repeats itself: odd details, overgeneralizations, misplottings.

> Told from the perspective of a new comer, to the "high society" party life that presides off the coast of New York City, it tells of an eventful summer centering on a man named Gatsby. The story follows him through a great journey. It starts years before the novel when he fell in love with Daisy, and then they were separated by the war. Their reunion is followed by a rediscovering of their feelings towards each other which ultimately brought the destruction of the couple and those closest to them.

The summaries don't seem to work; we write and re-write again.

Plot itself is a cultural construct, I say, and some English professors believe that there isn't a plot; others think that readers who share knowledge and values do plot similarly. So even plot—which we just took for granted—isn't a certainty. Neither are other certainties certain. History, for instance, what is that? "Facts," Wayne replies. "Finally, we have something we can hold onto." (Really?, I think. He doesn't know.) Even history doesn't exist in a vacuum, I say. Your facts are my myths. History too is located within a **rhetorical situation** that includes writer, reader, topic, and language/voice. What would happen to history if we place it in different rhetorical situations?

We find out by writing the story of Lyndon Baines Johnson. I supply the facts; the students write the story. One student comments that the story will be only as good as the facts I've supplied. (I appreciate the skepticism; they're learning.) Next the students write LBJ's story, but for an audience of six-year-olds. They complain that they don't know six-year-olds, that this is too hard. I remind them they were six once. They write.

Melissa drafts a text and then adds "<picture to be inserted>"; from her babysitting experiences, she knows that visuals capture the attention of the children. Verbally, Andrea notes, there were changes as she wrote for the new audience:

> I tried to write on the level of a six year old, by doing things such as shortening my sentences and simplifying things a tad.

But it is Jamie who articulates best the change in story caused by the change in audience.

> The history in the piece became very oversimplified to the point that a lot was left out. A 6 year old, on average, could not understand the ideas of government, war, fraud, legislation, and poverty. They could get a general picture by telling them simple thoughts, like poverty means the poor, but this is not the whole truth. So, essentially, you are not telling them the entire truth. I only wrote the things that a 6 year old would be prepared for. There's more to it than that.

The plot changes; truth is not a fixed object. It's a hard lesson to learn.

The Story of the Class: Take Three

Jamie's paper on *The Great Gatsby* shows how reading and writing from text play out in the class. Like the other students, Jamie reads the novel. She also writes some eight prompts on it in class—prompts that ask her, in addition to the ones listed previously, what her favorite line in the novel is; what the characters in the novel were doing some ten years later; if (and how) the students read the novel differently, had Fitzgerald used one of his other proposed titles (e.g., *The High Bouncing Lover* or *Under the Red, White, and Blue*). We debate in class: Is this merely a story of the '20s? Why is it considered a great novel? Why do they identify with Nick? Why do they think Daisy won't leave Tom? What does this say about America?

As the debate progresses, Jamie and the other students work on their drafts; their purpose, as I explain in the assignment sheet, is to construct the stories of *Gatsby* that they think are most important. Jamie brings her first draft into class and shares it with a group of peers. Jamie then rewrites the paper and is ready to submit it.

Jamie's paper is focused on two themes: the desolation in the novel, both personal and physical, and the ironic use of romance.

> It is true that Daisy appears to live a happy life, and she may seem as though she has done "gay and exciting things," but the truth appears in her statement to Nick, Jordan, Gatsby, and Tom: "What'll we do with ourselves this afternoon, and the day after that, and the next thirty years?" . . .

Generally, I find her "focus . . . clear, your argument well-supported." But I want some changes: in the transitions she neglects; in points that need to be articulated more fully; and more substantially, in her treatment of romance. "The main suggestion that I'd like to make is that you separate out the Tom and Myrtle false romance from the knight romance of Gatsby and Daisy. Since they are mirror images of each other, they both deserve attention, which requires a paragraph for each. Yes?" In the margins I admire Jamie's use of quotes, and occasionally I ask for more.

About three weeks later, a writing workshop in class: Students are asked to choose a passage that needs work and to revise. Much as in a studio, I walk around the class and observe the changes the writers are making as they make them, pointing out what I like, what I'd like more of: "Yes. More of that please." "Can you explain this?" "Remind us of your earlier point." In sum, it gives me a chance to comment and direct **as students write**. Jamie has already decided that she will use the *Gatsby* piece in her portfolio, so this is the piece she rewrites. She starts with the paragraph on romance.

> Medieval romance typically involves a private lovers' world, and *The Great Gatsby* contains many secret meeting places. Void of obnoxious guests, Gatsby's road house becomes a love nest where Daisy comes over quite

often in the afternoons. Tom and Myrtle have a secret apartment in the city,
but their romance is different from Gatsby's and Daisy's. Tom shows little
true affection for Myrtle, and their apartment is much less private, with
many guests. The medieval gardens also play an important scene for love.
Daisy and Gatsby set up a meeting in Nick's home as the cottage is transformed into a garden by filling it with a "greenhouse" of flowers (551). As
Mandel points out, "Daisy and Gatsby escape to Nick's house during a
party, Nick watches from the garden (107) and later lingers in the garden
(11) to talk to Gatsby and his beloved (111, 114)."

That paragraph becomes two. The first of these isn't changed very much,
though a sentence that sums up is appended at the end:

> Gatsby is transformed into the pure knightly figure who loves and adores
> Daisy unconditionally in their lovers' setting."

Tom and Myrtle's "romance," however, evolves from the two sentences
it originally received into the beginning of an elaborated paragraph. Though
the discourse isn't polished yet, the contrast between Gatsby and Tom is more
tightly drawn, the false image of romance more clearly articulated. Overall
Jamie constructs a theme of doubled romance, and at the end of the final draft
she raises an interesting question about how we define intimacy:

> The continuous theme of love and romance is slightly twisted with Tom and
> Myrtle, but they offer a kind of foil to the intimate relationship shared by
> Gatsby and Daisy.

I hadn't thought of Gatsby and Daisy as intimate, but given that the term
is over, it's a point we don't get to explore.

Representing the Stories: The Portfolios

Tell the readers about portfolios, one of my editors requests: explain how
they work, if they work, when they don't work. One to another, the portfolios look different to me, much as the students do. They include different
selections, so no two will be identical. But they have common organizing
elements that help me read.

- An annotated Table of Contents that signals me as to the contents
  and their arrangement
- An exhibit from a portfolio they composed before entering UNC
  Charlotte
- Three computer prompts
- Two of the four formal essays, complete with drafts
- A reflective essay

I look with pleasure at one Annotated Table of Contents:

PAPERS

- I chose "The Main Causes of the Civil War" from my June portfolio partly to be used as a contrast text to the academic paper I wrote this year, and partly because in most cases I prefer to write academically.
- The voice paper is my revolutionary piece. I broke out of my academic writing mold and wrote relaxed and conversationally; this was a milestone for me!
- The Great Gatsby Paper displays academia with creativity to interpret a story in your own way.

PROMPTS

- Prompt Four, Joan Didion's "Letter from California" summary. This prompt gives a good example of my writing style in the form of a concise, informative summary.
- Prompt 11 shows spontaneous creativity and thought.
- Our Lyndon B. Johnson exercise, writing for a five-year-old, shows a different facet of my thought process, creativity, and ability to write to different discourse communities.
- Prompt 18, a summarization and opinion piece on Toby Fulwiler's article, is another demonstration of a summary, however it includes my feelings and thoughts about his writing.
- The final free prompt we did is a "me" prompt using a conversational tone telling about my feelings and what I have learned in my first semester in college.

Melissa B.
November 23, 1993

When I read the portfolios, I see that the concept of story—of text as larger than literature but rooted in literature—began to take on the power for which I had wished. So while I'm reading the portfolios to assess the student work, I am able to assess my own. (Sometimes this is exhiliarating; other times disconcerting; all times instructive.) Stephanie includes a paper that she submitted both to history and to English 1103, a report on the Salem witch trials, grounded in a simple if horrific plot: Accusations were made and women were put to death. For Stephanie, it's also a set of competing stories: the Salem witch trials as mass hysteria, the Salem witch trials as East-meets-West class conflict, the Salem witch trials as misogyny legally sanctioned. Andrea and Angie have taken on another query related to story: How much, and when, do we trust the narrator? They have researched the Holocaust, asking what difference it makes when the story is narrated by a participant observer. They respect Elie Wiesel's account, but they have learned to distrust the personal account, to question its "truth." (Is this skepticism what we in the Academy induce, I wonder.)

How else to describe the portfolio? Like a story: The contents—the papers and prompts—provide a plot. To evaluate it? Against the scoring guide: Can they write from text? Do they write for different audiences appropriately? And guided by their own perceptions, their reflections. Sometimes these are shorter pieces, like the prompts; sometimes they are reflections that are added later to journal entries. But in this model of portfolio, the culminating piece is the Reflective Essay. In some of these essays, I am disappointed: They seem reflective in category only—short, skimpy, vague. (I wonder where the fault belongs, with me or them or with us both. I wonder how to get it right next time.) With several of the essays, I am pleased; they confirm for me what I had believed—revising was hard for Stephanie, gaining confidence in her writing was Angela's major task and working with a colleague helped her, Donald's strength is in academic rather than "personal" writing.

Excerpts from Stephanie's Reflective Essay also tell the story of the class.

I am staring at a blank computer screen trying to figure out what exactly you want in this essay. I know that some people think that I am an expert in the field of talking about myself, but discussing my writing is a different story. My writing seems so much more important, so much more personal. . . .

The in class prompts are next in my portfolio. To be honest, when Dr. Yancey said that we had to include prompts in our portfolio, I thought it was a lousy idea. What could one possibly learn about my writing in pieces that I did in fifteen minutes (besides the fact that I am the worst speller in the world)? But when I went through the twenty prompts, I noticed some really strange things. I notice that I am candidly honest in a way that I have only experienced with my journal writing. Maybe that has to due with trusting your teacher, or maybe it's the "sink or swim" attitude that was prevalent in the writing. I really didn't have the time to be witty or argumentive, just honest. And if I came across as witty or argumentive, then that was my honest reaction to the subject of the day. Although I have revised the prompts, I tried not to change any of the ideas that where presented within them. I believe that by not changing the content of these papers it gives the reader the sense of growing with me, of seeing how my thoughts changed over the course of the semester.

"The Hammock" is a very personal piece. Not only in the sense that it is about my boyfriend, but that I learned so much in the writing that piece about my persona. . . . My affection for this piece is displayed in the many rewrites I went through in order to make it as perfect as possible; this paper taught me how to revise.

The last paper, "Salem Witch Trials: A West Side Story," was originally written for a history paper (I've included the copy with my history professor comments). I finally was able to write a history paper and enjoy watching it unfold. "Salem" was written to a different discourse community then to I usually write (History v. English), and in a different style. Like all of the papers that I have included, this one also went through numerous rewrites.

Denouement

"The best ideas are transformative," I think, as I search for a way of concluding this story. In summary, it's about how we use reading and writing to learn about the world, to construct it. There are other interpretations as well: in particular, that this method of teaching of literature, as exemplified in this class, is characterized by specific techniques, by infusing it with many different kinds of writing, by connecting it to other discourses, by using structured computer prompts to generate those connections and insights, and by representing the learning in a coherent way in a portfolio of work characterized by selection and reflection. In reading the portfolios, too, I see each student doubly: as a member of our classroom community; as a developing writer with his or her own agenda.

As important, though, as I construct this story I see an interpretation more central to me, one about the power we have to teach and to learn and to learn from our teaching. And I understand the value of text, not just for what a particular text reveals or evokes, but also for the opportunity that it presents to us, as readers, as writers, as human beings.

And I take satisfaction in thinking that my students understood some of that, too. When asked on an evaluation form about the value of the texts that we used in class, one of them observed, "*It wasn't so much the texts that we used; it was how we used them.*"

(Yes, I think. That's what I thought, too.)

Pulling the portfolios into a pile I could remove to the car, I reflect on what I will change next time round, about how I will add Frost's "Design," about how we might read *The Age of Innocence* and see the movie, too (that's yet another story). Feeling watched, I see a child's blue eyes spying on me from around the still-barren stairway, hear another's child's voice from above, insisting rather than inquiring: "Is it time for decorating yet?"

(Yes, I think. Time for that, too.)

I use a course portfolio to replace the midterm and final examination. With the portfolio, I use multiple drafts and peer response groups.

Donald A. Daiker
Miami University (Ohio)

What I don't do is as important and useful as what I do: I don't assign only the Standard English Department Critical Essay; instead we write a wide variety of responses, including personal and creative ones. I don't lecture or talk to the walls; instead I talk with students, and write with students, and play with language and ideas with students. And I don't restrict discussion only to the work of art under examination; instead, I encourage students to draw into the novel or poem whatever they can.

Pat Murray
California State University—Northridge

22

Less as More
The Ten-Minute Writing Assignment as Enabling Constraint

William E. Coles, Jr.
University of Pittsburgh

Artificial limits create a crisis, which rouses the brain's resources:
the compulsion towards haste overthrows the ordinary precautions,
flings everything into top gear, and many things that are usually
hidden find themselves rushed into the open. Barriers break down.
Prisoners come out of their cells.

Ted Hughes,
Poetry in the Making

As a teacher of writing committed for years to the educational value of offering
writing to students as a mode of learning, a special way of thinking and coming
to know, I was clear my upper-division literature course entitled "Fantasy and
Romance" was going to have what in catalogese is known as "a writing
component." I was just as clear, however, that the size of the course (forty-five
students) and the amount of reading in it (over three thousand pages of text;
ten to fourteen books) meant that the writing I was going to have the students
do would have to be defined and understood in a very particular way. Given
the many things my department and the university hold me responsible to do
as a teacher, for me to have expected myself to read, let alone evaluate
thoughfully, a series of even very short papers, one on each of our readings,
say, would have been as wishfully unreasonable as imagining my students

would have had the time and energy to work at crafting that much writing that was ready to be read. The Requirement and Evaluation section of my syllabus for Fantasy and Romance the first term I taught it, therefore, read as follows:

> Your grade will be based on your performance on a number of short, in-class writing assignments (forty percent), on a midterm and final examination (fifty percent), and on your participation in class (ten percent). For most of the in-class writing assignments you will be given no more than five or ten minutes, sometimes at the beginning of a class period, sometimes at the end, and you will always be restricted in the number of sentences you may write (one, two, three at most). Sometimes you will be asked to prepare for these writing assignments in advance, sometimes not. The questions asked you will not have a correct as opposed to an incorrect answer ("Whom does Aragorn marry?"). Rather, they will be questions to which a number of intelligent responses are possible ("In what sense may *The Tombs of Atuan* be considered a feminist novel?"). I will grade the assignments F, P, or H (failure, passing, or honors), and though I will not write comments on any of these pieces of writing, I will give them back to you the period following the class in which you write them. No missed in-class writing assignments may be made up, and all missing assignments will be recorded as failure.
>
> I will not count spelling on any of your in-class written work, but grammar and punctuation will mean a great deal in how your work is evaluated. You will have to know how to set up a series or an opposition in a sentence, the difference between commas and semicolons, colons and dashes. And since you will be given a number of opportunities to see how complexity may be honored, you will be graded also on the development over the course of the term of your ability to write with precision and control under the pressure of time.

Such a description let my students know that they were going to do a lot of in-class writing and assured them that their teacher wasn't the type to dawdle when it came to evaluating their work, that they could in fact count on getting it back the very next period. But about all I say of *how* I'll evaluate that work is that grammar and punctuation are going to count heavily, and that since the students "will be given a number of opportunities to see how complexity may be honored," I'm going to grade them on their "development" with the form. The precise relation between the honoring of complexity and individual development is not articulated.

The same section of my syllabus for the same course (I continue to teach it at least once a year) is now, as one might expect, fuller and clearer. But, so far as I am concerned, the most important difference between my first way of talking to students about the ten-minute writing assignment and how I became able to talk to them about it has to do with my belief in the educational value of the form as I have learned to use it—a belief that may be traced out in *what* (not just in how much) I'm able to say about both how I want my students to understand the form and why as a class we're going to be handling it as we are:

> Your grade will be based on the *development* of your performance on a number of short, in-class writing assignments (fifty percent), on a take-home midterm and final examination (forty percent), and on the effectiveness with which you enter and contribute to our classroom conversation (ten percent). (Please notice that there is a distinction being made here between just talk and talk that is useful to us as a class.)
>
> The in-class writing assignments (there will be from fifteen to twenty over the course of the semester) are designed to give you the opportunity to develop the kinds of conceptual skills that are important in gaining and demonstrating command of a subject—such skills as the ability to infer and deduce; to paraphrase, summarize, classify, synthesize; to discover patterns; to make connections; to build models. Developing such skills under the pressure of time and within the restriction of space means developing your ability to move efficiently to the core of an issue, to train yourself in seeing quickly to the heart of things. For this reason, most of the in-class writing assignments will give you no more than ten minutes to work within, sometimes at the beginning of a class period, sometimes at the end, and you will always be restricted in the number of sentences you may write (one, two, three at most). Sometimes you will be asked to prepare for these writing assignments in advance ("Here is a paragraph, or here are two paragraphs, about which you will be asked to write something next period."), sometimes not ("Please take out a piece of paper and in no more than a single sentence explain where, given our discussion this period, we need to move next period."). These assignments may be about our readings, our classroom conversations, fantasy as a subject, or any of these in combination with any of the others.
>
> Most of the time the questions asked you will not have a correct as opposed to an incorrect answer ("Whom does Aragorn marry?"). Rather, they will be questions to which a number of intelligent responses are possible ("In what senses may *The Tombs of Atuan* be considered a feminist novel?"). I will grade the assignments N, P, or H (no credit, acceptable, or honors), and will give them back to you the period following the class in which you write them. I will not write comments on any of these pieces of writing, but we will go over examples in class of both adequate and inadequate responses. No missed in-class writing assignments may be made up, and all missing assignments will be recorded as failure.
>
> I will not count spelling on any of your in-class written work, but grammar, punctuation, and syntactical control, because they have to do with a writer's ability to acknowledge and handle complexity, will mean a great deal in how your work is evaluated. Though you will certainly have to know

how to set up a series or an opposition in a sentence, the difference between commas and semicolons, periods and dashes, more will be expected of you in your writing for this course than mechanically correct sentences, for a sentence can be correct and stupid or silly at the same time. And since you will be given a number of opportunities to see how complexity may be honored, how thoughtful or perceptive sentences may be distinguished from those that are superficial or obvious, you will be graded also on the *development* over the course of the term of your ability to write with precision and control under the pressure of time. It is expected, in other words, that you will incorporate more and more in your own writing the distinctions made in class between adequate and inadequate in-class writing.

In my revised syllabus I'm able to make the connections I do between the students' work with ten-minute writing assignments and the development of their abilities as thinkers generally, because I've learned myself more about how to ask the kinds of questions that give them a shot at doing that. I'm able to define "development" as the gradual incorporation into the students' writing of the "the distinctions made in class between adequate and inadequate writing," because I've found some ways of dealing with responses to the ten-minute writes that make the students' learning from them likely and, hence, make a demand for an enactment of that learning reasonable. In short, and as my rewritten syllabus I think suggests, the artificial limits of my situation as a teacher of literature had roused my brain's resources as a teacher of writing.

The kind of ten-minute writing assignment I've found to work best with my students (and no matter what the level or subject; I now use ten-minute writes with graduate students and in my composition as well as in my literature courses), is one that—my temptation here is to say—mandates thinking. Here is a assignment I used the first time I taught Fantasy and Romance:

> *In ten minutes and in no more than three sentences,* explain how it is that fairy tales can be interpreted differently by different people.

What that assignment resulted in, however, was a mass response, a number of barely differentiatable phrasings of the cliché that different people see differently, very few of which contained any specific reference to the material we'd been studying. Here is not just a more focused form of the same directive, but a more challenging one as well, and, as such, a potentially richer source of learning for students:

> Imagine someone who has read and heard everything you have read and heard in this course so far saying something like this:
>   "Readers can make fairy tales mean whatever they want them to."
> In ten minutes and in no more than two sentences, explain how this assertion may be said to be irresponsible.
> Write your sentences on this page.

And here is another of my first tries at a ten-minute write:

> In ten minutes and in no more than three sentences, explain which of the
> nine critical commentaries given you to read on fairy tales you like best.

Again, however, such an assignment is too easily addressed with the obvious; in this case, a list of dust-jacket terms of praise. The revised form of the assignment read:

> You have read and ranked in order of your preference nine critical commentaries on fairy tales. Record that ranking by number on this line (highest preference first) _____
>
> *In ten minutes and in no more than two sentences,* explain which of the nine critical commentaries on fairy tales given you to read is your *second* favorite. Be sure your response makes clear what you mean by "favorite," and why you rank your choice second rather than first or lower than second. (You may use any notes or texts you wish.)

It is not, of course, possible to mandate thinking with ten-minute writing assignments (or with anything else), but as my revisions suggest, it is possible to phrase them in such a way as to require considerably more than that students simply report what they have retained.

Even with very ordinary classroom procedures, and no matter what the subject, ten-minute writes can become richly enabling constraints. Consider, for example, the educational possibilities open to a teacher who decides to have students write for ten minutes on something they are assigned to read. "For the past week," one might imagine a teacher's saying, "we have been studying X [where X maybe anything form the work of Marx or Freud to ways of rebuilding automotive carburetors]. I am now giving you two statements about X [which may be two paragraphs, or chapters, or articles, etc.], and at the beginning of next period I am going to ask you to write for ten minutes on something involving X and these two statements."

Here are just a few of the ways in which that teacher may choose to initiate things the following period:

1. *In no more than a single sentence,* explain which of these two statements is for you the more correct (or useful, or important, etc.).

2. These two statements *apparently* contradict (or are in harmony with) each other. *In no more than two sentences,* explain how from another point of view they may be said to be in harmony with (or may be said to contradict) each other.

3. Here is a third paragraph, a third statement, about X. *In a single sentence,* explain which one of these two statements you have read this third statement is more in agreement with and what makes you say so?

4. The two statements given you to study are both statements about X. To judge from what each writer says about X, what would each say about Y? *Write no more than a single sentence.*

5. The two statements given you about X are not the only perspective from which X may be considered. *Write, in no more than three sentences,* what seems to you another important way of accounting for X.

6. Here, in this additional paragraph, is an account of a situation involving X. Which of the two writers you read for today would have the best way of explaining how this situation came to be (or way of remedying the problem this situation poses, or way of explaining what this situation is likely to develop into, etc.) and what makes you say so? Confine your answer *to no more than three sentences.*

Just as there are a number of kinds of ten-minute writing assignments, there are a number of uses for them. How many sentences one decides to allow students for the handling of a particular problem, for example (see directions 3 and 4 above), can help them experiment with more complicated sentence patterns than they might use all on their own. And no teacher will have any difficulty seeing the pedagogical value of the ten-minute write I give as an example in my revised Fantasy and Romance course description: "Please take out a piece of paper and in no more than a single sentence explain where, given our discussion this period, we need to move next period"—nor will any teacher have any trouble seeing ways of making his or her own use of the principle there: What's the *main* point of the lecture today? What's the most important thing you have learned this period? What question is raised by our conversation today? How does what we have been doing this period connect with what we did last period? Etc.

The ten-minute write can also be an efficient way not just of involving students with revision, but of enabling them to see the value of it. "Your ten minutes are up," I say several times a term in Fantasy and Romance. "Now, draw an X through what you have written. Next period turn in not just what you have drawn an X through, but a revision of it as well, the best three sentences you can write on the issue of the assignment. Type them out on the back of the page you've been working on." This last variation is a standard one for me, not just because some writing problems are more complicated than others, but in order that I may acknowledge how not all good thinking is fast thinking. (The midterm and final examinations I give in Fantasy and Romance are both take-home exams, papers in effect, for this same reason. Each has two questions and the students' responses to each question are limited to a single typewritten page, but in both cases the students have a week for the work.)

Because most students will have had virtually no experience with anything like the ten-minute write, and because, for this reason, students generally perform at first very badly with them, it is imperative that any teacher planning to use the form plan also some ways of helping students become more discriminating evaluators of such writing. In fact, I would go so far as to say that without such help students will experience the form as punitive rather than educational.

In Fantasy and Romance, I distribute some sample responses to the very first ten-minute write the students do, which I print on a copy of the same assignment the students have worked with:

N

Things in fairy tales have specific meanings for readers. To think otherwise is ridiculous.

N

Fairy stories connect with early childhood. We all clearly relate these basic themes, my friend doesn't seem to know this.

P

There's a range of interpretations of fairy tales outside which it seems illegitimate to go. It would be difficult to see "Water of Life," for example, as a story about the Vietnam War.

P

Fairy stories seem to connect with themes that even children can know about (good vs. evil). It is hard to see therefore how something children couldn't know about (such as political intrigue) could be a "meaning" of a given fairy story.

H

A particular fairy tale seems with its materials to set its own limits on how far an interpretation of it may be taken. "The Frog King," for example, may be read as a story about conflicting responsibilities (between two kinds of promises, the obligation one owes to self and to society, etc.) but not about, say, the power of beauty ("The Wonderful Musician").

H

Fairy tales seem to deal with living fundamentals (they use a "vocabulary" of things common to all ages and all cultures: sun, water, sickness, wealth and poverty, etc.). An interpretation which did not take these universal concerns into account would be possible but not to me convincing.

"Here," I say of that handout to my students, "is a sampling of the work you did in class last time. I thought you might appreciate seeing what it is I like, want, admire, respect, take seriously, give A's to, etc., and, conversely, what it is that I *cannot* take seriously, will not be able to give a passing grade in the course to, and so on. [I've not found it productive to have students discuss how to *grade* responses in literature courses. Conversation about writing degenerates quickly into unproductive argument about quality.] Please look over these samples and come to class next time prepared to have a conversation about what sorts of things you think you can do as a writer of ten-minute writes—remember, you're going to do about twenty of them—to do *well* in Fantasy and Romance, and what sorts of things you think you can avoid doing to avoid doing poorly.

"Please note that though I'll help you try to describe something you see, the ideas for this conversation are going to come from you, not from me. Since this is not a writing course, we'll be able to take no more than ten minutes for our conversation, so maybe you'd better come with some notes in order that we don't waste time."

Some of the "tips" my students have come up with from that sampling are (as our volunteer class secretary wrote them up):

1. Take the full ten minutes to work on your sentences. Don't just jot something down and spend the next five minutes looking out the window.

2. Use concrete evidence from the readings to explain your position— the more specific the better.

3. Act like you care whether somebody understands you or not.

4. You can get a lot of firepower into a sentence by using the kinds of parentheses that will say to a reader: This information is in here to show you I know what I'm talking about.

I have arranged, and in some cases created, the sample responses, particularly at the beginning of the course, that make it possible for students to see what they do of course. My N responses above, for instance, are paradigms of what the N work of a particular class looked like, rather than the work of particular students. (One of the two H responses is also made up, but could anyone say for sure which one?) My arranging of responses is also deliberate. From one point of view, for example, it might be said that the first N, P, and H responses all "say the same thing" (as it might be said of the second). They don't, of course. But rather than having my students realize just that a given way of seeing is limited, I want them to understand some ways of making it better than that—and to suggest also that I am willing to give them time to learn how to do this. (At this point I refer students again to the underlined word "development" in the course description, and explain that though a number of students have earned A's in Fantasy and Romance, in no case did a particular student's in-class writings add up to an A with simple arithmetic. Another way I try to take the terror out of what it is I'm grading on and care most about is by using the invented scale of H, P, and N rather than the more conventional, though also more poisoned, scale of A, B, C, D, and F.

More complicated writing/thinking problems can be handled later in the term as they become appropriate to a class as a whole. Here are the sample responses I worked with one term in Fantasy and Romance in order to address the problems of how a writer can go about providing substance for his or her substantives, and of how to use evidence tellingly as well as accurately, authoritatively as well as correctly:

H

Auden is my favorite critic, less for his total argument than for certain remarks that illuminate the genre of fairy tales for me ("no one conscious analysis can exhaust [their] meaning"). My second favorite is by Bettleheim, not because I totally buy his Freudian analysis of "The Frog King," but because it is so internally consistent and uses so much of the story (the ball *and* the well *and* the talk and appearance of the frog, etc.) that it clarifies, through its respect, the artistry of stories that I once saw as simple or even crude.

N

Fairy tales, for me, are an escape from this dog-eat-dog world and take me to an imaginary place where the good are justly rewarded and the bad are punished, i.e. giving me my childhood dreams. Lina Leonard is not first in my list of critics simply because she takes away the imaginary realm of fairy tales to interpret *everything* as an everyday occurrence.

What I like about the writing of the H response above is the way it succeeds in doing what the writing of the N response only gestures in the direction of doing: making distinctions ("less for . . . than for"; "not because . . . but because"), marshalling telling evidence ("the ball *and* the well *and* the talk and appearance of the frog, etc."), qualifying through appropriate modification ("through its respect"; "or even crude"), defining by means of verbal triangulation (as with the term "artistry"). And I like also the way such writing, in doing what it does, creates the image of a mind at work, shows how impressive a sensibility can be when it is passionately committed to doing justice to its subject, even if limited by time and space.

Or is it in some sense *because* of these limits that the mind there is able to show itself off so well—the way, as Frost claimed, rime can help make poetry poetry; the way the game of tennis is made possible through the use of a net; the way the artificial limits of my position as a teacher of literature roused my brain's resources as a teacher of writing? It just may be that to invite students to work with how the constraints of the ten-minute writing assignment can be seen as enabling is to help all of us, teachers and students alike, to use our minds in ways that others can learn from and so be heartened by.

I put writing at the center of my literature classroom. I want students to enlarge their understanding of themselves, our texts, and the contexts in which those texts are created and read. My writing-teacher sense of the importance of revision is key and finally what makes the re-seeing and larger understanding possible. I ask that students keep double-entry reading journals. As class discussions progress, they make follow-up entries that they revise into short position papers and longer analytical papers. Students come to "own" their readings, honing them from gut responses to full interpretations.

One English major, who began the semester by declaring that teachers had always *told* her what the literature meant, wrote a final paper on the constraints of the Gothic genre on Bronte's feminism in *Jane Eyre*. The paper really began in her reading journal as what she called "nitpicky observations": "Why wouldn't someone as hard-headed as Jane not just go find out right away what all that noise was in the attic?" More important than the final product was the pride this student took in developing and daring to offer an interpretation of her own.

Many of our colleagues who work primarily in literary studies design courses on fascinating topics, juxtaposing canonical and non-canonical texts, fiction and nonfiction, print and non-print media. But those who have not taught that much writing often think more about the critical statement their course is making and less about what it is they want students to be able to do with the texts—less about how those students can make statements for themselves. That is more how writing teachers think. We get our hands dirty with the messiness of students' efforts in progress and, finally, give theories of literary interpretation a run for their money in practice.

Christine Farris
Indiana University

23

Song of the Open Road
A Motorcycle Rider
Teaches Literature

Toby Fulwiler
University of Vermont

When you're the editor of the book, you're allowed a few liberties—later deadlines, more pages, deviant ideas. Which maybe explains how, in writing this chapter, I changed my mind about influences, believing at first I taught literature differently because I taught writing, only later realizing that it wasn't writing, but *riding* that's made the difference. Motorcycle riding, which I've been doing even longer than teaching writing.

Wait a minute. You teach literature differently because you ride a motorcycle?

This is not really so far-fetched as it sounds. Charlie Moran started me in this direction when he said he became a writing teacher instead of a literature teacher because he was interested in working "where the rubber hits the road." I naturally figured he was referring to the rubber of motorcycle tires. See, when you travel by motorcycle, everything is more difficult, less comfortable, slower, more considered. Putting on leathers, boots, helmets, gloves, packing the rain gear, strapping things down. Holding on, crouching low, mile after mile, the wind rush and engine rumble your stereo. Watching for gravel, water, ice on the corners, thunder and rain on the horizon, drivers who don't see you. Arriving, taking things off, stowing helmets, glasses, gloves. Unpacking, stretching, learning again the ground beneath your feet.

I still don't get it. What's all this got to do with teaching literature—that is your topic, right?

Well, you don't travel by motorcycle because it's faster, easier, or softer, but to learn the way and live the journey—to feel the pavement, to lean the corners, taste the wind, test your judgment—all that Robert Persig stuff. And you travel by motorcycle because it's more fun, taking the long way around, the blue highway, not the interstate, moving faster, arriving later, sure of your destination because you've learned the road that got you there.

So . . . ?

In other words, when I teach anything now, I slow down and attend as much to the journey as the destination—to the process as much as the product. I start with the writing, then add the reading. For a literature course, this approach may sound backwards, but I find that the writing focuses the reading, slows it down, creates and necessitates greater attention. Let me work that out for you.

Wait a minute. What do you mean, you "start with the writing"?

To plan my syllabus, I design the writing assignments in first (types, deadlines, activities). Then again, when I teach classes, I begin with writing for the first few minutes (questions, problems, insights).

> Start with writing. This course requires frequent informal writing: a daily journal and several letters. And it requires regular formal writing: two critical papers, a personal essay, and a work of your imagination (play, poem, story).

But reading, then grading all this student writing—in addition to reading texts and preparing lectures—that's a lot of work.

It depends on how it's handled. First, I get a lot of help by asking my students to read and critique each other's drafts and to assess their own writing. Second, I don't comment on all the writing. Third, I don't grade any of it individually. Instead, students keep all their written work in portfolios that are graded only at mid- and end-term.

> Follow with reading. "American Literature, Colonial to 1865" (sophomore survey for non-majors): William Carlos Williams's *In the American Grain*, Emerson's essays, Thoreau's *Walden*, Frederick Douglass's *Narrative*, Stowe's *Uncle Tom's Cabin*, Whitman's "Song of Myself," Melville's *Moby Dick*, Emily Dickinson, selected poems. (These to be a mix of individual paperbacks and copyright-free handouts.)

How do you choose which texts to study?

Some traditional ones that reflect my graduate school training, some oppositional, which reflect my current reading. Some what I know, some what I still want to learn. Very much because I think students will enjoy the texts and the approach.

Class clusters. Class will operate workshop-style, with daily meetings taking place in six groups of five students each. Form your groups first class, and find out who your group-mates are, why they're here, and what interests them. All class meetings will start out in these groups in which you'll share journal entries, paper drafts, insights, and ideas.

Groups sound great, but they don't work. Without supervision they digress, talk about other stuff—sports, parties.

These groups are the backbone of the course, so they're never left to drift— nor, however, are they carefully supervised. We start each group session with focused writing and conclude each session with some kind of report to the rest of us. When they sometimes digress, as good groups inevitably do, that's OK, because they're people and interested in each other. In fact, the groups I worry about are those that never digress—the ones that don't laugh. I want students to be comfortable in their groups—but not too comfortable, so at midterm I ask students to make new groups.

Journal writing. Keep a journal. Write outside of class about the readings, about last class, about issues on our minds. In addition, each class will start with a few minutes of private journal writing and cluster sharing. Other times, journal writing will take place in the middle or at the end of class, to raise questions, catch insights, brainstorm topics, and start papers.

You use up class time for writing?

The writing advances the discussion because it helps students recall, find, and focus information. I easily gain back the five or ten minutes by having a sharper discussion. (Yes, I write and share my writing too.)

Journal topics. Include in your journal the following: (1) in-class topics that prompt our discussion (*Moby Dick:* Why go to sea?); (2) responses to your reading: every time you finish reading a chapter, poem, or passage, write about it—summarize, interpret, evaluate—but always with specific text references; (3) make connections between this course and another course or between this course and your own life (my great-grandfather was a whaling captain; we have his log.)

So you'll have to collect and grade all this writing or else they won't do it.

Not exactly. But I'm always feeling a little trapped with journals—I want students to write honestly to themselves, yet I want to see what they've written. If I monitor journals too closely, it kills their honesty as well as my time. And if I don't monitor at all, it suggests the assignment isn't serious. I compromise by asking students to keep loose-leaf journals, and to share voluntary page selections with me.

Assessing journals. Hand in ten good journal entries three times in the next fifteen weeks, and ten percent of your grade will be an A. What's a good entry? More than a few lines and about any topic related to this class.

You give them A's no matter what they write, or how wrong their answers, so long as it's ten pages?

Essentially, yes. But remember, journals are not about right answers. Being able to be wrong is part of the purpose of journals—an idea practice book. Since they do the selecting from among lots of entries, they always give me pretty interesting stuff. By the way, you know (and they know) that ten percent won't change much, but everybody wants the points. (And, no, I don't really keep track of points or percentages—they know that too, but the incentive seems to work.)

> First class. Take as much loose-leaf paper (7 X 10) as you need and write: Why did you sign up for this class? (Share with a neighbor.) Describe your good or bad experiences with literature classes. (Share with nearby people.) What do you already know about American literature? (Volunteer to share with all of us.) What makes literature "American"? (At the front of the room, write a sentence on the overhead projector.) To conclude this class, introduce the people near you to the rest of the class.

You have them write first thing, first class?

I like to start fast and have students writing and talking rather than listening to me—acting rather than reacting, starting from where they are and moving outward toward my course. These questions do that. I also want to introduce different ways to share and respond, and to say: There are no rules, we can study literature any way we want. I do the obligatory stuff—calling role and handing out the syllabus—in the last five minutes.

> First assignment. Buy a loose-leaf notebook to hold these in-class writings—your journal is started: (1) write a letter (Dear Toby) sharing your reaction to this first class meeting (one page, typed, single space); (2) read the first three essays in Williams. [Week 1]

What happens if they don't do these assignments?

On days when a writing assignment is due, I put a bouncer at the door (a student with a clipboard and class list). Nobody gets in who doesn't have the paper. (Yes, we have a little fun here, and I drop the idea after a couple of weeks, but the message is clear: Do your homework.) If reading is due—which it usually is—the other students get on those who aren't prepared because the groups don't work very well.

> *In the American Grain.* As you read this William Carlos Williams collection of "historical interpretations," mark passages that especially interest you (for any reason). Write journal responses to these passages that will

start the small-group discussions. Each group plan to present one reading to the class (outline your responses on a transparency; limit your presentations to ten minutes; be prepared for five minutes of questions). [Weeks 1–3]

So what's your role when you've got the students doing all the work?

To kibitz, to ask or answer questions, to make suggestions or corrections, and especially to nod my head when I witness good work.

Emerson: "The American Scholar." Preface to the first critical paper: In journal, then in groups, discuss the effectiveness of Emerson's argument for a distinctly American literature. How will he (or you) know it when he (you) sees it? Make an outline of the organizational scheme of this essay, paying special attention to Emerson's logic and evidence to share with us and compare with others. [Week 4]

Shouldn't you be giving historical and contextual information to help students do this?

Yes. But keep in mind that they'll be progressively more interested in the information as they become more involved in Emerson's text. So I usually provide such background information in response to questions or in fifteen-minute mini-lectures when it seems most useful.

Drafts. Your first draft goes to the writing group (Tuesdays, 2–3 pages, typed double space, three copies). You'll need the draft plus the extra copies to get past the bouncer. Pass out extra copies, then read aloud, each in turn, and ask about focus, evidence, strong and weak passages, error. Discuss larger issues as a group; mark smaller issues in the margins and return to the writer. Before class ends, write out revision plans on the copy you hand in. The final draft is due the following week, with this first draft clipped behind and a cover note on top explaining why you changed what.

Wait, wait, wait! Not everyone knows how to teach writing. Not everyone has time to read all these papers. Not everyone can afford to spend class time on student writing—especially in a literature class.

When students read and discuss each other's interpretations of literature, they *are* studying literature. I promote serious interpretations by encouraging serious revision—which actually reduces the time and energy I spend on any given draft. For example, on first drafts, I skim-read without a pen in my hand, commenting only on their revision plan. I raise margin questions, but don't evaluate intermediate drafts. I make end-of-paper comments only, on final drafts. In other words, I consider class time devoted to student writing well spent.

Critical Paper #1. Identify, trace, and explain a theme or idea that occurs in more than one of the readings in Williams or Emerson. Make a claim and support it with evidence (passages, page numbers). Make it clear why this theme or idea is of some interest today (2–3 pages). [Weeks 4–5]

This sounds like pretty standard stuff.

It is. I think learning to read texts closely is an important skill. I was trained, as were most people my age, in close reading techniques (Ph.D., Wisconsin, 1973). However, I now think other literacy skills are equally important— which is why I make the other kinds of assignments.

> Letter to Toby #1. Look back through your journal, check your class notes, and think about what you've learned so far and how you've learned it. Write a letter (Dear Toby) commenting on your experience so far; conclude by suggesting what you want more or less of in the coming weeks. [Week 5]

OK, but if you treat their letters seriously, you'll have to change your syllabus.

I do, but always in reasonable ways. By now the student voices are strong, some of their work very good, classroom spirit is high, and we are used to being honest with each other. We usually enjoy negotiating some change— sometimes in reading selections, sometimes in writing assignments, often about deadlines. In fact, they are more likely to prod their classmates to work harder than ask me for more lectures.

> Letter to Henry David Thoreau. In classroom pairs: Write a short letter (Dear Henry) in which you explain to the author how one of his passages has affected you personally; ask him a question about this passage. Exchange letters with your partner and respond as if you were Henry David himself. Exchange, and write one more time about whatever is on your mind. (Make photocopies so that each writer has the complete set of letters; plan to show them to me in your midterm portfolio. [Week 6]

Role-playing sounds like high school.

Trust me here. Asking students to enter, defend, and even alter classic texts can be serious business. Once they begin writing, the playful purpose takes over in astonishing ways. Actually writing—as opposed to reading, talking, or staring—is an act of commitment. Students then both assert and defend their ideas. Writing to a real partner who responds and asks for responses also makes a difference.

> Personal Paper. Mark the passages in *Walden* about which you have strong thoughts (e.g., "Simplify, simplify, simplify") or personal associations (I've watched black and red ants battle many times). Make substantial journal entries about several of these. Develop one into a personal essay, in which you use the passage by Thoreau as your point of departure and move

into your own thoughts or experience with this passage and conclude with something that teaches us about both HDT and you. [Weeks 7–8]

You really expect students to be able to do this?

Keep in mind that it's midterm and your students have been writing in and sharing their journal entries every week. That you've written and shared with them your own entries. After seven weeks of this positive workshop atmosphere, they'll do good work. It would help, however, to share some student or professional samples of personal essays via handouts or transparencies or to share selected final essays with the entire class.

> Portfolio, Midterm. Include two finished papers (Analytic #1 and Personal); attach all prior drafts and selected journal entries, as well as any other writing that represents your learning in this course. Write a one-page (typed double space) self-assessment of the work so far: Which is strong? Which is not? Can you explain why? Identify what you need to work on in the second half of the course. [Week 8]

So you don't grade the papers individually as they come in? Which means you have to read them all over again?

Right. You'll be surprised by how fast and fair this procedure is: I review the papers quickly, but write nothing on them. I agree with upwards of eighty percent of their own assessments, which makes grading quite easy. Finally, I write each student a letter back agreeing or disagreeing with their assessment, adding some of my own. Each student understands that if his or her work continues at this level, this will be the final grade.

> *The Narrative of Frederick Douglass.* Questions for journal writing, research, and group discussion: Which passages in Douglass are most believable and which are not; explain why you have these opinions. Next class will meet in the library to investigate holdings of nineteenth-century periodicals. Try to locate and photocopy any article that sheds light on the racial climate of the late 1840's and 1850's. [Weeks 8–9]

This assignment assumes knowledge of the library and research skills.

You're right, and many won't have such knowledge and skills yet, so I've arranged for a reference librarian to brief them on this part of the library, while I establish a beachhead at a nearby table to help out where I can.

> *Uncle Tom's Cabin.* Library investigation continues: Locate any references to the publication of *Uncle Tom's Cabin* in 1852. Your informal writing assignment is to write a letter to the editor in response to one of the reviews, making your own case for or against the inflammatory nature of this novel. Include this letter in your final portfolio. Finally, in your journal, estimate for

yourself the political effectiveness of Stowe's novel compared to Douglass's autobiography. [Weeks 9–10]

Letter to Toby #2: Look back through your journal, check your class notes, and think about what you've learned so far and how you've learned it. Write a letter commenting on your experience so far; conclude by suggesting what you want more or less of in the final five weeks. [Week 10]

How do you respond to these letters?

After each letter to me, I write back to the whole class (Dear Classmates) and distribute the copies in the next class. In responding, I quote concerns from their letters and address any issue that's mentioned more than once. I usually conclude with a P.S. telling them candidly how I think the class is going.

Poem after Walt Whitman. Go outside and sit for a moment in the grass. Bring a few leaves of it back in. Examine one blade of grass: What does it look like? Feel like? Remind you of? Suggest? And so before we read Whitman's "Song of Myself" (the central metaphor is grass), write a poem and share it within your group; include the results in your final portfolio. [Weeks 11–13]

You're not supposed to teach creative writing. Why do you have them writing poems?

Most students, especially non-majors, have a great deal of difficulty with understanding poetry, believing writers plant hidden meanings and that only teachers can find them. I want them to write some poetry to experience how it's created and so to diminish the distance between themselves and the published poets.

Okay, but how, actually, do you get them to write a poem? They must be pretty bad.

Good or bad poems are not the point; I simply want to bring them closer to the form they're trying to understand. I do a lot of overhead projection work here, asking them to make lists of possible images, ideas suggested by the images, metaphors, active verbs, and we share these and try out different combinations—me modeling some feeble attempts on transparencies. To some it's a word game, others get quite serious. If they write some pleasing lines, they appreciate better what the masters have done. And this exercise also helps with the next assignment.

Imaginative Paper. Write this paper about something that strikes you as especially interesting in Douglass, Stowe, or Whitman. Construct this paper in the genre of either autobiography (play a role?), fiction (invent a setting, character, situation?), or poetry (include all three authors?), preferably after the fashion of the authors just studied. The most convincing papers will integrate that author's stylistic, thematic, and structural approaches in a single document. Good luck! [Weeks 12–13]

How on earth do you evaluate these creative papers?

These imaginative papers need to convey as much understanding of the authors as a critical paper—students are accountable for demonstrating these things, with the added difficulty of finding a new form to convey this information. These may be the most difficult papers to write, so I'll accept some added difficulty in assessing them—and certainly ask the students to help me here.

> Collaborative Take-home Questions. Group: Construct a take-home question for the final examination. The answer to this question should involve at least five of the eight authors studied. Next week, classmates will critique all questions, asking (1) Is it focused?, (2) Is it answerable from course readings?, and (3) Is it answerable in ten pages? Finally, select one of the questions and answer it in a collaboratively written final exam. (Due final exam date, all names signed, same credit for all authors.) [Week 12]

This way you receive six ten-page papers instead of thirty shorter ones? No complaints here. But what about the student who doesn't contribute?

For this one assignment it just doesn't matter—they're individually accountable in their journals and in all the other portfolio writing.

> *Moby Dick.* Keep a set of running journal entries about the progress of this novel. Note what interests you, what you understand, and what you do not. Your second analytical paper will be written about some aspect of this novel. Each period, one group will volunteer to pose the day's journal-writing question and lead the subsequent discussion. [Weeks 12–14]

> Emily Dickinson. Read the following poems carefully for next class, at which time each group will select one to read aloud (perform) in some way that involves contributions by all group members (this is a kind of "reader's theatre"). You will have five minutes for presenting your reading if you need it. [Week 15]

You have them do reader's theatre? Good idea. I've seen reader's theatre and it's interesting to watch readers examine a text closely, read it with their own emphasis; in fact, even when two groups perform the same text, the meaning always changes, depending on how it's read.

Yes, I find it an excellent end-of-the-term assignment. (In fact, I should probably do it earlier and more often than I do.)

> Critical Paper #2. Before you write this final analytical paper, review the results of your first critical paper and discuss with group-mates the major

difficulties in writing that paper. Include some aspect of *Moby Dick*, either by itself or in conjunction with one of the other works read in the course. (3–4 pages, typed double space.) [Weeks 13–14]

And is the second critical paper better?

Almost always, so long as they've done the reading—which with *Moby Dick* is sometimes a problem. Sometimes I think I should have them reading this novel all term long, but I've still never done it that way.

> Letter to Chris. Write a letter to Chris, the imaginary student who will occupy your seat in this course next year. Tell Chris what to expect and offer your secret for succeeding. (Open page limit; include in final portfolio.) [Week 15]

This sounds like a nice end-of-term synthesis. And then you actually deliver them to next year's class.

Sure—a real audience and purpose to this letter.

> Portfolio, Final. Include all work written for the course, in the order completed, excepting the final exam. If you revise one or more of your papers one last time, attach a note indicating the directions these revisions have taken. Finally, write a 1–2 page self-assessment, attach grade. [Due Week 15]

So reading these would be like at midterm, skimming and then writing a letter back to each student?

Yes, and now upwards of ninety percent of their assessments will probably agree with mine.

Do you always teach literature classes this way?

I learned to teach this way at Michigan Tech (1976–83), as I learned from mentors Britton, Emig, Elbow, and Macrorie the role of writing in learning. There I also began to conduct workshops for faculty across the curriculum, where only active, experiential learning works anyway. Since moving to Vermont, I only teach this way, never basing my classes on my lectures (those long answers to questions nobody asked). All my classes are workshop classes (where somebody is always asking questions, all of us trying to answer them).

The writing makes that much difference?

Yes, the writing gives the students their voices in the first place, and the confidence in their voices in the second. The writing starts and advances small-group discussions, pushes first-draft ideas out in public, and forces second-draft ideas into more precise sense and articulation. And their writing allows the students to both critique and participate in shaping the literary canon and, in the end, to enter that canon themselves.

So, to return to the motorcycle?

The writing is how we get there, I guess, the reading what's gotten to. Motorcycles—OK, and maybe writing courses—teach you to attend to the journey (the learning) as well as the destination (the knowledge). It goes without saying that the complete traveller needs both.

Well, you've almost convinced me to center my lit class on writing, but you've definitely convinced me that it's time to buy a motorcycle and learn to ride.

U ntil recently, I used only two kinds of student writing in literature classes. The first we know as "writing to learn": freewrites, journals, speculations. I wanted writers to engage a literary work to make their own discoveries and to establish their own questions. I privileged the language of the student learner in such writings; I did not tinker with the way they chose to use language as a personal discovery tool. The second we know as "writing to communicate"; critical essays, book reviews, writings for publication. I wanted writers to express to others what they have learned in studying literature. I privileged the language of the discourse community, the argumentative discourse valued by the academy, the academic discourse valued by the literary profession. Now, in addition to these two kinds of writing, I assign letters that I see as an intermediary between students' language (the language of novices, of outsiders) and academic discourse (the language of experts, of insiders). Letters are not written only for self-discovery but to other members of the learning community; these letters are not written as mature arguments ready for publication but as "rough drafts" of initial readings; these letters privilege the language of the classroom community. This language is a changing mixture of the language of the literature being read, the secondary sources, the teacher's voice, and the diverse students' voices. It assumes a collaborative context in which students are learning to read and write about literature rather than one that judges how far short they fall of meeting the standards of academic discourse and professional understanding.

In one recent class in Victorian literature, students wrote paired letters on a selection from J.S. Mill's *Autobiography*. Here is a brief excerpt from Sharon's initial letter to Debbie:

Dear Debbie,
    The last paragraph on page 243 talks about associations of pleasure with all things beneficial to the whole, and associations of pain to all things hurtful to it. But then Mill goes on to say "but there must always be something artificial and casual in associations thus produced." Why would Mill, one of the great spokesmen of Utilitarianism, call such learning by association "artificial and casual?" How else are we to learn to be social beings if we don't accept what's good brings good things to most people? . . . I hope you have better luck with this than I've had!
        Your friend,
        Sharon

Here is a small part of Debbie's seven-hundred word response to Sharon written a few days later:

Dear Sharon,
    I can understand how Mill's "casual and artificial" seems highly contradictory, but if you look closer, that is not what Mill says. In the next sentence Mill wrote, "The pains and pleasures thus forcibly associated with

things are not connected with them by any natural tie." So, if you think about it, how could Mill agree with the idea of drilling associations into pupil's minds like some sort of psychology experiment? He clearly states that these feelings of association are something that must be felt by the individual, and not just taught by the teacher. He was not discouraging learning by association, he was explaining that this type of learning without personal input was negative.

As I stated earlier, this whole theory is rather difficult to explain on paper, but I hope I have helped somewhat. I am pleased to say that I understand this whole philosophy a hundred times better than I did a few hours ago. I hope you do as well.

Best Wishes,
Debbie

And I hope so too. I wanted those letter exchanges to benefit the writer, the reader, and the entire classroom community in which the study of Mill's *Autobiography* took place. In writing about an academic subject in the form of the personal letter to a nonexpert audience, we write to each other using a middle language between the personal "writing to learn" and the public "writing to communicate."

Art Young
Clemson University

Afterword

Gerald Graff
University of Chicago

What do teachers of writing bring to the teaching of literature? If this lively collection is any indication, they bring a student-centered perspective that corrects without trying to replace the text-centered outlook that has traditionally marked the study of literature. The writers collected here have all benefitted from the radical rethinking of academic institutions that has come out of the maturation of composition and rhetoric studies since the early seventies. Several of these writers have been in the forefront of that rethinking, which challenges the very division between composition and literary study. *When Writing Teachers Teach Literature* eloquently exemplifies this challenge and presents a wealth of practical suggestions on how the comp/lit gulf can be crossed.

With apologies for my reductiveness, here are four propositions that seem to me broadly shared by the contributors:

1. Direct attention to students is compatible, not competitive, with close attention to literature. Far from diverting us from rigorous and loving attention to literary texts, concern for students and their experience is a precondition of improving the quality of their literary attention. In other words, pedagogy cannot be left to take care of itself, as even today most graduate programs still tend to assume.

2. Students will understand and appreciate literature more fully the more they write, both critically and creatively. Teachers who respect student writing for possessing literary qualities of its own will be more effective in helping students to appreciate the literary qualities of published literature, as well as helping them to write about those qualities.

3. Since writing is a more meaningful practice for students when addressed to real audiences, the standard literature class can profit

from group work, collaborative learning, peer tutoring, and other strategies in which students write to and for each other rather than only to and for their teachers. Such collaborative work recognizes that writing and reading are active processes, not inert products of mechanical skills that can be handed down by experts. Both writing and reading involve the active making of meaning by students in dialogue with other students, as well as the teacher. In short, the literature class needs to become a writing workshop, at least part of the time.

4. Though teachers cannot and should not simply abandon their classroom authority, good teaching involves a willingness on teachers' part to put their own authority and that of their subject matter into question. This means treating literary knowledge not as a set of correct answers (or right readings), but as a conversation whose terms are always open to renegotiation and challenge. To teach literature or writing, then, is not to hand down facts, precepts, or skills from above, but to bring into the foreground the contingent, constructed, and negotiated nature of these subjects. Turning a literature course into a writing workshop is a way of problematizing the teacher's authority without simply renouncing it.

I like these precepts, particularly their optimistic (but not naive or unrealistic) faith that academic literary study possesses a vast potential appeal to students that has barely begun to be tapped. You don't have to see literature professors as villains (as some compositionists have been prone to do) to agree that a certain self-absolving fatalism has marked the teaching of literature since excitement over the New Criticism began to wane in the 1960s.

I know that whenever I have asked my literature colleagues what they think their students may be getting from their courses, some admit quite candidly that they teach for the top ten percent of students, since, after all, the rest will just never "get it" and don't care. Some, on the other hand, react by defensively maintaining that their students are indeed getting it quite well. In either case, the implication is that literature teachers need not rethink the ways they have been doing things.

To be sure, it's unfair to single out literature professors for attitudes toward teaching that are all too pervasive across all the academic disciplines. In questioning these attitudes, compositionists are challenging an unspoken law of the academic ethos, which is that it's better not to ask what happens to our teachings when they get filtered through the minds of undergraduates. Recognition of the often hilarious discrepancy between what professors say and what their students hear is best confined to howler anecdotes that reinforce the prevailing cynicism about students.

In one such anecdote that came my way recently, a professor friend described being asked by a student on the first day why he is asking the class to read *poetry* when his course has been announced as one in *literature*. My friend told the story as yet another sorry illustration of the abysmal ignorance of today's students, as if there had not been a time when he or any of us didn't yet know that poetry is a subclass of literature. To be fair, when I challenged him on the point, my friend acknowledged having recently noticed in a local bookstore that "poetry" and "literature" indeed occupied separate sections, an illustration of how confusingly unstable such seemingly unambiguous categories can be. This is just the sort of anecdote that educators could learn from if we were to get off our high horse and start thinking pedagogically; that is, seeing the assumptions of the university from the point of view of students instead of that of professors.

What I mean by thinking pedagogically is incisively exemplified in the essay here by John Trimbur, who observes that his students "have very little idea why they've been asked over and over again in twelve years of schooling to take English and to read and study works of literature." Trimbur adds that students probably read the title "Introduction to Literature" as somehow belonging to an "undifferentiated" concept of "English" that "encompasses virtually everything they've been asked to do in the past in school" under the auspices of this mysterious rubric.

I agree with Trimbur. It has always seemed to me a rich joke on English professors that while we wrangle solemnly over whether to teach canonical or revisionist texts, many of our students see *both* kinds of text as instances of an undifferentiated substance called "literature" that they learn to endure in "English." Once the non-canonical Alice Walker gets assigned in a class, she automatically *becomes* canonical for students, especially those who are unaware of the struggle it took to get her there. At that point, Walker, like Shakespeare and Hawthorne, joins the ranks of things that one does in school, which is to say, things that are hard and not necessarily fun and that you may need *Cliffs Notes* to get you through.

For that matter, the very difference between composition and literature courses that is so politically charged for professors is probably imperceptible to many of our students. If so, this would be a fitting comment on the long struggle to elevate literary study above "mere" freshman composition so that people encountered at cocktail parties will finally stop saying, "Oh, you teach English. I guess I better watch my grammar." It would seem that, despite the best efforts of the literature faculty, that is still often the way students think of us. If this is the case, we teachers of "English" have only ourselves to blame, for, as Trimbur notes, we have always tended to presuppose rather than explain the concept, because those who don't understand it presumably never will, or because it would be just too humiliating at this late date to admit that our discipline is still virtually unintelligible to outsiders.

As Trimbur says, "of all the disciplines, English in general and literary studies in particular have been remarkably reticent about explaining to their charges what these fields are about, what kind of problems they investigate, and why they do so." Work like Trimbur's and the other contributors to this collection aims to put an end to this reticence by flushing these questions about what we do and why we do it out into the open and incorporating the questions themselves into our subject matter and pedagogy. In this respect, these writers manifest the reflexive self-consciousness that is encouraged by recent literary theorists, but they go these theorists one better by demanding that theory be enacted performatively in pedagogical practice instead of being left to freeze into yet another academic expertise.

I identify very strongly, then, with the general program espoused by the writers in this collection. At the same time, their program leaves me with several questions that seem worth pausing over here (at the risk of being a boring guest at Deborah H. Holdstein's dinner party), ones that remain very much in debate in discussions of pedagogy today.

Let's begin with the appeal these writers make to student experience as a corrective to the priest-like absorption in literary texts that presumably has characterized literature teaching. Setting aside the question of whether literature teachers are really quite as "priestly" about their subject as they are made out to be here (or whether some of the writers here may be touched by that trait as well), I find myself wondering what kind of terms these writers expect students to use in describing their literary experience.

To put the question crudely for the sake of getting it up front, should we want students to talk and write about literature in their own idiom, in that of their professors, or in some other register in between? Is provoking an animated and interested classroom discussion among students an end in itself, or is the point to move student discussion closer to the norm of professional discourse (journalistic, if not strictly academic) than it is likely to be at the start of the process? I sense implicit disagreements among the contributors on these questions, ones that can easily be papered over out of a need to close ranks against traditional educators.

Teachers often for many reasons feel ambivalent about asking students to acquire the discourses of the academy. Certainly to ask that students learn "our" talk risks giving the impression that "theirs" is inferior, implying a lack of respect for students' abilities. Then, too, some of the reluctance of teachers to socialize students into academic discourse communities may be rooted in the sheer difficulty of the project. Teachers of literature and composition often find it so difficult to arouse even minimal interest from their students that they may be tempted to settle for a lively class discussion, whether or not its terms and vocabulary approximate those of the academic community.

Students themselves often feel deeply ambivalent about trying on academic discourse, and for good reason, for the personal and vocational rewards of doing so are likely to seem far less obvious than the liabilities. Why learn to sound like an "intellectual" when it figures only to alienate you from your friends and relatives without necessarily qualifying you for a better job? Faced with such student resistance to using intellectual discourse, teachers may understandably forego this as an objective, at which point "getting them to talk" becomes the *goal* of the class discussion rather than its starting point.

Certainly too much traditional literature teaching has arrogantly proceeded as if the point is to get students to appreciate literature "as we do" without concern for the way "they" experience it. It should be possible to counteract such arrogance, however, not by giving up "our" discourse for "theirs," but by opening a dialogue between "ours" and "theirs." Such a dialogue seems to me badly needed in order to close the huge and disabling gulf between academic talk and student talk. Peter Elbow, in his essay in this collection, observes that though teachers and students may not have experienced *Othello* in the same way, "we are working in the same world here." But we are not working in the same world if students describe *Othello* as boring or cool while their teachers describe it as an "embodiment of humanistic values" or an "inscription of hegemonic discourse."

Let me make my own views on this issue clear at the outset. I think it's reasonable to expect students to acquire some degree of competence in talking and writing in the public idioms of journalistic and academic discussion, something that inevitably involves using the languages of argumentation, exposition, analysis, and generalization. I question whether grasping academic subjects is wholly separable from gaining competence in their vocabularies. Furthermore, such competence seems to me a precondition of student "empowerment" in an information-oriented society that increasingly rewards those who are able to move flexibly and articulately between different discourses and contexts and who can cogently size up, reformulate, and advance arguments.

In other words, I agree with Patricia Bizzell's defense of the project of socializing students into academic discourse. (Of course, the very term "academic discourse" risks making the thing sound specialized, arcane, and useless, when in fact academic literacy overlaps with that of television, newsreporting, government, business, and other occupations. I use the term here in this broader sense, as I think Bizzell does too.) As Bizzell writes:

> We cannot demystify academic discourse for students, cannot teach them to analyze it, until they already understand something about it from trying to use it in imitation of experienced practitioners, such as their professors. In other words, mastery of academic discourse must begin with socialization to the community's ways, in the same way that one enters any cultural group. (219)

Like Bizzell, I believe that we do no favor for students by protecting them from such "socialization," through a misguided belief that intellectual argumentation is inherently dehumanizing or repressive. In fact, such a tactic only places students in a double bind, since it discourages them from mastering the discourse that both the academy and society rewards, and for which their teachers have been rewarded.

Instead of encouraging students to experience literature as "they" and not "we" do, then, I would prefer to see teachers help students reformulate their experience in our academic and professional terms, even as we in turn learn to restate our experience in the light of students' vocabularies and insights. Kenneth A. Bruffee has usefully suggested how collaborative learning can be used to create "transition groups" in which students speak and write a kind of "boundary discourse," somewhere between their own and that of the academic disciplines. (23ff)

In literary studies, my view commits me to the belief that students should learn to speak and write some of the discourse of literary criticism (including literary theory), a discourse that I see as an extension of the general field of rhetoric and argumentation. For me it is argumentation that can bridge the notorious gulf between literary and composition studies and between both these studies and other disciplines. What potentially binds literature and composition teachers together, among other things, is an implicit commitment to teaching argumentation. Teachers who refuse this commitment to teaching argumentation are refusing to give students a set of instruments that they themselves control. In my view, then, it is not only reasonable but inevitable to expect students to some extent to imitate the discourse of their teachers—if only to acquire the power to contest that discourse.

Among the contributors here, Diana George and Saralinda Blanning seem to me the most unambiguous in holding that students should learn to speak and write the language of the academic discourse community of literary and cultural criticism. George and Blanning do want their students "to become engaged by the literature" they teach, but they "also want them to be able to identify and articulate intellectual questions and issues embodied in those texts." In other words, George and Blanning unabashedly want their students to be able to think and write like "them," the teachers.

Others here seem less comfortable with asking students to "articulate intellectual questions and issues," or they write as if such intellectualization can be depended on to emerge from the process of reading, writing, and classroom discussion. Douglas M. Tedards, for example, offers students the option of writing journal entries in either analytic or expressive-creative forms, as if it makes no great difference which form is chosen. Tedards writes of "the simple power of asking students to delve into the craft of poetry firsthand." I wish he had explored that power further, for in my experience such firsthand delving doesn't necessarily generate adequate categories for articulating it. There is a difference between saying that a poem "gave me bad vibes," as does Allyson Y., one of Tedards' students, and responding in the more "intellectual" register Tedards uses. Isn't it important to overcome that difference?

Like Tedards, Brad Peters seems to think that if we can only make the experience of literature and class discussion personally rewarding enough, this experience will somehow generate an adequate vocabulary for describing that experience. Here the quarrel between "expressivism" and "academic discourse" needs to be engaged and worked through. James Britton (as quoted by Peters) disparages the need for any preset "written model" and suggests that "the kind of internalization that comes from reading for reading's sake" will somehow "articulate, interlink with the . . . resources which have in general been recruited at the spoken level. . . ." I find Britton's formulation obscure, but he seems to be saying that personal experience itself generates the terms of its own description, obviating the need for set written models or for a socialization of the student into the academic discourse community of the kind recommended by Bizzell. This view sounds curiously reminiscent of the traditional humanist assumption that great texts ultimately read and teach themselves and therefore can be adequately appropriated by student readers without being supplemented by acculturation into critical discourse.

Though he invokes Britton, Peters actually adopts a different—and I think more useful—set of assumptions in his use of personal "companion texts" to mediate among "expressive" and "persuasive" and "expository writing." The personalized companion text becomes, as Peters puts it, the "soil in which the metalingual and theoretical substances of critical thinking" take root. Again, however, "metalingual and theoretical" discourse will not necessarily "take root" through the practice of personal writing, as if in some process of plant-like organic growth. Teachers need explicitly to encourage students to take such a plunge into metadiscourse, since for reasons I have already suggested they won't necessarily feel comfortable "getting meta" on their own.

As Peters states it, the problem is how to move from a classroom in which "the teacher does not impart wisdom and truth" but helps "the student to develop her own wisdom and truth." In his practice as described, however, I think what Peters really tries to do is help students redescribe their own wisdom and truth in the discourse of the teacher, something that changes the form and content of "their own" wisdom and truth without necessarily denaturing it (and may transform the teacher's discourse as well). Again, Bruffee's idea of "transition" discourse could help us avoid overdrawing or romanticizing the opposition between student-talk and teacher-talk.

Not all contributors seem sure, however, that overcoming this opposition is a good thing. Cheryl Glenn writes that "In theory, if not always in practice, we encourage our students to write the way *they* want to write, to say what *they* want to say, rather than to write for the sole purpose of pleasing us." Expressivism seems to have the upper hand here: Teachers should help students find their own voices, not impose ours. Glenn would seem to agree with Lynn Z. Bloom, who describes using creative assignments to undo the programmed expectation that students become "ventriloquists in the language of critical jargon, submerging their own voices in the process." (That would be wishful thinking for me!) On the other hand, Glenn writes about teaching Swift and other authors, subjects that it is not obvious undergraduates even "want" to have opinions about, much less write about. Glenn's description of her course makes sense only if the point is to enable rather than prevent student "ventriloquizing" of academic-intellectual registers.

Like Bloom, however, several contributors fear that analyzing literature conflicts with experiencing or performing it. Carl R. Lovitt opposes student journal writing to "the aims of academic literary study," as if those aims were so alienating that journals have to become "a separate space where students can explore private connections to literature. . . ." Lovitt is right to point out that "many of our students—including most of our English majors—will not devote their lives to literary study or become teachers of literature." True, and a salutary warning against overly professionalizing teaching. On the other hand, you don't have to become a professional literature teacher or critic to find the cultural and analytic discourses of literary study (which Lovitt himself employs) usefully applicable to real-life situations.

Citing Keith Fort, Charles Schuster suggests that requiring students "to analyze literature in terms of structure, form, and meaning in typical critical fashion" is merely "to condition students to think in terms of authority and hierarchy." Schuster therefore seeks to undo authority and hierarchy in his literature class by asking students to "perform texts" rather than analyze them, giving "assignments that require students to speak or write in the voice of a character or author."

I can identify with Schuster's desire to overcome the authority gap between teachers and students. I suspect, however, that replacing analysis and argument with "performative" discourse only increases the power differential between teachers and students, since it leaves the teachers exclusively in control of analysis and argument. It does little to empower students to suggest that they needn't master the modes of argumentation that we as teachers take for granted. Like Schuster, Brenda M. Greene asks her students to recreate and perform scenes from assigned literary texts "from the perspective of an underprivileged character." I think a more thoroughly performative pedagogy would try to close the gap between that underprivileged perspective and the argumentative discourse that teachers like Greene and Schuster use.

That, however, would mean overcoming students' alienation from academic intellectual discourse instead of identifying with it, recognizing that "empowering" students entails transferring control over such generalizing discourse from teachers to students. Again, it is difficult even to discuss the problem without sounding as if one thinks students are anti-intellectual and have no academically valid experience of their own. This in fact is the charge Trimbur levels at me when he says that my argument for "teaching the conflicts" treats students "as novices for whom the study of literature amounts to learning the practices of experts . . ." and thereby leaves "student experience" out.

I plead guilty to the charge of viewing most undergraduates as "novices," a word my dictionary defines as "a beginner in any occupation; an inexperienced person." I also own up to believing that studying literature involves "learning the practices of experts,"as long as the experts are not beyond challenge or are assumed to have nothing to learn from the "novices." If students and teachers are not in a novice/expert relationship, it is difficult to understand the existence of schooling.

Trimbur himself positions students as novices when he describes them as having "very little idea why they've been asked over and over again . . . to take English. . . ." Surely the vice of bad education lies not in treating students as novices but in doing nothing to help students *stop* being novices. Treating students as novices is not only proper but necessary, as long as this is seen as a stage in a process leading to something beyond.

If the point (as Trimbur argues) is to move students from simply exemplifying personal and cultural contradictions to describing and analyzing them *as* contradictions—and that seems to me precisely the point—then I see no way around the conclusion that the problem is how to help students move from student-speak to professor-speak more or less like the kind Trimbur writes; or, better still, to some hybrid discourse that would combine the strengths of both discourses even as it would differ for each student. Trimbur is surely right to suggest that this transition will not happen unless teachers *start* from where students already are. But the problem is to respect student experience even as we try to transform it into something different.

My own suggested strategy for dealing with the tensions between academic and student discourse is to foreground these very tensions in our writing and literature courses, and even use them to build bridges between the two. John Schilb (1994) has developed this idea in a critique of my work on "teaching the conflicts," suggesting that the conflicts we teach need to be broadened to include conflicts between students as well as between professors, and between nonacademic and academic discourses. Schilb describes several possible courses (including one he taught at Denison University) that bring the concerns of literature and composition together in ways that engage students in thinking about the relation of their own experiences to traditional intellectual culture.

Another course with similar goals is one on "Youth Cultures" taught by David Shumway of Carnegie Mellon University. Shumway's students read literary texts such as F. Scott Fitzgerald's *This Side of Paradise* and the poetry of Rupert Brooke, Edna St. Vincent Millay, and Wilfred Owen alongside jazz and rock music, films like *Love Finds Andy Hardy* and *I Was a Teenage Werewolf*, and comic books. In addition they read sociological accounts of student life such as Michael Moffatt's *Coming of Age in New*

Jersey, histories of practices such as Beth Bailey's study of dating, *From Front Porch to Back Seat,* and studies of subcultural semiotics such as Dick Hebdidge's *Subculture: The Meaning of Style.*

By turning youth subcultures into an object of study, Shumway legitimates those subcultures on their own terms, yet it also legitimates the academic culture and discourse through which they are analyzed. The course in effect asks students to assume a kind of double identity, partly still inside student culture and partly looking at that culture from outside, like an anthropologist or ethnographer. A dialogue is thereby opened in the student between the culture he or she has grown up with and the academic culture of analysis and argumentation. Out of such internal dialogues rich versions of Bruffee's transitional boundary discourse figure to grow.

To the suggestions offered by Schilb and Shumway, I would add a further one, which is that, in making the tensions between academic and student discourse an object of study, teachers should not shrink from forthrightly addressing the *dislike* that many students harbor for literature (poetry most notoriously). Such dislike is hardly unexpected in a culture where high literature and intellectual analysis have been marginal and often suspect. Students often feel coerced and therefore turned off by the presumption that many teachers convey that "we all love literature here, don't we—otherwise why would we be here?" Instead of engaging in this pretense, it seems better to confront anti-literary, anti-analytical prejudices directly by making them part of the course's subject matter where they can be explored.

Though I have disagreed with several of the contributors to this book, I like to think that these closing suggestions are in the spirit of their enterprise. On one overriding point I think we all agree, that (as Toby Fulwiler and Art Young write in their introduction) "the best teaching is not the mere transmission of knowledge but the transmission of the means of creating knowledge and the excitement that accompanies that."

Works Cited

Patricia Bizzell. 1992. *Academic Discourse and Critical Consciousness.* Pittsburgh: University of Pittsburgh Press.

Kenneth A. Bruffee. 1993. *Collaborative Learning: Higher Education, Interdependence, and the Authority of Knowledge.* Baltimore: Johns Hopkins University Press.

Schilb, John. 1994. "Composing Conflicts: A Writing Teacher's Perspective," in William E. Cain, editor, *Teaching the Conflicts: Gerald Graff, Curricular Reform, and the Culture Wars.* New York: Garland Publishing, Inc.

Contributors

Wendy Bishop teaches writing at Florida State University and writes essays and books about composition and creative writing (*Released into Language*, 1990; *The Subject is Writing*, 1993; *Colors of a Different Horse*, 1994) when she's not talking on e-mail and to her poetry writing group or finding out, from her daughter and son—Morgan and Tail—how to read new books and play new games.

Saralinda Blanning is currently an Instructor at Wright State University. She studied English Language and Literature and Creative Writing at the University of Michigan as an undergraduate and has an M.S. in Rhetoric and Technical Communication from Michigan Technological University. She has presented papers based on her work with the MTU Writing Center at the Midwest Writing Centers Association Conference and the National Conference on College Composition and Communication.

Lynn Z. Bloom has been immersed in biography and autobiography for thirty years as a teacher (currently, Professor of English and Aetna Chair of Writing at the University of Connecticut); biographer *(Doctor Spock*, 1972); editor (*Forbidden Diary*, 1980, and *Forbidden Family*, 1989); critic (numerous articles); and autobiographer ("Teaching College English as a Woman," "Growing Up with Dr. Spock," and others).

William E. Coles, Jr., is currently Professor of English and former Director of Composition at the University of Pittsburgh. He has published a number of books and articles on literature and on the teaching of writing, including *The Plural I* (1978), *What Makes Writing Good* (1985), and *Seeing Through Writing* (1988). He regularly conducts workshops on Writing Across the Curriculum for teachers of all educational levels.

Peter Elbow is Professor of English at UMass Amherst. He has taught at MIT, Franconia College, Evergreen State College, and SUNY Stony Brook—where he directed the Writing Program for five years. His books include *Oppositions in Chaucer* (1975), *Writing with Power* (1982), *Embracing Contraries* (1988), *What is English?* (1990), and a textbook with Pat Belanoff, *A Community of Writers* (1995). He has published numerous essays, and won the Braddock Award in 1986 for "The Shifting Relationships Between Speech and Writing."

Toby Fulwiler has directed the writing program at the University of Vermont since 1983. Before that he taught at Michigan Tech and the University of Wisconsin where, in 1973, he also received his Ph.D. in American Literature. He conducts writing workshops for teachers across the disciplines and teaches classes in first-year composition as well as "Personal Voice" and "Writing The New Yorker." His recent books include *The Working Writer* (1995) and *The Blair Handbook* (1994). He has also written *College Writing* (1992) and *Teaching with Writing* (1985) and edited *The Journal Book* (1987). And, in case you're interested, he rides a white BMW K100RS (1991).

Diana George is an Associate Professor of Humanities at Michigan Technological University where she directs the work of Humanities Department teaching assistants. She is co-author with John Trimbur of *Reading Culture* (1995). Her work has also appeared in such journals as *College Composition and Communication*, the *Journal of Advanced Composition*, *College English*, and the *Quarterly Journal of Film and Video*.

Cheryl Glenn is Associate Professor of English at Oregon State University, where she teaches writing whether she's teaching rhetorical history and theory, composition theory, British Literature, or grammar. Winner of a university teaching award, she has written (with Robert Connors) *The St. Martin's Guide to Teaching Writing* (1992), as well as various articles and chapters.

Gerald Graff, who taught at Northwestern University for twenty-five years and chaired the English Department there, is George M. Pullman Professor of English and Education at the University of Chicago and author of *Professing Literature: An Institutional History* (1987) and *Beyond the Culture Wars: How Teaching the Conflicts can Revitalize American Education* (1992). He has been a Guggenheim Fellow and a fellow at the Harvard Center for Literary and Cultural Studies and, in 1994–95, at the Center for Advanced Study in the Behavioral Sciences. He is currently at work on a book about students and academic discourse.

Brenda M. Greene is Associate Professor of English at Medgar Evers College, where she chairs the Department of Literature, Languages, and Philosophy and teaches composition and literature. Her research focuses on basic writing and writing across the curriculum. She has also taught and conducted research in African-American and modern literature. She served as Discussion Leader at the 1991 and 1992 NCTE Summer Institutes for the Teaching of Literature to Undergraduates and she was Program Chair for the 1994 Institute. Her articles have appeared in the *Journal of Basic Writing, the English Journal, Writing Centers in Context, The Journal of College Reading,* and *Community Review.* Greene is currently on the NCTE Editorial Board and has served on several CCCC committees, the NTCC Committee, and the NCTE College Section Steering Committee. Greene is also a key member of the National Black Writer's Steering Conference Committee.

Deborah H. Holdstein directs the writing program and coordinates the English program at Governors State University, University Park, Illinois. She is the author of *On Composition and Computers* (1987); co-editor with Cynthia Selfe of *Computers and Writing: Theory, Research, Practice* (1992); and numerous pamphlets and essays dealing with writing assessment, literature and critical theory, technology and composition, and other topics (although not necessarily all in the same essay).

Carl R. Lovitt is Associate Professor of English and Director of the Pearce Center for Professional Communication at Clemson University, where he teaches courses in the British novel and professional communication and directs assorted outreach programs. Having recently abandoned a lifelong study of murderers' narratives, he is currently co-editing, with Dixie Goswami, a volume of essays on international professional communication.

Charles Moran is Professor of English at the University of Massachusetts. He is Co-Director of the Western Massachusetts Writing Project; he is co-editor, with Anne Herrington, of *Writing, Teaching and Learning in the Disciplines* (1992); and co-editor, with Elizabeth Penfield, of *Conversations: Contemporary Critical Theory and the Teaching of Literature* (1990). With Kay Moran, he is co-parent of two scientist-musicians.

Richard J. Murphy, Jr., teaches composition and literature at Radford University where he has been a member of the English Department for fifteen years. He helped initiate and coordinate Radford's writing-across-the-curriculum program and co-authored a book on the history of its development (*Symbiosis: Writing and an Academic Culture*, 1993). He has published articles on teaching and writing in professional journals and a collection of autobiographical essays (*The Calculus of Intimacy: A Teaching Life*, 1994).

Thomas Newkirk is a Professor of English at the University of New Hampshire. For the past fifteen years he has directed the New Hampshire Writing Program, a summer institute for teachers. He has also written on literacy education at all grade levels. His most recent book is a co-edited collection, *Taking Stock: The Writing Process Movement in the 90s* (1994).

Brad Peters is Director of Composition at Texas Christian University. He has published studies on dramatic writing in the ESL classroom and acquisition of narrative skills among elementary students. He is currently researching new applications of genre theory in composition. He also works with discourse analysis in literature of the medieval mystics.

Linda H. Peterson is Chair of the English Department and co-director of the writing program at Yale University. Her recent publications include *Victorian Women Artists* and *Authors* (co-authored with Susan Casteras, 1994), "Sappho and the Making of Tennysonian Lyric" (1994), and "Writing Across the Curriculum and in the Freshman English Program" (1992).

James A. Reither teaches English at St. Thomas University in Fredericton, New Brunswick, Canada. He is aggressively engaged in an ongoing search for ways to help students—in their efforts to learn, write, and be—deal with the condition that the defining quality of their ethos is that they are ignorant.

Charles Schuster, Professor of English at the University of Wisconsin, Milwaukee, shared the 1992 CCCC Outstanding Book Award with Richard Bullock and John Trimbur for the *Politics of Writing Instruction: Postsecondary.* He has published extensively in books and journals and is President of the Council of Writing Program Administrators. His current research interests include the essay as genre, composition and performance, writing program administration, and graduate education.

Helen J. Schwartz, Professor of English at Indiana University–Purdue University at Indianapolis (IUPUI), has pioneered the use of computers in writing and literature since 1979, publishing her textbook *Interactive Writing* in 1985. Her software SEEN won an EDUCOM/NCRIPTAL award and is now being revised with a National Science Foundation grant for use as a multimedia program in mathematics. She has been active in CCC, MLA, and EDUCOM committees to support the integration of computers into educational practice and institutions and to further equity of access to computer-mediated learning. She is currently working on hypermedia software for distance education.

Jeffrey Sommers is Professor of English at Miami University–Middletown. He is author or co-author of three composition textbooks, including the forthcoming *The Two-Year College Reader.* He has published articles on portfolio assessment and responding to student writing in journals such as *WPA, Assessing Writing, CCC, Teaching English in the Two-Year College, Freshman English News,* and *Journal of Teaching Writing*; his work also appears in collections such as Anson's *Writing Response* and Belanoff and Dickson's *Portfolios: Process and Product.* He is co-editor of *New Directions in Portfolio Assessment* (1994) and serves as Secretary-Treasurer of the National Council of Writing Program Administrators.

Douglas M. Tedards, Associate Professor and previously Director of Writing at University of the Pacific (1982–88), currently teaches courses in composition and ninteenth and twentieth century American literature. His poetry has appeared in the *Florida Quarterly, The Georgia Review, San Fernando Poetry Journal, Mind in Motion, The Scroll,* and *Calliope.* His articles have been published in *California English* and the *Appalachian Journal.*

John Trimbur teaches writing and literature classes at Worcester Polytechnic Institute, where he also directs the Technical, Scientific, and Professional Communication program and the WPI Writing Across the Curriculum Project. He has published many articles on composition theory, cultural studies, and collaborative learning. His book *The Politics of Writing Instruction: Postsecondary* was named the CCCC Outstanding Book for 1992.

Joseph F. Trimmer is Professor of English at Ball State University where he teaches courses in writing and cultural studies. His scholarly books include *The National Book Award for Fiction: The First Twenty-five Years* (1978) and *Understanding Others: Cultural and Cross-Cultural Studies and the Teaching of Literature* (1992). His textbooks include *Fictions* (1994), *Writing with a Purpose* (1995), and *The Riverside Reader* (1996). In the summer he teaches at the Martha's Vineyard Institute on Teaching and Writing.

Kathleen Blake Yancey is Assistant Professor of English at the University of North Carolina at Charlotte, where she also co-directs the UNC Charlotte site of the National Writing Project. She has edited two collections of essays, *Portfolios in the Writing Classroom: An Introduction* (1992) and *Voice on Voice: Perspectives, Definitions, Inquiry* (1994); she also co-edits the journal *Assessing Writing*. Her current projects include linking genre theory, technology, and writing.

Art Young is Campbell Chair and Professor of English and Engineering at Clemson University in South Carolina, where he coordinates the communication-across-the-curriculum program. Throughout his thirty-year teaching career, he has frequently taught literature courses in the British Romantic and Victorian periods. In most ways, he remains an unrepentant Romantic who drives a convertible through midlife, eternally searching for his various selves along life's highways.